The Art of Co-Creation

Bryan R. Rill • Matti M. Hämäläinen

The Art of Co-Creation

A Guidebook for Practitioners

palgrave
macmillan

Bryan R. Rill
Rill Insights LLC
Florida, USA

Matti M. Hämäläinen
Riihi Consulting Ltd.
Espoo, Finland

ISBN 978-981-10-8499-7 ISBN 978-981-10-8500-0 (eBook)
https://doi.org/10.1007/978-981-10-8500-0

Library of Congress Control Number: 2018943292

Cover credit: Westend61

This Palgrave Macmillan imprint is published by the registered company Springer Nature Singapore Pte Ltd.
The registered company address is: 152 Beach Road, #21-01/04 Gateway East, Singapore 189721, Singapore

Preface

Co-creation is a trendy term used across the disciplines of business, design, and marketing to indicate new modes of engagement between people in order to either create shared value or unleash the creative potential of diverse groups. Its wide appeal has led to a proliferation of "co-creative" programs, yet an integrated perspective on how to design and facilitate such programs remains lacking. This book addresses this need, clarifying co-creation as an operational concept and providing a set of guidelines for professionals in design, education, and organizational change.

Our guidelines derive from the action research of the Co-Creation Initiative (CCI) at the School of Design, Hong Kong Polytechnic University, as well as practical applications in the School of Design, the Aalto-Tongji Design Factory in Shanghai, and in our design consulting practices. The primary author, Dr. Bryan Rill, founded the CCI in 2014. CCI has since evolved from a research initiative to an ongoing open source platform that aims to explore various aspects of co-creation.[1] All of our collaborators and participants openly share their experiences, philosophies, and best practices. Herein, we purposely contrast the industry standard of trademarking and protecting a toolkit for commercial gain. Instead, we share everything we have learned and continue to develop in the spirit of creative positive change. Co-creation is a powerful framework, and we want to give that to the world.

After several years of inquiry, our goal is to translate our learnings into an evocative and pragmatic "how-to" guidebook that enables professional working in their respective fields to design and implement co-creation. Given the right tools, skilled leaders and facilitators can utilize this approach to unleash the creative potential of their organizations. The principles herein integrate deep practical wisdom from some of the world's best designers, educators, and organizational change facilitators. The result is a co-creative framework for designing the space between (a field of collective knowledge) and the capacities (collective intelligence) that engender breakthrough insights.

As practicing professionals, we expect that our readership will understand many of the core concepts in this text. Given this, our aim is not to explain the fundamentals of design or facilitation, but rather build upon existing knowledge to help practitioners more effectively tap into the potential of the teams they work with.

We imagine two different pathways for reading this book. One is for professionals who are new to designing for and leading collective creativity. These readers will benefit from reading the book front to back, learning first how to prepare the conditions for co-creation and then how to implement it. Other more experienced readers may already have their own methods and be searching for new ones to add to their toolkit. These readers might jump straight into Part II, which focuses on facilitation (the *How*). Another audience will be veteran facilitators who have more techniques than they know what to do with, and they are looking for answers to questions they have been pondering for years. "Why do my techniques work in some contexts and not others?" "What processes underlay effective change initiatives?" "Is there something that makes sense of all?" We are familiar with these questions because they have been put to us many times, and this book answers them all. The short answer is that there is an underlying process architecture for co-creation. This book reveals and explains it, as well as how to organize techniques for optional flow and efficacy.

The guidelines in this manuscript will be valuable for business professionals who see design thinking as integral to innovation and culture change. Additionally, in the field of participatory design, there is a lack of facilitation training. Great designers are intuitively good at facilitation, but rarely are they self-reflective. As such, this book will be of particular value for designers who wish to improve upon their processes. We see the manuscript as the foundation for new educational programs in facilitating co-creation.

Although we do our best to explain co-creation with a conceptual model, in truth a large part of it is tacit knowledge. Because tacit knowledge is situationally dependent, it is difficult to put into language and transfer it to another person via written instruction. Thus a book is not the best medium to transfer tacit knowledge. You do not learn to play the violin or master archery by reading a book about archery or how to play the violin. Meetings do not change for the better if everyone reads a book about meetings. To develop tacit knowledge, you must go out and practice. The theory and guidelines herein point out the way, but it is up to each of you to walk it if you truly desire to master the art of co-creation.

On Creativity

We are about to take you on a journey into the creative process. For many, creativity is a mystery, a special talent that people have in different measures. Exemplary figures such as Albert Einstein and Hayao Miyazaki stand out and, as such, are studied in an attempt to figure out what makes them so special. While it is certainly true that some people are recognized as being more creative than others, we take the position that creativity is not an inborn trait that only a few people have. It is something that can be trained and designed for.

Children are an excellent example of creativity. Take any six-year-old into a craft room and you will find a wellspring of ideas. Some will make sense to an adult, while others seem pure fantasy. At eight years old, my two nieces were showing me how to build a spaceship out of cardboard and duct tape, and they still regularly run circles around me in terms of creative output. What happens to us as we grow up? The answer, unfortunately, is education. We enter into learning models that emphasize mastery of content with very specific learning outcomes. While creativity is encouraged, creative writing in college is quite different from a kindergarten classroom where play is still encouraged. Education is about developing skilled, disciplined workers in society. And we are very good at it. Either by the time we get into the workforce or shortly after, most people have been neatly molded into productive citizens. If they are not, they lose their job. Just ask the Japanese, who have a saying "The nail that sticks up gets hammered down." While their society allows for great creative freedom throughout university years, once a person enters the workforce, they must adapt quickly to a very structured system.

Structure can facilitate or hinder creativity. Our educational and work systems are structured in ways that transform creativity into productivity.

This is not a bad thing in and of itself. We need productivity. But we can no longer sacrifice the chaotic, fantastical creativity of children on the altar of success. We need to bring it back if we are to innovate, and there are structured ways of doing so. Design, for example, encourages creative play and has developed spaces and practices that bring it out in adults. Here we will go further and introduce gamestorming, presence, and other techniques to help recover the creativity we all once had. We look specifically at how to cultivate and unleash *collective* creativity—a special experience that requires a nuanced understanding of creativity. Our core approach is that creativity always resides in action. Imagination, acted out, is creativity. Therefore, co-creation can be considered to be a special form of collective action, the act of creating something together.

Within this text we use the metaphor of art to refer to creative processes, with the practicing/performance of this art being a journey. Art also refers to a set of skills that cannot be perfected, but only improved upon, implying that there is no "right" or "wrong," only "better" or "worse." Journey refers to an isolatable performance of this art, which results in improvement of your skills in addition to reaching your goals. The journey is the center of co-creation, the experience through which collective potential can be realized.

Outline of the Text

The first two chapters look at the value of co-creation and offer a definition of the term. The aim of these preliminary chapters is to illustrate the relevance of co-creation and to present a clear understanding of what co-creation is and is not. In Chap. 1 we focus on the *Why*, for without a clear purpose there is no point in attempting co-creation. In the second chapter, we introduce our models for co-creation. Taking a human-centered rather than process-oriented perspective, we argue that experience design separates true co-creation from other forms of collaboration and design thinking. Our focus on experience design for creative teams takes into account the knowledge and emotional aspects of the creative journey, as well as the importance of team dynamics when working with groups. It is attention to all three aspects that harnesses the full creative potential of teams.

The remainder of the text is laid out in three parts. "Part I: Preparing the Conditions" unpacks our *Space Between* model into its three components: People, Environment, and Process. This part focuses on the *What*, the raw ingredients needed for co-creation.

Part I also explains *Why* certain ingredients are needed and *Where* to place them in the overall experience design. We unpack our *Co-Creative Journey* model, the process architecture that helps create flow among program piece and maximizes the potential for creative breakthroughs. There we introduce the container, the felt environment of a creative team, and how to "set" a strong enough container to handle the dive into the Unknown. We also explain the intangibles of co-creation, the qualities in people and process that amplify creative output.

The guidelines offered in Part I focus on the design and planning of co-creative processes, from the intangibles to more observable aspects of program design such as the creative brief and gamification. Throughout we stress the need for the *Why* of any creative program to integrate with the needs of the larger strategic and cultural context. Without designing specifically for growth opportunities and integration of needs, co-creation easily loses its potential impact.

"Part II: Performing Co-creation" is the *How* of co-creation, putting theory into practice with a focus on facilitation. We illustrate the overall process and the knowledge, emotional, and interpersonal aspects of the experience that people go through, offering guidelines on how to create the impactful programs following our process architecture. Throughout Part II we refer to two stories that, while given fictional names and actors, derive from real-world scenarios. These stories, one of success and one of failure, highlight touchpoints that can make or break co-creation. By drawing attention to these touchpoints, we hope to improve the ability to recognize key shifts in a creative program and how to harness the potential of these moments. By the end of Part II readers will have all the guidelines necessary to design and implement co-creation.

"Part III: The Perfect Play" introduces resonant co-creation, the ideal to which we strive. Resonance is the product of a harmony among three elements: experience design, facilitation, and talent development. When and if resonance occurs, creative potential is amplified. Resonant co-creation is highly conducive to strategic innovation (breakthroughs) because it specifically designed to break through existing worldviews and ways of interacting, establishing a powerful collective intelligence from which truly innovative ideas can emerge.

We close the text with an Epilogue that raises questions about the future and the impact co-creation can have, leaving the reader an invitation to engage our community of practice. Here we consider the potential for co-creation as a centerpiece of inclusive work cultures, as a nuance upon design thinking, and as a force for social change.

Florida, USA — Bryan R. Rill
Espoo, Finland — Matti M. Hämäläinen

Note

1. We welcome participation in this community of practice. To learn more, please visit www.cocreation.world

Acknowledgments

The authors thank the Brains on the Beach community, Wisdom Peak, Khalsa Consultants, Bridge Fellowship, the nowhere group ltd., the Hong Kong Polytechnic University School of Design, the Aalto Design Factory, the Institute of Cultural Affairs, the MIT Ideation Lab, and all our other colleagues and friends for allowing us to observe and engage you in the creation of this guidebook. Special thanks go to Prof. Cees de Bont, Dean of the School of Design. You gave us the impetus, wisdom, and resources to make this happen. Deep gratitude also to the CCI team—Benjamin Butler, Max Willis, Kyulee (Kim), Liang Tan (Ricky), Yunan Zhang (Echo), and the MScMET students who volunteered their time and energy. Large or small, your contributions helped make this happen. Thank-you also to all our friends and colleagues who have been patient with our social experiments and endless questions. Without your support, this would not have been possible. We welcome continued dialogue and engagement in activities in the years to come. Finally, we could have never made it without the love, patience, and guidance of our better halves, Lisa and Meri.

The Art of Co-Creation was developed by Dr. Bryan Rill and Matti Hämäläinen at the Co-Creation Initiative. In the spirit of co-creation, we maintain an open source philosophy regarding our materials. Please feel free to use them. Our only request is that credit be given where it is due, and *no trademarking!* Co-creation is for everyone.

Contents

List of Figures

List of Tables

CHAPTER 1

Why Co-creation?

We are in a time of great rehabilitation. For a century, the workforce was designed around the concept of production with predictability, reliability, efficiency, and control being central values. In contemporary office spaces, the design of factory floors has neatly translated into square spaces filled with cubicles, each its own little production unit. Through education we have prepared the population for these environments, naturalizing them to the point that many people like their cubicle and personal niche within much larger systems. As long as they do what they were hired for, they have security, and there is no need to step outside that box. Or so the myth goes....

This business model works, especially for producing many of the products and services that our world runs on today. The problem for the people in this system is that it reduces the beautiful complexity of being human into something less, something along the lines of performance metrics and human capital. That, in turn, reduces human creativity. Herein lies the rub. It is no secret that innovation is the Holy Grail of business. Some would argue that innovation is the sole differentiator left in a global economy where it is easy to replicate the latest and greatest business strategy. Innovation is sorely needed to address the global challenges we face today, from food shortages to environmental destruction. Simply put, we are in a time of "innovate or die."

Many innovation models in business are excellent at producing incremental innovations, improvements upon existing products. The next iPhone will include the latest tech and a couple of new features that meet

B. R. Rill, M. M. Hämäläinen, *The Art of Co-Creation*,
https://doi.org/10.1007/978-981-10-8500-0_1

or shift the desires of consumers, but the concept of a smartphone is well established. This is not what we need, and it is not what companies and social entrepreneurs are calling for. What we need is strategic innovation—ideas that break the mold, chart entirely new territories, or find elegant solutions to complex problems. What we need are the ways and means to meet hopes and dreams. That is what this book is about.

Our answer to the innovation challenge is co-creation. It is based on one simple principle: harnessing the collective potential of groups can lead to breakthroughs wherein every participant is empowered. Collective creativity is a difference that makes the difference.

This book is meant to be a guide for practicing professionals who wish to implement co-creation into their design teams, organizations, or learning platforms. Throughout we will lay out the *What*, *When*, *Where*, and *How* of co-creation. Here we want to focus on the *Why*.

The *Why* is straightforward. We need people to be creative so that we can innovate. The tricky part is figuring out how to cultivate creativity in workspaces that, in general, kill it quite effectively. The good news is that we are recovering from industrial systems that stripped away the invitation to be fully human in the workplace. In many places workplace well-being is now a major factor in talent acquisition and retention. Companies like Steelcase and Herman Miller have entire research divisions focused on designing furniture that supports these spaces. Innovation labs, start-up commons, and DIY workspaces are filled with funky, comfortable furniture designed specifically to improve upon sense of well-being and inspire new ways of working. Books on spatial design focus on social interaction, flexibility, and other principles that fly in the face of the neatly ordered cubicles and desks. We will be discussing these principles to help you design your own creative spaces later in this book.

Creative spaces alone, however, are insufficient. The innovation landscape is littered with the remains of creative workspaces that go unused, or worse, reordered into neat rows. I encountered this phenomenon first-hand when teaching in the School of Design for the Hong Kong Polytechnic University. Our classroom had Steelcase Node chairs, rolling self-contained desks that can be easily configured into any or no arrangement. Due to the famous architect Zaha Hadid's design of Innovation Tower, our building had no square rooms. One might think this a dream come true for a design school. After all, designers pride themselves on being able to reinvent space. The reality was quite different. For months upon moving into the building, every elevator conversation contained talk of how inefficient the building was, with both teachers and students lamenting on how challenging it was to arrange the rooms "orderly." In my classroom students did their very best to arrange the Node chairs into lines in a grid. Every day I would force them to rearrange, and it took several weeks for them to understand that I was challenging the psychological structures that informed them of "proper" class formations.

While educators carefully evaluate content delivery in classrooms, *how* that content is delivered is actually the real lesson. When a class, or business meeting, is arranged with a teacher or leader at the head of the space and everyone else in front of them, the message is one of control and followership. Starting in schools, people learn how power works and what they need to do to wield it—that is, become the expert or boss. We continue this pattern throughout life, ever working longer and harder to climb the ladder to a position where we are the ones in control. This pattern, for good or bad, is deeply ingrained in how we understand "proper" educational and work spaces. It is not something we think consciously about, and when given a choice most people will default to it because it is comfortable. When a space violates the norm, people often feel uncomfortable, and least at first. This simple conditioning is why so many innovation spaces are left unused. What is needed is a set of practices, or a process, that encourages people to use space differently. Enter design thinking.

Design thinking is reshaping the landscape of innovation across multiple sectors, from business to education. As Tim Brown from IDEO states in his book *Change by Design*, "Design can help to improve our lives in the present. Design thinking can help us chart a path into the future."[1] Design thinking is a thought process and iterative pathway that brings structure to creativity with demonstrable outcomes. For businesses, "Design thinking can do for organic growth and innovation what TQM did for quality—take something we always have cared about and put tools and processes into the hands of managers to make it happen."[2]

Design thinking is an iterative, experimental learning process. It employs empathy, entropy, and creative reframing of spaces and ideas to shake up existing knowledge and shake out new ideas. Human-centered design, or co-design, is particularly salient for supporting creative teams because these approaches focus on people and their needs. In short, design "rehumanizes" the work of innovation.

The focus on the human experience as a starting point contrasts the analytical, economic logic of business. Reality, for the business manager, is precise and quantifiable. "Design assumes instead human experience, always messy, as its decision driver and sees true objectivity as an illusion. Reality, for designers, is always constructed by the people living it."[3] These two perspectives on reality are equally essential for innovation. As Ogilvie and Liedtka argue in *Designing for Growth*[4]:

> The future will require multiple tools in the managerial tool kit—a design suite especially tailored to starting up and growing businesses in an uncertain world, and an analytic one suited to running established businesses in a more stable one—not two opposing sets wielded by warring groups of people who can't communicate with each other.

Companies that have adopted design thinking create or send teams to spaces wherein the rules of normal offices are suspended and teams can interact on completely different premises. In these spaces teams often turn to design thinking processes such as those provided by Stanford, IDEO, or the Aalto Design Factory as a way of working. Design consultancies can also be hired to work with a team in either a design studio or a dedicated project space within the client organization. In both cases teams enter into physical and psychologically "other" spaces with the hopes that the processes in there will translate into innovative ideas that can be enacted back in the "regular" world. This oscillation between the known, controlled world or organizational life and the unknown, chaotic world of creativity is working to generate innovations large and small. It seems then that the combination of creative workspaces and design thinking is an answer to the innovation challenge. So why write this book?

If reality matched the argument I have just laid out, then there might not be a need for another book that praises the value of design thinking. Yet reality has a way of being difficult, and what works in theory often fails in practice. This is just as true for design thinking as for anything else. While the reasons are many, one of the main ones is the fact that humans are not robots. As Neil deGrasse Tyson aptly notes, "In science, when human behavior enters the equation, things go nonlinear. That's why Physics is easy and Sociology is hard."[5] Humans simply don't conform to mathematical models. That trait can frustrate the systems engineer, but it is also a source of our creativity.

An equally important factor is that the conditions of every project are different. Because the context and human elements of any project cannot be predicted, no formulaic implementation of a process will maximize creative outputs. In business, for example, the adoption of design thinking has led to strategic innovation, but often this occurs only when that process is facilitated by a gifted design thinker. What is it about that individual that makes or breaks a project? What are the attributes of the successful design lead and their process that set them apart? As much as design talks about understanding the user and designing *with* rather than *for*, a black box remains as to *how exactly* to do that well. Here we pose co-creation as an answer that can advance design thinking and its application to innovative projects across sectors.

Stories of Co-creation

Over the years we have learned that trying to explain co-creation conceptually can be quite challenging. It is better to show through example what it can do. To that end, we have chosen a cast of characters to illustrate co-creation throughout the text. Each of these we have either worked with closely or been inspired by, and we want to give credit where credit is due. The cast includes the Eliad Group and their program iLead+Design, the nowhere group ltd., the U.Lab and corresponding Theory U initiatives, the Presencing Institute, Brains on the Beach (BoB), the Institute for Cultural Affairs (ICA), Social Artists and the Building Creative Communities conference, the Stanford University d.school, IDEO, the Aalto-Tongji Design Factory, and our peers in and around the School of Design at the Hong Kong Polytechnic University in Hong Kong. This book exists only due to their amazing work, the relationships we have developed through our research and beyond, and the spirit of co-creation from which we have all operated. We are grateful.

It is through the exemplary work of these individuals and groups that we can answer the question, "Why co-creation?" In the spirit of "show don't tell," what follows is the first of our stories of co-creation.

iLead+Design by Aaron Eden

Building the iLead+Design program with my co-founders was one of my first consciously co-creative experiences. I've been intentionally developing co-creative spaces ever since. iLead+Design, now in its fifth year of operation, is a summer intensive program for high school age youth I started with co-conspirators Bob Cole of Middlebury Institute of International Studies and Sean Raymond of York School. The program brings together two or three small teams of participants, each with a dedicated coach. The teams explore social innovation and design thinking by working on real problems brought in by community partners. The program balances time between experiential workshops on relevant co-creative skills with on-problem work time and weaves team space and group space together to form a lattice of co-creation at multiple scales.

A unique aspect of the co-creative environment, and one that is often missing from our professional lives, was an explicit understanding of the importance of safety of expression and of iteration on ideas, regardless of origin. This is one of the most important aspects of co-creation, I believe, and one I have carried with me whenever trying to replicate the conditions of the iLead+Design container: a willingness to be vulnerable and to play with ideas regardless of how crazy they may seem, without judgment. Design thinking language such as "Yes, and." (rather than "no, but...") and "How might we?..." help keep creativity flowing and buffer against taking things personally.

Equally important, and similarly absent from most work environments I had previously inhabited, was an explicit understanding that process is as important as content. In other words, how we discuss things is as important as what we discuss, and being willing to reflect on and alter process at any given moment is as important for quality outcomes as discussing what the outcomes should be. For example, when offering ideas on how to meet a goal, if someone is attempting to evaluate each idea as it comes out, it was explicitly okay to say something like: "I wonder if we could try to get all ideas out before evaluating them, so we are sure to make it to those "leftover" ideas that sometimes prove extremely creative?" And similarly—and explicitly!—acceptable to suggest reasons for not doing that.

Finally (although not exhaustively, for the list could go on), there was continuous and purposeful reconnection to *Why* we were building what we were building. When a decision would come before us on how to shape the program, we would try to remember to evaluate the option based not only on what we were trying to build, but why we were trying to build it. Critically, the "Why" question was not only used in terms of why our "customers" would want it or benefit from it, but why we wanted it to exist in the world. Why were we there? What did we care about? Often in business endeavors, there is an unstated understanding that we leave our personal lives at home. While there are many aspects of our personal lives that do not enhance our endeavors while engaging in our work, why we do what we do can only be personal. If we leave that out of the picture, and only adopt the "Why" of the customer, or of the business we are working for, we block off the greatest source of drive and creativity we possess. We therefore explicitly referred back to our individual "Whys" as part of our process to help us make decisions collectively. In doing so, we routinely contacted to our individual drive, reinforced our connection to and understanding of each other, and enhanced the quality of our output.

To this day, as I build or support others in building co-creative containers, I look to ensure the presence or creation of these characteristics:

- having the right people in the room, to ensure sufficient autonomy;
- a feeling of safety to express all ideas, and a shared lexicon in service of that goal;
- an explicit understanding that process is equally as important as content and is similarly subject to discussion and improvement;
- and ultimately that everyone there understands why they show up each day and feels supported in checking in with that foundation to shape our understanding of each other and of a shared "Why" that we can calibrate output against at every stage of development.

With this culture of engagement permeating what we do, iLead+Design gets better every year, no matter who joins the fun.

End

It was through an iLead+Design program at the Green School in Bali, Indonesia, that we met Aaron Eden, the beginning of a relationship that opened our eyes to the power of co-creation in learning.[6] Aaron uses co-creation to transform education as we know it. It is the means to shift from command and control to self-directed education, a movement wherein parents and teachers partner with children to collectively imagine and realize their dreams.

In educational contexts, co-creation can transform learning processes while simultaneously driving social innovation. This is what we were part of at the Green School, bringing our design students from Hong Kong down to work with their K-12 students on social entrepreneurship projects throughout Indonesia. We helped teams redesign trash bins, address deforestation and the pollution created by palm oil plantations, build a mobile application for the biodiesel school bus, and more. The students benefited by being able to learn the capacities and skills needed to be entrepreneurs while working on real-world issues. The communities benefited from the results of their efforts. It was a win-win scenario.

At a larger scale, the ICA has been working co-creatively for decades on some of the most pressing challenges faced around the world. Their publication *Winds & Waves* highlights several cases annually, showing how transformational co-creation can be in community development and organizational change projects.[7] In 2016 alone, ICA Nepal built a new Disabled Service Center in Kathmandu to replace the facility destroyed by an earthquake. In Chile the ICA is developing programs for leaders and organizations to work with disabled people, including a School for Participative Leaders that builds the capacity for co-creation. In Peru a community development project is underway to co-create an entirely new economic system in the mountains.

The ICA's work with communities was so sought after by business that they developed the Technology of Participation (TOP), a training series that teaches leaders and facilitators ICA methods. When we first sat down with Larry Philbrook, who runs the TOP training at ICA Taiwan, there was an immediate recognition between their methods and those we had developed in the Co-Creation Initiative, our research program in the School of Design. TOP *is* co-creation, albeit from an organizational change perspective rather than design.

The ICA continues to work with communities and organizations to build the capacity for co-creation, and their facilitators work behind the scenes of many United Nations and NGO social innovation projects. Their work demonstrates how co-creation empowers communities and organizations to become agents of social change.

The role of co-creation in social change became more evident when I experienced it first hand at the 2017 Building Creative Communities conference in Colquitt, Georgia, USA. Colquitt is a tiny country town, known only for its peanuts, murals, and folk theater. It was a town that almost disappeared due to economic downturn, but was saved by the arts. Richard Geer, the inventor of Story Bridge, came down to Colquitt on the invitation of a very active community elder by the name of Joy Jinks.[8] Together they sought and received an Endowment of the Arts grant, which they used to fiscally support the growth of a unique art community. All around Colquitt are beautiful painted murals of farming life, and every year thousands of people from Georgia and North Florida flock to Colquitt to see Swamp Gravy, a Story Bridge performance. Swamp Gravy is a play co-created and acted out entirely by members of the local community. It gives them a voice, encouraging the community to write their own story and own it. Story Bridge has grown from these humble roots to become a community empowerment technique, and it can be used equally effectively in organizations to build and express culture.

The Building Creative Communities conference is the three-day event when Swamp Gravy is performed.[9] There Story Bridge is one of two frameworks that people experience and learn from to become agents of social change. The other is Social Artistry, an approach developed by Jean Houston.[10] Social Artistry is a model of consciousness and methodology to build capacities for creative leadership, with several useful techniques that we will explain later in this text. At BCCC Jan Sanders, an ICA and Social Artistry trainer, holds workshops and a train-the-trainer series for those interested in learning. Social Artistry is not co-creative in itself, but the capacities developed through it support co-creative leadership.

BCCC 2017 was held one week after the US Presidential election, and many of the participants came directly from the Women's March in Washington, DC. They were emotionally charged, and they found great inspiration in what Story Bridge and Social Artistry could do for them as agents of change. They came to learn tools and ways forward, and the community there became instantly co-creative to that end. It was a special moment that I will never forget, for I found myself in the midst of a newly forming civil rights movement. The air was charged with passion and commitment, and everyone praised co-creation as the vehicle for a new future.

The Co-creative Difference

These vignettes illustrate the fact that there is something special about co-creation that sets it apart. Whenever someone asks me what co-creation is, I respond by evoking a memory that most of us have. "Think back to a time when you were working with a few other people on a challenge, and you had a collective breakthrough. What was that experience like?" I then probe for what made that moment so special. "What made that possible? And how does that compare to other collaborative efforts?" These questions draw out some key characteristics of breakthrough experiences.

Foremost among answers is the sense of synergy among the collective, complemented often by trust and authenticity. Second, people felt like they were part of something larger than themselves, and that what they were doing mattered. This gave them a particularly strong drive to carry things forward. Lastly, people talk about emergence—the feeling that new ideas or solutions manifested out of thin air. Emergence is often complemented by a sense of joyful surprise—the "eureka" moment that accompanies an epiphany.

If you evaluate these statements carefully, what becomes apparent is that most of them are emotional. It is rarely the case that someone, when asked these questions, replies by commenting on the quality of the outcome. They focus on the quality of the *experience* that leads to great outcomes. Our team has been fortunate to have witnessed and participated in co-creation across several contexts. Indeed, it was participation in experiences like our colleagues' examples that inspired our inquiry. Being part of the process, we realized that the experiential aspects of collective creativity are really the key to fostering breakthroughs. Thus began our exploration of how to design for such moments.

As many readers of this text might relate to, we came to use the term co-creation only after having a profound experience of it and wondering how it occurred. The terms we use are our way of conceptualizing and sharing a process of fostering collective intelligence and then tapping the potential of that collective. Our ideas are not entirely novel, but rather part of a growing trend. In the September edition of Harvard Business Review, Anthony Scott suggests that the business world is shifting from the Third Era of Innovation (driven by venture capital) to the Fourth Era (driven by corporate catalysts in large companies).[11] This article paints a very interesting picture for established companies, as it suggests that we can unlock much more creativity, innovation, and therefore profit with *internal* creative processes. How to do that has been the subject of much interest, with consultancies like IDEO, Deloitte, Bain & Company, and others coming into companies and helping restructure or create an environment conducive to internal creativity.

The animated film company PIXAR is an exemplary illustration of collective creativity. PIXAR was founded on the premise of co-creation. They are campus based, and the founders have done an excellent job of establishing and preserving an environment that continuously generates creative expressions. If we imagine creativity to be a frequency, as Nick Udall from the nowhere group argues, then we might say that PIXAR "optimizes the frequency at which their organization operates."[12] We enjoy the "creativity as frequency" metaphor, for it suggests that we can tune ourselves and our teams to it. We call the optimal expression of collective creativity "resonant co-creation." Resonance, as we will explain in Chap. 12, is a harmonization of three "frequencies"—or elements of co-creation. When an experience design, its facilitation, and talent development harmonize with each other (play off and build upon each other perfectly), then the amplitude (creative potential) increases. PIXAR is one of the very few organizations that has made this part of their everyday working environment—an example to be lived up to.

Most organizations do not have their own campus-based model like PIXAR. Large organizations are more often robust systems that strive for maximal predictability, efficiency, and reliability. Success in these contexts requires more than just a good process with innovative results. It needs a good story to connect with potential users and cut through the organizational inertia that so often meets any change initiative. Strong narratives reach and engage stakeholders, facilitating the desire to adopt something new. In his explanation of the power of story, IDEO co-founder Tim Brown explains.[13]

> An experience that unfolds over time, engages participants, and allows them to tell their own stories will have resolved two of the biggest obstacles in the path of every new idea: gaining acceptance in one's own organization and getting it out into the world.

Brown highlights the fact that high levels of engagement (created by the story) and mutual empowerment are essential drivers for organizational innovation. These are both outcomes of co-creation, and in fact we do not consider a process co-creative without these experiential dimensions to the creative process. Co-creation is a vehicle to build empowered, creative teams with the capacity for breakthrough innovations that connect with the broader ecosystem and inspire change.

Co-creation can be a process led by an external consultant, and it can also be integral to a culture of innovation. One of our favorite quotes is "Culture eats strategy for breakfast." The quote is a play on the common misunderstanding of the relationship between culture and strategy. Culture is the broad set of relationships, beliefs, behaviors, and artifacts (tangible representations or products) shared among a group of people. In organizations, culture is the bedrock that everything else is built upon. Strategy may be a compelling vision and means to enact it, but strategy always occurs in a relationship with the larger culture. As Nick Udall notes in *Riding the Creative Rollercoaster*, a common challenge is that "strategies get lost in translation, as they are only seen and understood through ingrained cultural filters." Moreover, "most strategies are born out of the dominant culture, and in so doing replicate their self-limiting beliefs and patterns."[14] Thus, while a great amount of resource and attention is given to developing new strategy,

> The irony is that cultures of innovation are the only source of true and sustainable competitive advantage. Breakthrough strategies, therefore, emerge from an ecology of creative teams and are brought to life through cultures of innovation.[15]

Embedding co-creation as a way of working within an organization is an effective way to establish the ecology of creative teams needed for competitive advantage. Frederic Laloux's popular text *Reinventing Organizations* speaks specifically to this point.[16] His approach is co-creative and supports our argument for resonance as a key differentiator in strategic innovation initiatives.

Scharmer and Kaufer's text *Leading from the Emerging Future* contains many examples of organizational transformation and strategic innovations resulting from applications of the Theory U framework[17]—itself a co-creative process. Among these include the IDEAS Indonesia project, which resulted in a new form of governance by Bupati Suyoto; the Bronx Cooperative Development Initiative (BCDI), which employs an inclusive multi-stakeholder dialogue to drive development; and an initiative called the Global Well-Being and GNH Lab, aimed at improving well-being worldwide. Each of these was a strategic innovation in that they required abandoning existing models and co-creating entirely new ways of addressing challenges.

Our Value Proposition

Co-creation is a meta-level process that enhances collective creativity. Co-creation can fuel innovation, drive culture change, and harness the full creative potential of any team. Strategic innovation (breakthroughs) revitalizes organizations and can create entirely new markets. However, focus on pragmatism, control, and efficiency in businesses tends to stifle creativity. How then can businesses generate the types of innovations needed to thrive? The answer: co-creation.

Co-creation adds a nuance to design thinking that can evolve how it is understood and employed. That nuance is the focus on experience design for the creative team itself. In the field of design, teams are often assembled to create new products or services. Our argument is that we get the most out of our teams by designing growth experiences for them and integrating techniques from facilitation and leadership development. Throughout this text, we argue for the value of facilitation and capacity training programs in user-centered, co-design, and participatory design practices. IDEO's courses on design thinking are an opening to this exciting new area of development.[18] Building up on that, we pose co-creation as a framework that can improve upon design outcomes.

In the next chapter we will tease out what co-creation is and is not, offering our own research-based definition that brings more operational utility to the term. We argue that co-creation is an art rather than a science, and like art it involves practice and performance. Also, like the great actor or musician, the co-creative experience designer benefits from certain qualities that transcend process. The secret of the art lies in weaving together process, environment design, and human factors to establish the space between from which insight emerges and the collective intelligence to harness it.

There are many places where one can learn aspects of co-creation. Facilitator conferences, practice-centered conferences on social innovation, leadership development programs ... in each of these you can hear about or train in one or more of the philosophies or tools related to co-creation. Here our goal is to bring these together into a cohesive framework that is held together by the metaphor of a great artistic performance. The art lies in the weave, which we have found to be a nearly universal grammar, or process architecture, that underlies many trademarked approaches to innovation. In the next chapter we present the Co-Creative Journey and the Space Between models as the framing upon which many different facilitation techniques can be placed.

Notes

1. Brown and Katz, *Change by Design*, 150.
2. Ogilvie and Liedtka, *Designing for Growth*, Kindle Locations 169–171.
3. Ogilvie and Liedtka, *Designing for Growth*, Kindle Locations 290–294.
4. Ogilvie and Liedtka, *Designing for Growth*, Kindle Locations 451–453.
5. Neil deGrasse Tyson (@neiltyson) Twitter Post, Feb 5, 2016, https://twitter.com/neiltyson/status/695759776752496640?lang=en.
6. Learn more about the Green School at https://www.greenschool.org.
7. Institute of Cultural Affairs International. Winds & Waves. Vol 6. No 1. April 2016. www.ica-international.org.
8. More information on Story Bridge and its training is available at https://www.storybridge.space/training.
9. Learn more at http://bc3-colquittga.com.
10. http://jeanhoustonfoundation.org/social-artistry/.
11. Anthony, *The New Corporate Garage*, 44.
12. Udall, *Riding the Creative Rollercoaster*, Kindle Location 1503.
13. Brown and Katz. *Change by Design*, Kindle Location 136–137.
14. Udall, *Riding the Creative Rollercoaster*, 1548.
15. Udall, *Riding the Creative Rollercoaster*, 1556.
16. Laloux, *Reinventing Organizations.*
17. Scharmer and Kaufer, *Leading from the Emerging Future: from Ego-System to Eco-System Economies.*
18. IDEO offers several courses online at https://www.ideou.com/products/hello-design-thinking.

References

Anthony, Scott D. "The New Corporate Garage: Where Today's Most Innovative – and World-Changing – Thinking Is Taking Place (the Big Idea)." *Harvard Business Review* 90, no. 9 (2012): 44.

Brown, Tim, and Barry Katz. *Change by Design: How Design Thinking Transforms Organizations and Inspires Innovation*. Adobe Digital Edition ed. New York: Harper Collins e-books, 2009: Kindle Location 136–137.

Institute of Cultural Affairs International. *Winds & Waves.* Vol 6. No 1. April 2016. www.ica-international.org.

Laloux, Frederic. *Reinventing Organizations: A Guide to Creating Organizations Inspired by the Next Stage of Human Consciousness.* First edition. ed. Brussels, Belgium: Nelson Parker, 2014.

Ogilvie, Tim, and Jeann Liedtka. *Designing for Growth: A Design Thinking Toolkit for Managers.* Columbia Business School Publishing. Kindle Edition: Columbia University Press, 2011.

Scharmer, Otto, and Katrin Kaufer. *Leading from the Emerging Future from Ego-System to Eco-System Economies.* San Francisco, Calif: Berrett-Koehler Publishers, Inc., 2013.

Udall, N. *Riding the Creative Rollercoaster: How Leaders Evoke Creativity and Innovation.* Kogan Page, 2014: Kindle Location 1503.

CHAPTER 2

Understanding Co-creation

Background

"Co-Creation is everywhere," says Francis Gouillart in his 2010 blog entitled "the Co-Creation Effect."[1] Providing examples from Sony to the cities of London and Copenhagen, Gouillart illustrates the co-creation trend. Indeed, at the 2014 Business of Design Week in Hong Kong, co-creation was printed on over half of all the brochures. In the eight years since Gouillart's blog entry, the term has grown even more ubiquitous and more difficult to pin down. This is due in part to co-creation success stories of companies such as Nike + and Starbucks pointed out by Ramaswamy and Gouillart in their book *The Power of Co-Creation*. Everyone has jumped on the bandwagon, branding nearly every collaborative activity as "co-creative."

An examination of the literature reveals that co-creation has different applications. Co-creation is inclusive of multiple forms of collaboration and design thinking, but it is not defined *by* these. Co-creation is a general term used across multiple disciplines, principally design, organizational development, and marketing.

Depicted in Fig. 2.1, the innermost circle (*Co-creation*) includes approaches that are considered co-creative. These are value co-creation, resonant co-creation, and co-design. The approaches within the *Collaboration* layer include many features associated with co-creation and are understandably often mixed with co-creative processes. As we move farther away from the center, the approaches become less empowering and

B. R. Rill, M. M. Hämäläinen, *The Art of Co-Creation*,
https://doi.org/10.1007/978-981-10-8500-0_2

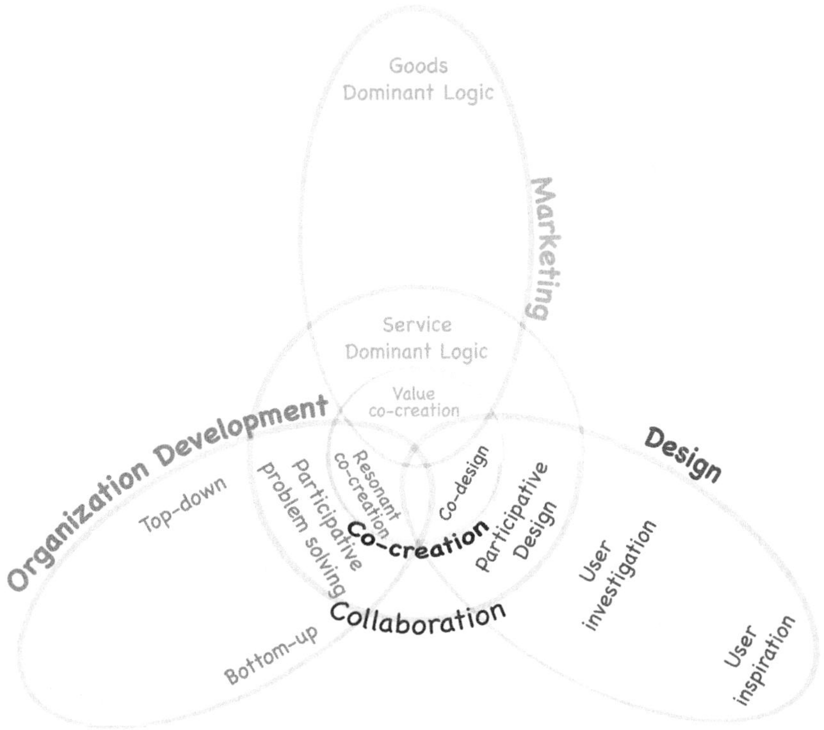

Fig. 2.1 Co-creation in three disciplines

more passive. Users and other stakeholders may be invited into the process to give inputs, but they are not actively participating in the creative process.

In each domain co-creation takes on a different nuance, perhaps best understood by what it *does* in these fields.

In Design

- Involve users in the design process (or)
- Utilize a wide range of experts (from different fields) within the design process
- Create a sense of community and brand loyalty through user engagement

In design, co-creation is a new gloss on the established practices of participatory and human-centered design. In the field of human-centric design, the term co-creation has referred to the participatory process between users and designers, or between different stakeholders. A distinction has been made between these two, by labeling the first as co-design and using co-creation for the latter.[2]

In *Change by Design*, Brown describes the co-design relationship, writing[3]:

> For the moment, the greatest opportunity lies in the middle space between the twentieth-century idea that companies created new products and customers passively consumed them and the futuristic vision in which consumers will design everything they need for themselves. What lies in the middle is an enhanced level of collaboration between creators and consumers, a blurring of the boundaries at the level of both companies and individuals. Individuals, rather than allowing themselves to be stereotyped as "consumers," "customers," or "users," can now think of themselves as active participants in the process of creation; organizations, by the same token, must become more comfortable with the erosion of the boundary between the proprietary and the public, between themselves and the people whose happiness, comfort, and welfare allow them to succeed.

In our work we conflate the two terms to simplify what has been a complex analysis of the relationships between designers, users, and stakeholders. The co-design journey planner (Fig. 2.2, next page) illustrates the range of possible relationships. Co-creation, as we define it, is a meta-level process that can be used across the entire range.

In Marketing

- Value co-creation is considered to be the process in which value is mutually created *between* the producer and consumer of a service
- According to the Service-Dominant Logic of Marketing, value is always created *during the use of* a product, not during the production

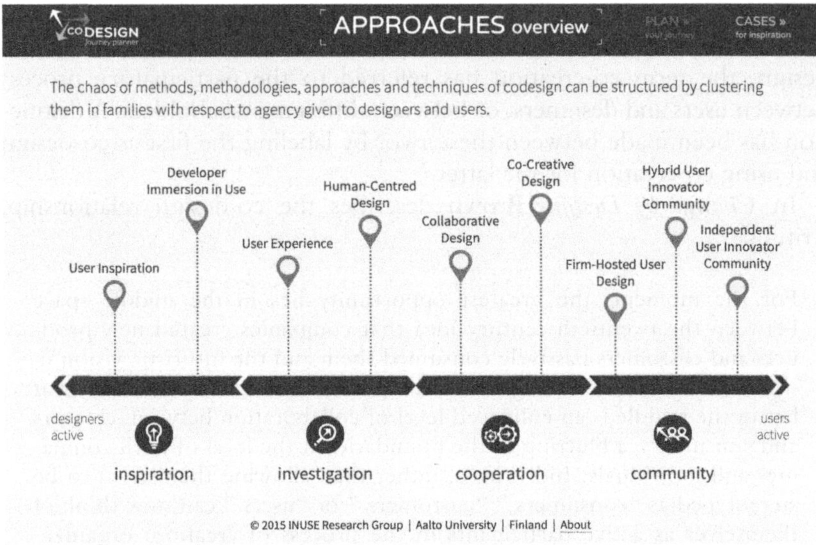

Fig. 2.2 Co-design journey planner. From the INUSE Research Group in Finland. Their website states: The Users and Innovation research group is a cross-Aalto team that creates in-depth knowledge on the role of users in socio-technical change. Our work focuses on user and designer practices, co-design arrangements, user innovation communities, and pathways of user contributions to innovative products. http://codesign.inuse.fi/approaches

C.K. Prahalad and V. Ramaswamy originally coined the term, defining co-creation as "the practice of developing systems, products, or services through collaboration with customers, managers, employees, and other company stakeholders."[4] Gouillart added to this definition, arguing that co-creation is a:

> theory of interactions. It involves changing the way the organization interacts with individuals, including employees, customers or any stakeholder. More specifically, co-creation involves setting up new modes of engagement for these individuals—platforms, in the jargon—that allow these individuals to insert themselves in the value chain of the organization. The idea of co-creation is to unleash the creative energy of many people, such that it transforms both their individual experience and the economics of the organization that enabled it.

His expansion of the definition made co-creation more inclusive, shifting the focus from producer-consumer collaboration to engagements among a wide range of people across the value chain.

However, ever since the introduction of Service-Dominant Logic as a new theory of marketing by Stephen L. Vargo and Robert Lusch in 2004, the field of marketing has designated the term co-creation for a very specific use. Even though the term co-creation has preexisted in Business and Management literature, currently the term is used to describe the process during which value is co-created between a service producer and a service consumer.[5]

In Organizational Development

- Foster innovation by tapping into the *collective insight* and potential of groups
- Generate *breakthrough solutions* when existing models fall short
- Bring together *diverse stakeholders* facing a common challenge

In Organization Science the terminology has evolved through another path, so as a term co-creation has been used only in very few occasions. However, the co-creation principle has received tremendous interest from the 1980s, and ever since it has been promoted as a competitive strategy, as a tool for organizational renewal, and as a management innovation.[6] Our colleague Benjamin Butler captures the essence of co-creation in organizational development, stating:

> Co-Creation touches on the most upstream part of an organisation as one can—the organisation's "mind." We see co-creation as tapping into the collective intelligence of a group or organisation in order create something new.

As this quote indicates, co-creation in organizational development is often an *internal* process of collective visioning and problem solving. There co-creation cannot be defined as a participatory process between producers and consumers. Instead, it is a creative process inclusive of stakeholders across a value chain defined by the organization.

Common Ground?

From our comparative analysis, we found that, on one hand, there are core tenets underlying all definitions of co-creation. A thorough and straightforward explanation of these comes from LegoViews, a blog dedicated to the LEGO® SERIOUS PLAY® framework for collective ideation.[7]

> The word co-creation is composed by two parts: a suffix, *co–* and the word *creation*. That *co–* may be explained in different ways, such as, *Collaborative* or *Collective*. The prefix comes from the Latin *cum*, meaning together and used in English to mean "together, mutually, in common."
>
> *Creation* is the act of *coming into being, producing, making*.
>
> The etymology of the world already highlights the key features of co-creation, which are the social, reciprocal dimension and the act of coming into being, creating, that is much more complex and abstract than production. The mix of those two words add another meaning, which is not only creating collectively, but creating something that has a value, for a mutually beneficial goal.

While we agree with this etymology of co-creation, the term is so general that it is frequently used without consideration of what it actually refers to. Quite often co-creation pops up as a format for a design workshop or panel at a conference, yet these events tend to miss the essence of co-creation and end up merely harvesting knowledge from various participants in an exclusive, controlling fashion. It seems at times that people expect for a dialogue to be co-creative just by labeling it as such. What this tells us is that many people simply do not understand what co-creation means or what it requires, and they use it because it sounds inclusive and/or attractive. We want to solve this problem by offering an operational definition of co-creation that is at once precise and empowering.

Definition

Given the overgeneralization of the term "co-creation," at the Co-Creation Initiative (CCI), we developed a specific set of inclusion and exclusion criteria that help define what it is and what it is not. Our efforts to be as specific as possible are in service of pragmatism. The particulars of this definition, as you will see, have direct impacts on program design.

Co-creation is a creative process that taps into the collective potential of groups to generate insights and innovation.

Specifically, it is:

1. A *process*, in which
2. Teams of *diverse stakeholders* are
3. *Actively* engaged in an
4. *Mutually empowering* act of

5. *Collective* creativity with
6. *Experiential* and
7. *Practical* outcomes

Co-creation rests upon a particular theory of interactions, wherein "stakeholders" are inclusive of both people on the "inside," the design or organizational team, and people on the "outside" of that team—users, employees, and others that *actively* contribute to the creative process. The role of the "outside" influence is specifically to bring in such external viewpoints and insight that may lead to reframing of ideas and the development of new perspectives. This type of participation often leads to a *creative disruption* that is followed by the formation of *collective insight*, which is the core element required for a co-creative solution to emerge. These two features are the most defining characteristics of the co-creative process, and they will be explained further in Chaps. 8 and 9 of this book.

What separates co-creation from crowdsourcing or other forms of end user involvement in the design process is the *type of interaction*. Co-creation requires direct group engagement, putting the major stakeholders (designers, consumers, managers, employees) into the same ideation space and collectively working together toward a goal with mutual value.[8] While crowdsourcing and mass collaboration do open up innovation by bringing in a wealth of ideas, what they lack is the experience of innovation with participants that co-creation provides. Successful programs such as the Nike +, My Starbucks Idea, and ITC's farming initiative in India created entirely new engagement platforms between the company and community, and continually learn from the engagement experiences among all participants.[9]

Co-creation is collaborative in that it meets Michael Schrage's, author of the book *Shared Minds*, definition of collaboration as

> the process of shared creation: two or more individuals with complementary skills interacting to create a shared understanding that none had previously possessed or could have come to on their own. Collaboration creates a shared meaning about a process, a product, or an event. In this sense, there is nothing routine about it. Something is there that wasn't there before.[10]

What collaboration is *not* is communication, coordination, or consensus. We agree with the article *Collaboration and the 3 C's*, which states[11]:

> Collaboration is distinct from each of the "C" words profiled above. Unlike communication, it is not about exchanging information. It is about using information to create something new. Unlike coordination, collaboration seeks divergent insight and spontaneity, not structural harmony. And unlike cooperation, collaboration thrives on differences and requires the sparks of dissent.

This perspective on collaboration contrasts the Merriam-Webster definition of it as "to work jointly with others," or "to cooperate with or willingly assist."[12] In co-creation, team dynamics shift from the common notion of collaborative—that is, working together—to formations that encourage independent or competitive tasks. Thus, while co-creation is a collective endeavor, it is not collaborative in the way that many understand it. This distinction is why we explain co-creation as "collective creativity" vs. "collaborative creativity."

The emphasis in co-creation on different forms of interactions among stakeholders over specific "how to" processes also separates it from design thinking.

In design terminology, User co-creation, a.k.a. co-design, is a participatory design process where the design process takes place in collaboration between the user(s) and the designer(s), whereas the design thinking process is all about *how* to design, and hence revolves around the designers rather than the users. While co-creation is also a process, we shift the emphasis to the design of interactive experiences among *all* stakeholders.

Finally, of our definition requires co-creation to integrate practical and experiential outcomes, with mutual empowerment being a core success criterion. Co-creation does not require consensus, which is very difficult to achieve with diverse groups. Instead, it requires empowerment, an experiential goal we feel central to all co-creative programs. Mutual empowerment is the felt sense that everyone has had a valued role to play in the process. When people feel valued, they will most often support a process they were part of even if they did not get what they personally wanted. In a successful co-creative program, people are encouraged to see the larger picture and the part they played. Empowerment translates into greater engagement in initiatives, increasing the likelihood of their success and impact.

To summarize, key differentiators include:

1. Team dynamics shift and are not always collaborative.

Co-creation is not *just* collaboration.

2. It emphasizes the use of a wide range or forms of interaction among stakeholders over specific "how to" processes.[13]

Co-creation is not design thinking.

3. It integrates practical and experiential outcomes, with mutual empowerment being a core success criterion.

Co-creation is not brainstorming, spitballing, or a typical team meeting.

Leveraging Experience Design

Co-creation is not specific to any one discipline, but is rather a process that can add value and increase innovative potential through ***intentional experience design***. The "ah ha" moment of an insight cannot be designed, but it can be designed for.

The key to successful co-creation lies in creating and holding a field of potential that we call "the space between" (Fig. 2.3).

The space between is the place from which new ideas emerge. It is the product of a well-designed experience that takes into consideration the knowledge, emotional, and interpersonal aspects of the overall experience

Fig. 2.3 The space between

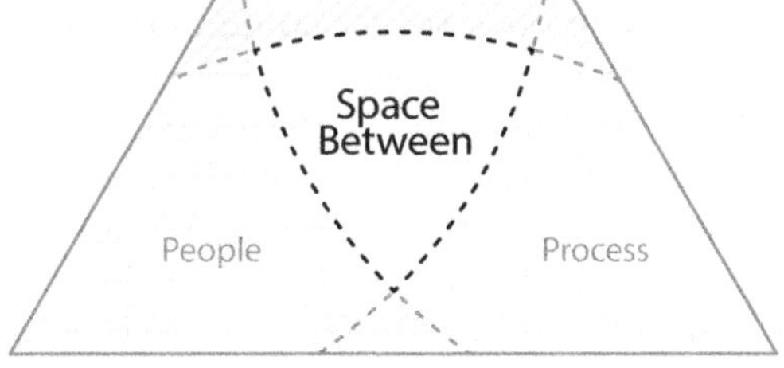

that the people go through during a creative journey. We refer to the person who designs and leads this journey as an experience designer, or *Xd* for short. The *Xd* may be a consultant, facilitator, organizational leader, designer, educator, or anyone else creating and supporting collectively creative processes. It is their task to create and "hold" the space between, which is:

- A source of creative potential
- Collectively empowering
- Temporal
- Designed

Creating this space requires setting the right conditions for success. The Space Between model (below) illustrates the three major components (PEP – People, Environment, Process) of co-creative experience design. We depict the components as curved triangles within the pyramid to convey the notion that each flexibly supports the space between. There is room to stretch to accommodate the needs of any project.

There will be times, for example, when an *Xd* does not have any control over the environment, or when they do not have an opportunity for the stakeholder interactions they desire. In such cases they, and their offering, must "flex" to the situation. This model allows for such agility.

Additionally, the three aspects are not mutually exclusive, as indicated by overlapping borders. In Part I (Preparing the Conditions) of this text, we offer a series of guidelines for creating the space between. Many of these guidelines could be placed in more than one of the core components, a facet of experience design that emphasizes the fluidity and interdependencies between People, Environment, and Process (Fig. 2.4, next page).

The story of how the Space Between model came about is instructive. It began in one of the many dialogues we had with James Bishop, co-founder of Brains on the Beach (BoB for short)—a community of organizational change consultants based in Asia. BoB and the CCI share the values of an open source community of practice and have worked closely together to solve a challenge James put to us one evening. "We intuitively know which tools and processes to use in the moment, and sometimes this means being willing to ask a question or take the dialogue in a different direction than the original plan. What we don't know is what's happening at the point of that decision, and the exact conditions or reasons we've chosen to do this, other than … it feels right to do and so. And it usually is."

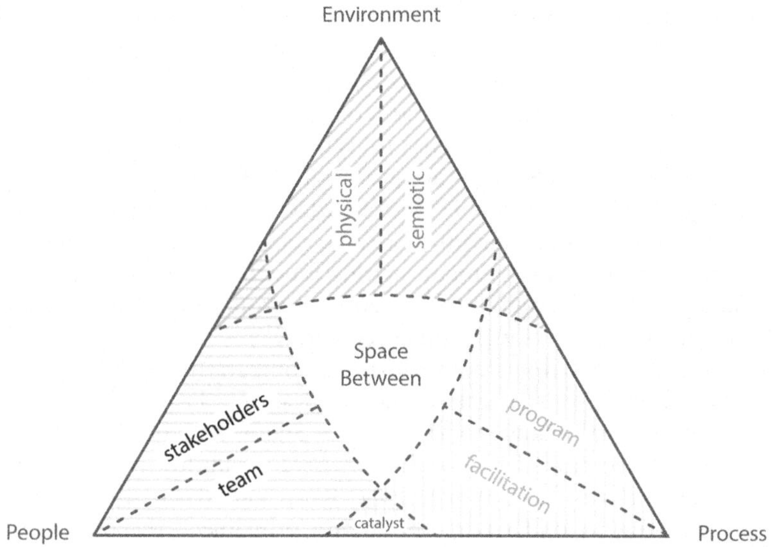

Fig. 2.4 Space Between model

Figuring out what was happening behind the scenes became a pillar of our research at CCI, weaving tightly within our larger objective of designing cultures of innovation. Our team spent two years closely looking at the interrelationships between creative leadership, spatial design, organizational change, and design thinking.

Three revelations came out of our research. First, we realized that successful programs were ones that carefully considered the interactions between people, process, and environment. Each discipline that we looked into (business, design, psychology, facilitation) had philosophies and techniques, but none put them all together in a way that maximized the potential benefits. From this insight we sought out to create the integrative, cross-disciplinary model offered here.

Our first conceptualization took a systems thinking angle, and the Space Between model was born. The space between is a powerful context for the emergence of new ideas. How well that space is "held" determines the potentiality of the system—with greater potential leading to more breakthrough insights.

In time, however, we realized that a systemic metaphor was inadequate. Creativity cannot be engineered, and creative performance does not follow the mathematical premises of systems thinking. If it did, we could reliably predict breakthroughs, an objective that has proven to be elusive.

Creativity, as we have found in design, follows art more closely than science. Unpredictability, chaos, and serendipitous moments of inspiration are absolutely essential. It occurred to us that the metaphor of a theatrical or musical performance holds the three aspects (PEP) together in a cohesive framework. A memorable performance is the result of a synergy between its constituent elements. Creative expression is a particular interaction between the environment, actors/musicians, director, script, and the audience that can only be achieved with proper preparation and performing attitude. Just as it is with co-creation.

Our second revelation stemmed from a comparative analysis of several different approaches to catalyzing innovation. From the "Double Diamond" design thinking model created by Stanford to the "Breakthrough by Design" trademarked way of the nowhere group ltd., we studied not only the techniques used but *Why*, *How*, *When*, and *Where* they were used. We were trying to understand the design principles—the philosophical and practical rationale—that underlie their works. What we discovered is that the experience of co-creation, which we articulate metaphorically as an artistic journey, has an underlying grammar. This grammar—or process architecture—is expressed throughout many innovation and change models. Although the names differ by trademark, understanding this grammar makes it possible for any designer or facilitator to orchestrate creative performance. Part II (Performing Co-creation) of this text explains how to use this theoretical framework in practice.

Our third revelation came out of the CCI Sessions, biweekly physical and virtual peer coaching dialogues wherein different change catalysts and designers spoke candidly about their experiences and what issues they faced. One of our group, a strategic consultant in Hong Kong, asked "What is necessary for true large scale change to take place?" Her question stemmed from frustration in her previous career with a global consulting firm that has robust (and expensive) organizational change programs. In her experience, the vast majority of change initiatives failed. "Why?" is a question echoed by many change catalysts, each of whom doing their very best for their clients.

Two years and many dialogues later, we can answer that question. While there are several contributing factors, a couple stand out above the others. The first is leadership. Change initiatives that start and stay with mid-level management and HR (human resources) are likely to fail, unless by some miracle they match perfectly with the vision of the leadership. A better approach is to begin with leadership, get their sanctioning, and involve them in the process. Co-creation, as we see it, requires commitment and active participation by senior leadership. If the people who have the power to make decisions and allocate resources are not in the room, it might as well be a shell game. Creative programs which generate outcomes that are greeted with no enthusiasm or ignored altogether by leadership are counterproductive. People who invest themselves into a process want to see their efforts realized. When this does not occur, they become quickly disillusioned and even skeptical. In a worst-case scenario, pessimism becomes part of the organizational culture.

Organizational culture is a second factor that can hamper or help co-creation. I was trained originally as a cultural anthropologist, which is perhaps why I jumped on the opportunity when the Prof. Cees de Bont, the Dean of the School of Design at Hong Kong PolyU, challenged me to figure out how to build a culture of innovation. “Sure! Culture is my thing.” I replied. As it turns out, it is my understanding of culture that has helped me understand what I call “Structural Resistance.” Culture is complex and often misunderstood in the business world. Culture is not a set of institutional practices that highlight the fun things people do at work or the social projects they are involved in. It’s not the celebratory moments. In organizational life, culture is the values, beliefs, and relations that structure people’s behaviors and interactions. It is the foundation upon which everything else rests, including strategy. Nic Turner, co-founder of the nowhere group ltd., talks about culture and strategy as existing in a virtuous circle, one supporting the other.[14] When one is not in the service of the other, for example, the culture not supporting a strategic change initiative, that initiative will meet structural resistance and likely fail. We will discuss this point in detail in Chap. 5, wherein we consider the lines of integration conducive to co-creation. For now we emphasize the fact that culture must support co-creative outputs if innovation or organizational change are to succeed.

The Co-Creative Journey

The co-creative journey reflects a balance of constructive exploration, systems thinking, and artistic performance. Like an improvisational play, it is both a designed experience and open to serendipity. At its heart lies a worldview taken from the Asian cultures in which this model was developed. In this worldview, the universe is understood as a dynamic interaction, a dance of sorts, between the forces of entropy and order. Depicted in the yin/yang symbol, light and dark, entropy and order are constantly consuming and creating the other. Order requires chaos, and vice versa. This worldview does not look at chaos as evil, but rather as a source of renewal. The lesson is that entropy—which often manifests as chaos—can be channeled to positive ends.

Another way of framing the co-creative journey is as a movement between the *Known* and the *Unknown*. The Known is based on the past. If you think about it, all expertise exists in past tense—it is based on the accumulation of experiences (our own or others) that have already happened.[15] This is the particular strength of the Known.

The Unknown, by contrast, is based on a *potential* future. Since the future hasn't happened yet, we can't possibly know it. This is why it's nearly impossible to give a client "deliverables" for a creative process. While we can guarantee an experience, to say that we can guarantee the outcomes is to state that nothing creative will occur. The reason is simple. Creativity requires newness. It requires us entering into the Unknown and exploring the potential that lies therein.

This movement between the Known and the Unknown is a journey. Both expertise and exploration are necessary components, and the journey is an oscillation between the two (Fig. 2.5, next page).[16]

The figure (next page) depicts the co-creative journey from the Known through the Unknown to create the New. Cultivating creative insights requires stakeholders to undergo a journey together from the world of their existing expertise into spaces of new potential. This is notoriously difficult, because it can require letting go of the very things that got us hired and have led to our success...expertise. It requires leaders moving from a position of dominating space to holding the space for others. And it requires developing core internal capacities and interpersonal skills so that teams can engage each other co-creatively.

When grounded in PACE—awareness (presence), high levels of trust generated by evolved teams (authenticity), willingness to take risks (courage), and thinking of the whole (eco-centered mindset)—co-creation has the potential to transform organizational culture and generate breakthrough innovations. This is co-creation at its best, and throughout this text, we will explain the additional value gained by investing in personal and organizational capacity building.

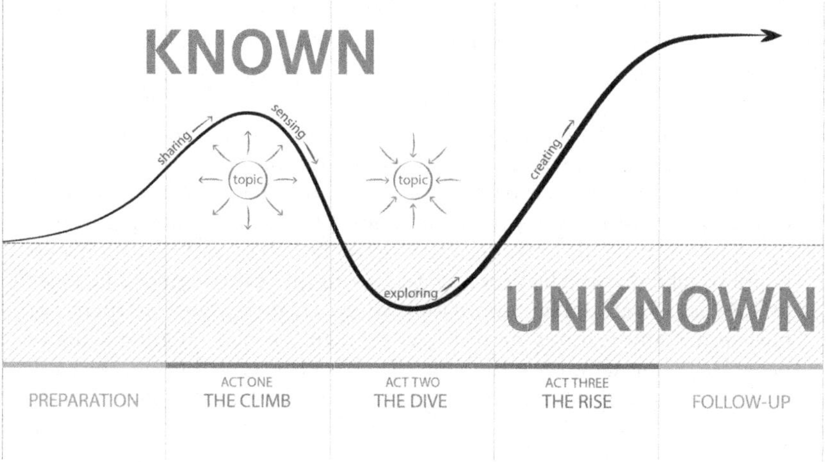

Fig. 2.5 The Co-Creative Journey

Aspects of the Journey

Our definition of co-creation requires both practical and experiential outcomes. Here is why. As anyone who has been through a creative process can tell you, creativity is a rollercoaster with highs and lows, moments of incredible flow and moments of profound frustration. Sometimes breakdowns are needed to generate breakthroughs.

The co-creative journey is not just one of knowledge. The oscillation between the Known and the Unknown is also emotional and interpersonal (Fig. 2.6).

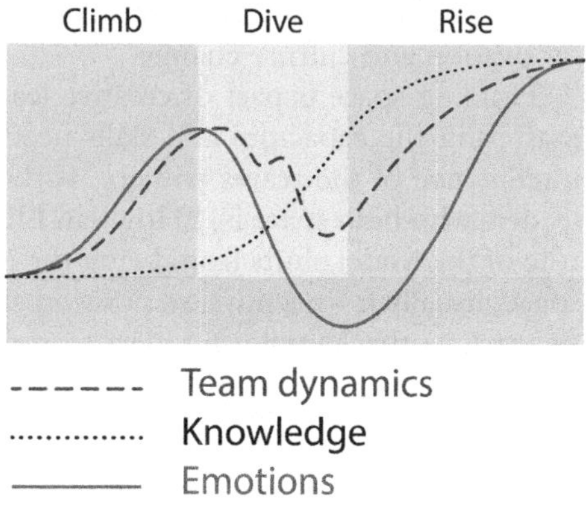

Fig. 2.6 Experiential aspects of co-creation. Act I is the Climb, Act 2 the Dive, and Act 3 the Rise

A well-designed experience takes into consideration the knowledge, emotions, and team dynamics of the creative process. In *Change by Design*, Tim Brown explains[17]:

> When a fresh team ventures out into the field to collect information, it is full of optimism. The process of synthesis—the ordering of data and the search for patterns—can be frustrating as important decisions seem to ride on the most insubstantial of hunches. But then things begin to pick up. The ideation process becomes more tangible, and new concepts begin to take shape. The process peaks when the team begins to produce prototypes. Even if they don't look so good, don't work properly, or have too many features or too few, they are visible, tangible signs of progress. Eventually, once the right idea has been agreed upon, the project team settles down to a state of pragmatic optimism punctuated by moments of extreme panic. The scary bits never completely go away, but the experienced design thinker knows what to expect and is not undone by the occasional emotional slump. Design thinking is rarely a graceful leap from height to height; it tests our emotional constitution and challenges our collaborative skills, but it can reward perseverance with spectacular results.

Each experiential component requires special considerations and tools for maximizing the potential creative output of the group. In the language of leadership development, the art requires "creating the container" and "holding the space." Creating the container is establishing a safe, authentic space wherein people can open themselves up and take risks. By "safe" we are not implying a space wherein no one gets their feelings hurt. On the contrary, "safe" is a space of mutual respect where people can express what they feel freely without fear of consequences outside that space. No one is going to get fired, for example, for challenging their boss. PACE (above) establishes a very specific kind of container conducive to strategic innovation and culture change.

Holding space is part of creative leadership, and benefits greatly from mastering the capacities and skills needed to fully tap into the collective intelligence of the teams you are working with. The central question for leaders who hold space is, "How can I help my team be at their best?" The role of the leader shifts from being the person who dominates the creative space, usually from a physical position at the head of the space, to creating spaces for other people and ideas to come forth.

If and when people develop the resources to be at their best in a creative process, amazing things can happen. When a team goes through this journey collectively, they come out with renewed energy within and between themselves, deeper respect, understanding, and insight. Co-creation can be transformative, meeting and often exceeding experiential goals such as team bonding, improved communication, and improved performance. That alone makes it worthwhile, yet co-creative projects done right also tend to exceed the practical aims. In our final chapter, *Striving for Resonance*, we look at what makes for a truly breakthrough performance where everything seems to work like magic and innovation manifests from seemingly nowhere.

Three Acts

Having looked at the overall journal and its components, we can now take a glance at what each part of the journey entails. This overview is intentionally minimalist, so that we can get on with the *How to* design and implement co-creation. Chapter 5 unpacks the co-creative journey in greater detail.

In co-creation what we strive for is a powerful experience of creative synergy that leads to deep insights and possibly breakthrough innovations. The co-creative journey in Fig. 2.5 depicts movement through several stages, with the three "acts" representing a multi-segment creative program. A segment can range from a half day to several months, context dependent. The process begins with PREPARATION, inclusive of stakeholder dialogues, framing the challenge, and other steps necessary to design bespoke co-creative programs.

ACT I—THE CLIMB—is an input stage aimed at opening up people's minds with new information. In their text on gamestorming, Gray et al. give this stage a keyword of "divergence."[18] The driving principles are knowledge transmission and team bonding, with the latter being equally important. Co-creation is an emotional rollercoaster. Strong interpersonal bonding in the beginning enables the team to navigate the Unknown better and often leads to prosocial behaviors in the workplace long after the program.

ACT II—THE DIVE—is exploration, reframing the subject from different perspectives. It is the journey into the Unknown. ACT II is when serious games, presencing, dialogue, and other techniques shift understanding from received notions to new ideas. Among facilitators there are a wide range of possible activities to use. Some facilitators prefer to keep the group in dynamic motion from one activity to the next, tapping into energy and creative tension using gameplay mechanics. Others concentrate on identifying and deeply exploring each aspect of the problem and the posed solutions. Co-creation is successful when the conditions for it (e.g. respect, trust, engagement, awareness) are set correctly and the energy of the group is managed to meet the best possible outcomes for the program. It is in ACT II that seeds of collaborative potential first manifest, and the keyword is "emergence."

ACT III—THE RISE—is the movement toward outcomes, with keyword "convergence." It focuses the collective energy toward initiatives that engage and mutually benefit all of the participants. It is the prototyping stage, in which designs and action plans are formed. ACT III brings clarity to whether the process has been co-creative or not. Co-creation is evident when all of the members of a team remain engaged and take collective ownership of an idea. The outcomes of co-creation are those ideas with the most energy behind them. Not everyone will be happy with everything, but ideally everyone understands and is committed to the way forward.

FOLLOW-UP is needed for any co-creative program, for often the outcomes of the program are only arenas of action with first steps charted. From there the team/organization must pull together the right resources and commit to action. FOLLOW-UP can consist of further facilitation, consulting, coaching, or a number of activities that support the team/organization meet its goals. These activities may or may not be co-creative, depending on how that group wishes to work.

The Co-creative Difference

In this chapter, we have presented our understanding of co-creation and illustrations of the Space Between and the Co-Creative Journey. Framing co-creation as *experience design for the innovation journey* is the unique angle in this text that truly separates co-creation from other enactments of design thinking. Contrasting the design thinking focus on "how to," our experience-centered model adds a humanistic dimension to creative processes and highlights the value of integrating skills and tools from other disciplines such as leadership development and change facilitation.

To use an architectural metaphor, we have laid the foundation and framed the house. You have seen blueprints and the AutoCAD layouts that give you a general idea, but many of the details are still to come. We unpack these details for you in the coming chapters, beginning with a deeper consideration of the people involved in and affected by co-creation. To close this chapter, let us consider the effect this model of co-creation can have in design and beyond.

Co-creation in User-Centric Design

When we think about how the design process has evolved in the past few decades, perhaps the most visible changes relate to the user involvement within the process. In the past it was clear that the role of the Designer was to design a product, while the role of the User was to use it. Today, however, we see the users getting involved in the design process as inspirators, initiators, consultants, co-designers, and so on. Even though the users are no longer seen as only passive consumers, their contribution to the design process can vary a lot. We can classify a design process as ***designer-driven***, ***user-driven***, or ***co-design***, according to the level of designer/user involvement, as illustrated in the figure below. Intuitively it is clear that co-creation is performed at the sweet spot of co-design, where designers and users participate with roughly equal contributions to the design process (Fig. 2.7).

Fig. 2.7 Designer-user participation

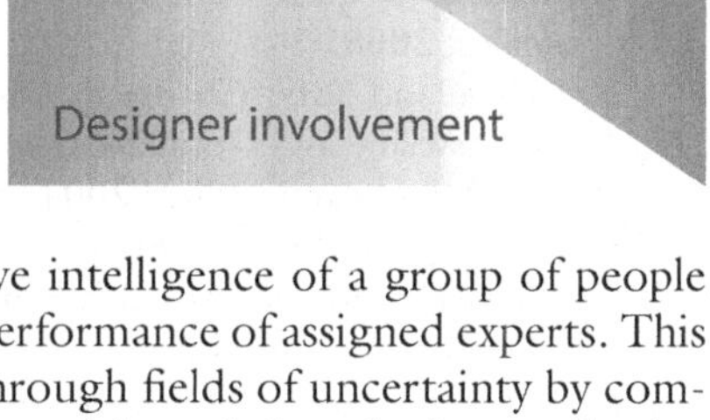

Co-creation builds on the collective intelligence of a group of people rather than relying on the individual performance of assigned experts. This approach enables the group to rush through fields of uncertainty by committing to an iterative process of internal knowledge sharing, collective decision-making, and constructive experimentation. This organic way of design encourages the group to create a *shared base of reference* through which they can operate collectively and to generate *shared knowledge*, which they—as a group—can apply to perform design.

Co-creation, however, is not limited to co-design. Co-creation as a process can take place without any user involvement—as long as the process is based on a collective performance of a diverse bunch of stakeholders who work together toward a common goal. Indeed, such a process might benefit from the presence of actual users, but even without their involvement, the process can be very co-creative. At the other end of the spectrum from the design studio, a closed community of activists can develop non-commercial solutions that fit their niche needs without involving any professional designers in the process. Obviously, this development can also be done in a co-creative manner.

As final note, even though there are clear benefits for involving certain types of stakeholders in a design process, co-creation as a process is not limited to any specific combination of participants. Diversity of participants increases the complexity and internal tension within a process, so it makes sense to keep the number of participants to a small enough level so that the process can be successfully executed. And of course, experienced *Xd* can find ways to steer very complex processes to their goals, while novice managers can find it difficult to deal with even small levels of friction between co-creators. Finding the right balance is the trick that makes some teams triumph, while others fail. *How to* design for balance is what we turn to now.

Notes

1. Gouillart, Francis, "The Co-Creation Effect," accessed March 27, 2010, http://francisgouillart.com/wordpress/?p=720.
2. Elizabeth Sanders and Pieter Jan Stappers describe the use of this term in the field of quite well in their article *Co-creation and the new landscapes of design*, 2008.
3. Brown and Katz, *Change by Design*, 59–60.
4. Ramaswamy and Gouillart, *The Power of Co-Creation*, 4. See also Prahalad and Ramaswamy, 2002, 2004.
5. See Vargo and Lusch, *Evolving to a New Dominant Logic for Marketing*, or Prahalad and Ramaswamy, *The Co-creation connection* and *Co-creation experiences: The next practice in value creation.*
6. See, for example, Dougherty, *A practice-centered model of organizational renewal through product innovation.* For organizational renewal, see Hamel, Doz, and Prahalad, *Collaborate with your competitors and win.* For Competition, see Hamel, G. (2006). *The why, what, and how of management innovation.* See also Mandle and Mandle, *The Co-Creative Meeting.*

7. LEGO® SERIOUS PLAY® is itself a co-creative methodology. Its definition can be found at the LegoViews blog. http://legoviews.com/2014/05/03/co-creation-the-power-of-conversations-1/. For an additional comprehensive analysis of the term, see Frow et al. (2011, 2015).
8. An ideation space does not have to be face to face. Communication technologies have enabled multiple forms of virtual and mixed mode engagements.
9. Ramaswamy and Gouillart, *The Power of Co-Creation*.
10. Schrage, *Shared Minds: The New Technologies of Collaboration*.
11. Denise, *Collaboration* Vs. *C-Three (Cooperation, Coordination, and Communication)*.
12. https://www.merriam-webster.com/dictionary/collaborate.
13. Design thinking can be a co-creative process, and we would say that it often is. However, in many cases it is executed by "The Master Designer" who merely squeezes information out of users and experts.
14. Nic Turner is one of the co-founders of the nowhere group ltd. More on the virtuous cycle can be read in their book *Riding the Creative Rollercoaster*.
15. The Presencing Institute has a nice illustration of thinking from the past vs. thinking from the emerging future. www.presencing.com.
16. The consulting firm nowhere group ltd. has written a book that depict this journey as a creative rollercoaster, and analogy that we find compelling.
17. Brown and Katz, *Change by Design*, 64–66.
18. Gray et al., *Gamestorming*.

References

Brown, Tim, and Barry Katz. *Change by Design: How Design Thinking Transforms Organizations and Inspires Innovation*. Adobe Digital Edition ed. New York: Harper Collins e-books, 2009: Kindle Location 136–137.

Denise, Leo. "Collaboration Vs. C-Three (Cooperation, Coordination, and Communication)." In *INNOVATING*: The Rensselaerville Institute, n.d.

Dougherty, Deborah. "A Practice-Centered Model of Organizational Renewal through Product Innovation." *Strategic Management Journal* 13, no. S1 (1992): 77–92.

Frow, Pennie, Adrian Payne, and Kaj Storbacka. "Co-Creation: A Typology and Conceptual Framework." Paper Presented at the Proceedings of ANZMAC, 2011.

Frow, Pennie, Suvi Nenonen, Adrian Payne, and Kaj Storbacka. "Managing Co-Creation Design: A Strategic Approach to Innovation." *British Journal of Management* 26, no. 3 (2015): 463–483.

Gray, David, Sunni Brown, and James Macanufo. *Gamestorming: A Playbook for Innovators, Rulebreakers, and Changemakers*. Sebastopol, CA: O'Reilly, 2010.

Hamel, Gary, Yves L. Doz, and Coimbatore K. Prahalad. "Collaborate with Your Competitors and Win." *Harvard Business Review* 67, no. 1 (1989): 133–139.

Hamel, Gary. "The Why, What, and How of Management Innovation." *Harvard Business Review* 84, no. 2 (2006): 72.

Mandl, Christoph E., Markus Hauser, and Hanna Mandl. *The Co-Creative Meeting Practicing Consensual Effectivity in Organizations.* Berlin; New York: Springer, 2013.

Prahalad, Coimbatore K, and Venkatram Ramaswamy. "The Co-Creation Connection." *Strategy and Business* (2002): 50–61.

Prahalad, Coimbatore K, and Venkat Ramaswamy. "Co-Creating Unique Value with Customers." *Strategy & Leadership* 32, no. 3 (2004a): 4–9.

Prahalad, Coimbatore K., and Venkat Ramaswamy. "Co-Creation Experiences: The Next Practice in Value Creation." *Journal of Interactive Marketing* 18, no. 3 (2004b): 5–14.

Ramaswamy, Venkat, and Francis J. Gouillart. *The Power of Co-Creation: Build It with Them to Boost Growth, Productivity, and Profits.* Simon and Schuster, 2010.

Sanders, Elizabeth B.-N., and Pieter Jan Stappers. "Co-Creation and the New Landscapes of Design." *Co-Design* 4, no. 1 (2008): 5–18.

Schrage, Michael. *Shared Minds: The New Technologies of Collaboration.* First Edition: Random House, 1990.

Udall, N. *Riding the Creative Rollercoaster: How Leaders Evoke Creativity and Innovation.* Kogan Page, 2014: Kindle Location 1503.

Vargo, Stephen L., and Robert F. Lusch. "Evolving to a New Dominant Logic for Marketing." *Journal of Marketing* 68, no. 1 (2004): 1–17.

PART I

Preparing the Conditions

CHAPTER 3

Working with People

Co-creation is a human-centered process, so we begin to unpack the *How to* with a focus on people. "People" consists of stakeholders and the participants in a program, facilitator included (Fig. 3.1).

Fig. 3.1 People

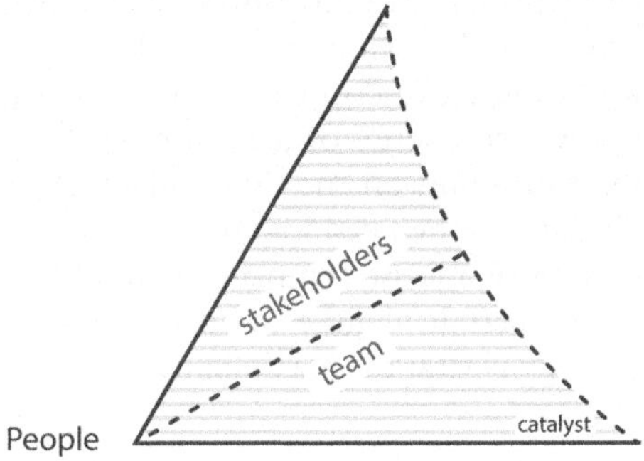

In this chapter, we will look closely at understanding and working with people, from the art of stakeholder interviews to co-creating a compelling needs story. Highlighted with vignettes of typical stakeholder dialogues, we show the reader not only what to consider but also how to go about it in the real world. We also introduce the value of the "virus"—a disruptive influence to creative processes. In co-creation, this means purposefully including people in the process that are outside of the worldview of the

B. R. Rill, M. M. Hämäläinen, *The Art of Co-Creation*,
https://doi.org/10.1007/978-981-10-8500-0_3

design or business team. We then offer techniques to manage that influence toward positive outcomes.

Introducing stakeholders leads to a discussion of team selection and dynamics—the *Who* of collective creativity. Creating teams is not formulaic. Each context and challenge demands a different type of team, sometimes with clearly set roles and others with purposeful ambiguity. In addition to introducing guidelines for team formation, we consider variables that can affect team performance and offer practical advice on how to work with diverse people. Above all, we emphasize engagement by all participants as one of the keys to successful co-creation. Without engagement, which itself is created by the compelling needs story, participants lack the energy and commitment required to manage working with uncertainty and the follow-up needed to realize the ideas that come forth in creative work.

Working with dynamic teams requires certain qualities in the experience designer (*Xd*). Great designers and organizational leaders do this intuitively, but can it be developed? We argue that it can, given the purposeful cultivation of qualities such as awareness, empathy, humility, and trust. Through a set of vignettes, we share the wisdom of veteran facilitators who speak of intangibles such as working with energy, being the midwife, and knowing when to let go of a process design. Rather than following a prescriptive process, we argue that skilled *Xd* enter into and follow the energy of a group. They must be flexible enough to change their program on the fly to adapt to the group's needs. This perspective illuminates the need for anyone who applies design thinking to realize that it is more a loose template than a blueprint. True co-creation is iterative with a certain degree of chaos built in. The ability to work with playful entropy is vital for maximizing the potential of co-creation.

Working with Stakeholders

"Ninety percent of all the work is in the preparation," Nic Turner once said to me. Nic, who has been catalyzing breakthrough innovations in major corporations for over 20 years, knows what he is talking about. His statement illuminates the importance of taking the time to understand stakeholders and design a program for them. Co-creation, in his perspective, is all bespoke.

Given that user-centered and participatory design practices involve, to different degrees, the end user of products or services into the design process, the field of design also highly values stakeholder needs and perspectives. Across these contexts the people involved in a co-creative process can be anyone internal or external to an organization. This compels us to refrain from the term "user" throughout this text, an attempt to avoid reducing participants in creative processes to the commercial ends "user" connotes.[1] "Stakeholder" is a more apt term because it is inclusive of all the people involved in and affected by a process or product throughout the value chain.

This inclusive definition of the stakeholder is the starting point for our exploration of bespoke program design. We begin by considering the complexity of needs and perspectives that exists in any diverse group of stakeholders. To understand these and create momentum, we then look into the art of stakeholder interviews, illuminating important guidelines such as building rapport, using context-specific language, establishing constraints and success criteria, and then co-creating a compelling needs story. Throughout this text we introduce each guideline by indenting and setting it in italics, as below. This convention will help readers skim through to specific points of interest.

Guideline (Example)

Beginnings

In design, a project often starts with the question "Who are the stakeholders and what are their needs?" It is followed by "What are the opportunities?" and "What is the product or service that you want to create?" These questions arise out of a desire on the part of the designer or entrepreneur for an opportunity to make something of value.

In organizations it is just as important for an *Xd* to ask these questions. Yet for the *Xd* the inquiry stems from a different place, and the services to deliver are most often a facilitated process, coaching, or training. An *Xd*'s work often begins in a dialogue with a person within an organization that has a need and is looking for outside help. Although it is a gross oversimplification, the *Xd* is dealing with either a burning platform situation, in which the organization must make change or else face negative consequences, or a theory of abundance situation, where the organization assumes (or has) resources and is interested in exploring potential. Strategic innovation, mergers and buyouts, changes in leadership, communication platforms, culture building, scaling, collaborative enterprises, reorganization, and start-ups, among many other situations, all fall under these two broad categories.

Understand Needs

Understanding the specific needs of the client/project is the first step in program design. Co-creation may or may not be the best way forward, and to determine that one must first identify whether or not the needs demand collective ideation. In design there are a variety of methods to identify needs, from the realization while using a product or service that it could be done better to ethnographic observation of people in everyday life. Designers will often research an area, looking at what others have done and identifying gaps or areas where something new enables another opportunity (e.g. technology innovation). They are actively looking for or trying to create needs because this is what drives the industry. For designers, co-creation is most useful when they involve other people in their design process. This can be users, but here we want to draw attention to *all* potential stakeholders in a design process. Unless you are designing by yourself, that means the people around you in the design team. In almost all design studios, teams rely on collective ideation. Thus in design there is an almost inherent need for co-creative practices.

In organizations, needs are everywhere. Finding them begins simply by listening to a conversation at the lounge or drink station. You can also turn to organizational ethnography and other assessment methods to identify unspoken needs. Many change consultants begin their work with assessment of the situation, identifying what is working well, what's facing challenges, and what is not working. From this assessment they can then offer services.

Finding a need does not indicate understanding of it. Nor is any one person's explanation holistic, including your own initial interpretation as an *Xd*. The anthropologist Clifford Geertz once challenged the field by making the point that ethnographic observations are similarly incomplete.[2] In his famous analysis of a Balinese cock (rooster) fight, he interviewed different participants and onlookers, asking them what was happening and what they thought of it. The answers revealed a wide array of interpretations, including completely different descriptions of what everyone was watching. The "facts" of the situation were few and the perspectives many.

Since Geertz turned the idea of "objective" observation on its head, we have come to understand that the vast majority of our lived experience and the so-called rational decisions that we make are in fact based on emotional reactions that are in themselves based on past events. We are a product of our experiences. Studies show that 70–80% of our decisions are reactive, which we layer with "reason."[3] Facilitation techniques such as the focused conversation method by the Institute for Cultural Affairs are tools that help catalysts tease out what parts of a dialogue or decision are objective and which parts are reactive. We look closer at this and other methods for dialogue in Part II. The point here is that no one, no matter how observant, can completely understand a complex situation. For one, our own experiences bias our perspective. Moreover, we can only see from so many angles, and most of the time there is more to consider than we sense.

So what can we do? The answer is relatively simple … we talk to people. Talking is "relatively" simple because, while the act itself is pretty easy, *how to* talk with them is more of an art form. Once the needs and perspectives of various stakeholders are understood, at that point you can decide if co-creation is the best tool for the job.

Hold Stakeholder Interviews

A stakeholder interview is a process of discovery. It is a process wherein the *Xd* is trying to identify not only where a person is at, but where they can go that is relevant to them and the larger situation. In design, this might be imagining the user journey if they had the product or service being conceptualized. In organizations, the *Xd* is trying to assess a situation and many different perspectives of it. This is complicated by the fact that for any complex situation we can examine it on three levels: the "I" (individual), "We" (group/team), and "It" (culture, organization, society).

The best metaphor for the overall aim of stakeholder interviews I have heard comes from Otto Scharmer.[4] He refers to the process as imagining that you have a video camera, and you are trying to observe a subject/object from as many different vantage points as you can. Following Geertz's argument, the camera is each person's individual perspective, limited by the lenses and depth of field it has. Looking at something with different lenses (perspectives) creates a more holistic comprehension. The challenge for individuals, Scharmer notes, is to get the camera out of their own head, to "zoom out" of their own perspective and see the larger whole.

We are not arguing here for the *Xd* to be able to extract the lenses from stakeholders' heads, but rather to listen to the various angles offered to create a composite of sorts—a picture "whole enough" to decide what type of program best serves the client or design project's needs. To illustrate the point and introduce further guidelines for stakeholder dialogues, let's us look at a real-world case.

Building a Community of Practice in Thailand

This project began when Peter—our fictional main character—reached out to the Co-Creation Initiative seeking help to establish a community of practice based on co-creative principles. Peter is a charismatic visionary who has dedicated himself to bringing social innovation to his small community in Thailand. His vision is grand, he has a lifetime of experience building businesses and making connections, and he was ready to form a core team to help realize his vision.

Our stakeholder dialogues began with myself and partners listening to Peter's vision in weekly Skype calls. To understand the scope of his vision, we deeply listened (listening without internal commentary), asked clarifying questions on details, and inquired into his motivations and visions for the future. We also spent some time just getting to know Peter. Where was he from? How did he end up in Thailand? What is his favorite thing to do with his children, who are now in an international school there? How does the community interact with foreigners? What is happening in local politics? Each of these questions helped us not only understand what he was telling us but also shed light on who Peter was and the broader context in which his vision was situated.

After several virtual meetings, we felt the need to get a better sense of the context. We made arrangements to visit Thailand and one of the potential partners. These visits gave us a lot more information than Peter could express, maturing our understanding and pointing out some inconsistencies between what we encountered and what we were being told. The site visits also served two other ends. One, they demonstrated our professionalism and commitment to the project. Two, they were an opportunity to meet in person, which deepened relationships and provided further contextual information.

As a team we reached an alignment of understanding and a unified vision for the best way forward. Our process was co-creative in that we all contributed and reached a consensus on the best way forward with each of us contributing an essential, yet different part. The next step was to help Peter with coaching that would bring more clarity to his role in the vision and, from there, create a compelling needs story that would attract the people needed to co-create the envisioned community.

This story illustrates several aspects of stakeholder dialogues. Our initial aim was to understand the needs and underlying issues of the situation, providing critical information for us to decide if and how we could help. The next several guidelines are about how to do that well.

Establish Rapport

Good rapport is a relationship in which you can have an open, honest dialogue with a person. We accomplish this by being genuinely interested in the lives of others. Human beings are amazingly sensitive creatures. We all want to be listened to, and often the people around us have heard it all and aren't that interested anymore. When someone new comes along and is receptive, it's quite common for people to open up and share details they may not even tell their closest colleagues. This happens when there is trust that you are not pursuing an agenda that might take advantage of them or misuse the information they provide. If your motivations are suspect, rapport is very difficult to establish. The best way to come across is to be authentic. For the professional facilitator, this means serving the groups' needs without vested interest in outcome. For the design lead or business manager, who do have vested interests, an inclusive attitude that truly invites and respects the views of others on their team works to establish rapport. In our example above, we began establishing rapport by asking personal questions about Peter's family and the local cultural context. Even though our dialogue was virtual, we were trying to connect on the personal level.

Use Context-Specific Language

Context-specific language is also helpful in stakeholder dialogues, especially when trying to communicate value. At CCI we struggled with this every time someone asked us what co-creation was. All of our attempts to explain it conceptually seemed to fail. This led us to define co-creation, as we did in Chap. 2, by discussing what it does before explaining what it is. We also found that analogies work well. For some audiences the analogy of improvisational jazz resonates with their experience of co-creation. For others football is a better analogy, and we draw comparisons to the German team that won the last World Cup. Collaborative art is also a good analogy, wherein the whole is an expression greater than the sum of its parts. In each case we find the language that makes sense within culture and worldview of the people we speak with. Speaking with terms from theoretical physics to an accountant likely will not help your attempts to communicate.

As we see from the story, questions are the bulk of stakeholder interviews. But what makes for a good question? The art of interviews is far too large for the scope of this text, but in the space we have, we can offer a few guidelines that make a significant difference in the quality of information you receive.

Open vs. Leading Questions

Derived from qualitative methodology, better contextual information comes from open questions, reserving leading questions to times when your intent is to guide a person's answers. An open question is one that does not confine the answer. These are generally the first questions you ask, when you are trying to get a very broad sense of the situation. "What is your vision?" is one example. "Why" and "How" questions are also very open, and these are some of the best tools you can use. Why and How questions explore the problem space, exposing needs and motivations that go along with the challenge scenario. If you ask "Why?," or some variant of it, five times, in most cases you will dig down to the root of the issue at hand. From there you can begin to think of the way forward with a much deeper comprehension.

Leading questions automatically bias the answer by guiding the person you are talking with in a certain direction. "What do you think the best choice is, X or Y?" forces the respondent to choose between only two options, when there very well be a third. "You don't like the new HR manager, do you?" is a more obvious manipulation. Leading questions are not good when you are inquiring into the scope of someone's perspective. They are good, however, in coaching contexts where you might be trying to steer a person toward an outcome. Coaching is all about asking the right question at the right time, and a skilled coach can do this to help people in a range of situations. Coaching, like therapy, is goal oriented. In these contexts leading questions are essential. In information-gathering contexts, by contrast, leading questions often generate poor knowledge bases that reflect the preconceived ideas of the inquirer (you).

Coaching

Coaching techniques are useful not only to help someone find direction or motivation but also to raise engagement and reframe an issue. Provocative questions such as "What are you creating now and what do you want to create?" encourage people to think deeply about their actions and the impacts these actions have. This is a particularly powerful question to use when dealing with a creative disruption—a person whom you have brought into the process specifically for their outside perspective but whom can also cause interpersonal conflict if not managed correctly. More commonly this question is put to leaders who are seeking to create change, or to people when they feel "stuck."

Like interviewing, coaching is an art that has its own library of resources. In co-creation we select a subset of coaching techniques that are particularly salient to the process.[5] For stakeholder interviews, challenging core assumptions is a coaching technique conducive to the process of identifying the true needs and motivations. In our dialogues with Peter, we used this technique to probe for where he was reactive. We needed to know his trigger points and how he might respond to criticism or challenge. He took this well because we had already established rapport, without which our gentle prodding may not have been well-received.

Our dialogues with Peter were receptive without judgment, a position from which we could ask sensitive questions and get honest answers. A relationship in which you are seen as authentic, open, respectful, and non-judgmental opens doors and establishes the trust needed to catalyze co-creation. From this position we are able to engage in a truly co-creative dialogue with the stakeholder, one in which we are looking at the situation and exploring what "we" can do together.[6]

The ultimate goal of stakeholder dialogues is to explore, uncovering the current reality and imagining a future one. It is all too easy for these conversations to stay in "blue-sky" thinking—a stratosphere of possibilities lacking the constraints of reality. If left there, co-creative programs can end up generating more blue-sky ideas with little hope of realization. To increase the likelihood of actualization, we need to come back to the ground and talk about details.

Check Capacity

Checking capacity is a guideline focused on identifying what kind of support a project has. The following are five open-ended questions that check capacity.

- What is the level of investment of people coming into the process?
- What resources are available?
- Who makes the decisions?
- What are the givens?
- What is non-negotiable?

The answers begin to reveal both resources and constraints that surround a project. They help us, as experience designers, understand what we can and can't do, what we need to be striving for, and what are the boundaries that we steer participants back from if necessary. This information, when shared with a team, can help bring focus at a critical juncture as they narrow the field of possibilities from everything to the chosen few that make it to prototyping.

Set Success Criteria

In co-creation, any program has at least two sets of outcomes. The first, practical goals, are desired outcomes. These are usually stated in terms of tangible products, services, or measurable change. Some design-based examples might be a new product line, a new form of customer interaction in a hotel reception area, or a new theme park experience at Disney. Organizational change examples might be a new vision statement, a merger platform, an improved sense of workplace well-being, or better performance metrics. In some cases the practical goal may be experiential, such as a team building workshop or company retreat. Practical goals are outcomes that people can see, touch, or measure in some way.

The second set of outcomes are experiential. We rarely see experiential intentions, such as personal growth or an emotional breakthrough, given consideration in program design. Yet we value these as essential for any process to be considered co-creative. The reason for this is because co-creation is a human-centered process wherein creative insights come from the *experience of* the space between. This mutually empowering experience is a centerpiece of the co-creative journey, without which the process is, at best, an imperfect design iteration. Although empowering and other internal experiences are a *felt* reality that cannot be seen or measured easily, they are a core success criteria in that they are essential to unleashing collective creativity.

The Creative Brief

The creative brief is the point where information translates into the action that generates the energy to move forward. A creative brief is the crafting of a compelling needs story, a breakthrough question, a challenge, or an opportunity scenario. The creative brief can take on a similar form to a design brief, a document that outlines the challenge or opportunity, the constraints, resources, timeline, and team. Alternatively, a creative brief can be a single phrase, a question, or a story. In all versions, the creative brief is meant to do one thing above all others—create engagement. The centerpiece of the brief must be something that attracts the interest of people who want and are able to work on it. It can be a burning bridge statement, such as "we must do X or else face Y." It can be visionary, such as "Let's design a human voyage to Mars!" It can be opportunistic, such as "Let's figure out a subtle game mechanic that differentiates our mobile gaming app." Whatever it says, it must be compelling. Therein lies its power to attract the *right* people to the co-creative process. Margaret Mead's famous quote, "Never doubt that a small group of thoughtful, committed people can change the world; indeed, it's the only thing that ever has," illuminates the needs for committed people. The only way to get people internally motivated is to make your story compelling.

The creative brief also situates the challenge or opportunity. We have encountered two very different philosophies toward the creative brief, and both work in different circumstances. In one version the creative brief is limited to the compelling needs story or breakthrough question, generating energy and interest without mentioning constraints. Those details come later. Inspirational speakers excel at this. A second approach is to frame the challenge scenario within a document that contains more specifics, especially the success criteria, capacity, constraints, and other project relevant details. Design projects are structured around their equivalent—the design brief. How much or little detail is needed for the brief can be negotiated in stakeholder interviews, but for the *Xd* it is beneficial to fill in as much of the detailed version as possible. This makes it much easier to design a program within the constraints and opportunities available.

Creating a Composite

To finish our section on stakeholder interviews, we zoom out from content and approach to look at a few broader guidelines that affect the quality of information we receive.

Tag Team Interviews

To begin, it is beneficial to have more than one person doing stakeholder interviews. We each have our own strengths and weaknesses. By working collaboratively with interviews, we can play off each other's strengths to create a more holistic understanding of what we hear in dialogues. This ability increases as a team of catalysts or interviewers work together over time. A good team learns to value the insights others reach that they might have missed.

Conduct Multiple Interviews

Interviewing more than one stakeholder is another means to create a holistic picture. Different people will provide different perceptions of a situation, and through the act of juxtaposing those perceptions the *Xd* is able to create a composite. This can be a long and arduous process, depending on the number of people involved and what you are trying to understand. At one end of the spectrum, such as organizational ethnography, qualitative methods and data analysis software may be required. Design and market research are less formal and "lighter" versions of ethnography. The advantage of these methods lies in the quality and quantity of data gathered, stemming from interviews and other forms of data collection. The disadvantage is how long it takes to gather and interpret all the data—ranging from a few weeks to a few years.

Explore the Context

Whenever possible, it brings great value to gather contextual information outside of interviews. The information people give is always biased, motivated by their own or someone they represent's interests. Observation will always reveal more than what is told. In design, researchers are instructed to gather as much observational data as possible, even things that seem completely irrelevant to the project. These snippets of information are then posted to the wall in the project room until there is what seems to be a huge disorganized mess. From this chaos comes insights that can seriously impact a project or program, so it is worth the time to gather as much as you can.

One important thing to look for is contextual information that indicates how the culture (organizational or otherwise) and strategy affects and could be affected by the process you are being asked to catalyze. "The road to hell is paved by good intentions" is a well-known saying because it is all too common for people to mean well but have no concept of how their vision articulates with reality. A vision is far more likely to succeed if we have an understanding of where structural resistance originates, and can make working with that part of the co-creative process.

In many cases, the inquiry phase is limited to a series of interviews and site visits such as those we had with Peter's project. Our composite was by no means as complete as we would have liked, but it was enough for us to initially frame the challenge. It was our 0.80 version, a term in design which indicates a rough prototype that is just good enough to take action and see how it evolves.

In our work with Peter, our composite understanding turned out to be different from what he framed the challenge to be. The only way we learned this was through ongoing dialogues over the course of two months, a time period in which things on the ground changed. This is not uncommon in the fluid reality we live in, and it demonstrates why a part of stakeholder dialogues is *ongoing status checks*. It is wise to establish regular communications with as many of the key stakeholders as possible. This, combined with site visits and conversations with people there that surround the potential process, provides robust contextual information.

Returning to Nic Turner's statement that 90% of all the work lies in the preparation, what becomes evident is the fact that a large part of this work lies in continuous stakeholder dialogues. When Nic runs a creative program, he is constantly soliciting inputs and feedback from key stakeholders and adjusting on the fly to meet ever-changing needs and dynamics. He is able to do this only because he took the time to develop a relationship with good rapport, deeply listened to a variety of stakeholders, and truly understands not only where his clients are but where they need to go. All of this comes before you ever set foot into a program or workshop space.

Team Selection and Dynamics

If you have a toolbox that only contains screwdrivers, chances are that you will not be able to complete any operations besides tightening and loosening screws. It doesn't matter how good the screwdrivers are, or even how many different types you have—the range of tasks you can accomplish with it will be very limited. In a similar way, if you have a team that consists solely of engineers, or only people from the production unit, chances are that even on your best day, you will not be able to complete assignments that would require knowledge, skills, or understanding from outside of their range of expertise. If instead you have a variety of different types of tools at hand, and you know how to use them, you have a much greater chance to succeed.

Selecting members for a team is analogous to selecting the tools for a toolbox. You will need to have a general understanding of *what type of issues your team might need to cover*, based on which you should know *which skills are essential* for solving the challenge. Front row skills might deserve more attention in the team selection process than the less vocal ones, as their impact will be greater on the process outcome. Then again, it only takes one wrong note to destroy a complete chord, so even the second flute needs to know how to play their part well enough to keep the team out of the bushes. In addition to looking at individual tools, you will also need to consider the various *combinations of tools* that can be required for producing an effective outcome. If key players are a mismatch for one reason or another, your team might be facing difficulties in finding a common tune. For example, a seasoned production engineer might be a good partner for a novice industrial designer, just as an established designer might be a fine pair for a young engineer, as both combinations have a more experienced person adding professional expertise and insight to the state-of-art skill provided by their younger colleagues. If the teams were set up differently, there would be a good chance that the egos of the senior experts would end up in a collision course, and the two newbies would not get the support nor guidance they would need to be able to reach their full potential.

For a toolbox to be useful, it needs to provide a wide range of tools. And it is good to remember that even a tool that is not of the best quality will add to the usefulness of the toolbox, if the tool extends the range covered by the set. An effective team is small in size, and wide in diversity. This diversity should extend through several dimensions (as described below), and the diversity should be somewhat deliberate, so that its effects can be monitored and controlled during the journey (Fig. 3.2).[7]

Fig. 3.2 Diverse teams. Each member should add to the diversity of the team

Building Diversity and Tension

Substantive conflict between individual team members is a driving force that pushes the team to aim high and look outside the box. This type of conflict is caused by differences in *what we know*, which can be traced back to the educational background (horizontal diversity) along with level and type of experience (vertical diversity) the people in question have. And since it is a favorable type of conflict, we should deliberately try to build suitable *substantive diversity* into our teams. Another form of diversity can be labeled as *demographic diversity*, and it stands for the many differences in *who we are* and *how we behave*. These differences can be traced back to the personalities, cultural backgrounds, and other types of demographic variances. Even though they can spark interpersonal conflicts, they can simultaneously contribute to the creative tension of the team.

The distinction between good and bad kinds of tension helps us design effective teams.[8] Teams with unresolved interpersonal conflicts will fail. Then again, the teams that have no interpersonal conflicts, nor substantive conflicts, will produce only trivial and boring results, which will not lead them anywhere. What is desired are teams that have substantive conflicts and who can manage their interpersonal issues. They will generally produce good results and triumph. This is because they use creative tension to boost their efforts and to take them—as a team—to a level of performance that individual members of the team would not have been able to reach on their own.

If you want to build a team that is both *willing* and *able* to push boundaries and exceed expectations, you will need to pay special attention to the range and scope of talents and personalities you have at hand when selecting members for the team. As diversity is a mandatory requirement for a co-creative team, it is good to keep in mind that diversity will create tension, and tension in turn will cause conflicts. The team will need to be prepared to handle conflict appropriately.

It is also important to understand that one should not even try to avoid creating these types of conflicts. In fact, conflicts have a special function in both team building and in knowledge production. First, any kind of internal conflict will give the team a chance to tackle and solve it together. Solving a problem together will help the team members understand each other better, bringing conflicting individuals closer to each other. This serves as a positive signal to the rest of the team as well and undoubtedly will have a positive impact on the team's performance.

Any substantive conflicts—conflicts between what people *know*—will push the conflicting individuals to get more information to support their own perspectives. This process will bring new knowledge to the team, increase the awareness of what others know, and expand the areas of shared knowledge within the team. Eventually, if the conflicts get resolved appropriately, the experience will again bring the team members closer together. So instead of avoiding conflicts, you should prepare yourself and your team to confront them as soon as they emerge—and preferably in a constructive way, as challenges that will help build the team.

Forms of Collaboration

The co-creation process brings certain requirements for how the journey is conducted, which again might affect the team composition and the choice of leadership style. Collaboration between different fields can be built in several ways, and each of these styles/approaches has their strengths and weaknesses. Below (Fig. 3.3) is an illustration of four complementary

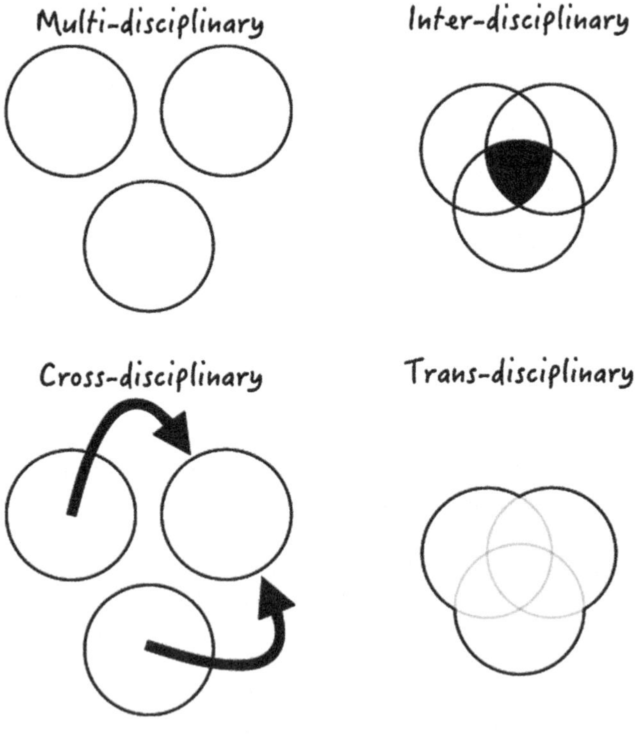

Fig. 3.3 Four types of collaboration

approaches to utilizing diversity across disciplines. *Multi-disciplinarity* refers to situations where there are individuals from multiple fields of expertise present within an organization, which makes it possible to use them as a resource in issues they are familiar with. Even though multidisciplinarity within an organization enables collaboration across different fields, in many cases the administrative boundaries along with physical separation create barriers between field-specific organizational units. The result is siloing, reducing the chance of interaction between individuals from different fields.

When a task can benefit from the expertise of another field, a suitable expert can be found from another unit and invited to contribute to the project. In this case, *cross-disciplinary* experts are used to applying their skills to an issue within another field. For example, if a cognitive psychologist is consulted to solve a problem related to the interface of a remote controller, or when a production engineer makes changes to the layout of cash registers in a supermarket, they are both applying their expertise to a situation in a different domain. Since they are working within another field, their contribution is cross-disciplinary.

In some cases, the need for certain type of expertise from another field becomes so common that it produces a need for *trans-disciplinary* expertise—expertise that integrates strengths from several traditional fields. The talented professionals produced by trans-disciplinary educational programs tend to dilute the borders between two or more disciplines. This creates expertise that is typically wider than in the traditional fields, but doesn't need to reach very deep into the domains. For example, Design Psychology and Industrial Economics are trans-disciplinary fields that combine characteristics from two complementary domains to educate trans-disciplinary professionals.

When the complexity of a task or situation demands for something more than just a simple application of expertise, there might be a need for a joint team effort. *Interdisciplinary* tasks are ones that require simultaneous utilization of expertise from several fields. Common examples of this type of collaboration would be a design team creating a new product concept by experts of marketing, engineering, and sociology, or a task force creating an organization development program by combining the expertise from human resources department, from their health service provider, and from their management team. Co-creation is most often interdisciplinary collaboration, but we shift to other forms as needed.

These four forms are intended to illustrate the complexity of collaboration and to help in planning and structuring any collaborative activities. In Part II we will tell more about how collaboration can be orchestrated in its different forms.

Creative Leadership

One of our favorite metaphors for co-creation is that it is like improvisational jazz, with the participants being the musicians. To play improv jazz, each artist must be a skilled musician. As we saw in the discussion of team dynamics, the people gathered are the right people, each contributing valued skills to the program. The second thing you need for good improv jazz is flow. The musicians listen and feel what each other is playing, intuitively responding to changes in tempo and passing the solo. How do we facilitate such flow? Continuing the metaphor, here we share with you a set of methods to tune your instruments, the participants and yourself, a bit differently to encourage flow and creative inspiration. Then we can perform together and make some music.

In the opening chapter we asked the question, "What are the attributes of the successful *Xd* and their process that set them apart?" Then in Chap. 2 we introduced creative leadership as being inclusive of "creating the container" and "holding space." What is needed to enact these guidelines? Our answer is part philosophical and part practical example. We draw attention to the qualities of creative leadership, focusing on how one can develop and embody these capacities in their practice.

Working with the Intangibles

Creating a container and holding space are what we refer to as "intangibles" of the creative process. They are intangible because they cannot be quantitatively measured.[9] Yet they are qualitatively experienced, often described in terms of "energy." Energy is a reference to the sense of interpersonal connection, as in the "vibe" of a group or space. A space, or group, can be said to have "good" or "bad" energy based on the perceived sense of safety or trust. A strong container then is one with "good" energy—a space where people feel comfortable being authentic with each other and trust the process.

Energy also refers to momentum, the felt sense of "having a lot of" or "not having" drive or engagement. If we consider the metaphor of the creative process as a rollercoaster, a lot of energy is needed in order to propel the team through the Unknown and into the New. That energy is developed in *Act I: The Known* through a mix of engagements, knowledge sharing, and social bonding. Music provides a useful analogy for this movement. Most songs have a chorus, verse, and break, each of which has its own particular energy. Songs are movements between energetic peaks and valleys, much like the creative process.

A good container consists of both conceptualizations of energy, and creative leaders intuitively know how to work with these. At their best, they create purposeful spaces that hold the engagement and inspire people to test their boundaries, step into the Unknown, and do things they might have thought impossible before. How they do that, in terms of process design and facilitation, is a subject for later chapters. Here we focus on the *capacity for* sensing and working with the energy of creative spaces. For a creative leader to work with energy, they benefit from developing the capacities of awareness (presence), empathy, trust, and humility. These internal capacities enable the project lead or facilitator to work with the intangibles of the creative process.

Awareness is an observational skill that we all have. It is our basic ability to notice what is occurring, and it can be further developed through intentional cultivation. As an example, presence is being keenly aware of what is happening within and around oneself in each passing moment. It includes suspension, creating a quality of mind that is best described as still or quiet. As Jon Kabat-Zinn explains, "if you bring a certain kind of open, moment-to-moment, nonjudgmental awareness to what you're attending to, you'll begin to develop a more penetrative awareness that sees beyond the surface of what's going on in your field of awareness."[10]

Sensing where things can go may seem to be a mystical quality of great facilitators, but it is actually an application of presence. Kabat-Zinn describes this application as deep listening, a shedding preconceived notions and historical patterns of understanding to sense a larger field of potential change. When presence is combined with attention to potential, the combination is what Senge et al. call "presencing."[11]

> The word Presencing means to sense, tune in, and act from one's highest future potential—the future that depends on us to bring it into being. Presencing blends the words "presence" and "sensing" and works through "seeing from our deepest source."

Presencing is tuning in not only to the group but also to the larger whole and the field of potential that surrounds any creative process. In his text on leadership, Peter Senge writes,[12]

> All learning is about how we interact in the world and the types of capacities that develop from our interactions. What differs is the depth of the awareness and the consequent source of action. If awareness never reaches beyond superficial events and current circumstances, actions will be reactions. If, on the other hand, we penetrate more deeply to see the larger wholes that generate "what is" and our own connection to this wholeness, the source and effectiveness of our actions can change dramatically.

The "wholes" Senge refers to are the systems in which creative processes take place—design teams, organizations, social and ecological systems. On the largest level the whole is the universe itself, the field in which the infinite interconnected chains of cause and effect create our reality.

Senge's idea was further developed in Otto Scharmer's *Leading from the Emerging Future*—a text that became the foundation for the ongoing Theory U course offered online via edX and the Presencing Institute. In these works, Scharmer and colleagues write about leaning in to potential futures. This is what we mean by the Unknown—a space where creative potentials reside and can manifest into tangible reality—insights and innovations. Highly present leaders and *Xd* can "sense" this field of potential and guide a team or organization toward it.

Awareness is also needed to understand organizational and interpersonal dynamics. All communication is situated within contexts that influence both their transmission and reception of information. A dysfunctional relationship among peers, a history of failed change initiatives, and design lead with a bad reputation … all of these are factors that can have negative impacts on creative processes if not accounted for. To illustrate just how complex a single social interaction is, the sociolinguist Dell Hymes came up with the anachronism SPEAKING.[13]

- Setting and Scene—The physical, social, and historical context of interaction
- Participants—Who is interacting, their roles, and relative power dynamics among them
- Ends—Purpose, goals, and outcomes of the interaction
- Act Sequence—The structure of communication (form) and order of interactions

- Key—Clues that establish the "tone, manner, or spirit" of the interaction
- Instrumentalities—Forms and styles of speech
- Norms—Social rules governing the event and participants' actions and reactions, that is, organizational culture
- Genre—The kind of interaction, for example, a brainstorming session, a strategy meeting, and a team building dialogue

The more an *Xd* is aware of and understands these dynamics, the more agile they can be when designing and holding the space for creativity. Nick Udall, the Chair of the Council on New Forms of Leadership at the Davos World Economic Forum, considers a high degree of awareness to be central to what he calls "fourth realm, or evocative, leadership." He states,[14]

> Now, it's not intellect that makes a great leader—although it helps. Rather it's the quality of their consciousness—their personal and systemic awareness. This arises from knowing that how we see the world can only ever be based on our own filters, lenses and biases. There is no one truth. We can only look at things from where we are. Walking through the world creatively requires multiple perspectives because it's in the weave that innovation happens…
>
> This quality of consciousness recognizes that we do not understand what we see; rather we see what we understand. The world can only, therefore, be subjective. Mastery requires us to enquire consciously into this subjectivity, to realize that we have been conditioned to look through our consciousness and not at it … It is only through a shift in our consciousness that new external possibilities, resources, innovations and pathways become knowable and available to us.

Nick's argument further supports the proposition that no one person can convey a holistic perspective because we experience and understand only a small slice of reality. We live in a subjective world. The ability to recognize this fact and look into how our own internal biases filter reality is an act of presence commonly known as self-awareness. Presence then is not just about being highly aware of what is happing around you. It is also being highly aware of what happens within. The more we are aware of our own filters, the easier it is to see and accept other peoples and weave them together to create something new.[15] Therein lies the heart of creativity. In *Making the Mindful Leader*, Jeremy Hunter of the Peter F. Drucker School of Management writes,

> Because mindfulness training focuses on how leaders use their attention, it is not just another construct to stand alongside the many other arms of leadership research and practice, but both a perspective and a systematic method that helps leaders better understand and transform their own minds. Such an internal shift changes both how a leader sees the world, how he potentially acts and the results those actions bring about. What marks mindfulness training out from other leadership training interventions is the fact that the shift in attentional capacity can be trained and embedded in the context of everyday action. Furthermore the effectiveness of such training is borne out by marked biological changes.

Be the Tuning Fork

Awareness of internal states leads us to our next principle—setting and maintaining an intention. In co-creation, as in other forms of facilitation, the *Xd* is part of the group. The *Xd* is a stakeholder in the process in that their vested interests are helping the group reach the goals set out for the creative program. The implication of this is that the *Xd* is a tuning fork for the other stakeholders. The quality of intention brought into the creative space can and does impact the process. For this reason, it is essential to prepare oneself to be in the right state of mind. Presence training helps in the regard, but is not a requirement. What is required is a particular perspective, and checking in with oneself to ensure that you are maintaining an internal stance of service.

Being the Midwife

One of the central tenets of facilitation is the analogy of the midwife. On being a midwife, the Tao of Leadership states[16]:

> The wise leader does not intervene unnecessarily. The leader's presence is felt but often the group runs itself. Lesser leaders do a lot, say a lot, have followers, and form cults. Even worse ones use fear to energize the group and force to overcome resistance. Only the most dreadful leaders have bad reputation.

> Remember that you are facilitating another person's process. It is not your process. Do not intrude. Do not control. Do not force your own needs and insights into the foreground. If you do not trust a person's process, that person will not trust you.
>
> Imagine that you are a midwife: you are assisting at someone else's birth. Do so without show or fuss. Facilitate what is happening rather than what you think ought to be happening. If you must take the lead, lead so that the mother is helped, yet still free and in charge.
>
> When the baby is born, the mother will rightly say: "We did it ourselves!"

There are many lessons we can take from this passage. Being present enables a clear perspective on what is happening and the needs of the group. This awareness, when combined with empathy and trust, underlies being a midwife. Empathy is being tuned into the emotional dynamics of the group and placing their needs ahead of one's own. Empathy is inclusive of caring for the group, but at the same time being non-attached to any particular outcome. This is a central guideline of good facilitation, a rule of thumb to be observed so that the facilitator does not hijack the process in service whatever he or she thinks is best. Facilitation is service to the group, requiring a surrender of one's own notions.

By acting as an outside catalyst without any personally invested interest in outcome, facilitators gain the trust of the group they work with. What the creative leader personally wants is rather irrelevant if they are seeking to hold the space and catalyze a creative process for others. If the leader cannot see beyond his or her own process and tune into the energy and needs to the group, there is a very real chance of losing engagement—which in turn affects creative output.

The philosophical stance of being the midwife may not be applicable on all instances of co-creation, for the *Xd* can be one of the core stakeholders—a leader in an organization or a design project lead. It may very well be your process, so the facilitators' value of non-attachment to outcome may not apply. Having said that, what we can take from this story as universally relevant is the emphasis on presence empathy, and trust.

Trust is a two-way street. The *Xd* needs the group to place trust in them, but equally the *Xd* must have trust for the group and their process. "Trust the process" and "trust the team" are two expressions we learned from our collaboration with Brains on the Beach. At first they might seem counterintuitive. After all, as process designers, aren't we the experts whose experience others should rely upon and follow? The answer is "yes" and "no." Our experience as leaders, catalysts, and facilitators helps us to understand challenges and design a program. Ideally, from the start that design process was co-creative, weaving our expertise and theirs together to create a process that is in service of their needs. As a facilitator of co-creation, you can be part of the process without controlling it. Creative processes have a life of their own, with dynamics playing out that could not have been fully anticipated. The *Xd* cannot, and should not, try to control these forces. Rather, as Nick Udall implied with the title of his book on creative leadership, the task is to ride the creative rollercoaster.

Letting Go of Process

The ultimate expression of trust is the capacity for a creative leader to let go of their process. This is perhaps a difficult pill to swallow, especially for design and system thinkers. Both disciplines have developed elegant and productive processes that are now codified as models. These are taught in many cases with the belief that the process can guarantee results if followed correctly. If this were a chemistry lab experiment, we would agree. But it is not. Humans are complex creatures with shifting needs and capacities, and when you put a bunch of them in a process together, things go nonlinear.

At the moments when people in a process simply aren't doing "what they are supposed to be doing"—that is, in accordance with the carefully designed program—creative leaders have four choices. They can adopt the Dory motto of "just keep swimming .... swimming swimming swimming..." and plow onward with their process.[17] They can give up and mentally check out while the group does whatever it wants. They can pay close attention to the energy and process that the group is in, be present to where it can go, and support that movement. Or they can be present to the group and its energy, moving with it while also gently steering it toward the program goals. Trusting the process—which this is an example of—does not mean trust the predetermined process that you came in with, but rather trust the process that is occurring. Letting go is an act of trust.

The first two of these choices we don't recommend. The result is usually that either the strongest ego in the room "wins," and/or people lose interest and become disillusioned with the creative process and its leadership. Neither are empowering outcomes. Co-creation benefits from the second two choices, both of which are based on the creative leader tuning into the needs and direction of the group and then responding. This is "conscious" leadership, acting with full awareness of what is happening in the space and how that in turn articulates with larger program or organizational goals. Whether the creative leader moves wholly with the group or gently steers the flow depends on the context and needs of the program.

The lesson is one of awareness and flexibility. Good facilitators can change their program on the fly to adapt to the group's needs. This brings us to our final consideration—humility.

Stay Humble

One of the more challenging lessons for any expert to accept is that a process or program is not about them. No one, except perhaps academics, cares how much you know unless that knowledge is helpful or relevant to them. For creative leaders, your process is only as good as its ability to empower others and tap into the collective potential of the team. Perhaps you are the next Steve Jobs, and through power of will and insight, you can lead a team to innovate the next iPhone. Yet Jobs was a very difficult man to get along with, and his innovation style was certainly not co-creative.

Contrasting the inspirational leader model is one wherein the creative leader is nearly invisible. Larry Philbrook, a veteran facilitation trainer from the Institute for Cultural Affairs, once told me that great facilitation is when everything seems easy. At CCI we were fortunate to have worked with gifted facilitators, because when we first started researching them we thought "You get paid *how much* for this?" It all looked so easy. Only after trying it ourselves did we realize just how much work goes into making a process look simple.

Humor aside, staying humble is not easy to do. It requires a mastery over one's own ego and the ability to put it aside for a time. It all comes back to awareness, both external (sensing the energy) and internal (sensing the ego), and acting on that awareness in a way that serves the needs of the client.

The Art and the Practice

Creative leadership is both an art and a practice. The art lies in crafting and holding the space for innovation and then working with the dynamics of the group to help them achieve what is needed. The practice is the personal cultivation of the capacities that support the art. While there is a lifetime of learning one can take on to develop themselves as creative leaders, here we have drawn attention to those qualities that have the greatest impact on co-creation. We expect readers to have training in many of the associated skills and capacities, and have provided references for those who desire to look further. Our aim has been to make the case that co-creation begins within oneself rather than in a process and to highlight the salience of capacity building for creative leaders.

Returning to the metaphor of performance theater, great actors and great directors have qualities that transcend the script and set. Some of these come naturally, and we will always have charismatic leaders that catalyze teams to new levels of creative output. These factors we cannot control. Others though we can. We can develop our capacities for observation, presence, empathy, trust, and humility. When we do so we are not only bettering ourselves, but we are also better serving the needs of our clients.

Notes

1. The commercial connotation derives from UX (User experience) design and is slowly changing its meaning as users become more internally involved in design processes.
2. Geertz, *The Interpretation of Cultures.*
3. Damásio, *Descartes' Error: Emotion, Reason, and the Human Brain.*
4. From the Edx course *u.lab: Leading From the Emerging Future.* Accessible at https://www.edx.org/course/u-lab-leading-emerging-future-mitx-15-671-1x-0.
5. Coaching techniques are vital in challenging given ideas in the problem or solution space. If we want to find anything new, we must take apart existing constructs. Chapter 9 discusses this in detail.
6. "Together" does not mean the *Xd* becomes an invested part of the team. Rather, it refers to an alignment generated wherein the *Xd* and stakeholder are looking at the possible future and exploring where that might go if they work together.
7. For descriptions of common roles, see, for example, Belbin's model (http://www.belbin.com/).
8. For example, Eisenhardt, K. M., J. L. Kahwajy and L. J. Bourgeois Iii (1997). "How management teams can have a good fight." Harvard Business Review 75(4): 77–85.

9. At CCI we spent a year trying to develop measures. We found that we can measure factors related to these concepts, such as risk taking or divergent thinking. None, however, could reliably tell us what a "good" container or holding space was. These are subjective experiences.
10. Kabat-Zinn *in* Senge, *Presence: Exploring Profound Change in People, Organizations, and Society*, Kindle Location 719.
11. https://www.presencing.com/presencing.
12. Senge, *Presence: Exploring Profound Change in People, Organizations, and Society*, Kindle Location 200.
13. Hymes, *Foundations in Sociolinguistics.*
14. Udall, *Riding the Creative Rollercoaster*, Kindle Location 773–776.
15. Hunter and Chaskalson, *Making the Mindful Leader.*
16. Heider, *The Tao of Leadership*, Kindle Locations 305–306.
17. A humorous line from the movie *Finding Nemo.*

References

Damásio, António. *Descartes' Error: Emotion, Reason, and the Human Brain.* Penguin, 2005.

Geertz, Clifford. *The Interpretation of Cultures: Selected Essays.* USA: Basic Books, 1973.

Heider, John. *The Tao of Leadership: Lao Tzu's Tao De Ching Adapted for a New Age.* Atlanta, GA: Humanics New Age, 1985.

Hunter, J., and M. Chaskalson. "Making the Mindful Leader." In *The Wiley-Blackwell Handbook of the Psychology of Leadership, Change, and Organizational Development*, edited by H. S. Leonard, R. Lewis, A. M. Freedman and J. Passmore, 195–220. Oxford: John Wiley & Sons, 2013.

Hymes, Dell. *Foundations in Sociolinguistics: An Ethnographic Approach.* Philadelphia: University of Pennsylvania Press, 1974.

Scharmer, Otto, and Katrin Kaufer. *Leading from the Emerging Future from Ego-System to Eco-System Economies.* San Francisco, CA: Berrett-Koehler Publishers, Inc., 2013.

Senge, Peter M. Presence: An Exploration of Profound Change in People, Organizations, and Society (Kindle Locations 85–87). The Crown Publishing Group. Kindle Edition, n.d.

Udall, N. *Riding the Creative Rollercoaster: How Leaders Evoke Creativity and Innovation.* Kogan Page, 2014. Kindle Edition.

CHAPTER 4

Staging the Environment

If you have ever been to a creative retreat, you probably remember the space. As an example, in most mid to large organizational "retreats," you might walk into a large ballroom filled with roundtables that hold 8–12 people, a projector or two that will inevitably be used for PowerPoint presentations, a podium for keynote speakers, and flip charts for each table. Creative meetings within organizations often use the board room or something similar, with a central oval table that everyone sits around so that they can give attention to PowerPoint and/or whiteboard presentations. The creative retreat/meeting is filled with inputs from a variety of speakers, roundtable discussions with or without cross-fertilization of ideas, and eventually a capture session to identify the most salient issues/directions to pursue.

These events make me cringe, and I must admit that I avoid them like a plague. Why? Because, as many of you know from experience, they are a huge waste of time. This is not due to lack of good intent. Organizations spend a lot of time and money gathering their people together for such events, and they can be fun. Occasionally they can be productive as well. At the very least they serve as an opportunity to bring everyone together and share ideas (or complain), build teams, and onboard to the latest mission and vision statements. They are wasteful in that they are not reaching their creative potential. The opportunity for creativity is effectively killed by the form of the space from the onset. And if that doesn't do the job, the predictable flow of activities and structural arrangement of power and people certainly does. Creativity is killed because these large events mimic,

B. R. Rill, M. M. Hämäläinen, *The Art of Co-Creation*,
https://doi.org/10.1007/978-981-10-8500-0_4

in most cases, the classrooms we were all educated in. Both contexts quietly reinforce power relations and distance between leaders and everyone else. While the overt aim is knowledge sharing, the subtext is one that expects everyone to be passive recipients.

At the end of such programs, most people have heard the loudest, most powerful egos in the room, perhaps they have contributed in some way, and there is a set of one to three "outcomes" to be considered for action by leadership. If these outcomes are acted on, the meeting may be seen as productive and empowering for those that contributed to crafting it. If not, the gradual sense of having wasted valuable work time settles in, and people eventually lose all respect for creative programs and the facilitators who run them.

By contrast, you may have had the privilege of attending a creative retreat hosted by an organization which intentionally created an environment that encouraged novel forms of interaction, play, and creativity. Design firms, innovation labs, creative commons, start-up communities, and incubators, among others, commonly have dedicated spaces for creative teams to work that allow for and enable teams to redesign their working space according to their needs. Increasingly, large organizations have adopted the concept of workplace well-being, and now you can find funky, comfortable, non-conforming furniture and spaces in everything from university libraries to corporate offices in Hong Kong.[1] In most cases these spaces are designed to hold only a small team while the rest of the workspace meets more traditional norms, but in others an entire workspace can be transformed. The basic premise behind designing for workplace well-being is creating a space where people want to come to work and interact with their peers. More interactions lead to a stronger sense of community and more novel intersections where creativity can surface.

Creative programs in these spaces can take on any number of forms. In some cases the format might follow the stereotype of PowerPoint presentations and inputs, discussion, and capture of outcomes. In a design studio the team may cover every inch of wall space with post-it notes, pictures, and strings connecting together observations, spend days debating what they see and what to do, make a prototype, watch it fail or succeed in user testing, then throw it out or iterate the design until it is viable. A creative consultant can come in and get rid of all the furniture except for chairs, put people in a circle, and play card games with them to help them work through ideas. The possibilities are endless.

What are the differences between these two types of environments? The answer—experience design. In most cases, people who coordinate creative programs are consciously thinking about social bonding, ensuring smooth communication, and (hopefully) maximizing the quality of interactions. Designers, event planners, human relations staff, leaders, and facilitators all want to get the most out of the participants in a program. This desire is constrained by the facilities available, and in a ballroom there are only so many options to choose from. Life is much easier when given a space designed to be creative from the onset. Yet even in these settings the environment is not always used to its full potential. The reason can be a lack of concern, but more often it is a lack of awareness of the impact environment design has upon experience.

What Is an Environment?

Of all the factors that contribute to the efficacy of creative programs, environment is one of the most important yet least considered elements that can make or break a program the moment it begins. The environment people walk into shapes their experience. Subtle adjustments in infrastructure and implementation of communication strategies have wide-ranging, positive consequences for organizational creativity. Whenever we speak of environment, it is a combination of material infrastructures, technologies, philosophies, action strategies, and most importantly people, who together form a space, define the practice within that space, and actuate it. The physical and semiotic interface is essentially a gateway to the opening of communication lines, the initiation of collaboration, and of co-creation. It is impactful to give the environment a message that gives permissions and sets the stage for the activities to take place (Fig. 4.1).

Fig. 4.1 The environment

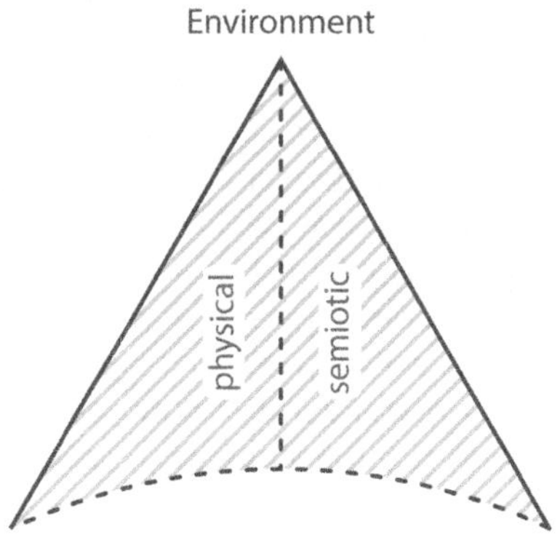

In *Make Space: How to Set the Stage for Creative Collaboration*, authors Doorley and Witthoft state,

> Space is the "body language" of an organization. Intentional or not, the form, functionality, and garnish of a space reenact the culture, behaviors, and priorities of the people within it. This suggests that a space designer is simultaneously a cultural translator and a builder. That said, space design has its own grammar that can be tweaked to bolster desirable habits.[2]

Using this concept of space, in this chapter we offer insight into how to stage the environment so that it acts as a catalyst for the co-creation process. We draw on research from design schools to furniture manufacturers to illustrate the core principles for designing creative spaces: flexibility, multimedia tools, information and communication technologies (ICT), open collaboration zones, moveable and writeable walls, non-spaces, culture hubs, and interplay areas. Taken together, these principles encourage communication, creative play, and culture building while also providing spaces to get away when needed.

People respond to extremely subtle cues in their environment, both physical and semiotic. While the physical aspects of environment design (listed above) are enabling, the symbolic "ideoscape" of that environment can *suggest* ways of working within that context. Several of our guidelines will help *Xd* understand how to subconsciously cue participants toward co-creative behaviors.

We conclude this chapter with an emphasis on uniqueness and legacy. Co-creation is a rare place of trust and sharing. Making this explicit will speed up innovation capacity by increasing levels of trust and willingness to be authentic. An effective way to create this "container" is through ritual and culture building. Rituals encourage "stepping into" different modes of interaction and behavior, increase group solidarity, convey key information or rules of behavior, and encourage designed behaviors. Rituals are the central mechanism through which culture is created and conveyed. You have to go no further than an Apple product rollout to see the power of ritual. It is hard to forget the iconic image of Steve Jobs walking out onto a stage wearing his blue jeans and black turtleneck, backed by a massive screen that contained only the Apple logo while he spoke. It is no coincidence that his turtleneck resembled the collar of a Catholic priest, nor the single icon glowing much like a Holy Cross backlit by the sun through stained glass windows. Jobs was intentionally copying the environment of a Catholic church, drawing on the physical and symbolic aspects of environment design to deliver his speeches with maximum impact. Clearly it worked.

Spatial Design

Collaboration spaces, collaboration technologies, and socially engaging environments have long been the subject of research and experiments aimed at re-defining the modern workplace to foster innovation and support collaborations within organizations.[3] These studies identify three foundation elements of a collaboration space: a built, tangible environment, an electronic collaborative working environment, and a social space or place, referring to interactions for building shared mental spaces. We will discuss each of these elements and the interactions between them that maximize the potential of the environment. But first we need to step back and look at spatial design from a broader perspective, examining how space affects experience and vice versa.

Cultured Spaces

Environment design begins by thinking about the experience you want people to have and the space you have to create that experience in. The first consideration beyond "Do we have a dedicated space?" and "What does it look like?" is the fact that spaces are not blank canvases or experience neutral areas. Rather, spaces carry cultural values taught to us from infancy.

Education plays a key role in training people how to think and behave. In school classrooms we were taught not only content but also social norms and cultural expectations. We learn these rules so well that they become unconscious, and we follow them throughout life without further instructions. These unconscious mental schema help us in many situations. For example, most people automatically understand how to behave in different settings. We all know what a classroom is, and when in one we take on the appropriate behaviors designated by our role in the space. When a person deviates from the expected norm, we apply social pressure to bring them "in line." Alternatively, we can avoid them. In either case, "deviance" is acting in a way that does not conform to the code of conduct. The point is that space and normative behavior are connected. Space design and the structure of an organization's physical premises are often the "regulating logic" of the internal organization. We not only control the flow of movement and personnel, establishing control relationships in the layout of a space,[4] but we can encourage interpersonal communication and knowledge transfer between participants of that space through our design.[5]

The tendency for people to automatically adapt to their environment is the "chameleon effect."[6] It is based on a set of cues given to us by our environments—both the physical and social context. These cues are not inherent features of space. Places only have meaning because we *give* them meaning in social contexts. It is because we create these rules and share them with others that people learn how to behave in a space. For the *Xd*, this leads to two guidelines:

Know the Influence of Your Cultural Environment

Awareness of the cultural significance of a space is informative of how people can be expected to act in it. As an example, if you hold a creative program in a classroom and assume a position at the front of the room, the participants assume (unconsciously) that you have taken the role of teacher. If you sit in a circle with them, the message is entirely different. But does a circle mean the same thing in Hong Kong as it does in New York? Don't assume. Figure it out.

Shape Your Environment

We can create new meanings of space and use these to our advantage to encourage desired behaviors. Rules in designed environments can act as catalysts to help people step out of their normal roles and into a new, creative, one. Take on the role of shaping the environment and you may be surprised at what people can be and do.

Before going too crazy with environment redesign, a word of caution is in order. People have expectations of the physical environment, and if they encounter a space that is too far outside those expectations, it can cause stress. If a room, for example, contains no familiar objects or has been constructed in an novel way, it can make the people in it very uncomfortable. The example of our asymmetrical classroom at the Hong Kong Polytechnic University with the Steelcase Node chairs illustrates this point. Week after week the students tried to arrange their chairs into configurations that they perceived as "normal." In creative programs this stress may be desirable, or it may not. In our experience we have used extreme settings when purposefully trying to destabilize norms, and it does work. The closing section of this chapter on ritual will speak more to this point. In many cases though such extremes are not desirable.

The Social Workspace

In recent years, spatial design has shifted to encourage well-being and the social interactions that lie at the heart of creativity. This modification requires a new conceptualization of the workplace. While previously the concept of productivity in enterprise was imagined in relation to hours spent working at one's desk, modern enterprises, in particular those associated with knowledge economy, are developing toward a situation in which workers have more choice and decision-making as to when and where they work.[7] The future-forward thinking office space is no more an air-tight casket stocked with faceless cubicles. Rather, the individual worker's cubicle has been transformed into a new office layout which facilitates communication and interaction between colleagues and departments. The most advanced businesses and collaboration teams are implementing interaction design for creativity and ingenuity, not just experimenting with open-plan workplaces and providing ergonomic furniture or variable office hours, but introducing completely new concepts for participatory labor, management, networking, and communication services.

The integration of social activity spaces into organizations and workplaces has been successful.[8] In education, these spaces foster active learning, social interactions, and a sense of belonging. They can also be used as co-working spaces. In business—where innovation is a catchphrase—terms such as playbour (play + labor), hackathon, and enterprise gamification attempt to capture a new kind of social productivity.[9] Supporting such activities has led to a rethink in workplace layout, with shared offices, informal meeting areas, play spaces, the café, and the lounge providing areas for workers and management to relax and have the casual encounter. These "off-time" interactions enhance productivity, collaboration, and well-being. Enhancing performance now takes the seemingly counterintuitive route of providing for, even encouraging a certain inefficiency, which extends to spatial design practice as well. The designer of a collaboration space has succeeded when the limitations of the material infrastructures do not inhibit or restrict but, in the best case, actually transform our life in the workplace.

Work is more than tasks and activities carried out in offices or meeting rooms. It is also the relationships between people and conversations by the coffee machine that result in knowledge sharing.[10] Physical spaces have a major impact on the social environment, enabling or disabling such fundamental aspects of culture as having a place to be, to meet, and to learn from others. A "social workspace" is one that has dedicated spaces for these encounters. A well-designed social workspace balances physical, social, and virtual spaces.[11] It also consists of more than tangible objects, having shared practices and rituals that increase the sense of community and belonging. A Friday afternoon cocktail hour or Monday team breakfasts are examples of small organizational acts that enable discussion of non-work topics in a friendly atmosphere. The lesson is that physical structures and social practices work together to hinder or support informal interactions that cultivate stronger relationships and knowledge sharing, both of which are essential in co-creation.[12]

Third Places

In the International Finance Center in Hong Kong, the Starbucks on the second floor sees a constant flow of business men and women, shoppers, and tourists. The small satellite tables with two to four chairs are almost always full, many times with people in deep dialogue. A great many engagements and opportunities take place at this and thousands of other coffee lounges around the world. Why is this? Why are millions of professionals choosing to meet in a loud coffee bar or cafés rather than in their office or a conference room?

The answer is that coffee lounges and cafés are "third places." The first place being home, the second being work, third places are intermediate spaces, social spaces, places of leisure.[13] Third places, and in particular cafés, are places of shared experience based on communal awareness, lively face-to-face discussion, philosophical debate, unpredictable and unplanned encounters, and an established egalitarian social norm.[14] They are perfect for co-creation because both the physical and social aspects of the environment encourage co-creative behaviors. Consider, for example, the need for multiple perspectives in a creative dialogue. In the social space of the lounge, dissenting or unique views are the most appreciated, because they provide a different perspective than the relations the day to day. Indeed, lively discussion is a part of what makes the third place atmosphere appealing. Participants feel they are part of something emerging, a café culture.

This is in part directly related to café culture's historic place in the formation of concrete political and philosophical ideas, even revolution.

There are several guidelines we can take from third places to help us design creative environments. First, the relaxed, playful attitude encouraged by a café leads to a sense of belonging. This egalitarian, inclusive element of the third place is essential to incite collaboration and participation among those who might normally remain passive. Another aspect which fuses team building and groupthinking is the simple communal awareness that arises from the experience of participation in the social space: the shared physical experience of coffee or tea at the bar, or the shared experience of Wi-Fi use in the cafe.

While the concept of "working" in a café has many different perspectives, some more introverted than others, we recommend the social activity of "placemaking." This form of spatial participation revolves around encouraging social interactions, serendipitous exchanges, and availability for interactions with strangers. While a creative program is a guided experience, the very nature of the café environment can allow the experience to take shape in a relaxed, spontaneous atmosphere, which is one of the foundations of innovation and collaboration.

Affordances

Up to this point we have argued that an environment is much more than a room with tables and chairs. It is a powerful shaper of experience, a fact often overlooked or underestimated. Now that we have made our case, the question remains as to how to design a co-creative environment.

In design terminology, what we need to identify are the "affordances" that encourage creative behaviors. An affordance is an attribute of something that influences the use of that thing. The classroom or café *affords* certain behaviors based upon our unconscious mental schema of these environments. We adjust our behaviors because we interpret affordances of the space that silently guide our behavior and ways of working.

Let's look at the example of rolling walls. In the book *Make Space*, a work from Stanford's famous d.school, there is a blueprint for glass walls set onto rollers. Four of these can be brought together to make a small enclosed but see-through space. Alternatively, they can be put in an L shape or straight line and also be used as writing surfaces with whiteboard pens. The team at the d.school was experimenting with the concept of a wall. They transformed it from something that typically divides people or creates privacy into a flexible surface that can be used in different arrangements for open, public uses. The use of glass and rollers created new affordances—and encouraged novel behaviors as a result.

Another example is the Steelcase office in Hong Kong. Their office is at once a living advertisement for their furniture and the environment that they work in. It has desks that convert from sitting to standing, lounge chairs with ergonomic arm rests for a laptop, standing workstations with only a short divider between the sides, "campfire" enclosures, and small roundtables with writable surfaces. Meeting rooms can be reserved through an application by anyone at any time, and the digital system keeps usage data that tells everyone what rooms are free and when in order to maximize availability and usage. No one at the Steelcase office has their own desk. Rather, they rotate daily based how they feel like working that day. All of this is possible because the Steelcase designers carefully thought about affordances. They intentionally wanted to create a social workspace that facilitates well-being and serendipitous encounters. You can do the same with or without Steelcase's high end furniture by just considering what you can do in an environment to affect behavior.

With the theory mostly behind us, we are ready for spatial design guidelines for co-creative environments. Before we do though, there is one last point to make. You can never expect people to use a space as you have designed it. While you or someone else may have designed a space for a particular reason, ultimately the use of that space is up to its inhabitants. Space is in fact performed by its occupants, rather than defined by an architect or designer.[15] The occupants of a space are as much participants as they are observers, as every member has the ability to influence and contribute to the overall use (performance) of it. Having said that, we can now present guidelines that integrate an understanding of space as a negotiated reality that, like a theater play or concert, is a co-created experience.

Designing the Physical Environment

Our relationships within work, between co-workers both present and virtual, require new physical structures, and as such the material of our physical workplace needs to anticipate the dynamic roles and relations which may arise from the very innovation it seeks to encourage, without, as Idenburg suggests, "endlessly moving furniture around."[16] To do this we design spaces that encourage (afford) shifts in both the quantity and quality of social interactions.

In their recent text on co-creative meetings, Mandl et al. state that,

> ...adequate meeting rooms are of utmost importance in co-creative organizations. Such meeting rooms are ... stimulating, peaceful environments. Such rooms are bright, have windows and natural light, and are spacious enough for participants to stand up, walk around and examine flipcharts or information posted in the room. The high ceilings create feelings of openness and generosity, as opposed to small rooms with constricting, dark paneled ceilings. Empty, uninhabited rooms with bare, white walls and only essential furniture invite participants to fill this space with their own ideas. Such rooms are simple, inconspicuous and not distracting.[17]

The authors' argument flows from the fact that many successful co-creative meetings are held in such environments, with the central feature being a circle of chairs in a mostly empty space.

Use Circles

Circles are a starting point for three reasons. First, they are easy to use anywhere. Second, they have a socially leveling effect—eliminating hierarchy to make everyone an equal participant. That is an essential step in creating the container for co-creation. Third, circles encourage greater engagement. It is hard to hide in a circle or secretly text under the table top, and everyone's face can be seen. This makes everyone equally vulnerable, which tends to invite deeper dialogues.

While it can be common for one or two people to dominate dialogue even in a circle, the arrangement suggests a lack of a power center. This affordance opens new interactional spaces, subconsciously cueing opportunity for all to speak if they choose to. A good *Xd* uses the physical circle as a central space to reinforce decentered collaboration. The result of doing this is outcomes that originate from the intersection of ideas in the space between speakers.

The spatial arrangement of the circle establishes a mindset that can extend into other collaborative activities. Open Spaces and World Café are two examples of this.[18] In Open Spaces, a large central circle is used for overall group meeting times, but then people move freely between breakout discussion groups where there is no set physical form. They may take a walk, go to lunch, or use a classroom, but in each of these the issues being discussed are primary. If someone does not like the way a conversation is going, they are free to leave and listen to another. In World Café, groups sit at circular tables, but orchestrated movement among groups enables a cross-fertilization of ideas and another means to destabilize power relationships.

A circle of chairs in a spacious, minimalistic room works well in many situations. Yet there are many other things we can do to enhance the potential of an environment. Design research into collaborative work spaces, such as Aalto University's Future Learning Environments Project, the Aalto Design Factory, Stanford's d.school, Steelcase's WorkSpace Futures research, and the ProWork study, reveals a set of core features of innovative environments. Spatial design guidelines include:

- Flexibility
- Multimedia tools
- ICT
- Open collaboration zones
- Moveable and writeable walls
- Non-spaces
- Culture hubs
- Interplay areas

Taken together, these design principles encourage communication, creative play, and culture building while also providing spaces to get away when needed.

Let's break this down. We will use the design for the CCI within the School of Design at PolyU as our example. CCI was fortunate to be given a large space at the top of Innovation Tower, an architectural design by Zaha Hadid. The beauty of the design was accompanied by asymmetrical spaces and low ceilings. In our space, the 13th floor, over half of all the wall space was long angular windows providing a spectacular view of Hong Kong. Because it was a multiuse space, we had very strict constraints. First, we are not allowed to structurally modify the space in any way. Second, everything we used had to be able to be moved so the space could be set up with hundreds of chairs and tables for events (much like a ballroom). Given these constraints, we went to work to create an environment that afforded the space between and emergent creativity. Drawing on design research, the layout adopted an open zone approach like the Steelcase office. Each zone had a different spatial design and resources, and participants could be organized into project teams that could move between zones based upon the needs of the tasks at hand.

In order to choose furniture and assemblages for the future projected needs, we imagined what exactly CCI participants would be doing in the space. They would be communicating, of course, but physically they would be standing, sitting, and lounging. At times they would be moving things around, gathering in a circle, or forming small groups. Other times they might be sitting still, or lying on the floor in meditation or visualization exercises. Thus we needed, initially, groups of non-hierarchical furniture, arranged in areas which support the four main poses: standing areas, seating arrangements, reclining, and lounge-type groupings. As many of the CCI activities would involve writing, drawing, and using portable screen devices, all of the areas needed accompanying support tables. The areas needed to be open to flow, augmented by portable whiteboard easels that could be moved between spaces. Seating must be easily and quickly rearrangeable to allow a change in orientation to participate in projection media utilizing the CCI wall space. The following image illustrates the design (Fig. 4.2).

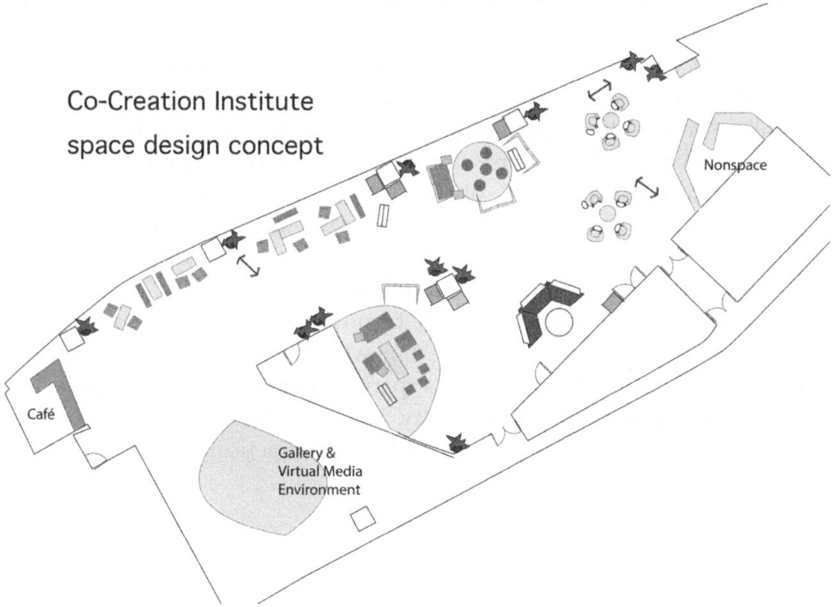

Fig. 4.2 Co-Creation Institute design

The CCI spatial design used the theory of affordances to create a collaborative working environment that balanced privacy and proximity. Portable L-shaped "walls" were used to create the sense of privacy, allowing people to share in small groups ideas and talk about topics they may not wish to share with the larger group. Yet these "walls" were partially see-through and lightweight. The ability to see others working creates a sense of closeness and enhances non-verbal communication, which influences communication patterns, cooperation, and social interactions. People respond well when they work in an environment that balances visibility with privacy.

Caves and Commons

Creativity benefits from having both "Commons" (community gathering spaces) and "Caves" (non-spaces where an individual or small team can work in privacy). This is especially true in co-creation, where people are often asked to shift from one form of teamwork to another. Because co-creation is not always collaborative, dedicated or reworkable spaces are necessary. Furthermore, giving permission to shift between spaces as one needs is equally important to having the spaces.

Some places have enough rooms to accommodate different workflows. Creative environments where only one room is given to work with require flexibility. To decide on furniture and arrive at the constellations needed for a space with such a diverse user and usage profile as co-creation, we maintain that most, if not all, objects in the space be portable, at least to some extent. The facilitators should be able to choose from a repertoire of arrangements for different activities, and users must be able to rearrange these elements spontaneously depending on their needs.

Fortunately, lightweight moveable furniture is a pretty common feature of most spaces. Having it is great, but what you do with it is far more influential. Caves and Commons is a spatial arrangement based on the balance between privacy and community. Yet as we have discussed, community is often formed more by informal social interactions than it is through planned engagements.

Designed Third Places

We can design third places, or "culture hubs," within workspaces to encourage social interactions. Water coolers, copy machines, lounges, and cafes are all "magnet" spaces that encourage socialization. They are places where people often hang out, switch from formal to informal dialogues, and form relationships. In terms of size, the smaller the physical distance between people, the more likely they are to interact. Physical proximity also adds the ability to share tacit (firsthand, experiential) knowledge, which is key to forming shared understandings. In addition to building trust, cooperation, and creativity, informal social spaces strengthen the sense of community and feed positivity into the culture. What is not to like?

Designing a creative environment to have an informal social space is actually quite simple. Provide a constant supply of refreshments and position these to afford social interactions. Breaks can be designed as another form of interaction and can often lead to valuable connections and insights. In addition to the social element, the refreshment area must have what people want. Coffee, tea, and water are non-negotiable necessities if you want to keep people happy and productive.

Interplay Spaces

Interplay spaces are a form of culture hubs that mix play with work. Whether it is table football, a gaming room with a PlayStation 4, or an arts and crafts workshop, spaces that encourage play open up altogether new creative territory. When we were children we all loved to play games. As adults, we tend to enjoy more complex games, but there is a space within us that still relates to the simple pleasures of childhood. Any space or activity that takes us back to our childhood also unlocks the creative potential that all children possess. I am often reminded of the tremendous creativity of children by my two nieces, both of whom have immense talent. By age six they were competing in Odyssey of the Mind, a creative theater school program. My nieces were part of a team who developed a spaceship that traveled to the future…not a bad feat. When we, as adults in creative teams, allow ourselves to go back to that time, magic can happen. Not only do we tap into our inherit creativity, but we also radically alter our interactions with others. We have fun, even with our bosses and other colleagues whom we might not get along with so well. Interplay spaces, by their design, give permission to be silly, to laugh, and to fail with no consequence.

Environment designs such as interplay spaces are one way to give permissions for people to take on a different role. Spatial design can also be used as a social lubricant to help introverts or those who experience collaboration as a totally new and different environment that makes them uncomfortable and reluctant to participate. The café is one example of an environment that relaxes and opens communications. We can also draw inspiration from a nightclub or evening lounge. In these cases there are couple more guidelines to consider.

Unorthodox Spatial Design

An environment that breaks the norm subconsciously cues people to follow suit. In Bali, Indonesia, for example, people spend a lot of time in raised, open-aired wooden platforms with bamboo flooring and a thatch roof. Many restaurants have these with some small cushions. People sitting in them are forced to sit in a lounged position, and you can easily see the effect on their behavior. They are relaxed. The nightclub dance floor or the velvet couches in the back of a martini bar blanketed in red lighting equally encourage stepping into different behaviors. In each of these environments the spatial design, music, lighting, and arrangement of objects are carefully constructed to afford an experience.

Use Multimedia Technologies Sparingly

Music and lighting are technologies that you can use to set the mood—establishing subtle permissions and encouraging creative or prosocial behaviors. In the modern workspace we also have need for ICT and multimedia tools. There is a lot of hype about innovation labs and technology-enhanced learning environments (TELE) filled with the latest and greatest technologies. Immersive multimedia, responsive environments, and ambient intelligence sit at the forefront of the future collaboration spaces. The ideas behind these are exciting, but studies show that the collaborative experience does not match the expectation in nearly all cases. At CCI we have firsthand experience with this—we designed a high-tech innovation environment based on the principles of co-creation. The Cloud Lounge, as our name suggests, was an immersive multimedia cloud-based collaboration environment that integrated the latest interactive ICT with a coffee café concept. To this day, it is one of the best designed innovative concepts out there, even though it was never finished. The reason it was not finished was due to limitations of existing technology-driven innovation labs, and until certain design challenges are overcome, it would not be possible to realize our vision. Perhaps one day when ambient intelligence is more advanced, we will pursue its completion. For now the vision is on hold because we realized that technology gets in the way of creativity more often than it helps.

We are not arguing for a technology-free creative environment. There are some technologies that are absolutely indispensable, such as computers. Creative teams need to use the internet for their research and communication. Software is needed for design, evaluation, reporting, and many other tasks. Social media is growing more and more valuable in sharing ideas and crowdsourcing solutions. Smartphone cameras capture priceless moments of teamwork and play. And who can go without the projector or monitor for those beloved PowerPoint presentations? These are all standard and accepted technology tools in creative programs. What we caution against is being too heavily into the "technology first" mindset that lies behind the funding of so many innovation labs. Technology does not have a causal effect on creativity. More technology does not equal better collaboration or better solutions. In a recent study of innovations labs, Lewis and Moultrie found that the single greatest factor on delivery of successful results was facilitation.[19] Participants invariably reported that the facilitated process within the innovation lab was most important to outcomes. New and interactive media elements helped establish the sense of "this is the future" among participants, but it did not affect productivity. Moreover, given the rapid pace of technology change, these labs become quickly outdated. In all research cases, the labs stated that they wish they had developed more low-tech, flexible media environments.

High-tech interactive environments also create the need for training in the use of them. Interestingly, Lewis and Moultrie found that facilitators received training more in usage of the technology kit than in any particular process or facilitator skills. Concluding their study, they stated,

> Facilitation remains arguably the most important aspect of even the most high-tech laboratory, and surprisingly this was the area where the research revealed the least well developed set of heuristics for determining good and bad practice in different applications.[20]

Educational technology-enhanced learning environments (TELE) often face this challenge. At our university we had a multimillion dollar classroom sponsored by Microsoft. To use it we had to go through a training series and be certified. The room itself was very cool, with modular tables, three projectors, and smart whiteboards that allowed us to transfer content from the computer screen to the smart whiteboard and vice versa. We could do a range of functions from grabbing text off internet pages and marking it up with digital pens to hosting anonymous student feedback sessions while lecturing. We used the room for two years, and by the end we found that the enhanced technologies actually impaired our ability to interact with and engage our students. Besides, the students all felt that the tech was old news, even though it was only a few years old. The fact is, by the time the space was funded and built, it *was* old tech.

The point of these stories is to argue that most interactive technology, in its current form, can and does take away from the creative process. More equals less in the case of co-creation. What matters in collective creativity is what comes out of catalyzing novel intersections between people and knowledge. Technologies that support this must be people, not technology, oriented. For now, some of the best tools we have are post-it notes, flip charts, games, and face-to-face human interactions. We encourage the continued development of new and novel tools, with one basic rule of thumb to use as a criterion. If it helps people interact creatively, then it is good. If it takes more than a few minutes to explain and get people using it, then you might want to hold off. Creative teams can be trained to use new interactive technologies and can benefit from this training, but most of the time we are not in this situation. In the design studio and corporate office, people want to get things done without having to learn a new interface. Our job is to facilitate their process as seamlessly as possible, which means minimizing non-essential activities.

How we stage our environment given the resources at hand contributes to our ability to deliver the co-creative experience. We have looked at environment as a cultured, social, and physical space. Our design guidelines thus far have been focused on the tangible and spatial aspects of the environment. Now we turn to another set of tools to shape experience—semiotics.

Semiotic Design

The experience of any environment is a psychological one. Our internal mental models are constantly filtering and reacting to the outside world, creating through the process a unique, personalized experience of reality. Shared culture, whether ethnic, ideological, or organizational, allows for people to have similar experiences, but no two people ever have exactly the same experience. This is simply because we all have different life experiences that shaped our internal models. In other words, our filters shape our reality, and everyone has different filters. This is why good communication is so challenging, a point that we will return to in great detail as we discuss creative facilitation.

As an example, think of the last time you and your significant other had a difference of opinion about a shared experience. Since we are writing about environment design, let's reflect on an interior design conversation. What pattern, color, or layout was chosen to create the mood of the room? What differences in opinion did you have and where do those ideas come from? Who was the "decider"? In the case of my wife and I, it is quite simple. She always politely asks me what I think of this or that and then asks me which one I would go with. I start listing ideas, which she immediately vets. We work well together because we are married and share similar values, but I am under no delusion about who is really in charge of design decisions. It is not me.

My wife's ability to quickly vet my design ideas does not come solely from her status as my wife, although that is certainly a factor. It comes from the fact that she has developed her internal schema by spending a lot of time looking at interior design and fashion. She and I have different schema that filter how we experience particular colors and layouts, but I trust her judgment because she intuitively knows how to choose design elements that create the experience we both enjoy. Part of her interior design sensibility focuses on spatial design, but another part takes into consideration the psychological effects of color, lighting, and signs. The color theme of our home is blues, light tan, and soft white colors because it reminds us of the beach we love so much.

Most people can relate to this story because they have one just like it. If you look around any home, what you find is a designed environment where different areas are supposed to create specific experiences. Homes are an easy example because we all have one, and we can each tell our friends about the theme of a particular space. The same is true for any organizational environment. What makes the environment is not only the spatial design, but, like a home, the colors, pictures, signs, and objects within it that convey meaning. The study of such signs and their use or interpretation is called "semiotics."

Semiotics is especially important for designers because it helps them understand the relationships between signs, what they stand for, and the people who interpret them. "Signs" are more than what we can convey with words. Semiotics defines signs in the broadest possible sense as being anything capable of standing for something else. The coy fish in Japan, for example, symbolizes perseverance for its ability to swim upstream, and the Apple logo conveys a sense of higher social status throughout Asia and India.

We have already looked at how aspects of spatial design function as signs to establish a certain atmosphere or suggest ways of working. The reason a spatial design can afford behaviors is due to the semiotic associations given to that design. With this perspective we can better understand why a circle of chairs represents egalitarianism. The circle is a sign for the idea. But what happens when an understanding of a spatial design, such as the circle, is not shared by all? What happens when, in a cross-cultural environment, we cannot assume common mental schema? We have found that, even in contexts with people from the same cultural and organizational background, it can be a mistake to assume shared understandings. Moreover, although people may understand the role of something like a circle, they may choose to ignore or take advantage of the context for their own purposes. In these circumstances it is advantageous to cue what types of behaviors are and are not appropriate. This can be done subtly or more overtly. The former we term "semiotic priming."

Semiotic Priming

Semiotic priming is the use of signs (symbols, images, quotes, colors, furniture arrangements, etc.) in an environment to help set the container—to establish the atmosphere—thus framing the type of experience people can expect to have in the environment. Semiotic priming does not need to be explicit, such as posters listing rules of behavior. Humans will naturally respond to cues subconsciously based on their internal schema. When they do not have an internal model of what to do, most people look to those around them and follow the group behaviors. This behavioral trait is to our advantage as experience designers.

Luxury branding provides a great example of semiotic priming. If you look at the advertisements in Central Hong Kong, a common feature is one or two young models looking fantastic as they wear, hold, or drink whatever is being advertised. While it is not explicit, the message is that if you buy the product you can live like the people portrayed. You can be fun, sexy, and a member of a social class higher than the one you are likely living. Walt Disney's innovation is another legendary example. In Orlando, Florida, Walt Disney World has a series of underground tunnels to hide all of the workers and facilities necessary to keep the amusement park running. The guests are never to see this, enabling them to suspend their reality as they enjoy the various attractions. Every aspect of that environment is carefully designed to encourage leaving the real world behind and entering into fantasy, from the sculpted bushes to the cast of characters walking around inviting you into their reality.

At CCI we also used semiotic priming, taking advantage of the built environment to create a unique and memorable atmosphere. We were fortunate to have uncluttered white walls that could be used as projection surfaces or canvases for post-it notes and flip chart paper. On these we would poject background images or visual metaphors. The white, minimalist design eliminated necessary distractions or color choices that some people might not like. The windows overlooking Hong Kong gave the space, even with its low ceiling, a sense of expansiveness and of being someplace special. People always commented on how amazing it was to work in a space so different from their normal office.

Emphasize Uniqueness

Co-creation is a rare place of trust and sharing. Emphasizing uniqueness, and making it explicit, will speed up innovation capacity by increasing levels of trust and willingness to be authentic. At CCI we added to the environment given to us with a spatial design that broke from everyday norms and intentionally primed guests into dialogues about the space and encouraged them to play within it.

In one program, for example, participants walked in to find a series of workstations bordered by tall portable poster stands. We gave them balls of string, popsicle sticks, rubber bands, and index cards and then told them to represent their ideas three dimensionally inside the poster stands. They had to build their ideas into a space they had never seen before. While at first many found this challenging, they all rose to it and ended up creatively using the space to reimagine the relationship between concepts. In the same event, we set up projectors around the room with no content showing during any inputs. The content, high-resolution images of natural landscapes, was projected only during breaks. This exercise was based on attention restoration therapy (ART), a theory which holds that looking at natural landscapes relaxes the cognitive forebrain and allows for other, more gestalt, processes to work. These are just two small examples of things that you can do with an environment to both semiotically prime participants and make it unique. Doing so opens people to the novel ways of being and working that we encourage in co-creative programs. The best recommendation we can give you, other than the tips here and directing you to design psychology readings, is to suggest that you play with what you have and solicit feedback specifically about the how the space *felt*. It is the felt sense of the space that informs whether or not you have created a good container. When you receive similar reports from multiple participants, you know that you have given the right cues to align people into a shared experience. A successful environment is one in which people feel safe enough to contribute freely and authentically, relax and have some fun, and even stretch their boundaries a bit.

Semiotic priming is a subtle, background art similar to creating a theatrical stage. You are making the set upon which the actors, your participants, will perform the space. Ideally everyone there will respond to the environment as you have hoped for. However, it is wise to remember that every person has a different set of mental models that filter their experience of the environment. Due to this, there is no one set of design guidelines for semiotic priming or any other aspect of spatial design. As an *Xd*, you must calibrate your design to the people and context you work in.

Using Posters and Signs

Overt, explicit medium is another means you can use to calibrate your participants to the way you want them to work. At CCI we liked to use posters with famous quotes by people who inspire us, placing these around the room without ever directly bringing them up. Inevitably people would comment on them, opening up a dialogue about the significance of any particular quote. That was a less subtle but still indirect way of encouraging behaviors.

Create a Social Contract

The most direct way to shape behavior when staging the environment is to establish working guidelines—a social contract. Contrasting subconscious cues, this guideline draws attention to "rules of play." Rules are beneficial because co-creative environments may be radically different from the norm. Instructions on what to do and how to act increase comfort, decreasing the time required for establishing social cohesion.[21] Specific guidelines help by removing the need to interpret the rules of engagement. Instead of acting based on internal schema, people are given a standard that they can align to. In most cases people will follow the guidelines you give them, so long as they are not too strict or complex.

Facilitators use a wide variety of guidelines in their work, but a common one is the rules of dialogue. To date our favorite presentation comes from the Theory U illustrations of the levels of listening and dialogue.[22] We have seen this redesigned and used in several different consulting and educational contexts, and the premise is a set of very simple rules that help people have an authentic, respectful, empathetic, and creative dialogue. Later we will explore these and other principles of good dialogue. Our present argument is that behavioral guidelines provide a framework for how to behave in ways that brings out the best in oneself and in others. Posting such guidelines in co-creative spaces makes it very clear what is expected from participants.

In summary semiotic design, through both subtle and overt means, is a means to create an entry point into the co-creative experience. Entries are crucial in setting the container, for they not only establish the permissions and guidelines for behavior, but also act to sever the tie to the "normal" world. In our final section to this chapter, we consider how severance and ritual can be used to create dramatic and impactful environments.

The Power of Ritual

For thousands of years cultures have been using ritual environments to shape behavior. Imagine being at the Egyptian pyramids and witnessing a Pharaoh being entombed. With such majestic and impressive architecture, it is no wonder the people then thought of the rulers as Gods. Today we still create monumental architecture and hold large-scale rituals to create, express, and share culture. Churches, concert stages, and football stadiums are all ritual environments. So also are the conference hall and classroom. In each of these spaces, from large and grand to a small and square, we regularly conduct rituals.

The word "ritual" may evoke images of cultural acts like religious ceremonies and rites of man or womanhood, and indeed these are rituals. But rituals are much more pervasive in our lives than these signature moments. A ritual is a series of actions followed in a prescribed order in a specific place. Rituals are also symbolic acts, where signs are manipulated by participants. Consider a football (soccer) match between Manchester United and Chelsea. The fans all gather in a specific place (the stadium or the pub), wear their jerseys (symbolic acts), sing team songs (also symbolic acts), and cheer for their team to win (conditioned behaviors). The match itself is also has ritual elements, from the introduction of the teams to the rules of the game. Any game is ritualistic, and so also are most of our everyday behaviors. Brushing your teeth, having coffee with colleagues, and running meetings...these are all rituals.

There are lot of theories about why we have rituals, from creating and sharing culture to social control and managing uncertainty. Each of these ideas has its merits, and ritual can be all of these at once. For the *Xd*, a basic understanding of ritual can help them understand how to shape the environment and when to implement different techniques.

Design Rituals

Highly symbolic and embodied (requiring physical involvement) rituals can be used to join the space, express membership, and trigger behaviors. Highly symbolic activities are those that involve the explicit creation and engagement with symbols. Creating a team logo, a company brand, or a collective piece of art is highly symbolic. We will describe these and other techniques in Part II. Here we are speaking to the preparation for such activities, wherein the participants are doing something that gives them a sense of togetherness, or community.

If you plan to use ritual, the environment for it must be carefully designed beforehand. This can be as simple as making sure a room has the right tables, chairs, and writing surfaces, or as complex as an elaborate interior design that makes the space unforgettable. The more unique you design the environment, the more memorable it is. Furthermore, we can improve upon how memorable an environment is by making the experience within in it multi-sensory. The most memorable rituals are ones in which people are fully engaged, using their mind, senses, and bodily interaction. Think of the difference between watching theater and being *in* theater. The embodied experience is much more impactful that spectatorship, and we encourage you to think of ways that you can design ritual environments to invite full participation.

Co-create Mythology

Rituals can also be the vehicle for creating and transmitting the mythology of a group. Some time ago I read Harrison Owen's writings, and I was shocked when he told the story of his first academic paper being rejected for suggesting that organizations had a mythology.[23] At the time, the 1980s, companies had strategy, not culture. It was heresy to suggest that they also had a mythology. Today Owen's argument has won out, and most people see organizational culture as rooted in its own mythology that we call purpose and vision. A mythology is a people's or organization's sense of self and relation to the world around it. It is a worldview that is created by members of the culture and shared through rituals. In many organizations, the people creating the myth (vision, purpose) sit at the top, the executives or design lead. They share the myth through internal marketing, human relations, and special events like creative retreats.

This is great for top-down dissemination, but it has a real BIG problem. When people are not part of creating something, it is hard to convince them to adopt it. There are many cases where an organizational vision is compelling enough to draw people to it, and they want to buy into the myth. But there are many more cases where organizations decide to change their purpose and vision behind closed doors, and when they try to disseminate it throughout the culture, it is met with resistance. That resistance can come from a variety of factors, but some core reasons are people not believing the organization in what it says it is trying to be (disillusionment), not understanding the message, perceiving the change to be extra (and unnecessary) work, and not being involved in the creation of the new culture they are being asked to embody.

The top-down, or closed-door, approach to creating a mythology is common across every organizational culture we have seen. It can work, but for co-creation it is of little value. We argue that having real, meaningful impact requires designing rituals in which the people themselves create the meaning and then displaying the artifacts of that creation in the environment to give it culture. When people are engaged in the creation of something as important as purpose and values, or a statement of co-working agreements, they are far more likely to implement and follow the rules they helped create. People want to have a role that they perceive as valued, so give them one. Empower them as co-creators of the environment by designing rituals in which they can create their own artifacts. When these objects, physical and symbolic, are then displayed in the environment, it reminds them of their membership in the group and what they have accomplished. It also gently reminds them of the agreements that have been made.

What they co-create can be anything that you can display artifacts from. It can be as simple as a team logo or as complex as a theatrical performance. The important thing is that you are creating culture in a shared social bonding experience. While it may not be possible to create full-fledged culture in a short-term program, even small acts of ritual and bonding set the co-creative process apart and give it a uniqueness that can inspire participants. For program designers and facilitators, it can also become a signature of your work that attracts new clients.

Ritual Disruption

In our earlier discussion of spatial design, we mentioned the possibility of creating spaces that purposefully disrupt people's expectations and norms, warning that taking spatial design too far can cause considerable discomfort. We also wrote that at times this is exactly what you want to do. The time when disruption is most influential is when you want to catalyze a breakthrough. Most of the techniques for this are facilitated, but these techniques need to be staged correctly for them to work. Enter ritual....

Ritual is most often used, as we have explained above, to create a sense of shared culture and deepen social bonds while empowering people by engaging them in the creative process. There is a special type of ritual, however, that serves a different purpose. These are rites of passage, used in cultures to facilitate life transitions such as from child to adult. Rites of passage are dramatic events with three distinct stages: separation, liminality, and aggregation. Separation is the break from a previous reality, a departure from the normal world and roles one had into a new space. People naturally resist separation because they are being forced to leave their comfort zones. Separation is thus an uncomfortable, even painful process.

Liminality is the transition space, the threshold time between a previous role or place and a new one not yet known. In liminal spaces, people must navigate the unknown and acquire new knowledge that will enable them to leave the threshold and return to society in a new role. In tribal cultures, this is when the elders would take young boys or girls off into a special place and teach them what it means to be a man or woman.

Aggregation is the return to the world you came from, but with new knowledge and a new role. It marks the completion of a life transition, the adoption of new responsibilities and behaviors. In our common media culture, it is the returning hero or heroine after having passed through a series of trials to master their gift and return that to society.

Although you may not have ever thought of it this way before, rites of passage are integral to innovation. Take, for example, the design studio or innovation lab. A team is assembled and must leave their normal working environment and go to a new place (separation). This place is most likely organized differently from what they are used to, encouraging them to experiment with their surroundings and learn new ways of working (liminality). While in the studio or lab, they are encouraged and pressured to think and act differently, to come up with new ideas (liminality). If the team has a breakthrough, they rapidly prototype it and start testing it with potential users (trials). After several iterations, they develop a product or service that has real value. They leave the studio or lab with new knowledge, new relations, and something new to offer (aggregation).

We see the co-creative process as a collective movement between the Known, the Unknown, and the New that in many ways parallels rites of passage. Because this movement begins with separation, it is essential that the environment people walk into helps to achieve the break from the norm. The more the environment can be used to disrupt expectations, the more likely it is that you can get participants into new ways of working and interacting. Mind you, this is not the "ease into it," or comfortable approach. Disruptions cause discomfort, and you must be able to manage these toward productive outcomes.

Nic Turner once told me of an event the nowhere group held that did this beautifully. The client, a large multinational corporation, asked the team to organize a co-creative conference. They reserved a hotel ballroom with tall ceilings. Nowhere was very secretive about the event, not letting anyone know what to expect. When the 300 or so participants walked in, they were likely expecting a room filled with roundtables, a couple projectors, and flip charts. Instead, they were greeted by a massive Native American teepee (pyramid tent) in the center of the room, and no tables or chairs. No one had any idea what to do. The nowhere team used that stark break from reality as a catalyst to their program.

There are other ways to create separation without forceful disruption, ranging from the off-site leadership retreat in a remote natural setting to a design studio setup. How much or how little disruption is needed is case dependent, which is why you must really understand the stakeholders and what is right for them. In each of the cases above, the environment plays a key role in the efficacy of ritual. Just as actors need a theater and a stage, so too does co-creation need an environment that enables and reinforces the activities taking place within it. Ritual provides a natural bridge between the design of environments to process design. Ritual is at once spatial and behavioral, entered into and enacted. It is thus the perfect place for us to reflect on what we have written about environment design and cross the threshold into process design in the next chapter.

Conclusions

Staging the environment for co-creation requires careful consideration of the experience that you wish to create and how the physical and semiotic resources you have can be best put to that end. We have argued that the environment people walk into profoundly shapes their experience, providing several guidelines to help you design more impactful spaces. From circles of chairs to elaborate rituals, we have illustrated how subtle and overt adjustments in the environment have wide-ranging, positive consequences for business and project realization.

While we praise unique, flexible, and socially engaging spatial design, it is prudent for us to also make the point that a creatively built, tangible environment alone is ineffective at generating innovation. The simplistic upgrade to business practice or training seminar, a rearrangement of schedules or furniture, does not equate directly to a more productive, healthy work or learning environment. Contemporary organizations are littered with the remnants of failed or partially implemented programs for innovation and change.[24] What is needed are the practices that go along with the environment. Businesses, schools, and research and training facilities which do not develop the core exercises for communication, team building, idea incubation, and true innovation benefit little from superficial restructuring. The most important elements of the co-creation paradigm are the people and activities we enable through our work, and this does not require spending a lot of money on environment design.

At the end of the day you must work with what you have, so it may be the case that you are asked to facilitate a creative program in a ballroom filled with circular tables and projectors for PowerPoint presentations. Or, if you are lucky, you will be able to work in an environment like one of the examples in this chapter. In either case, it is not what you have that makes the difference. It is what you do with what you have. Making the best use of available resources is an integral part of process design, the subject of our next chapter. Metaphorically speaking, now that we have our actors ("Working with People") and the set is built ("Staging the Environment"), we can turn to the final part of preparation—the script.

Notes

1. Kuo, Jeannette, A-typical plan: projects and essays on identity, flexibility and atmosphere in the office building.
2. Doorley & Witthoft, *Make Space, 38.*
3. See, for example, Nenonen (2004), Nenonen et al. (2009), Lewis and Moultrie (2005), Streitz et al. (2005).
4. See Foucault (1995), Leclerq-Vandelannoitte (2013).
5. Fabbri and Charue-Duboc (2013).
6. Chartrand and Bargh, *The Chameleon Effect*, 1999.
7. Oldenburg (2013), Kuo (2013).
8. Fawkes (2013), Boman and Gullström (2013).
9. Kuo (2013), Idenburg (n.d.).
10. Kolko, Thoughts on Interaction Design.
11. Nenonen, Future Learning Environments.
12. A good example of a well-designed social workspace is netWork Oasis. See Kakko et al. (2006).
13. Oldenburg, Celebrating the Third Place.
14. Tjora and Scambler (2013), Henriksen et al. (2013).
15. Banke et al. (2004).
16. Idenburg, *Workspheres.*
17. Mandl et al., The Co-Creative Meeting, 55.
18. Owen (1997), World Café, the. "Who We Are." http://www.theworld-cafe.com/about.html.
19. Lewis and Moultrie, The Organizational Innovation Laboratory, 73–83.
20. Ibid., 81.
21. An alternative to providing guidelines is to co-create them with participants, establishing a social contract. We will discuss this as a facilitation technique in coming chapters.
22. Scharmer, *Theory U.*
23. Harrison Owen is the founder of Open Space Technology, one of the first co-creative engagements.
24. Banke et al. (2004).

References

Banke, P., I. Hague, T. L. Hansen, and E.-C. Norskov. "Moving Beyond Rhetoric: Creativity, Organisations and Performance." In *Action Research in Workplace Innovation and Regional Development*, edited by Werner and Peter Totterdill Fricke, 263–286, 2004.

Boman, Magnus, and Cha Gullström. *Technical Foresight Report: Mediated Futures.* Brussels: European Institute of Innovation and Technology, 2013.

Chartrand, Tanya L., and John A. Bargh. "The Chameleon Effect: The Perception–Behavior Link and Social Interaction." *Journal of Personality and Social Psychology* 76, no. 6 (1999): 893.

Doorley, S., and Scott Witthoft. *Make Space: How to Set the Stage for Creative Collaboration*. New York: John Wiley & Sons, 2012.

Fabbri, J., and F. Charue-Duboc. "The Role of Physical Space in Collaborative Workplaces Hosting Entrepreneurs." In *Materiality and Space: Organizations, Artefacts and Practices*, edited by F. Vaujany and N. Mitev, 117–134. Basingstoke: Palgrave Macmillan, 2013.

Fawkes, Piers. *Future of Work, Psfk Labs Report*. New York: PSFK Publishing, 2013.

Foucault, Michel. *Discipline and Punish: The Birth of the Prison*. 2nd ed. New York, NY: Vintage Books, 1995.

Henriksen, I. M., Skjolsvold T., and I. Gronning. "The Cafe Community." In *Cafe Society* edited by Torja and Scrambler, 87–102. New York: Palgrave Macmillan, 2013.

Idenburg, Florian. "Workspheres." In *A-Typical Plan: Projects and Essays on Identity, Flexibility and Atmosphere in the Office Building*, edited by Jeannette Kuo, 116–118. Zurich: Park Books, n.d.

Kakko, Ilka, Mika Lavikainen, and Tatiana Glotova. "Network Oasis: New Practices for Emergent Collaborative Working Environments." In *Network-Centric Collaboration and Supporting Fireworks*, edited by L. Camarnha-Matos, H. Afsarmanesh and M. Ollus. Ifip International Federation for Information Processing, 333–342. Boston: Springer, 2006.

Kolko, Jon. *Thoughts on Interaction Design: A Collection of Reflections*. Burlington, MA: Morgan Kaufmann, 2010.

Kuo, Jeannette. *A-Typical Plan: Projects and Essays on Identity, Flexibility and Atmosphere in the Office Building*. Zurich: Park Books, 2013.

Leclercq-Vandelannoitte, Aurélie. "Beyond Panoptic Enclosures? On the Spatiotemporal Dimension of Organizational Control as Induced by Mobile Information Systems Materiality and Space Trial Access." In *Materiality and Space: Organizations, Artefacts and Practices*, edited by F. Vaujany and N. Mitev, 197–215. Basingstoke: Palgrave Macmillan, 2013.

Lewis, Michael, and James Moultrie. The Organizational Innovation Laboratory. *Creativity and Innovation Management* 14, no. 1 (2005): 73–83.

Mandl, Christoph E., Markus Hauser, and Hanna Mandl. *The Co-Creative Meeting Practicing Consensual Effectivity in Organizations*. Berlin; New York: Springer, 2013.

Nenonen, Suvi. *Future Learning Environments: Finnish Insights*. Aalto University, 2004.

Nenonen, Suvi, Kaisa Airo, Petra Bosch, Renate Fruchter, Satu Koivisto, Nils Gersberg, Peggie Rothe, Virpi Ruohomäki, and Matti Vartiainen. "Managing Workplace Resources for Knowledge Work." In *ProWork Project: Helsinki University of Technology*, Stanford University, NTNU (Norway), 2009.

Oldenburg, Ray. *Celebrating the Third Place: Inspiring Stories About the Great Good Places at the Heart of Our Communities.* Boston: De Capo Press, 2009.

Oldenburg, Ray. "The Café as a Third Place." In *Café Society*, edited by Aksel Tjora and Graham Scambler, 7–21. New York: Palgrave Macmillan US, 2013.

Owen, Harrison. *Open Space Technology: A User's Guide.* 2nd ed. San Francisco, CA: Berrett-Koehler Publishers, 1997.

Scharmer, Claus Otto. *Theory U: Leading from the Future as It Emerges: The Social Technology of Presencing.* Cambridge, MA: Society for Organizational Learning, 2009.

Streitz, Norbert, Carsten Magerkurth, and Thorsten Prante. "From Information Design to Experience Design: Smart Artefacts and the Disappearing Computer." *Interactions* 12, no. 4 (2005): 21–25.

Tjora, Aksel, and Graham Scambler. *Café Society.* First edition. ed. New York, NY: Palgrave Macmillan, 2013.

CHAPTER 5

Process Design I: Building Containers

Fig. 5.1 Process

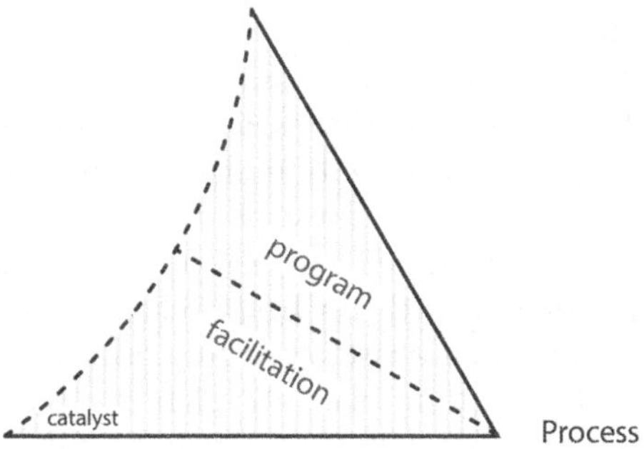

In improvisational theater, actors create a performance from a few constituent elements that they are given to work with. If you have ever seen the comedy show "Whose Line Is It Anyway," you have witnessed the creative genius of actors who entertain a crowd by creating comedy from elements chosen by the host and guests. Their job is hard, for they have no idea when they come onto the stage what they will be working with. It could be a lasso, giant banana, and cell phone. Or it could be a cardboard cutout of New York City, a martini glass, and a paragraph from a Broadway special. No one ever knew if the improv would be a success or failure, which was part of why it was so funny.

B. R. Rill, M. M. Hämäläinen, *The Art of Co-Creation*,
https://doi.org/10.1007/978-981-10-8500-0_5

In co-creation we are fortunate to have a bit more structure to work with, but our job is not unlike that of improvisational actors at times. The co-creative facilitator, like an actor, performs and must be able to improvise when conditions change. Our structure—or script—is called "process."

Process consists of the *design* and the *facilitation* of a multi-segment program, as well as all other activities that run in conjunction with a co-creative program (Fig. 5.1). Process, then, is not temporally constrained to a multi-segment program in one locality. It can occur mixed mode (face-to-face and virtual), asynchronously, or in parallel (e.g. coaching or team building exercises in addition to facilitated programs).

When leading a creative program, achieving both the practical and experiential outcomes is the foremost consideration. "How to" create this experience lies in the design and facilitation of the program. Because in this book we separate co-creation into planning (Part I) and facilitation (Part II), we must also divide up guidelines that, in practice, apply to both Parts. Our division creates two sets of guidelines: (1) guidelines for program design and planning and (2) guidelines for the facilitation of a program. The separation helps us divide our insights into stages, but we acknowledge that in real life the boundaries between planning and doing are less clear. Given this, you can expect to see some of the philosophical points and guidelines offered here elaborated further in Part II, where we discuss how to implement them. In this chapter we introduce guidelines that apply to the planning phase, occurring prior to actually leading a program.

The starting place for planning a co-creative program lies in the perspective that collective creativity and insight are *emergent* properties of a designed experience. Introduced in Chap. 2, here we go further into the nature of this experience and how to design for it. Setting the container—establishing a community space of trust, clarity, engagement, and safety—is the first step and vital. Without this, co-creation is nearly impossible, and creating this container begins long before the program itself. Given how vital the container is for co-creation, we dedicate this entire chapter to understanding what a good container is and how to prepare it.

Building upon this foundation, in Chap. 6 we present our guidelines for process design in light of the conceptual framework of a co-creative journey. The journey illustration is a grammar—or process architecture—upon which many different methods can be placed. Unpacking this model further, we introduce the experience design principles that support this journey. Careful consideration of each of these non-quantifiable, seemingly intangible aspects of experience design is part of the secret sauce of co-creation. It is not so much the specific program pieces offered that lead to creative breakthroughs, but rather managing energy and encouraging people to take risks collectively as they explore the Unknown in pursuit of the New.

An understanding of the intangibles helps us lay out the more tangible aspects of program design. We will introduce several principles that guide our own planning efforts. This is by no means a comprehensive list of considerations, nor are these guidelines concrete requirements. While helping maximize results by showing how to put techniques into a larger framework, we encourage each leader, facilitator, or designer to use the tools they are most comfortable with. Our goal is to help *Xd* create a synergy between program components that increases collective potential and the ability to harness it toward productive outcomes.

Synergy often results from a mix of hard work, fun, and a sense of community. Process then is not just the program that people go through, but the total context in which they encounter each other and the challenge. To illustrate this point, we share an experience from the BoB community of practice. In 2016 BoB took a team of professional consultants to Laos to help local NGOs. What we learned was that the most important outcome of the effort was not the outcome for the NGOs. Rather, it was the growth opportunity for the team of consultants. The BoB story illustrates the professional development potential of co-creation, and we stress growth as an important design principle in itself. If you plan and prepare people for growth, their engagement and efforts will be markedly improved.

We close Chap. 6 by looking closely at our primary objective—moments of insight. We consider the capacities and process necessary to create optimal conditions for insights to manifest, as well as the cultural and biological barriers to creativity. Co-creation, we argue, is a process that uses an oscillation between the Known and the Unknown to breakthrough these obstacles and release the full potential available.

The Container

If collective creativity and insight are emergent properties of a designed experience, then what is that experience? The experience is that of collectively tapping into the space between—the informational and interintentional field from which insights come forth.[1] The space between is where all the creative potential people bring with them engages the potential of everyone else. It is from the intersections that novel ideas emerge. When recognized and acted upon, these emergent ideas can become innovations.

If we take a moment to reflect upon our own creative experiences, we each have at least one memory of being in a group context where insights seem to manifest out of thin air. Perhaps it was a flash insight into a problem that the team had been mulling on for a long time. Perhaps it was a way forward from a seemingly intractable group conflict. Or perhaps it was a meeting where ideas seemed to build upon each other effortlessly, building energy as it went along. In these cases, the moment of breakthrough felt *collective*, and it showed on people's faces or in their expressions. The right side of Fig. 5.2 (below) illustrates collective intelligence. In this visual, insights emerge from novel intersections in the space *between* the different actors (circles). Collective intelligence is the *capacity* for the group to hold and explore the space between, then act on emergent insights.

The image on the left, by contrast, depicts a dialogue where, even though the group is in a circle, one actor (black circle) dominates. As you can see, his or her dominance greatly reduces the communication channels (dotted arrows), which in turn reduces novel intersections and the likelihood of collective insights.

A key identifier of collective intelligence is that there is no sense of personal ownership. If you asked someone there whose idea it was, the answer is that it came from multiple sources. While it may be possible to identify the specific contributors, sometimes it seems that the insight emerged

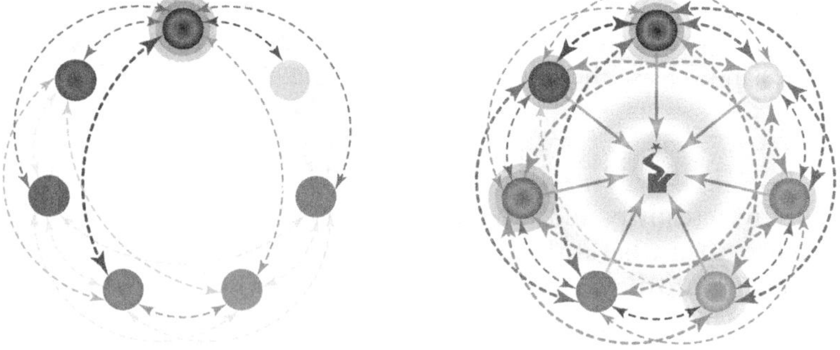

Fig. 5.2 Collective intelligence

from something greater than the group. It might have. The whole *is* more than the group membership. It is the group in context with each other, the creative program, the organization, the challenge they are facing, and even the broader social and ecological systems that we all are part of. Insight can come from anywhere in this larger field of interrelationships, which is why it is beneficial to invite and recognize all of these influences in co-creative programs. The space between is where it all comes together.

In our experience, the space between does not develop in most collaborative endeavors. The reason for this is that creating and holding the space between takes great care. Without careful planning and constant maintenance, it can easily collapse back into routine ways of being and doing.

Preparing a creative team for the space between begins with setting the container. Throughout the opening chapters we have mentioned the container several times. In Chap. 2 we described the container as a safe, authentic space wherein people can open themselves up and take risks. In Chap. 4 we mentioned several aspects of environment design that help set a strong container. Here we bring it all together into one place, for the container is absolutely critical to co-creation.

The container is the interpersonal, felt environment in which people work. It is the group context that participants and *Xd* contribute to and experience. To understand the ingredients of a good container, it is helpful to consider its opposite. A bad container is an environment—an experiential context—characterized by fear and separation. The current state of global politics is a prime example. The world is at a turning point between two very different styles of governance. One style prefers networked collaboration, dialogue, and compromise. Trying to understand and work with one another to tackle global challenges underlies this style. Collaboration and compromise are time consuming and can seem inefficient, but when decisions are made they have the support of a group that tends to respect one another as (more or less) equals. This style requires a willingness to engage in multi-stakeholder dialogues, patience, and empathy. It favors collective representation and actions.

The contrasting style is classic authoritarian leadership, characterized by an emphasis on isolationist policies and nationalism. The authoritarian style is supported by fear tactics and separation in that it makes everyone else the "enemy" of the state. The common answer in the face of perceived threats (fabricated or real) is a show of strength.

Fear and separation are valuable weapons in a divide and conquer mindset. Whether in global politics or in workplace dynamics, seeding suspicions about others and encouraging competition is a powerful tool to get people to do what you want. They are levers that resourceful leaders often use to reach their ends. The problem with this approach is that fear and separation are tools used by people in power to keep, use, and increase their power. They are not methods that serve the larger whole or empower everyone, and for every winner there are many losers.

In general, competition has a positive effect on creativity, but how you do it is key. Authoritarian, fear-based approaches often have the effect of demoralizing the people you are trying to encourage. "Innovate or else" strategies tend to produce only small, incremental changes because people are too afraid of what will happen if their ideas fail. Since creativity benefits from failing and trying again, a fear of failure is a sure way to hamper any creative efforts. It is a container wherein no one wants to stick their neck out too far. And so what you get in such environments is very predictable, very mediocre performance.

Even in the absence of an explicitly authoritarian culture, establishing a good container can be difficult. In most situations, it is the everyday cultural norms of protectiveness, carefulness, and comfort zones that prevent people from exploring new forms of being together as co-workers. People are typically pretty good at what they do and they already have friend groups, so why would they invest the time and energy into doing things any differently? This is a fair question for an *Xd* to ask, because it is an organizational reality. We cannot expect people to change just because we think it is good idea, no matter how much evidence we can bring to bear. *They* must believe it too.

A good container requires a real effort and desire to create it, which is why having a compelling needs story is so important. People simply will not change how they do things or explore new social forms unless there is a good reason for them to do it. A bad container can be as simple as a task group assigned by leadership without the team knowing why they were chosen. Or it could be a team that is engaged in a challenge, but they can't stand working with someone else on the team and the facilitator (if they have one) is not managing that conflict well. In these and other cases of a bad container, there is always some issue or dynamic that hinders rather than encourages creativity. While tensions can be good, in bad containers tensions cause a loss of energy and productivity.

What we want is a container that can transform the energy of tensions into a positive force. A good container is characterized by community (togetherness), trust, safety, engagement, and clear expectations. A successful environment is one in which people feel safe enough to contribute freely and authentically, relax and have some fun, and even stretch their boundaries a bit. "Safe" is a space of mutual respect and empathy where people can express what they feel freely without fear of consequences outside that space. The veteran process consultant Ed Schein said, "The group has to become a container to legitimize saying things that would ordinarily in polite society be considered to be rude or bad etiquette and therefore don't say things to each other."[2] A safe container is thus one in which we can leave social norms aside to a certain degree and be honest (authentic) with one another. Yet it is also one in which respect for each other's feelings and the process discourage overly disrupting behaviors.

There is a delicate balance between encouraging disruption and maintaining group cohesion and flow. Setting the container goes a long way in navigating this balance. In *Riding the Creative Rollercoaster*, Nick Udall writes,

> These containers, spaces and working practices need to be strong enough to hold the uncertainty and emotion that emerges when we disrupt the status quo. They need to be safe enough to speak the truth. They must create the openness and trust needed to step into the unknown. They need to be subtle and still enough to catch glimpses of 'the new'. And they need to be skillful enough to transform creative sparks into innovations.

In this description, a good container is one in which the team has bonded to the point of being able to handle disruption. If someone that you consider a friend or close colleague, with whom you have established trust, disrupts your experience, it is usually ok. Your relationship is strong enough to handle it and you can see how the disruption might be helpful. If, by contrast, someone that you don't trust causes a disruption, things can go downhill quickly. It is also very difficult to regain trust once lost. To prevent potentially negative disruptions, strong interpersonal bonds must be developed at the onset of a co-creative program.

Nick also draws attention to subtlety and stillness as necessary to catch glimpses of the new. He is referring to presence and the observational skills we discussed in the section on creative leadership. Stillness, a calm awareness, brings with it a greater capacity to identify potential insights than the mind filled with thoughts. The need for calm is why we build in moments of stillness into co-creative programs, a point we will return to shortly.

The passage also refers to transformation of creative insight into innovation. A good container has a particular energy that makes transformation possible. It has the felt sense of a "good energy" or "vibe," an indication of strong team bonding and leadership necessary to manage the uncertainty of the unknown. The energy is also a sense of momentum to move—to manifest potential into action. This latent potential manifests when properly supported, which is part skillful facilitation and partly the internal capacities of participants.

The Pillars of Co-creation

Our description of a good container consists of mutually perceptible features of the container. People can make signs of these attributes to describe their working spaces, and facilitators often use such signs as semiotic cues to establish the working environment. The Circle of Trust Touchstones developed by Parker J. Palmer and the Center for Courage & Renewal are one example of this practice. The Touchstones include, among others:

- Give and receive welcome
- Be present as fully as possible
- Speak your truth in ways that respect other people's truth
- Attend your own inner teacher
- When the going gets rough, turn to wonder

According to their pamphlet, facilitators at the Center for Courage & Renewal "use these Touchstones to define clear boundaries in a Circle of Trust, the kind of boundaries that create a safe space…they can be adapted to support any place where we want to honor the integrity of the individual and build relational trust."[3] What the authors offer is a set of guidelines for establishing a good container.

IDEO offers something similar, but crafted specifically for design teams. In their brainstorming rooms, the rules are written on the walls:

- Defer judgment
- Encourage wild ideas
- Stay focused on the topic
- Build on the ideas of others

The last rule, according to Brown, "is right up there with "Thou shalt not kill" and "Honor thy father and thy mother," as it ensures that every participant is invested in the last idea put forward and has the chance to move it along."[4]

These two sets of guidelines complement each other nicely, bringing into consideration both what to do and how to be in a creative context. The overlap between the Touchstones, IDEO's guidelines, and the principles we developed from research in Hong Kong only serves to strengthen our collective argument that a good container must have certain qualities. Yet, other than putting up nice posters, how can we support and enhance these qualities? It is one thing to instruct people to be present and to respect other's ideas without judgment, but how does anyone actually embody those principles?

There are several resources to aid facilitator development, with foci on creating the container and cultivating the necessary personal skills to facilitate groups to where they need to go. The International Association of Facilitators (IAF) and the Institute for Cultural Affairs (ICA) are two organizations that provide training, and we include resources throughout this text.[5] Yet while there is a wide variety of training available for facilitators, there is very little offered on preparing the internal states of program participants. Usually this work falls under the categories of professional development or coaching, which can make growth training appear to be only for people in leadership positions. The truth is that any such training is fantastic, and we can get even better returns from our processes if we share it with the entire team.

It may be a lot, too much in most cases, to approach a client and say, "We need to do professional development for the whole team before we get started with your challenge." If you can get away with that, go for it. A more reasonable approach is to ask for a little leeway to build capacity building into the program while simultaneously tackling the challenge.

When asked what difference it will make that justifies investing their time and money, a short comparative inquiry can be useful. You might reply with questions, such as "Can you remember the last really good creative meeting you had? What did it feel like? Why was it so successful?" The client will identify a few aspects of that experience, which usually includes a sense of enjoying the team dynamic, good energy, feeling valued and respected, and so on. Then ask the client to recall a bad meeting and what made it so bad. They might reply by listing external forces that interrupted the flow, internal group dynamics, or other factors that made the meeting dysfunctional. Their narrative will often include emotional or judgmental statements like "I was bored," "It was frustrating because no one listened to me," or "Those people are idiots." After hearing these tales, direct the client's attention to the differences that made the difference. You may ask this directly, with "What was the difference between these two experiences?" Or you can be a bit more guiding, with questions such as "How did people show up to the meeting?" or "Do you feel like the group had respect for each other?" Whatever techniques you use, the point is to shed light on the fact that how people "show up"—which is a statement describing their attitude, degree of preparedness, and how they treat others—has a major impact on how the meetings went. In most cases what is drawn to light is the fact that it is not as much what people were *doing* as much as how they were *being* that made the difference between a good and bad creative meeting. Teams comprised of people that come in with the right internal attitude and consideration for others tend to do much better than teams dominated by egos and entrenched positions. Once this point is clear to the client, you can close the dialogue by stating that the capacity building component helps people show up at their best for co-creation.

In co-creative programs, we find that performance benefits from purposeful cultivation of four internal capacities. These "Pillars of Co-Creation" are presence, authenticity, courage, and an eco-centered mindset. "PACE"—as we call it—is analogous to structural supports for a building. You can build a house without them, but it won't be as stable. For individuals, these are capacities that can be developed with proper training and practice.

Presence, as discussed in the section in Chap. 3 on creative leadership, is a skillful awareness that enables people to calmly observe their internal states and process information in the moment without constant chatter from the mind about the past and the future. When applied in group dynamics, presence creates an internal space between thoughts, a slight pause in which a person can evaluate the range of possible reactions and choose what they feel most appropriate. This has huge implications for dialogue, and we will discuss this at length in Part II.

Presencing, an application of awareness when exploring the UNKNOWN, significantly impacts the ability to notice and act upon potentials—thus improving the ability to innovate. It is our experience that an expansion of awareness is necessary to break free from the tendency of the human mind to act based on preconceived mental models. Combined with the human tendency to act from habit, the vast majority of thinking and doing is reactive rather than proactive. Collective action is the same, rendering it difficult to innovate. Simply put, "if awareness never reaches beyond superficial events and current circumstances, actions will be reactions"—Peter Senge.[6] Presence is important throughout the creative journey, from dialogues to the critical reframing of understandings necessary to generate new ideas. As we navigate the contours of this journey in Part II, we will make note of just how much presence is a differentiator that leads to deeper insights and transformative outcomes.

The second pillar is authenticity, being honest with yourself and others. Authentic interactions lead to a high level of trust generated by evolved teams. Authenticity as an attitude *within* people is what cultivates trust *between* people. Despite the obvious value of authenticity, there is an important distinction to be made between being authentic and authentic leadership. This distinction arose from a dialogue with a CEO of a Chinese company in Hong Kong. In the dialogue we were discussing authenticity in the context of a Chinese company owned by a family in which the eldest son inherited the leadership. The son thought of himself as an authentic leader, which he understood as being open and honest with others. In truth he was quite frank and open, but he was a terrible CEO. The point of the story is that being authentic is not the same as being an authentic leader. What the young CEO was missing was the "leadership" part. An authentic leader must be completely honest with himself regarding his or her abilities to lead and then make the right decision from that place of awareness. In the case of the Chinese company, the CEO would be authentically leading if he recognized his weaknesses and turned his position over to someone more competent. For co-creation, authentic leadership means acting from an equally self-aware space and then being honest with the group about your capacities and limitations.

Courage is the third pillar. Courage is the willingness to take risk, to carry on in the face of fear and uncertainty. It is an attitude that sees failure as a learning opportunity rather than as a stopping point. It is the exact opposite from the pervasive attitude in fear-driven contexts, where people are afraid to do anything that could result in failure. Fear of failure is especially pronounced in Asian cultures that use shame as a mechanism for social control. Failure results in shame, which most Asians will avoid at all costs. When working with groups with this cultural composition, a willingness to take risks cannot be expected. Establishing the perception of safety, however, will bring the courage out from people. What we are saying here is that most people, in the right circumstance, can and are willing to be courageous. This is true cross-culturally, but cultural norms impose different constraints on people's willingness to take risks. In Western cultural contexts it may be completely unnecessary to encourage risk taking. You may have the opposite situation! In our experience working with predominately Asian teams, courage must be drawn out by giving permissions and by setting a safe container. Once the genie is out of the box, people are amazingly creative and freely contribute a much greater range of ideas to any creative process. They are also more capable of handling failure, an inevitable and necessary part of innovation. ***Remember: the design motto "fail faster" only works when people are open to failure and what they can learn from it.***

The fourth pillar is an eco-centered mindset. In its simplest form, an eco-centered mindset is thinking of the whole. Leaders are expected to think of the whole, but it benefits all team members to do the same. In practice, this might be a shift from an attitude of "What can I do to show how creative I am?" to "What can I do to support the creativity of my shy team member?" The first is an ego-centered perspective, focused entirely upon the individual. The second is an eco-centered perspective, focused on the "We" rather than "I." The shift from "Me" to "We" benefits co-creation greatly because it puts the collective effort first. This attitude makes it infinitely more likely that all participants will feel a sense of value and empowerment, which encourages everyone to make a serious contribution. If the process becomes centered on one or two individuals, the others can and often do fall into the background as "supporters" or "observers." The creative potential of the whole is reduced to the most powerful egos in the room.

On a larger scale, eco-systems thinking is a core feature of conscious business and sustainable practices. It is acting, as an individual, team, or organization, in ways that carefully consider surrounding systems. For teams, it is being aware of and considerate to the effects of behaviors and actions on the team, its process, and the organizational or target audience it is acting on behalf of. The larger scale adds the dimension of "It" to the "Me" and "We." Taken together, eco-systems thinking looks at any action on these three "levels" of analysis. In organizational change, for example, any initiative would need to consider the personal, team, and organizational impacts of the initiative. In design, eco-systems thinking might consider how a product meets the needs of a target audience, but also how sourcing the materials to produce it affects eco-systems. The team might also consider what happens after the life of the product has expired. Where does it go? Does it decompose? How will it affect our grandchildren? Eco-systems thinking can be large or small, but the core feature of all scales is awareness and consideration for something larger than oneself.

When grounded in PACE—presence (awareness), high levels of trust generated by evolved teams (authenticity), willingness to take risks (courage), and an eco-centered mindset (thinking of the whole)—co-creation has the potential to transform organizational culture and generate breakthrough innovations. It does this by shifting the place from which people act and how they interact with each other. The scale to which the team can embody the pillars of co-creation will vary, dependent upon a range of factors from personal histories to the amount of time you have to prepare the team. You may have coaching and mentoring built into a long-term co-creative change initiative, in which you can create the space for this type of personal and team development. Or you may have to work with a group you have never met in a one-day co-creative workshop, in which case you have no control over how they prepare. You can, however, control how they enter the space and establish an environment that encourages them to adopt PACE as a way of being in the temporal creative space.

Designing the entry and the environment is what we call "Setting the Container." It is the first and most critical part of a co-creative program and begins before the team ever enters into a physical space together. Setting the container is the first opportunity to put the pillars of co-creation into place, and how you do so depends on the type of program. The pillars have value in contexts where you need people to engage one another with respect, awareness, and appreciation, from leadership retreats to day-to-day operations in an organization. Because of the broadly applicable benefits of PACE, we offer guidelines on its implementation throughout Parts I and II of this text.

Setting the Container

Setting the container begins within the *Xd*, specifically the worldview and attitude they bring to bear in every engagement. Just as there are different styles of leadership, there are different styles of facilitation. An *Xd* can choose what suits them and the program at hand, and there are a range of possibilities. The *Xd* is at their best when they model the behaviors they expect others to embody. The Circle of Trust Touchstones and IDEO's rules are two examples. For co-creation, we recommend the facilitation guidelines offered by the ICA. These five guidelines are[7] thus:

Inclusiveness
Invite many perspectives, accept all ideas, involve everyone. No one has all the answers or the answer. Honor and encourage diversity. Give consideration to everyone in the group and the organization, including yourself; express your own feelings and opinions.

Participation with Profound Respect
Listen for understanding with deep sensitivity to allow others to participate. Put aside judgments and assumptions so you are free to hear others. Provide a safe and inviting environment. Support the group with open-ended, generative questions, open and honest communication which adds to a sense of community.

Discovery Process
Have a clear intention, yet be open to outcome. Let go of judgments so you can stay open and learn with your whole self. Use your intuition, both left and right brain, and your multiple intelligences.

Context for Understanding and Commitment
Be mindful and present, resolve to make a difference, ask helpful questions, and take personal responsibility for the group's decision around a common mission/purpose.

Facilitative Style
Speak to be heard and understood. Acknowledge self-organization, which you cannot control, with deep appreciation for where the group is. Your responsibility is for process rather than the result. Acknowledge diversity and creativity.

The ICA facilitation guidelines are an embodiment of PACE. As we discussed in "Working with People" chapter, the facilitator is a tuning fork for the creative program. People may or may not specifically look at you as a role model, but they will be influenced by how you present yourself.

Stakeholder Dialogues

Every program begins with a conversation between the *Xd* and a stakeholder. It could be that the stakeholder is also the program sponsor, or it could be one of many dialogues with different stakeholders that lead up to a proposal for a program. In all cases it is wise to embody whatever guidelines suit your personal leadership or facilitation style, as these initial encounters will largely determine what people think of your abilities as an *Xd*.

Stakeholder dialogues are where initial expectations are set, and these are set primarily from the impressions made. These impressions derive partly from an *Xd*'s reputation and the materials they present, but more critical is the relationship formed during initial dialogues. Here there can be a notable difference between design and organizational change consulting. In design a person's reputation may be enough for others to simply trust their ability to lead a creative team. Designers can be eccentric and demanding, and these behaviors are acceptable as long as they produce results. Extreme characters may be quite desirable, just as they are in fashion and the arts, for their unique perspective. This sets a very particulate type of container—one centered on that person's way of doing things. Participants are either "on board" or not, for better or worse.

Organizational change consultants can also operate this way, but more common is the desire to use whatever will work best for the client. The client-centered perspective benefits from appreciative, inclusive dialogues that focus on building rapport and a good relationship. The co-creative container is first set when the dialogue becomes one of what "we" can do together. "We" statements indicate a relationship; thus it is the quality of that relationship that determines the initial quality of the container. If the *Xd* embodies how they run a creative program and they get the contract, then the client has implicitly agreed and committed to a particular way of doing things. The *Xd* may need to draw out these agreements more formally later, but the container is being formed from the very first interactions.

Because the container begins to take shape in stakeholder dialogues, it is critical that these interactions are of quality. Part of the quality comes from how each person shows up and engages each other. Equally important is taking the time to jointly explore the challenge. Co-creation does not benefit from quick sales tactics or fancy brochures. Such interactions are transactional, bereft of the "co" part of co-creation. They seem shallow because they are. Co-creation requires that both the stakeholder and the *Xd* are engaged in the issue at hand, and co-creation begins when the both parties begin to explore how they can proceed together.

In both design and organizational change, the quality and depth of initial conversations has a significant impact on the creative process. Not only are people feeling each other out, but also as the dialogue advances they address most of the issues that eventually become integrated into the design or creative brief. What is the challenge? How do we approach it? Who needs to be involved? How long will we work on this? What resources can we allocate? In good stakeholder dialogues, the *Xd*, the program sponsor, and whomever else can be involved in the planning explore the *Why, What, How, When*, and *Who*. These dialogues can range from an hour lunch to months of ongoing conversations, and through them expectations are set. These expectations, along with the relationships formed, are the initial pieces of the container. The rest is set in the lead-up to and in Act I of a co-creative process.

Leading Up

In the planning stage, we must take account of our resources and work with what we have. The tremendous variation of circumstance makes it impossible to lay out every scenario. However, if there is enough time and resources available, a few things can really make a difference. An essential item is the creative brief.

A creative brief lays out the agreements made during stakeholder dialogues and can also contain a roadmap of the creative process. It may be a formal, public document shared among all stakeholders, a proposal created by the *Xd* and signed off on by the sponsor, or a simple memorandum of understanding with little detail. While there is quite a variety of forms possible, the key ingredients are:

- Program description
- Rationale
- Desired results
- Commitments made

It can help if the brief also includes information on the *How* (the process itself), *Who* will be involved, assessment criteria, key points and milestones, relationship to organizational strategy, and any other useful information. How much or little is included in the creative brief is determined largely by the client. Some will ask for very detailed descriptions of every activity, what it does, and what outcomes can be expected. Others need only a minimal explanation to sign off on.

Whether explicitly laid out in a document or not, for the *Xd* all the core components of a creative brief are critical to setting the container. A sense of clarity comes from clear expectations and the program description. Engagement comes from a compelling rationale and commitments. And commitment from leadership is an especially important element that boosts creative performance. As Brown notes,[8]

> What is needed is a serious commitment from the top of the corporate pyramid, and it will be repaid by better ideas from the base. Any promising experiment should have a chance to gain organizational support in the form of a project sustained by appropriate resources and driven by definable goals.

Commitment, engagement, and clarity are necessary ingredients for a good program. If you have clarity and engagement yet lack any commitment to acting on results, a program can be amazing and then wholly discouraging for the participants who worked so hard only to see their outcomes neglected. It is detrimental to a creative program and all future attempts at innovation if a team feels that their time and efforts are wasted by insensitive leadership. If you have commitment to results but a lack of collective engagement, then the outcomes will derive only from those who asserted themselves most powerfully in the program. Others may feel left out or resist the outcomes. If you have clarity but no engagement, you could end up with a very long and boring dialogue with little enthusiasm. The chance of innovation is very small with unmotivated teams.

To summarize, a good creative brief does a few basic things. It sets clear expectations and provides an overview of what people should expect. It creates engagement with a powerful challenge or question, motivating participants to *want to* be involved. And it indicates the value of the team effort by committing resources and actions. These actions help create a good container before the program ever begins.

> Design challenges are not only a great way to unleash the power of competition, they also create stories around an idea, transforming people from passive onlookers into engaged participants.[9]

In an ideal scenario, leading up also affords the opportunity to get to know the team and organizational culture. If time and resource permits, dialogues with every stakeholder help to establish relationships, understand the varying motivations and backgrounds, and then design a program bespoke to the participants. Processes concerned only with the knowledge journey and its outputs too often neglect the emotional and group dynamics of collective creativity. If, however, we pay attention to personal histories, relationships, and motivations, we can design engagements with more nuance. The better you know your people, the more you have to work with as an experience designer. Moreover, establishing professional relationships wherein you are trusted as a facilitator and/or consultant increases the likelihood of sustained work. This can translate to more projects with a company and their affiliates. Moreover, longer engagements create more opportunity for impact over time and an evolving trust. These are required for processes such as organizational culture change. In sum, take the time to build professional relationships. They pay off.

Integration of Needs

The enthusiasm toward and potential impact of a creative program are greatly enhanced if needs are integrated between parts and wholes. Integration of needs refers to the value chain—ensuring that the various needs of different stakeholders and participants are met. A high degree of integration helps establish a very strong container imbued with the eco-systems perceptive.

In Chap. 3 we noted the salience of looking for contextual information that indicates how culture (organizational or otherwise) and strategy affect and could be affected by the process you are being asked to lead. A colleague who works for the United Nations once told us that in any change initiative there will be winners and losers. The success of the initiative often depends on how hidden stakeholders respond. If the perceived losers are not compensated, they can and do derail change efforts.

Co-creative programs *in isolation* often result in suboptimal solutions that can lead to failed initiatives. Co-creation is most effective when a program is both *supported by* and *integrated within* the broader system in which it occurs. Support by leadership and enabling organizational structures (rather than the all too common disabling bureaucracy) will either foster or hinder collective creativity.

There is a circular relationship between culture and strategy. Culture—being the relationships, beliefs, and artifacts that structure behaviors and the organizational environment—is the context in which a strategy is enacted. No strategy, no matter how well conceived, will succeed if it does not take culture into account. The two exist in a feedback loop, ideally supporting each other's existence. They *require* each other if an organization is to be healthy. Given this, a co-creative program needs to be informed by an understanding of culture of the stakeholders for whom the process is directed. To this end Designers create personas, user journey maps, and mock environments. Change consultants use a variety of assessments before making recommendations. In both fields, efforts to understand the broader context enable the integration of needs.

As we have seen, co-creation can be enacted on the micro-scale to meet certain challenges/opportunities, as part of a culture of innovation, as a change initiative, or to meet other ends. The type and scale of program affords certain opportunities for and sets constraints on the integration of needs. It may be the case that integration of needs is determined early on in stakeholder dialogues, in which case it can be made known through the creative brief. This early effort pays off by generating energy around the project and ensuring participants feel that their efforts have relevance in the larger picture.

In design, ethnographic and other research *during* the project cycle brings the cultural understanding necessary to integrate the needs of the project with those of end users. Design projects that skip over this phase are hit-or-miss, dependent almost entirely on how well the vision of the design team articulates with real people once it's developed. Without a robust understanding of the target users (or stakeholders), chances of a success are diminished. For this reason, value chain analysis is taught as a core part of the design process. Often the idea chosen to further develop is the one that best integrates needs across the value chain.

In other circumstances—a one- or two-day creative workshop, for example—there may not have been time or resource for a thorough cultural analysis. Integration of needs can occur at the very end of a program as participants are evaluating the choices they have come to. In such cases the *Xd* must trust the group, relying upon their understanding of the larger whole and how well (or not) their choices integrate needs.

While most *Xd* would prefer to have contextual information and a clear integration of needs before any program begins, it is hard to make an argument for one method over the other. They all produce results. The important thing is not the specific when or how, but that you take the time to do it. Integrating needs generates energy and engagement for a project, eases concerns by ensuring stakeholders needs have been considered, and increases the likelihood that the outcomes can be successfully implemented.

Guidelines for Integrating Needs

Bring All Client Pieces Together into the Larger Collective Engagement

Clients often want to have their own input sessions or activities interspersed with a program. These can be inputs from leadership on organizational mission, an HR presentation, a design masterclass, lecture, or any other matter of importance the client wants to share with the group assembled. Often the mindset is that these prices will be added on to the program rather than integrated within it. Rather than accommodating this need, we suggest bringing all pieces into the program that you facilitate. Doing so allows you to manage the flow and creates a sense of continuity for participants.

Time and Quality Management Are Essential for Meeting and Integrating Needs

There will always be trade-offs between time given and expected outcomes. While in the past it might have been possible to ask a client for a week-long process with their leadership team, in the current organizational consulting climate it is hard to get more than one or two days. Design is fortunate to have longer timelines that afford more in-depth processes like cultural research and iterative ideation processes, but designers also feel the pressure of high expectations and fast approaching deadlines.

In an ideal scenario, an *Xd* could implement every guideline we offer in this book. Yet this is unlikely except in the rare scenarios where the *Xd* is working with a someone who understands, believes in, and is willing to dedicate resources for higher-quality outcomes. In the majority of circumstances, trade-offs are necessary. Being completely realistic, a one- or two-day event cannot lead to well-explored outcomes and action plans. At most, short programs can generate some insights and arenas of action.

Manage Expectations

It is vital to manage expectations *before* facilitating a program. One way of doing so is to lay out, in writing, what different commitments can deliver:

1. One Day =
2. Two Days =
3. Three Days =

Communication is key, ensuring that both the *Xd* and the program sponsor(s) know what to expect going into a program. Even if you ran a great program, a simple misunderstanding here can lead to the program being perceived as irrelevant or unproductive simply because it did not integrate needs.

Spread the Wealth

The best co-creative programs have relevant outcomes for all stakeholders. These include:

1. Professional development outcomes (for the team and individuals).
2. Organizational/client practical outcomes.

People enjoy engaging in activities that they can see making a difference in their organization and in their own lives. It is not hard to sell a program that will lead to greater work-life balance, or a new product or service that generates profits. It is hard to sell program where people do not see how their efforts will be realized. While this point should be self-evident, an often-overlooked need is communicating how outcomes will be relevant to *all* stakeholders, especially the creative team. If the outcomes are not seen as including or impacting the team working on them, it is hard for them to care. Thus, while leaders may see the benefits of a particulate program or outcome, it is essential that they convey their understanding. This effort is best done in the creative brief or as an introduction to the program, encouraging buy-in from participants before engaging the challenge.

Effective programs have both practical and growth outcomes. Unless it is the *explicit* practical and experiential desired outcome, team building as a result is disappointing. The reason for this is simple. When participants engage in co-creation, they want to make an impact. If this impact is denied from them, they lose faith in the process (and leadership). We have witnessed the devastating effects of an amazingly co-creative program empowering participants to the point of tears, only to have their ideas "taken into consideration" by senior leadership. When the leadership stated this at the close of the program, it was like watching a balloon lose all its air. The collective energy and enthusiasm in the room vanished in seconds. The leadership later rejected all the recommendations of the group, putting a quick end to what could have been a positive culture change. They told us that the program was a good team building experience, but that was not what we sold it as. In this case the leadership itself failed to integrate needs by reversing their stance on commitment to outcomes, rendering those outcomes irrelevant. Such circumstances are unfortunate, and the best way to avoid them is to manage expectations beforehand. If the sponsor changes course, the consequence then lies solely on their shoulders. In design, where you may be both *Xd* and sponsor, the burden of responsibility lies with you. If you make promises to your team, uphold them.

End with Sanctioned Steps Forward

Integrating of needs benefits from making it publicly known that the program will end with sanctioned steps forward. As the example above illustrates, if the sponsor is not willing to act upon the outcomes, the loss of energy can be damaging. Sanctioning, even if it is only in the form of the leadership checking in with the process and giving a thumbs up, empowers participants because they feel that they are making a real impact.

Trace Integration Lines

The impact of any design or change initiative occurs on many levels. We can integrate needs by tracing integration lines, connecting the program to the larger picture (eco-system). It is helpful to ask questions that draw out this information, such as:

1. What is the relevance for Me, We, and It?

2. How does the co-creative program intersect with the organization or team vision?
3. What will the impact of the program be six months from now?

The answers to these help situate the particular instance of a co-creative program and its desired outcomes within the larger context.

As an example, let's consider the potential impact of Amazon Prime. For me, an end user, Amazon Prime brings several benefits to my life at a low cost. I can watch or listen to a vast online library of media, I get free two-day shipping on purchases, and I earn 5% of my spending back as reward points to use toward future purchases. This is all great for me because I like Amazon. But how does it influence my other behaviors and the broader context of online consumerism? With Amazon Prime I no longer need Netflix, so I will cancel it. I am also more likely to shop on Amazon than other online sites, shifting my consumption patterns toward one central provider. That makes Amazon more money while saving me money. Win win! But Netflix and all of the other online merchants I might have gone to for shopping are losers. This example shows the kind of analysis that design teams do, looking at impact across a vast value chain. The objective is to trace cause-effect relationships among stakeholders to make sure that there is enough value created by proceeding with the design for people to want and adopt it.

This method is easily adapted to organizational change. In the process of integrating needs, we can navigate the value and impact chain by using a framework that helps me, or my team, "see" from different angles. One tool, Theme-Centered Interaction (TCI), encourages dialogue from different perceptual positions. Their website explains[10]:

> In group processes, interests of the individual subjects (**I**), the developing relational pattern of the group (**WE**) and the problem at hand, the theme (**IT**) must be in dynamical balance. This is symbolised by a triangle where individual, group and theme form the corners. Whenever one corner dominates, there are negative side effects. E.g. when the theme dominates, this may be a sign that people hide problems, no group feeling and no personal relationships develop. In WE-centered groups, individual views and needs are suppressed and group dynamics may get so overwhelming that no work is done. The theme gives communication a productive focus, but it must be balanced with the other needs. The "WE" of the group develops from centering around a theme, that is why TCI is termed "theme-centered."

> The triangle itself is placed in a circle, symbolising the **GLOBE**, that is the organisational, physical, structural, social, political, ecological *surroundings*, in a narrow and wider sense, which condition and influence the team work of the group, and which in turn are influenced by the work of the group. The globe can create disturbances and it can upset dynamical balance, shifting weight to one corner of the triangle. Thus one must always be conscious of the globe and the constraints it produces and take it into account.

The TCI model is one of many visualizations of eco-systems thinking. What is nice about their framework is that it also provides a method for facilitating dialogues that shift from one perspective to another, in doing so greatly enriching the shared knowledge base. As such, it is a useful tool throughout a co-creative process, used whenever a perspective check or a reframing of insight is needed.

We include their framework in this section on setting the container because it is useful in how an *Xd* can think about and design a co-creative program. The model can be used at any time to check how integrated our own (and hence our programs) perspective is. It is infinitely valuable to look at ourselves and our processes on different levels of analysis to ensure that we are providing what our clients and teams need.

Onboarding

If all goes well, by the time you begin a co-creative program, the container is fairly well set. Through stakeholder dialogues and lead-up preparations, you have worked closely with the sponsors and developed a creative brief that contains all of the key ingredients. It is a powerful brief that people are excited about and see as relevant to both themselves and the larger whole. You have the trust of the leadership and the team, and it is time to move into "Act I: The Rise." The final time to set the container is in this beginning of the creative program. It may seem strange to read that your last chance to set the container is at the onset, but it is true. If time and resource permits the type of preparations we have discussed, most of the work is already done. If, however, you are running a program with minimal previous engagement with the participants, then it is critical to set the container early on in this opening Act.

Consider that would happen if you failed to create an experiential space wherein people feel safe to express themselves fully, without trust or authentic interactions. Or a program where people show up and they have no idea why they are there. What type of creative output can you expect from them? Perhaps they will stay in what they consider a safe space by being overly polite and avoiding all conflict. Perhaps they begin arguing and refuse to compromise. Or perhaps one person takes on a leader role and everyone else becomes subservient to their ideas. None of these are co-creative. Nor can a group dynamic like this survive the deep exploration and challenges of "Act II: The Dive."

For us, "onboarding" refers specifically to the time when the team first comes together in a collective engagement.[11] Onboarding is metaphorically similar to getting on a rollercoaster ride together in an amusement park. A group has gathered in an environment designed specifically to cue them to a particular experience. All the signs around indicate the thrill and fun of the coming experience. As they wait in line, they have an opportunity to talk and get to know one another, sharing their expectations and fears. They are soon split into smaller groups and put into a container that will "hold" them throughout their journey. Together they climb up the steep ascent, then dive down and around the many curves and loops of the coaster. At times it is terrifying, others exhilarating. The energy is pumping until the ride slows and finally comes to a stop. Everyone gets out, having shared a tremendous experience, with smile and nods.

One of the reasons rollercoaster rides are so enjoyable lies in the onboarding to them. Without the designed environment, the signs illustrating what to expect, the chart of rules telling people how to behave, and the cue that raises expectation and excitement, rollercoasters simply would not be as much fun. All of these elements serve to set a container, reinforced by the very tangible containers people are put into for the ride. In co-creation, the *Xd* must make containers with similar qualities. Just like an amusement park, we must convince people to feel safe with and trust our process (the rollercoaster) while at the same time bonding them together and raising excitement.

Conclusions

We have come to a point where the line blurs between planning and facilitation. We understand that, for the reader, natural questions at this point are, "What do I do to set the container in Act I?" and "How can I encourage a PACE mindset?" We are anxious to answer these questions, but those answers we feel belong more naturally in Part II of the text, where we focus on facilitation. If you have a burning desire to look at onboarding techniques, we invite you to skip directly to Chap. 8. However, techniques to set the container do not exist in isolation. They are one part of a much larger picture that puts them in context. We encourage you join us in looking closer at this picture before picking up the co-creative paintbrush.

In the planning stage we take a wide angle simply because the variation of co-creative possibilities prevents us from sketching out a process blueprint. In this section we have argued for the need for a strong container, described its qualities, and offered guidelines that are useful while planning for co-creation. Here we use broad brush stokes to lay out the overarching principles that come into sharper focus in the context of a specific co-creative initiative. We turn now to the three ACTS of the co-creative journey that serve as the framing upon which an *Xd* can build programs. Looking at the overall process architecture sheds more light on the role of the container and how to best shape it for different programs.

Notes

1. "Interintentional" means a space in which the different participants' intentions intersect with each other. This layer exists alongside the knowledge, emotions, and other forms of "information" present in the space between.
2. Schein is referring to Bill Isaacs work on what is necessary for deep, open dialogue. Schein, U.Lab online course, Interview #6.
3. Touchstones and quote taken from a handout at the 2016 Ashoka Exchange. More information is available at www.couragerenewal.org/approach.
4. Brown, *Change by Design*, 78.
5. See more at https://www.iaf-world.org/site/, http://www.ica-usa.org.
6. Senge, *The Fifth Discipline*.
7. http://www.ica-international.org/ica-worldwide/ica-taiwan/.
8. Brown, *Change by Design*, 75.
9. Brown, *Change by Design*, 145.
10. http://www.ruth-cohn-institute.org/home.html.
11. The preparation for this, which we address in the coming section, occurs prior to the first group engagement, using dialogue, coaching, and other tasks to facilitate an optimally prepared state.

References

Brown, Tim, and Barry Katz. *Change by Design: How Design Thinking Transforms Organizations and Inspires Innovation.* Adobe Digital Edition ed. New York: Harper Collins e-books, 2009.

Senge, Peter M. *The Fifth Discipline: The Art and Practice of the Learning Organization.* New York, NY: Doubleday, 1994.

CHAPTER 6

Process Design II: Designing for Breakthroughs

In the beginning of this book we told you that there is nearly universal grammar—or process architecture—that underlies facilitating creative breakthroughs. What if we told you that, in hindsight, the grammar is obvious? If you react with curiosity mixed with a bit of skepticism, we don't blame you. In fact, we felt the same way when we first discovered it. "How can something so ubiquitous to catalyzing creativity *not* be headline news?" we thought. And then, being researchers, we started doubting our initial insight.

Two years later, after a prolonged comparative analysis and inquiry that took us from design thinking through knowledge management, interaction design, the human potential movement, gestalt psychology, leadership coaching, change facilitation, organizational development, and consciousness studies, we were still left with a very basic form that seemed to be a common denominator. This form is the sine wave—a pattern and movement that is ubiquitous to the natural and human world. From waves in the ocean to the human voice, sine waves are an integral part of our universe. Perhaps we should not be so surprised then that the creative process also moves like a wave. In our history, a great many innovations have come from biomimicry—designing based on forms found in the natural world—so why not creativity itself?

If you have doubts, think about your last creative insight. Whether you are conscious of it or not, it probably began with a lot of thinking about something. The brainstorming meeting at work, the plumbing

B. R. Rill, M. M. Hämäläinen, *The Art of Co-Creation*,
https://doi.org/10.1007/978-981-10-8500-0_6

challenge at home, or the design meeting where the team had to come up with possible solutions. Each of these is an input that requires a lot of energy and an increase of overall information and processing. When energy accumulates it swells up to a crest—the first high point of the creative journey. Then we take a break, let the steam off, and recover from the effort of the first stage. We relax, and in our "off" mental state the information gestates. This happens when we sleep, when we take walks in the woods or on the beach, and when we sit back in our office chair and toss a tennis ball idly against the wall. Like a wave that has passed, our energy is calm. This is the trough—the space of potential and unknowing in which we process, consciously and subconsciously, the knowledge generated in the first stage of the creative process. Creativity studies show that it is often in these still moments that insights occur.[1] They can come as a flash or as a slow boil, but an insight brings with it new energy. It compels us to act again before we lose sight of it. That energy propels us upward once again, and we use it to create plans and prototypes. This stage is the rise, the transformation of ideas into action (Fig. 6.1).

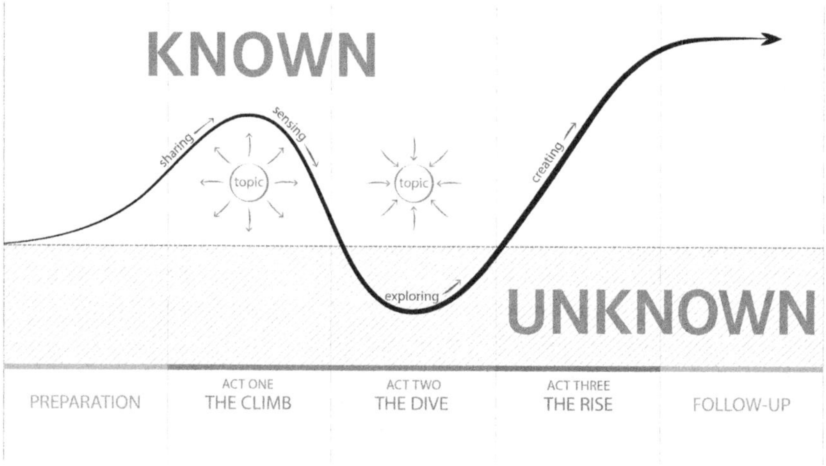

Fig. 6.1 The Co-Creative Journey

This three-stage movement lies at the heart of our model of co-creation. Our model, like several others, reflects the insight of the German physiologist Hermann von Helmholtz.[2] He developed a three-stage model of creativity: saturation, incubation, and illumination. In the language of serious gameplay—another valuable model for creativity—the core movement in each of the three stages are "Divergence, Emergence, and Convergence," respectively.[3]

Jacob Getzels expanded this model into five stages—insight, saturation, incubation, illumination, and verification—which are now part of the DNA of design thinking. A guideline derived from design thinking is to *use the three movements in both problem spaces and solution spaces.* In the problem space—the stage when the team is defining the challenge itself—one must remember that the initial question (or problem) might not be what needs to be addressed. It is helpful to explore the problem deeply, using tools to probe the true needs rather than symptoms. Tools such as the Five Whys or the d.school's Why-How laddering[4] use questions to dig deeper one layer at a time, often revealing underlying issues that the client may or may not have perceived. Both of these are methodologies that help clarify user needs by first expanding upon the initial challenge scenario (divergence), exploring the underlying issues and bringing the real needs into sharp focus (emergence), and then defining the appropriate problem to work on (convergence).

Only after the problem space is thoroughly explored and clarified does the team move into the solution space, where the team again applies the three-stage process to develop answers or innovations. This is one guideline that may need to be explained to clients whom are not familiar with design thinking. When faced with a challenge scenario, people tend to move directly toward solutions without deeply considering the nature of the problem or even if they are asking the right question. Applying the three movements to the challenge itself often leads to a reframing of it, opening new spaces for insight and innovation.

The nowhere group took Getzels' model one step further, arguing that creativity is born of the oscillation between the Known and the Unknown throughout the five-stage process. We agree. As far as we have seen from our research into design and consulting practices, this model is elegant in that it truly captures the essence of the creative journey.

The advantage of using an underlying grammar—or process architecture—for designing co-creative programs is that it provides a framework that helps us place the techniques we know into an optimal arrangement. By optimal, we mean a form and flow of activities that create a good container, the space between, and then harness the insights that come forth.

There are several experience design principles that help accomplish these goals. They include maintaining rapport, mutual empowerment, the energy arc, the four levers, entrainment and flow. We call these "intangibles," mainly because they cannot be directly measured with any scientific instruments. Yet people feel these, sometimes consciously and sometimes not. For the catalyst, they are ingredients in the secret sauce. They are our hidden tools that amplify creative potential.

The "Intangibles" of Experience Design

The aforementioned theories are primarily centered on the knowledge journey. While knowledge outcomes (innovation, solutions, etc.) are often perceived to be the most important (and at times *only*) aspect of a creative process, such a narrow perspective limits what is possible. By underemphasizing the emotional and interpersonal aspects of the journey, process designers focused on knowledge outcomes do not fully tap into and harness creative potential. To get the most out of oneself and a team, it is wise to look beyond the obvious and ask what else influences creativity. What other factors should we consider when designing an experience? Our answer is to give equal emphasis to all three aspects of the creative journey, designing with the intangibles in mind.

Rapport

Rapport, a term we introduced in Chap. 3, is the quality of a good relationship, characterized by agreement, mutual understanding, or empathy. It is a sense of trust and willingness to communicate. As simple as it sounds, establishing and maintaining rapport is not easy. Rapport is best established while setting the container, and there are two key principles to consider:

- *Empower people by ensuring that they each have equal voice/representation and a sense of making a real contribution.*
- *Ensure that everyone feels (not just thinks) their value.*

There is no better way to develop a good relationship with someone than to listen to them and show your appreciation for their contribution. Appreciative inquiry is an asset-based approach and it works almost universally. People have a lot of different motivations, and appreciative inquiry is not about judging them or identifying "problems." It is listening for the positives and building upon those. This is not to say that you can't judge another person's inputs, but rather that the quality of attention you bring to the listening affects your relationship. If you start off with what is good, chances are you will have better rapport.

Appreciative inquiry begins in stakeholder interviews and continues throughout a co-creative process. By integrating this and other similar empathy-driven dialogical techniques, you achieve two important experiential outcomes. The first is cultivating rapport. As long as people feel that they are contributing and that their contribution has real value, they will put effort into maintaining the relationship. People also feel empowered, the second intangible.

Empowerment

Empowerment, specifically mutual empowerment, is one of our core success criteria for calling any collective effort co-creative. Empowerment is visceral, embodied. You don't think that you are empowered. You feel it. For most people, it is the feeling of being valued. It is good, not just as a thought, but *physically*. Empowerment shows in a person's posture, in how they talk, and the energy they bring. Empowered people may appear happy, driven, even angry, but they are active and engaged. That is what we want as *Xd*, for it is the core energy that we harness and guide toward the desired outcomes. When that sense of empowerment is shared by an entire team, the energy is exponentially greater. This is great not only for us as *Xd* in terms of having raw energy to work with, but also for the team in that they are more engaged with the process and with each other. In most cases that translates into strong team building, a sense of ownership, and improved outcomes.

A corresponding principle is that *we cannot expect it for participants to be engaged all the time*. No matter how empowered a person feels, they only have so much energy. Given this, it is natural for the level of engagement to fluctuate in any program. We have all been in situations where we are excited and want everyone to share that excitement, only to look around and see a couple people partially or completely disengaged. In the modern world, a telltale sign of this is the head down, eyes locked onto a mobile device. One reaction is to be offended. "Clearly this person doesn't care!" we might think or comment. While you might be right, another possibility is that he or she is looking something up, or responding to a message that they feel the need to reply to. They might even be doing their best to manage a crisis while still paying partial attention to you. The point is that we don't know why a person has diverted their attention away, and it is not fair to judge them for it without knowing more of the circumstances. A more relaxed attitude is to accept the fact that engagement will vary, and that this behavior is quite natural. As long as people are contributing, allow them to do so in their own way.

The Energy Arc

Just as our personal energy oscillates, so too does a program's. We call the overall energetic movements of a creative program the "energy arc." The concept reflects the fact that a creative process is somewhat of a rollercoaster. It has peaks and valleys in each of the three aspects of the overall creative journey: knowledge, emotions, and team dynamics. These aspects have their own energetic contours, and the skillful *Xd* knows when and how to manipulate these to guide the group toward outcomes.

The Co-Creative Journey illustration depicts the overall energy arc as a sine wave, and we can plan what techniques to use and when to use them by placing them on this energetic "map." Having said that, while one visual is useful, in reality things are a bit more complex. Breaking down the overall journey into its components revels that the energetic contours vary, with emotions, knowledge, and team dynamics each having their own pattern. The three journeys visual (Fig. 6.2) is one possible rendition of these patterns, but by no means is it the only possibility. What we are faced

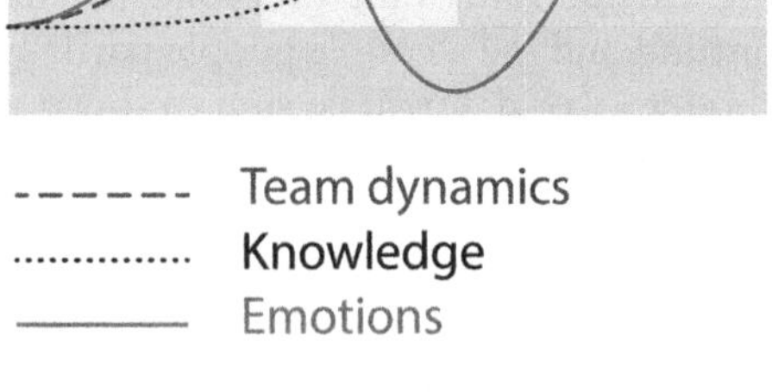

Fig. 6.2 The three journeys

with is the realization that we must plan for and accommodate fluctuations in each dimension. How do we do this?

Our answer is to design a program based upon the oscillation between the Known and the Unknown, taking into consideration which emotional and team dynamics can best assist the knowledge journey. In Act I, for example, we have a few aims. For the knowledge aspect, our goal is to increase the overall amount of knowledge in the collective space, to fill the field with ideas from every possible source. To do this we can plan key inputs, research, and then brainstorming. Concurrently, we need to set the container and build strong interpersonal bonds among the participants. We might begin Act I with check-in circles where everyone shares their "why" and expectations coming in. We complement this with socialization games to tease out personality types that can help us compose diverse and workable teams. We are also thinking of the emotional states of participants. Act I is the beginning of the journey, and we want people to be excited and engaged. Deep sharing and games build authenticity, trust, and a sense of play to set a positive emotional tone.

Act II, the Dive, is an entirely different context than Act I. It has a unique energy signature and thus requires different types of activities. The feeling of the Unknown is an important consideration when planning what to do. The Unknown, by its very nature, is often uncomfortable. While some people relish in not knowing, most human beings like their comfort zones. We call these "comfort zones" because they are based on what we already know and like. The problem with comfort zones is that they hinder creativity. They are not very open to novelty or the emotions that inevitably come with stepping out of comfort into the Unknown. Expertise, so highly cherished in our society, is a particularly tough comfort zone to work with because it also comes with a justified ego. Asking an expert to let go of the very thing that got them their status—knowing—makes them *very* uncomfortable. Given this fact of the Unknown, it is critical that we, as experience designers, take steps to manage the emotional and interpersonal dynamics of uncertainty.

It is in the Unknown that you will learn how strong the container is. A strong container is like driving a 4WD safari truck into the outback. The people in it know that they can rely on the vehicle to keep them safe and navigate the terrain. If these same people were in a 2WD sedan, they might spend their entire time wondering when and how bad they were going to get stranded in the wilderness. We don't want the participants, who have placed their trust in us, to feel lost in the wilderness. We want them to explore it and discover new things.

To help people step into the Unknown with a degree of confidence, setting the container in before and during Act I is the first step. Complementing this are tools to use while they are in the Unknown that help them manage uncertainty and interpersonal tensions. Emotional check-ins at the beginning and end of each day establish a valuable interpersonal space. This simple exercise deepens the social space by exposing the basic humanness of us all. By sharing our vulnerabilities and strengths, our moments of excitement and confusion, we bond with one another.

If someone needs a time out from the group dynamic, give them one. A "Caves and Commons" spatial design affords time and space for anyone to step out of the group dynamics and enjoy private time as needed. You may or may not be able to create this physical space, but giving permissions for anyone to step out is equally powerful. Whatever tools you use, our recommendation is to *create ventilation points.* Co-creation is an emotional rollercoaster. High levels of engagement = intense emotions. Create space for these to be expressed or else they can become destructive.

Managing potentially destructive behaviors is an art form in itself. We will share some of the techniques we use in Part II, where we take you through the journey from a facilitation perspective. In the planning stage, all we can do is establish a container strong enough to handle disruption.

In addition to a strong container, a lot of energy is needed to navigate the Unknown. Like a rollercoaster, the energy created in the climb (Act I) must carry the team through the Unknown until a new energy comes along (insight, inspiration) to catalyze the rise (Act III) out of the space of potential with new ideas.

Act II, the Dive, begins with exploration and ends with emergence. For the knowledge aspect of the journey, our goal is to problematize and reframe the understandings established in Act I. An *Xd* can use many different techniques for this, including serious games, presencing, dialogue, and others to shift understanding from received notions to new ideas. Some facilitators prefer to keep the group in dynamic motion from one activity to the next, tapping into energy and creative tension using gameplay mechanics. Others concentrate on identifying and deeply exploring each aspect of the problem and the posed solutions. Both approaches are good as long as they meet the goal of exploring and identifying new potentials to act upon.

Act III, the Rise, begins when new ideas emerge from the Unknown. This moments carry with them a particularly powerful energy—that of potential beginning to manifest. Peter Senge and Otto Scharmer stress the need for "crystallizing intent," an appropriate metaphor for the process of focusing energy toward productive outcomes.[5] The knowledge aspect of the journey raises the challenge of determining which possibilities should be pursued, and at this point it is valuable to use techniques such as Theme-Centered Interaction and value chain analysis to determine feasibility and viability. As a team goes through these vetting processes, there will surely be ideas eliminated that some people felt strongly about. To ensure continued engagement in the outcomes, the *Xd* must do their best to reassure the value of every participant's contributions. Maintaining the sense of mutual empowerment and the excitement that comes with it in Act III is a constant challenge, but one that is necessary if collective ownership is sought. When managed well, participants come out of Act III with a sense that their contribution was valued and integrated into whatever outcomes came from the effort. The result is perceived to be truly co-created.

When an *Xd* is aware of and able to influence each aspect of the co-creative journey, it is possible to use the different energies (knowledge, emotional, interpersonal) to build purposeful moments. These can be purposefully calm and reflective, dynamic and emotionally intense, fast, slow, or anything in-between. The range of experiences you are able catalyze will depend on how well you perceive and learn to work with these energies. In Part II we will expand on these points further, offering additional techniques and illustrating their use.

The Four Levers

While planning a co-creative program, it helps to think of energy as one of the four levers that you can play with to influence the group experience. The other levers are time, space, and information. Each of these can increase or decrease energy, flow, and emotional tension.

- **Energy** is the felt sense of collective engagement and creative movement, as well as the personal "vibe" of individuals and the group. *Xd* manipulate energy when they set the container, by their own presence (being the tuning fork), and with all of the tools and techniques they bring to a program. It is important to recognize the fact that everything affects energy, including a wide range of personal, interpersonal, and organizational factors outside the influence of the catalyst. For this reason energy is the most fickle of the levers, requiring the most attention and care.

- **Time** is inclusive of both observable, measurable time and the perceived sense of time. The latter is quite often completely at odds with observable time. In flow states, for example, large amounts of measurable time seem to pass in an instant. When a person is bored, by contrast, measurable time seems to pass incredibly slow. Both are valuable for *Xd*. We may want things to seem slow, perhaps when deeply evaluating an idea. In other points we may manipulate time to kick a group out of a process that is going nowhere and force the energy back up. And of course, we love when time "disappears," indicative of the flow states from which creative insights emerge.
- **Space** consists of the physical and semiotic environment, a lever so important that we dedicated an entire chapter to it. In addition to what is offered there, we can add that space is a perceived sense of comfort in relation to others. Because spatial relations between people and objects are culturally defined, space is a lever that can be used to shift emotional and team dynamics quite effectively. The circle, for example, is an effective tool to level out hierarchies. If you have some people stand on their chairs and others lie on the floor, that dynamic will shift once again to hierarchy simply due to the different elevations. How close people are to one another has an impact on how they communicate (or not), with physical closeness (if voluntary) often correlating to a greater sense of trust. Involuntary closeness, by contrast, can have the opposite effect. Here culture plays a critical role, and it is important to know cultural understandings of space before manipulating this lever.
- **Information** is the knowledge that groups create and interact with. Novel ideas emerge by creating intersections between knowledge shared by individuals and groups. The ideation space in which knowledge is shared is what we call the "field." As *Xd* our primary goal is often the creation and support of this field. Additionally, it is the *Xd* role to support the movements between the Known and Unknown, facilitating divergence, emergence, and convergence through a variety of methods.

The four levers are a useful way to look at the vast array of facilitative and consulting methods available today. They are not an exhaustive list of variables that can influence the group experience, but they do bring a sense of focus that some *Xd*, like us, find valuable. It is not unlike creating a recipe in which four types of ingredients come together to create something delicious.

As with cooking ingredients, the four levers are not independent from one another. They are interdependent, with each having the capacity to affect the others. We use them to *create a fluctuation between tension and release, an oscillation that stimulates breakthroughs.* The foremost of these is the oscillation between the Known and the Unknown, but the same principle can be applied in many contexts. You might use the four levers to purposefully instigate creative tension between team members, forcing them to create resolutions that they might otherwise avoid. A simple way to do this is to give a team a challenge topic to discuss, then reduce the amount of time they have to reach a conclusion. As time runs out, team dynamics will shift rapidly to deliver.

By contrast, silence and time away from others can also be a powerful tool. Create opportunities for people to check out (or be removed by the catalyst) of the group process, which consequently affects the group dynamic and gives time for all parties (individuals and the team) to work in different modes. *Creating conditions for reflection is necessary for creative breakthroughs.* Reflection enables reframing, release, and growth, all of which are healthy components of any creative process.

Entrainment and Flow

Our final intangible—entrainment—is a truly remarkable facet of a collective engagement. Entrainment, in its simplest form, is a synchronization to a rhythm outside oneself. This is easy to spot at a musical event, when a large number of people move in synch with the percussive rhythm. Drum circles also rely upon entrainment, with one or two lead drummers serving as rhythmic anchors for everyone else to play to. If you have ever taken music lessons, entrainment is the reason why you always play better when in the company of a skilled teacher.

Our brain waves can be entrained to periodic tactile, audio, and visual stimuli. Such entrainment induces different states of consciousness, from the deep meditative state of theta wave entrainment to the more creative and visionary state of gamma wave entrainment. There are a number of media that help people gain more control over their states of consciousness, from binaural beats to devices like the Neuro light.[6]

Entrainment is useful for our purposes. We have found that, given the right circumstances, people will entrain to each other. In one study, researchers found that:

> Behavioral studies have shown that engaging individuals in synchronized activity, be it walking, singing, playing musical games, or rocking, is a remarkably simple and effective way of increasing subsequent cooperation between those individuals. Thus, important aspects of human culture and social functioning appear to be linked by the remarkably simple phenomenon of synchronization and its basis in entrainment.[7]

From subjective reports the team also found that most people experienced a self/other merging that is commonly reported in musical entrainment. In such moments, the individual ego is transcended by a sense of the collective.

This finding has incredible value for co-creation, which encourages acting from the whole (the eco-centered perspective). The question then is how do we facilitate entrainment? The research team also asked this question, and they found that *the sweet spot for interaction is not too hard, and not too easy.* These findings support Csikszentmihalyi's theory that to achieve a flow state, a balance must be struck between the challenge of the task and the skill of the performer. If the task is too easy or too difficult, flow cannot occur.[8]

Being in flow requires less cognitive control, which results in a decrease in overall thinking and more prosocial behaviors. People get "in the groove" with one another and the task at hand, which is exactly what we want. To facilitate flow by means of entrainment, integrate musical games and other physical activities that require synchronized performance. The challenge level needs to be in the sweet spot of interaction, absorbing full attention while not being impossibly difficult. We recommend using entrainment techniques throughout a creative program, especially in the bonding phase of Act I and prior to any collective thinking challenge. By getting the team in flow with each other, it shifts the energy from a bunch of individuals to a collective expression that can then be harnessed and directed toward productive outcomes.

Program Design

Co-creation is at its best when we take a holistic approach to process design. A holistic perspective takes all three aspects of the creative journey into account, resulting in program pieces that maximize impact and outcomes by fulling tapping into the resources and energy that people bring. Keeping the intangibles of experience design in the back of our mind when designing creative programs will help to ensure optimal results. Complementing these are a set of more tangible design guidelines. We call these "tangible" because they take on an observable form in a creative program.

In our discussion of "Setting the Container," we introduced the several such guidelines that can be enacted through research and dialogues. A good creative brief is the tangible product of these early efforts. Once we have a creative brief that defines the scope of our engagement and desired outcomes, there are several additional guidelines that can help in the planning stage.

Flex and Flow

Facilitators are familiar with the tension between quality and quantity. In an ideal world, our clients, schools, or design studios give us all the time and resource we need to deliver our best. In reality, we must work within constraints. Rarely do we get everything, or even most, of what we feel necessary. Thus we make do with what have, squeezing as many activities into a narrow time window as possible or being realistic and setting lesser expectations. We flex our programs to what is possible with what is given, often asking what is the minimal resource needed to achieve the maximal impact.

There are a lot of guidelines in this book, a palette of possibilities from which *Xd* can choose what suits them and their programs best. Deciding which ones to implement can be challenging. The Space Between and Co-Creative Journey models are a core framework, or architecture, to help *Xd* make these choices and weave program pieces together.

A program can flex in terms of time, depth, and which aspects to stress, but the objective of creating the space between remains. The Space Between model helps design for that experience by highlighting what to consider when working with people, designing environments, and preparing a creative program. The model is a systems perspective of all the possibilities (system components) and how they come into play (interactions).

The Co-Creative Journey is of value when planning what program pieces to include and where to put them in the timeline. The model helps create and maintain fluidity among components of a program. The visual continuity of a sine wave implies a very basic formula—the outputs of one activity become the inputs of the next. Program flow is created through such continuity, and participants will move from one activity to the next as long as they feel (consciously or subconsciously) the momentum created by following this formula. There may be times when you want to purposefully disrupt the sense of flow, but even these moments can be built into the larger engagement.

What we strive to avoid is a breakdown of energy and momentum due to a misplaced or misunderstood program piece. In moments such as these, the quality of awareness and the number of alternative tools an *Xd* has available can determine what happens next. If he or she notices the loss of engagement and/or energy, they can flex the program by changing it on the fly. Experienced *Xd* are quite skilled at this. They know that no matter how well a program was designed, things will often unfold in ways that require adjustments. The most skilled *Xd* can flex to wherever the group is moving and simultaneously maintain the overall flow toward productive outcomes.

Build Momentum Throughout the Program to Reach Breakthroughs

When waves collide there are a few things that can happen. One outcome is that they merge their energies together, resulting in larger wave. Another is destructive interference, when the waves clash and cancel each other out. A third outcome is that they simply cross, and each carries on its own path independent of the other. Breakthroughs come from an increase in momentum—a magnification of creative force. What is broken through are preconceived understandings and established norms for doing things, each of which as a very strong energy to maintain the status quo. To get through those we need insights that have enough energy to shatter the old and make way for the new.

The energy needed for a creative breakthrough comes from building momentum throughout a program. Jumping straight into possible solutions, a common tendency for people simply because they are excited to be of value, is not the best approach. It is analogous to going to a movie and watching the climax in the opening scene. A better approach is to use their enthusiasm to set the container, building the bonds necessary to get through the stress of the Unknown. These efforts will serve to align the group, bringing their individual energies together to form a larger, more powerful wave (force) to apply to the challenge. The combination of a strong force, a strong container (to hold that force together), and movement (from the group or the *Xd*) facilitates breakthroughs.

Serious Gameplay

In recent years gamification has become popular, spreading far beyond the bounds of games for pure pleasure. Serious gameplay is the result of applying the principles of gamification to business, educational, and creative processes. Because they are fun and interactive, games are a social and creative lubricant. Moreover, they are a powerful facilitation framework. Serious games provide everything needed to facilitate a group toward outcomes, making them a solid stand-alone tool as well as being an excellent piece in a co-creative program.

We were fortunate to develop the Co-Creation Initiative within the context of a multimedia design department at the Hong Kong Polytechnic University. Our colleague, Dr. Hanna Wirman, teaches game design and has developed materials that help translate game mechanics into real-world, social gaming contexts. We learned a lot from her and our consulting colleagues from BoB, who regularly gamify their workshops. From our exposure to serious gameplay, we derive two core guidelines for designing and using games.

Five Components of a Game: A game is a world, with rules, constraints, goals, story, and characters. Video games often contain all five elements. They create immersive worlds with characters that the player must interact with to advance through a story. Reaching the final goals entails a series of obstacles and challenges, each with different constraints that the player must master to succeed. Constraints also include the gameplay mechanics themselves, such as the buttons and movement axes on a controller or the movements that a chess piece can make. In design we might call these the affordances of a product or service. Constraints create and limit what we can do—a key consideration when designing games.

For non-gamers, sports is another example. Football (soccer in the USA) has a world—the field (pitch). In this world there are specific rules that players (characters) must follow to meet their goals (scoring) in order to win the game. The players are constrained by the physical properties of the field, the rules, and other players whose aim is to prevent them from scoring goals. Each team has its own story, a personal history and mythology, that they and their fans bring to the game.

In our university program orientation, we put students into teams and had them design real-world games that we could actually play, giving them only this basic guideline and 24 hours. The faculty was always amazed at the level of creativity they demonstrated in this exercise, which for us was a both a bonding tool and a first dip into team design processes. Our observations of BoB revealed a similar level of enthusiasm among professional consultants, coaches, and trainers. In both contexts we found that almost everyone enjoys playing games. Since games are ubiquitous cross-culturally, all people have an inherit understanding of the mechanics that allows them to adopt whatever game structure you provide with minimal instructions. This cultural fact saves a tremendous amount of time, which is why serious games are an especially valuable tool for short programs.

Games are great in that they are easy to teach, quickly generate a high degree of engagement, encourage friendly competition, and cultivate pro-social behaviors. Additionally, they are fun, which can be a lifesaver when you need to take the pressure off and bring some lightness (not being too serious) to a process.

Leveling Up! People love to rise to a challenge. Increasing difficulty with requisite rewards (per game) is a positive stimulus (fun competition). Leveling up is a very simple progression mechanic that is used in many games to maintain engagement. Think of any classic 2D scrolling game like Mario Brothers or Donkey Kong, and you might remember the fun of progressively more difficult challenges. As kids we spent countless hours fully immersed in these challenges. These were perhaps our first true experiences of flow states.

Modern-day game design still relies on leveling as a progression mechanic in many games. It is an effective mechanic because many people thrive on challenges. If the challenge is an appropriate difficulty—not too hard and not too easy—it facilitates flow states. In time, however, what begins as a challenge gets easier, and the player may come out of flow. Game designers use leveling to kick up the challenge just enough to maintain the flow state, resulting in longer engagement and overall satisfaction with the game.

Serious gameplay also benefits from integrating leveling into our designs. As with video games, most people respond to leveling with greater engagement at the task given. Unlike video games, however, the user is not choosing the game that best suits their style. Some people do not like increasingly difficult challenges, nor the sense of competition that comes with it. The observant *Xd* notices these participants and helps them have a valued role without the need for pressure.

Leveling can also be an emergency tool. I recall one creative workshop where the chosen program piece had fallen flat. The participants did the activity, but it was clear that they grew quickly bored with it. In a side conversation with the lead catalyst, I recommended leveling as an option rather than ending the piece and moving on to a different activity. This was the first time we had thought of this possibility, and in a couple minutes we decided on how to step up the challenge. Without telling the participants that we had just made it up, we announced an impromptu Level Up! challenge for teams that had met the original goals. It worked, resulting in some teams continuing to work on the first challenge and others pushing themselves to meet the new one. All of the teams were then engaged. In that moment we had an epiphany. Leveling could be used at any time to increase engagement without any need for prior explanation. Also, it was an ideal way to introduce new rules or exercises that we may have forgotten to include in the original program design. Level Up! is the perfect excuse to modify a program on the fly.

Now that we have shared one of our closely held secrets, we hope that people do not suspect a lack of planning or disorganization on our part any time they hear Level Up! It is a tool best thought out beforehand so that leveling is purposefully part of a program piece. It just happens to also be a valuable tool for those moments when you need a spark and you want it to appear seamless in the overall flow of your program.

KISS (Keep It Simple, Stupid)

Misunderstanding of instructions is an easy way to lose energy in a program. "Keep It Simple, Stupid" is a statement about clarity and simplicity. Whether we are talking about a product, service, design process, or creative exercise, it is paramount to make engagement as simple as possible. Taking the extra time to create instructions that facilitate engagement acknowledges the fact that that people have a lot of responsibilities that require a great deal of attention, and consciously not adding to their mental load by asking them to figure out an exercise. Participants appreciate the effort, and the reduced cognitive load translates into more energy for the actual task.

Good instructions follow a few basic guidelines:

- Make it easy by providing clear, easy-to-follow instructions for everything.
- Use pictures to represent concepts as often as possible.
- Be prepared to convey instructions in different ways.

People have different styles of learning, which means that in any group some people will easily understand verbal instructions, while others need to read or see visuals that capture the essence of the concepts. Talking participants through a slideshow that contains both written instructions and illustrations neatly delivers to all three learning styles. Here is an example (Fig. 6.3):

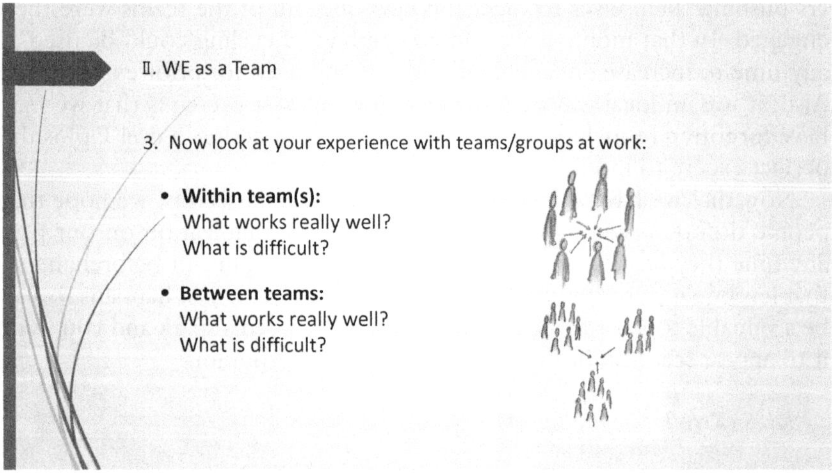

Fig. 6.3 Facilitation slide

To make this slide we had the help of a graphic illustrator, a valuable resource for any program. Graphic illustrators bring instructions to life with unique and customized visuals that often capture the essence of what you are trying to do better than you could ever explain it. In the above example, the images clearly and simply convey how we wanted the teams to discuss. There was no need for further written instructions.

A word of caution is necessary here. Do not fall into the trap of "Death by PowerPoint"—a phrase that captures the experience of being bored to death by poorly designed slide shows. A need for facilitation slides is *not* the same thing as spelling out every possible detail. Follow the KISS guideline and keep your slides minimal, clear, and easy to read. Your audience will thank you.

Purposeful Disruption (Entropy)

Chaos is bad, right? It disrupts activities, makes people uncomfortable, and can even derail a program. So why on Earth would we purposefully introduce entropy to an otherwise orderly process? The answer is that we need it. As potentially dangerous to a program as it can be, disruption is nonetheless an integral part of the creative process.

In our theory of co-creation, we adopt an Asian perspective on the relationship between order and chaos. Depicted in the yin/yang symbol, the concepts of entropy and order coexist in a dynamic balance. One *requires* the other to exist. The balance is dynamic in that each aspect is always trying to take over the other. When they do this simultaneously, the balance is maintained. When one aspect is more pronounced than the other, the balance is lost. In nature, as in human systems, the balance will eventually restore itself. This is why systems that are overly lawful always succumb to periods of tremendous chaos. Likewise, chaos cannot go on unabated. Order must be restored.

Asian cultural perspectives on entropy differ from Western cultures. In Japan, for example, the Edo was a historical period in which social status was strictly prescribed. Violations could bear the penalty of death. Yet, at the same time, specific areas throughout Japan were designated as outside this system. It was in these "anything goes" areas, run by the merchant class and *yakuza* (mafia), that the now famous *ukiyo-e* (paintings of the "floating world"), woodblock print, and many other arts first flourished. The fact that some of the most vibrant creativity in Japanese history emerged from chaotic contexts is instructive. In Western societies we call similar expressions "counterculture," and they always exist in a tumulus relationship with larger society. Rather than accepting them as natural, the dominant order continuously tries to repress or eliminate counterculture, depicting such expressions as "morally corrupt" or "evil." Notably, every effort to crush a countercultural movement has resulted in it growing stronger, a point that our leaders still seem to miss.

Politics aside, the lessons we learn from observing the relationship between order and entropy in society are applicable to creative processes. One of the distinguishing features of our definition is that we require entropy for a process to be called co-creative. When we first presented our ideas to a committee of design professionals, our colleague Ernesto spoke of this force as a "virus." The virus, he said, is an outside entity (usually a person) that comes into a system and disrupts it. That disruption forces the system to adapt, which in design is a healthy process.

Disruption can be healthy when it acts as a catalyst for dislodging or reframing existing understandings or entrenched ways of doing things. It is most useful in "Act II: The Dive," the stage in which the team is exploring and challenging ideas in search of insights. In design, disruption most often comes from including end users or others outside the core team in the design process. The degrees of involvement differ from participatory design to co-design, ranging from limited user inputs to designing together throughout the process. In other contexts, the virus can be stakeholders from different positions in the value chain, such as a front desk worker in an executive board meeting. The objective is to invite agents into the creative process that see and experience the world from a different perspective than the creative team. We encourage these actors to speak freely, challenging the status quo in an effort to improve upon the ideas being generated.

While disruption can be a good catalyst, that does not mean that disruption = good. Entropy has its place in creativity, but it cannot be allowed to take over. The key is to make space for disruption in a way that serves the group instead of purely self-interest. Managing that balance leads us to our next guideline…

Prepare Tools for Challenge Scenarios

"How do you handle someone who hijacks your process for their own ends?" This was one of our main operational questions as we developed this guidebook. The question stems from the fact that we had to work with a particular individual who was famous for completely taking over any environment he walked into. We were not alone in this struggle, and "hijackers" are a common problem in most organizations. There are variety of reasons why someone can become a hijacker, from having a huge ego to being disgruntled about the coffee that morning. Even the best of us can succumb to being "that" person, so the first point to make is that hijackers are not evil. They may be just the disruption you need.

What do you do though when they don't want to be a positive disruptive force? Or when the power of their presence overwhelms the ability for others to contribute? Or when someone in the program thinks they can facilitate better than you and tells you so? Or when the company boss disagrees with where the group is going and tries to impose his or her will on the process? These are challenge scenarios that we all face sooner or later. While we may not always be able to manage such moments as gracefully as we would like, there are a few ways that we can be prepared for them.

In ideation processes, silent brainstorming is an effective tool to ensure that everyone has the opportunity to contribute. In silent brainstorming, people write out their ideas on paper, which are later shared in the group context. Silence prevents any voices from dominating the process. Anonymous silent brainstorming is a nuance that works especially well in contexts where people do not want to be identified or take ownership of an idea. This happens frequently in Asia, where people are sensitive to shame. A bad idea can be perceived as shameful, leading to an aversion to "throwing out" ideas into the group for discussion. Anonymity prevents the chance for shame, thus encouraging full participation.

Anonymous silent brainstorming is also valuable when offering critiques. In most cases, we don't want to make our colleagues feel stupid, even if their ideas are not the best. Avoidance of critique can lead to acceptance of poor concepts, especially when the idea comes from someone that occupies a more powerful organizational position than the source of the critique. We try to eliminate such hierarchies in co-creation, but people are inherently sensitive to power relations. Anonymous silent brainstorming is a means around this challenge, enabling honest critique.

The marketplace is another technique for social leveling and fair evaluation. Marketplaces can be run in variety of ways, but the core concept is to allow people to visit, learn about, and then indicate their preference among a range of ideas. One example is to have each team design a threefold presentation of their idea. A representative speaker is chosen from each team, and their job is to pitch the idea to everyone else. People are allowed to walk freely among the presentation tables that are spread throughout the room, listening to each pitch at their convenience. After a period of time (30 minutes to one hour), everyone indicates their preference by voting with fake money. The tables with the most fake money indicate the ideas that have the most appeal and energy behind them. This does not mean that the tables with the most money are necessarily the best ideas. It means they are the most accepted ideas that people are willing to work on. One team might have brilliant idea, but if the person pitching it was previously a hijacker, they might get voted out. Alternatively, a team with a poor idea may have a great salesman/woman that garners a few more votes than it should have. In the end, it all works out by having a few "winners" that go on for more careful consideration. In the process of selection the marketplace levels out personal biases and helps control dominant personas.

Team reformation is a third tool to manage challenge scenarios. Depending on the message you want to send, a reformation can be explicitly in response to a poor team dynamic, such as a hijacker that is clearly making others uncomfortable. Reforming the team is in these cases a direct response that is meant to convey dissatisfaction with the current dynamic. Alternatively, reformation can be a more subtle act. Seemingly random (but not really) reformations can shift team dynamics without the potential conflict of a more explicit approach. We can make a reformation seem random by acting as if we were arbitrarily choosing new teams or by drawing names from a common pool and "fixing" the draw. In either case it is wise to consider whom would be the best counterbalance for the egos you are trying to manage, and get them together.

In most creative contexts, we are not aiming for teams that get along perfectly together, but rather diverse teams that build upon the strengths of the others. We need creative tension. Given this, it is perfectly natural to reform teams whenever we feel the need to shift the dynamic in ways that encourage more creativity. Reformation is thus valuable not only for managing powerful egos but also for encouraging shy people to contribute more or the breaking up of consensus among friendly colleagues.

Our final guideline for managing challenges is to *know when to let go of expectations.* We try to control outcomes when we expect certain things to come of our work. This is not always possible, for any number of reasons. Our colleague Jimbo Clark from InnoGreat told us of the moment when he learned this lesson.[9] He was facilitating a creative team, and the leader who sponsored the program continually hijacked the process. At first Jimbo was upset. This leader was not paying attention to where there group energy was moving. He wanted to force the group to where *he* wanted them to go. Jimbo pulled the leader aside and tried to explain to him his sense of where things could go, but to no avail. The leader got his way, and the program did not deliver the results hoped for. Jimbo was frustrated, feeling like somehow he had failed to deliver.

In reflection, Jimbo realized that the problem was not the failure of the program, but rather his frustration and sense of disappointment in himself. His feelings stemmed not from what the leader did, but rather from his own expectations. He was expecting to be able to facilitate the process without interference, and when that was taken away, it led to his frustration and eventual sense of failure. And then he let it go…

The wisdom that Jimbo shared with us was simple yet profound. *It is not your process. It is not their process. It is OUR process.* When we facilitate a program, we have been invited into the team and are temporarily a part of the team. Like a midwife, we are part of the process by virtue of our assisting the delivery, but it is not our pregnancy or baby. Our role as facilitators is to take the limited time that we have and find a way to get the team to discover and encapsulate the best of themselves. Their best thinking. Their best attitudes. Their best relationships. A part of being the best is being authentic and making space for authentic interaction (even if I view that as "hijacking" at the time).

There are times when leaders are putting themselves and others at risk, and need to be challenged, placated, dealt with, included, or excluded. The question Jimbo asks himself in such moments is, "How can I as a facilitator leave the leader and the team with agreements and understandings that will transform the organization as much as they can or want it to transform?"

There is no need to be personally invested in the outcome because of a particular attitude that Jimbo prepares and brings with him.

> I am not creating an new reality for myself. I am the one person who will walk away from all of this when the program is finished. I am helping them to create the best new vision and plan that they can imagine and agree to. When a leader responds negatively, it could be that the vision, the planning, the ideas are going beyond her or his capacity to imagine or lead. So together we need to find ways of grounding things so that we land on consensus rather than discord.
>
> Learning to dance with those emotions and not judge them in others or myself creates more space for me to be present. And as a temporary member of the team, my grounding shifts the grounding of the group, which is probably the greatest gift I can give to the team in those moments.

An *Xd* may or may not be in a situation where he or she can walk away from the program when it is finished (e.g. it is your design or leadership team), but the attitude that Jimbo brings is still highly applicable. He speaks in terms of finding what "we" need to do together to succeed, co-owning the process while doing his best to remain present and refrain from judgment. Jimbo's attitude enables him to be fully engaged as part of a process without having too strong attachments to particular outcomes, and that is part of what makes him such a great facilitator.

To summarize, even though we design processes and experiences, our designs are bespoke to the needs of the client. We co-create with them, resulting in an initial program or process blueprint that is theirs to enact with our guidance. The actual process is not the design you begin with, but rather what happens when people (including yourself) populate the blueprint and bring it to life. Our job is to be present to and steer the group energy to where it needs to go. When we are able to let go of our expectations and facilitate with agility, we mitigate the sense of personal responsibility when things go in a different direction.

Co-facilitate Whenever Possible

Consulting and creative facilitation are often solo enterprises. It can be challenging to explain the need for and cost of two or more catalysts to a client. And yet having a partner is rewarding in many ways that warrant the extra cost whenever possible.

First, a partner catches the blind spots in your facilitation. Regardless of how good any of us are at designing and facilitating processes, we are all biased. No human being can see things from every possible angle, and our awareness is filtered by our beliefs, past experiences, and culture. Having a second perspective in the environment greatly enhances awareness, which can have critical impacts on a program. Two facilitators affords more observation and interaction with working groups. A partner can also help read the energy of the room or particular individuals and offer alternative ways of moving forward.

In every program that we have facilitated, having a partner (or two) has led to more effective delivery. Partners offer a different perspective and also allow for role switching to play off one another's strengths. James and Jimbo from BoB are quite the dynamic duo. Jimbo is the high-energy showman and James is the empathic listener. They can easily switch places, or facilitate a program solo, but it is much more impressive when they work together. They have different energies, and people respond to that. By collaborating, they have more options to orchestrate the energy of the group through the creative journey.

We each have strengths and weaknesses, and co-facilitating can make both catalysts more effective. Doing so requires a good relationship and deep knowledge of one another as catalysis, something that the BoB team has. Co-facilitation can go wrong if the understanding and trust are not there, so this guideline is one to follow only when you have a sense of synergy with your partner.

The Catalyst

In chemistry a catalyst is a substance that causes or facilitates a chemical reaction. We like the term because it indicates an agent of change, a supporting element that transforms a process or environment. In co-creation, the catalyst is the person who triggers a breakthrough. Depicted in the Space Between model, he or she sits in the boundary zone between *Process* and *People* (Fig. 6.4).

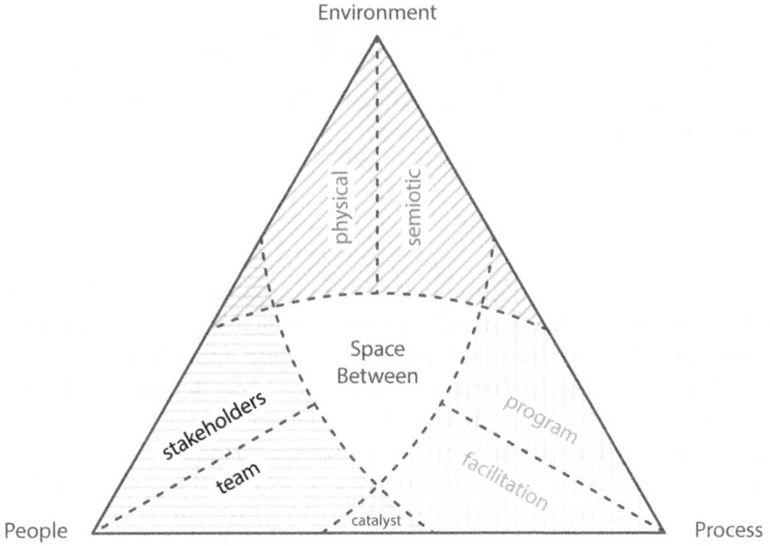

Fig. 6.4 The Space Between model

The reason for this placement is because the catalyst can be anyone. It can be the facilitator, a team member, or another stakeholder who created the space for the co-creation program. While we like to think of ourselves as catalysts, we stress the need to see outside our own role and encourage others to play this part. In that we are aware of and support the conditions for it, the emergence of a catalyst is the result of our process.

Nic Turner once told me that the reason the nowhere catalysts wear all black is because they want to be invisible. The sense of empowerment in a group is far greater when they perceive *themselves* to be source of energy and change. The less we, as the guides of their experience, are visible, the more we contribute to their sense of empowerment. Even better is when we truly aren't the catalyst… when someone else steps into that role and drives the reaction. Like a good coach, our goal is to help people feel that they did it all on their own.

Additionally, throughout a co-creative journey there can be more than one catalyst, each triggering a sudden insight or course shift. A champion in one moment does not mean that person can be expected to be so in every moment. Creating spaces for multiple actors to step up and be the catalyst further enhances the sense of collective empowerment, replacing narratives of "I" did it with "We" did it. That is co-creation.

Complementary Processes

There are times when we run parallel processes to complement a co-creative program. When there is a need and resource, complementary processes can include the following:

Sensing Journeys

Design researchers use ethnography to understand users in their natural context (everyday life). Sensing journeys are inclusive of observation and participation "in the shoes" of others to develop empathy for user needs. In co-design, sensing journeys also help us connect deeply with the other stakeholders on the design team. These journeys into the lived reality of others provide vital information that generates insights.

Empathy is key to a sensing journey. It is one thing to observe the behaviors of others, and quite another to feel what life is like from their point of view. Both are valuable information, but the latter is far more critical to understanding if and how a potential user might interact with product or service.

In organizational change, it is common for the leadership to decide on a new mission statement or strategy and then ask their internal communications team to disseminate the message throughout the organization. A mistake is making these changes from a purely logical perspective, without considering how it feels to be the subject of change. Empathic change initiatives take extra time for sensing journeys that explore the experiential reality of various stockholders throughout the organization. When complemented by such understanding, change initiatives can be much more effective.

A great application of sensing journeys can be seen in an Apple product release. An iPhone video presentation begins with everyday people holding the phone, dressed in casual clothing, expressing how it *feels* to them. Statements such as “I feel classy” to “It makes me so happy!” or “It’s beautiful” are all emotional expressions that subtly cue us to want the product so that we can feel the same way. After about 60 seconds of this, the video switches to a technical presentation of the phone’s capacities and build. The actors change from everyday users to someone who looks like they work in the tech department of product design. He or she explains the raw power of the phone and all of its cool upgrades. This part of the video is for the techies in the audience, and also the “logical” piece. Like product commercials before the 1950s, the advertisement describes all the practical reasons why we should buy it.

What these videos show is that Apple is very skilled at triggering both logical and emotional responses. They cue both sets of drivers to purchase their products. The reason they can do this is because Apple dedicates a lot of resources to sensing journeys, researching their target market and creating accurate user personas for their design team. The iPhone is a result of solid participatory design methodologies.

Input Sessions

The need for inputs from key information sources or stakeholders whom are outside the creative process itself is common. However, it is often not possible to have everyone valuable to a co-creative program participating for the duration. Input sessions are where experts or other valuable resources are brought into the program for short durations.

In co-creation it is best to integrate input sessions into the larger flow of the program, making it as seamless as possible rather than a separate instance. Given this, it is often necessary to consult and even coach the input provider on how the overall engagement is structured. The input providers can then tailor their delivery to suit the environment. When it does not make your team uncomfortable, you can invite input providers to come early to the program and just observe the team. That too will help them flex their input to the group and the energy of the moment.

Modern communication technologies afford a range of additional forms of engagement, from a remote call-in to full videoconferencing. These technologies are changing rapidly, continually enhancing the quality of interactions. This is very good news for co-creative teams. With platforms such as Zoom, Google Hangouts, or proprietary systems like those by Steelcase, virtual teams can use the contributions of parallel teams as inputs to work synchronously or asynchronously.

As one example, during the BoB Care program in Laos we experimented with multiple teams. The ground team in Laos was incredibly busy with sensing journeys, networking, and consulting a group of local NGOs. We fed our information to teams in Hong Kong and Taiwan at the end of each day, asking them to research and discuss possible solutions to the issues we were identifying. They would meet both physically and virtually using Skype or Google Hangouts and then send us their feedback the next day. The result was that the ground team had access to resources that we could not otherwise access. Together we co-created solutions without ever being physical present with each other.

The virtualization of meetings and inputs has opened up new spaces for interaction, and we encourage catalysts to experiment with new communication technologies as they become available. The trick is balancing the learning curve with the value of inputs in new modalities. The most effective platforms are ones that require minimal training to use. If you can teach your team in a few hours, or if they can learn it on their own though video tutorials in a day, then it is not too hard to implement. If it requires several days of specialized training, then only a few will learn it and they can be administrators for everyone else.

We evaluate platforms on the quality of engagement they provide and ease of use. Because we interact with each other as people and not as intersecting ideas, anything that creates a greater sense of being present in the space is preferred. When designing forms of interaction for a creative process, it is paramount that you decide what communication technologies to use well beforehand. It takes time to learn and experiment with the possibilities, not to mention onboarding the team to a platform. Decide early on who will use the platform and offer training to ensure proficiency *before* you begin the team engagement.

Breakout Teams

Team dynamics often shift in co-creation in order to maximize productivity. Breaking out certain participants to task forces that can work separately and then bring their work back to the collective is a means to multitask in a program.

The BoB Care Laos project is an example of one type of breakout teams. These teams were dedicated from the onset to operate asynchronously with the ground team. At no point did the three teams interact face-to-face, a fact that both enabled the teams to develop their own workflow and prevented the cohesion that could have happened if we did have direct, synchronous contact. Ideally, we would have had a pre-Laos gathering to bond the teams and post-Laos sessions to collectively work through ideas. If BoB Care programs were longer processes, we would have taken these steps, but in this instance the project was charity work with a one-week timespan. We did what we could in that time.

Breakout teams afford different modes of interaction that can be beneficial to co-creation. As discussed in Chap. 3 ("Working with People"), there may be times when we do not want collaboration. Perhaps it benefits the overall co-creative process to have breakout teams that compete with each other. Or perhaps we need a breakout team that operates under the guidance of a leader with the other members supporting that directive. Co-creation is wonderfully empowering as an overall process, but it can also be messy and inefficient at times. Breakout teams allow us to change the *modus opernadi* as needed. The key thing to remember is to bring the breakout teams and the products of their work back into the larger co-creative engagement, returning to mutual empowerment and collective ownership.

Providing Growth Opportunities

We have reached our final process design guideline, saving the best for last. Although placed at the end of the design and planning part of this book, we personally feel that this guideline is among the most important to implement.

As counterintuitive as it sounds, sometimes the most important outcome of a co-creative program is not the outcomes for the client. It is the personal and professional growth of the participants. The reason why we include experiential outcomes as a requisite goal of co-creation is because providing growth opportunities will bring out the absolute best from your team.

Laos

The BoB Care Laos project was the context in which we realized the full implications of providing growth opportunities.[10] BoB Care is a charity program that they host annually. For the past seven years, BoB has been assembling volunteer teams of professional coaches and consultants to help large clients with one of their pressing issues. This was a special program, the first attempt by BoB to work with multiple NGOs simultaneously. It was also the first implementation of virtual breakout teams to support our efforts. The ground team in Laos, led by James Bishop, consisted of eight consultants from all over the world. We had another 12 consultants assisting virtually in two teams. Each had offered, at their own expense, to help these NGOs. The program, as amazing as it was, is beyond the scope of this story. In the end the team was able to offer some constructive advice to the NGOs, with the main suggestion being shifting away from charity models to sustainable enterprises. Various members of the BoB team offered continued support for these efforts beyond the scope of our visit, another act of service to the cash-strapped and overloaded NGOs.

The question that kept occurring to us was, "Why would these professional consultants work for free?" When we put this question to each team member, their answers caught us by surprise. We were expecting to hear that this was an opportunity to network with peers, to learn new facilitation and consulting techniques from one another, and even the brand value of charity projects in their professional portfolios. These were, after all, the primary motivations for the broader BoB network to gather a few times annually in one- or two-day open source sharing events (BoB Create). What surprised us was the ubiquitous emphasis on the personal growth dimension. Every person who came said that they had transformed *as a human being*.

This outcome transcends the more pragmatic motivations we expected. Our epiphany was realizing just how much time and money people are willing to commit to personal growth. The price tag for Laos ranged from US$2500 to US$10,000, if you consider actual cost plus opportunity cost. That is a lot of money, but no one even flinched at their cost. The price was clearly justified by the perceived value of the growth opportunity.

Designing for Growth

The Laos project is instructive. The first lesson we can take from it is that designing for growth greatly increases willingness to participate and ensuing engagement. People want to be part of things that make a positive impact on others (e.g. the NGOs), and they are even more interested if it also benefits them. The value lies partially in psychic utility—a form of non-material capital that brings a sense of significance to our actions. Moreover, value is created when people expand as human beings by helping others. Through such efforts we grow past the boundaries of our selfish egos and begin to interact with the world from an eco-centered perspective. You get when you give.

The second lesson is one of design. The Laos team had tremendous synergy, even though only a few of the members had ever met before. Although there were certainly moments of tension, James managed these adeptly. In our conversations about his process design, James taught us that synergy often results from a mix of hard work, fun, and a sense of community. The Laos project had all three dimensions. We did not begin with a design brief, but rather a night out and drinks. Each day we worked for eight to ten hours with the NGOs, and then another two on our own. Yet even with 12-hour work days, we visited several amazing sites and enjoyed our short time in Laos. James kept the mood light even when the team was hard at work. Although everyone was given permission to check out as needed, no one ever did. The team stayed deeply engaged and committed to delivering results, which required stretching their boundaries and working in new, co-creative modes of interaction. In addition to the existing sense of community that BoB has developed over the years, the collective struggle served to strongly bond the team and NGOs as a micro community. Bonding by struggling and overcoming challenges is a page out of the leadership development handbook that applies to co-creation. Combining this struggle with fun and community activities supports a strong container and growth opportunities for everyone.

Finally, growth can occur in program or as the result of complementary processes. Preparing the participants through skills training and coaching can have significant impact. Courses in appreciative inquiry and presence (applied mindfulness), for example, enable participants to engage each other with the same qualities that make a good facilitator. They become more open, flexible, and creative as a result. Coaching leaders in the art of holding rather than dominating space is vital to creating a space of mutual empowerment where teams can cross over a threshold into new spaces of possibility. Whenever possible, we strongly encourage capacity building that supports co-creation. It pays huge dividends, cultivating a particular synergy that we call "resonant co-creation." Resonant co-creation results from mastery of the creative process by both the catalysts and the team. The guidelines here help with creating resonance, but the true art lies in doing rather than planning. We return to the subject of mastery in Chap. 11, after we have looked at the art of facilitating co-creation in Part II.

Moments of Insight

We bring this chapter to a close by looking closely at our objective—insight itself. The primary goal of most creative processes is to facilitate moments of insight. The insights sought can be centered on product or service design, innovation, culture change, communication, vision, and even addressing global challenges. The *What* (desired outcomes) will vary, but the *How* (process) is fairly consistent. That is why we can write this book. There is a unifying framework for cultivating insights, by design.

Our approach builds upon design thinking. But what about design thinking makes it so special for cultivating moments of insight? Tim Brown answers by describing design thinking as a capacity for integrative thinking. Drawing on Roger Martin's *The Opposable Mind*,[11] Brown argues that integrative thinking is "the ability shared by many of them to hold multiple ideas in tension to reach new solutions … Integrative thinkers know how to widen the scope of issues salient to the problem. They resist the 'either/or' in favor of the 'both/and' and see nonlinear and multidirectional relationships as a source of inspiration, not contradiction."[12] For Brown, complexity is key to insight. Design thinkers, like the successful managers of Martin's study, "allow complexity to exist, at least as they search for solutions, because complexity is the most reliable source of creative opportunities."[13] He further argues "The skills that make for a great design thinker—the ability to spot patterns in the mess of complex inputs; to synthesize new ideas from fragmented parts; to empathize with people different from ourselves—can all be learned."[14] We agree. The capacities of design thinkers (empathy and integrative thinking) combined with PACE (presence, authenticity, courage, eco-centered mindset) all support collectively creativity.

Insights are elusive and can appear at any time from any place, but we can create optimal conditions for them.

> Inspiration always involves an element of chance, but, as Louis Pasteur observed in a famous lecture of 1854, "Chance only favors the prepared mind." Certain themes and variations—techniques of observation, principles of empathy, and efforts to move beyond the individual—can all be thought of as ways of preparing the mind of the design thinker to find insight.[15]

As this passage indicates, optimal conditions are the result of processes that help prepare the individual or group to find inspiration. Co-creation is one such process that can break through the Known to find the Holy Grail (insight) in the vast Unknown.

A lesson that we have learned about this journey is that the most profound insights do not arise during the active exploration of the Unknown, but rather in incubation periods. Nick Udall describes this experience well[16]:

> We will have all experienced incubation when we let our minds wander, or when we intentionally stop thinking about a problem or a question we are holding. For some of us this incubation phase transitions into the next phase when we are shaving, or are in the shower, or having a bath. For others it may be when they go for a walk or a run. Whatever our different experiences, these are all examples of 'illuminations', or 'Ahas', when the solution or optimal way forward 'pops' or 'flips'—as if a light is now shining brightly on something that was previously hidden and out of sight, making it now in-sight. Finally, we intellectually verify our creative in-sight by testing its robustness and appropriateness. This oscillation is the essence of the creative process.

Creating and preserving this oscillation—the dance between the Known and the Unknown—lies at the center of the art of co-creation. This art requires being vigilant, for it is all too easy to default back to the Known. Nick calls this "flatlining," explaining that[17]:

> We just happen to also be very good at collapsing the creative process and diminishing this frequency back towards a flatline. There are many ways in which we do this: the fear of the unknown, being unfamiliar with not-knowing, feeling over-exposed and vulnerable, only focusing on the tangible, being overly controlling, emotionally over-reacting, judging others, pushing too hard too quick … and so on. We have been conditioned to flatline, as our educational systems focus almost entirely on the known, at the expense of knowing how to embrace, value and work with the unknown.

Flatlining is not solely the result of conditioning. It is also an inherit feature of our brains. Human cognition makes sense of the world by creating cognitive schema, mental models of reality based on experiences. If a child touches a hot stove, a schema is created that associates the two events (stove—burn). That schema protects the child from future accidents by giving them predictive model of what will happen if they touch another stove. Throughout our life we build many thousands of cognitive schema, each modeling interactions between things in ways that help simplify and streamline the complexity of being.

Once established, mental models condition how we perceive new events. Our cognitive schemas become conceptual boxes. When we encounter something new, the first thing we do is try to put it in an existing box. If it is similar enough, there is no need to change the box. When we say "it tastes like chicken," for example, we are fitting a new taste experience into a preexisting model. If the experience is different but still relatable, we adapt our schema to accommodate the new experience. Only when an experience is completely novel—so different that no box we have fits—do we create new cognitive schema.

The challenge to creativity is that mental models are comfortable. We like them, and when they are challenged or disputed, we feel uncertain or uncomfortable. This is a perfectly natural response. There will always be a handful of people that are naturally good at thinking "outside the box," able to challenge their own and other's concepts. Most of us, however, do not fall in this category. Most human beings are creatures of habit, choosing comfort (staying in Known boxes) over divergent or disruptive thinking.

The resilience of cognitive schema is why we must go to great ends to disrupt them. You can't just tell a group to "Think outside of the box" and expect much to happen. Giving permission to think and behave differently is certainly helpful in loosening up creative juices, but truly diving into and exploring the UNKNOWN requires careful preparation and specialized techniques that guide people to a space where they feel comfortable stepping out of and challenging their cognitive schema.

Closing Matters

The Art of Co-Creation attempts to advance the application of design thinking by shifting focus from primarily knowledge management processes to experience design. Our work stresses the need to design the overall engagement and create a good container before ever setting foot into a room with a team. We draw attention to and empathy for the experience of the design team itself, with the proposition that careful attention their experiences will lead to more creative outcomes. This principle is equality true for any creative team, from corporate leadership to school boards. Co-creation is a meta-level process that brings value not only to design teams but to any process where mutually empowering, collective creativity is desired.

In Part I we have provided an overall framework, centered on the Space Between and Co-Creative Journey models, that Levels Up! your process design. By integrating this framework into your practice, you will be able to design more effective programs that unleash your team's creativity and deliver innovative ideas. How well these preparations are made has a significant impact on the quality of co-creation. There is a lot to consider when designing an experience, and you may find that the clear majority of your efforts come prior to any facilitation. For us, preoccupation with the design is a good sign. It is indicative of an experience designer who is deeply committed to using co-creation to meet the needs of their clients or teams. The first half of this book has been dedicated to the design and preparation of co-creative processes.

In Part II we put theory into practice with a shift in focus to the *How*—the facilitation of the co-creative journey. There we introduce specialized techniques for each stage of the journey—the tools needed to harness the full potential of a team and create optimal conditions for insight to emerge. In Part II you will also find experience design blueprints and other templates that can either serve as a starting point or add a new dimension to your practice.

Notes

1. See Weisberg, *Creativity*, or Runco and Steven, *The Encyclopedia of Creativity*.
2. Udall has an excellent discussion of the theoretical background in *Riding the Creative Rollercoaster*, 1248.
3. Gray et al., *Gamestorming*.
4. This is one of many method cards made available by the d.school under the Creative Commons NonCommercial-Sharealike 4.0 International License. Available at https://dschool.stanford.edu/resources/the-bootcamp-bootleg.

5. Scharmer and Kaufer. *Leading from the Emerging Future from Ego-System to Eco-System Economies.*
6. http://www.theneurolight.com.
7. Fairhurst et al. (2012), Merker et al. (2009).
8. Csikszentmihalyi, *Flow.*
9. Jimbo Clark is the developer of the "Thinking In & Out of the Box" ideation framework and one of the founders of Brains on the Beach. Learn more at www.innoGreat.com.
10. The engagement with Laos stems from qualitative research the CCI team was conducting on the BoB Create programs. We went with the team to observe how BoB designed and led the overall program, interviewing the clients, team members, and project lead (James Bishop).
11. Martin, *The Opposable Mind.*
12. Brown, *Change by Design*, 85–86.
13. Ibid.
14. Ibid.
15. Ibid., 62.
16. Udall, *Riding the Creative Rollercoaster*, 1276.
17. Ibid.

References

Brown, Tim, and Barry Katz. *Change by Design: How Design Thinking Transforms Organizations and Inspires Innovation.* Adobe Digital Edition ed. New York: Harper Collins e-books, 2009.

Csikszentmihalyi, M. *Flow: The Psychology of Optimal Experience.* New York: Harper & Row, 1990.

Fairhurst, Merle T., Petr Janata, and Peter E. Keller. "Being and Feeling in Sync with an Adaptive Virtual Partner: Brain Mechanisms Underlying Dynamic Cooperativity." *Cerebral Cortex* 23, no. 11 (2012): 2592–2600.

Gray, David, Sunni Brown, and James Macanufo. *Gamestorming: A Playbook for Innovators, Rulebreakers, and Changemakers.* Sebastopol, CA: O'Reilly 2010.

Martin, Roger. *The Opposable Mind: How Successful Leaders Win through Integrative Thinking.* Boston: Harvard Business Review Press, 2007.

Merker, B. H., G. S. Madison, and P. Eckerdal. "On the Role and Origin of Isochrony in Human Rhythmic Entrainment." *Cortex* 45 (2009): 4–17.

Runco, Mark A., and Steven R. Pritzker, eds. *Encyclopedia of Creativity.* Second Edition ed. London: Elsevier Inc., 2011.

Scharmer, Otto, and Katrin Kaufer. *Leading from the Emerging Future from Ego-System to Eco-System Economies.* San Francisco, CA: Berrett-Koehler Publishers, Inc., 2013.

Udall, N. *Riding the Creative Rollercoaster: How Leaders Evoke Creativity and Innovation.* Kogan Page, 2014: Kindle Edition.

Weisberg, Robert W. *Creativity: Understanding Innovation in Problem Solving, Science, Invention, and the Arts.* Hoboken, NJ: John Wiley & Sons, 2006.

PART II

Performing Co-creation

While the first part of this book looks at the required conditions and planning for co-creation, the second part will focus on the co-creation process cycle itself, outlining the general stages of the process and giving practical instructions for experience designers (*Xd*) to facilitate such a process. Building on the metaphor of an explorative journey, we illustrate how the later stages of the journey build on the previous ones and how even a petty issue that arose early in the process can grow into a huge problem if not attended to soon enough.

Every journey is preceded by preparation and followed by a cleanup. As your experience increases, the preparation becomes easier to perform, and the various simultaneous steps turn into intuitive routines. But even when the steps have become familiar, the preparation is always different from the previous ones. Every time, you gain more experience in performing the process, deeper understanding of the consequences of each action, and more knowledge about the underlying requirements of each step.

You might also learn to appreciate the period of mental transition from everyday life to the performance-oriented mindset required for this journey. This transition is inevitably toward a point that requires readiness. And as the journey comes closer, your mind becomes more and more aware of the many issues that might affect its execution.

The "how-to" instructions provided in the following five chapters are aimed at facilitators of co-creative journeys, since their contribution is always crucial to the success of the process. In each chapter, we complement our philosophical points with practical guidelines for leading and facilitating the co-creation process during that stage. In Part II, we also offer vignettes (short stories) that will run in parallel with the journey. These stories, drawn from real-world experiences in design and business, portray two companies that represent good and bad ways of performing co-creation. In our stories, *ACME Ltd*—A Company that Makes Everything—is the successful company, and *ACAN Ltd*, A Company that Achieves Nothing, is the one that doesn't perform so well. For each part of the journey, we include vignettes from ACME and/or ACAN to highlight different nuances related to the art of facilitation. These examples help us to draw out and describe co-creative guidelines related to that segment of the journey.

Throughout Part II, we will look closely at the three interwoven aspects of the overall creative journey. The first aspect is that of knowledge, for it is primarily knowledge that we are working with to facilitate innovation. The emotional journey is the second aspect. Creative processes are an emotional rollercoaster, with highs and lows. The facilitator must compliment knowledge creation with an appreciation for personal psychology if they are to maximize creative outputs. We pay special attention to key moments, such as the Red Curve Transition (a collective emotional breakdown or breakthrough), as touchpoints where facilitation can make the difference between launching a team into the next Act or flatlining. And when you put diverse people together in a collective process such as co-creation, each individual then interacts with others, opening up a third aspect of the journey—team dynamics. Interpersonal relationships and tensions must be managed to ensure the team stays on track. Taking all three aspects of the journey into consideration is a key part of co-creative experience design that we will model in our writing by making explicit what principles and guidelines relate to each aspect.

In Chap. 7 we describe "Packing the Backpack," the specific preparations needed, in light of a case study—the ACME design process. We also offer a set of experience design roadmaps that *Xd* can use in their own work. In Chaps. 8, 9, and 10, we describe the three Acts of the Co-Creative Journey—the Climb, the Dive, and the Rise—and how each one of them can be led. In Chap. 11 we explain the activities that take place after a co-creative journey. This follow-up ensures that outcomes are captured and utilized appropriately. Refining the shared experience in the follow-up also facilitates learning, growth, and improved team and organizational performance.

What Is Knowledge and Why Should I Care?

From a knowledge management perspective, the first two Acts of a co-creative journey focus on generating *collective knowledge*, while the third Act exploits this new knowledge through *collective intelligence*. Collective intelligence is the capacity for a team to hold and tap into the space between, allowing for insights to emerge from the shared informational field and then crystallizing those insights into actionable plans and/or prototypes.

Post-journey stages (the follow-up and then planning and preparing for the next project or iteration) focus on sustaining knowledge and preparing the organization to produce more. Because of this complex evolution cycle of collective knowledge, it is crucial to understand the basic nature of individual and collective knowledge. The characteristics of knowledge (below) inform our efforts to tap into and harness the creative potential of the people and teams we work with.

Our definition of individual knowledge is based on the perspective that knowledge is a characteristic of a person, which cannot be separated from that individual. Similarly, collective knowledge cannot be separated from the group that it belongs to. From the perspective of collective knowledge evolution, each one of the three Acts of the co-creative journey has a specific function in *knowledge generation*. The other stages (pre- and post-journey) play vital roles in *knowledge management*.

Characteristics of Knowledge
Since knowledge in its different forms plays a crucial role in our perception of the co-creation process, we have specified the following key characteristics of knowledge. These will help to understand how to manage different forms of knowledge.

Knowledge is alive, which means that it constantly evolves along with its carriers. Hence it makes sense to expect dynamic rather than static behavior of it when making plans for applying it somewhere. Experience brings more depth to knowledge, and therefore the expert opinion of a professional might change quite radically during a project. A testimonial written beforehand might be outdated as soon as a project has started. So knowledge is best applied while it is

(*continued*)

(continued)

still fresh, and one should rely on the source that has the most recent knowledge available.

Knowledge cannot be transferred, since the transmitter of knowledge does not experience a loss of knowledge when somebody receives it. This is mostly a semantic issue, yet a very important one. In fact, the amount of knowledge cannot decrease; it can only increase (with the exception of brain injuries or such). Hence it would be much more accurate to talk about ***knowledge sharing***, during which the total amount of knowledge always increases.

Knowledge accumulates, meaning that new knowledge always builds on previous knowledge rather than replacing it. When knowledge is shared, the receiver always produces new knowledge—which is her version of the original, shared knowledge. In such a process, the knowledge always transforms. We visually portray this accumulation as the rising wave in Act I of the co-creative journey. The analogy represents reaching a critical mass of knowledge before taking the dive into the unknown.

Knowledge cannot be captured or harvested, at least without capturing or harvesting its owner. It is of course possible to capture different kind of snapshots of knowledge, but it would be foolish to think that they would equal the knowledge itself. Many companies have created different types of knowledge portals or knowledge repositories, in which they claim to have captured knowledge from their organization. The existence of such platforms does not need to be questioned, only the usefulness of the knowledge they claim to capture.

We can illustrate this point with an example from physical world. If a rich person owns 50 cars and wants to build a storage for them, he or she would undoubtedly not accept a photo album as a storage unit. It is possible to store photos of all the cars inside that album, in which case it would be an accurate statement to say that all 50 cars are stored inside this album, but photos are not the actual cars. Such an album might bring some value to its owner, for example, it could make it easier to keep track of the cars' locations, but regardless of

(*continued*)

(continued)

how much value it could add, nobody would ever even consider replacing a garage with an album. The same is true for knowledge.

The point is, it is always better for a person, especially a decision-maker, to be part of the co-creative process rather than reading a summary report. Participation is the only way to truly "know" what the creative team does.

Collective knowledge is different in nature from individual knowledge. The knowledge within a team is valuable only if the team members are *willing* and *able* to apply their personal knowledge collectively. Therefore, it is accurate to say that collective knowledge has three dimensions—the *what*, the *who*, and the *how*. The *what*—or the cognitive dimension—is equal to the sum total of personal knowledge (held by each individual) within a collective knowledge network. Without relevant individual knowledge, the team members cannot add much to the collective effort. The *who*—or the coordinative dimension—describes how well the members of a network are aware of each other's personal knowledge, so that they can utilize this knowledge collectively. If people are not aware of each other's skills, they will not be able to utilize those. The *how*—or the social dimension—tells how effectively the knowledge can be harnessed through the social connections within a collective knowledge network. If team members are holding back, their knowledge cannot be effectively used for collective goals. This is why authentic dialogue is absolutely critical.

Our point here is that knowledge cannot be viewed in isolation from the people and relationships from which it derives. It is because of this fact that co-creative experience design must take into consideration all three aspects of the experience-knowledge, emotions, and team dynamics. Looking solely at the *what* (knowledge) dehumanizes creativity, and people are not robots. We all respond much better if we are treated as fully human, with all of our sensitivity and complexity.

Process Objectives

Before jumping into the details, it might help to have a very concise overview of our process objectives, broken down by stage. During the preparatory stages (Part I and Chap. 7), the objective is to ***design and build a foundation for co-creation***. This happens by designing optimal conditions and creating a suitable container that will enable the co-creative process to take place.

The objectives in the first Act (The Climb) of the co-creative journey are to:

1. Finalize setting the container
2. Share knowledge
3. Build capacity

In knowledge management terms, these objectives could be called *sparking the collective intelligence*. This process is very similar to ***team building***. Collective intelligence is ignited through sharing individual knowledge within the team, building trust between team members, and developing the willingness and skills needed to operate collectively as a team.

In the second Act (The Dive), the goals are to:

1. Feed and expand the collective knowledge
2. Cultivate collective intelligence

This happens through complementary processes. We expand collective knowledge by gathering new information from outside the team and by generating new knowledge through a cycle of exploration, experimentation, and validation. Act II is where we challenge the Known-knowledge based on past experience and explore the Unknown for the New. To do that we must simultaneously cultivate collective intelligence, the capacity to tap into and harness the potential latent in the space between.

The goals of the third Act (The Rise) are to:

1. Apply the collective intelligence
2. Create the New

This means that the collective knowledge of the co-creative team is focused to create solutions that match the original creative brief. In the field of design, these solutions might take form as testable service models or prototypes. In organizational development, the solutions could be implemented as a pilot program for executing changes within the organization.

Post-processing (follow-up) takes place right after the co-creative cycle has been completed. The objective for this stage is to harvest the collective knowledge and collective intelligence produced during the creative journey. We identify the results from all three ACTs in terms of both tangible and intangible outputs. Taking an action learning approach, we reflect and create feedback loops that help us and our organizations continually grow. The result is a culture of innovation that will make the next co-creation journey easier, more efficient, and higher in quality.

Let's begin…

CHAPTER 7

Preparing for the Journey

In Part I of this guidebook, we offered an overview of co-creative experience design, unpacking the Space Between and Co-Creative Journey models as a process architecture. This general framework helps the *Xd* choose activities and plan the timing, creating coherence and flow to their designs. In addition to preparing the conditions for a journey, a more selective preparation needs to be made before the journey can begin. This category we have labeled as "Packing the backpack," since it revolves around the element of selection. As we move from the general considerations of Part I to specific preparations, we use ACME Ltd—A Company that Makes Everything—and ACAN Ltd, A Company That Achieves Nothing as illustrations.

When leaving for an expedition, you may not know where you will end up in the end, or what route you will take, or even how long you will stay. Regardless of this uncertainty, you will need to make many early choices that cannot be changed after the journey has started. "Packing the backpack" refers to these choices, and to the art of making them wisely. Once the stage has been set, and the backpacks have been packed, the journey can begin.

Why Preparation?

A big part of the excitement, and the anxiety, related to the experience of a creative journey begins during the preparation. Depending on the expected difficulty and duration of the journey, the preparation could be

B. R. Rill, M. M. Hämäläinen, *The Art of Co-Creation*,
https://doi.org/10.1007/978-981-10-8500-0_7

very quick and easy, or very hard and demanding. Regardless, you will probably make a list of items that you consider packing with you. You might rehearse some maneuvers that could become useful during the journey. You might exercise your body and mind to endure the known and unknown challenges that will lie ahead. You might call your mates to find out what steps they are taking in preparation. You can relive some of your experiences from previous trips and try to figure out how you could be better prepared for them next time. You may try to envision some parts of the journey and go through them in your mind. For these reasons, the preparation is an indispensable part of the journey.

More experienced travelers/participants understand the value of good preparation, and even though they might not need to go through as many steps as when they were novice, they will know how big of a difference the preparation can make for the success of the journey. Given this, it is good practice to match any newcomers with more experienced mentors, so that they can gain from their experience and better prepare themselves for the journey.

Training, Recovering, and Improving

As this book reveals, co-creation is complex and requires the *Xd* to develop a suite of skills. Honing your skills is similar to the athletic process to training, and we encourage readers to look at their own growth as one might prepare for a marathon. Nobody runs a marathon without first running some shorter legs, and by doing so building readiness for the big challenge step by step. It is a good idea to begin with smaller engagements before taking on large projects. Practice with workshops, facilitating individual program pieces, and peer coaching are good training for the co-creative *Xd*. Once fluent with these aspects independently, it then becomes easier to weave them all together into a larger engagement.

Also, not every journey leads to a favorable outcome. Depending on the level of ambition, the success rate of such endeavors varies significantly. It is worth understanding that many journeys do fail, and these failures have consequences. A failed journey might leave a permanent mark on its participants, and some people might never recover from very negative emotions related to their experience. On the other hand, a failed journey can act as an exercise and motive for improving your personal or collaborative skills, which in turn might end up producing less tangible but more sustainable outcomes in the form of experience-based learning. We have stated before that co-creation is tacit knowledge; thus it is to be expected that this book is just a starting point. The real learning will come from your experiences delivering co-creative programs.

An insight we can take from the training analogy is that of recovery. One thing that is often forgotten when exercising one's abilities is to reserve enough time for proper recovery. Exercises consume energy, and it always takes some time to bring back this energy. Development takes place during the recovery periods, not during the exercises. In sports, this phenomenon is known as *supercompensation.* This should be taken into consideration during the journey as well as after it has been completed, for we need both ourselves and our participants to be performing at their best.

Supercompensation in Physical Training and in Co-creation
Supercompensation is a theory about physical development of muscles, which was introduced and developed by Russian scientist Nikolai Yakovlev in 1949–1959. This well-accepted theory, illustrated in Fig. 7.1, describes how the development of physical characteristics such as speed or power takes place through training. This theory explains that physical development occurs through a mechanism known as supercompensation, which in fact happens *after* an exercise is over, and the body is recovering from it. The strain of the exercise itself produces only fatigue, which triggers a recovery period. If the recovery has sufficient time and other conditions are in order, the phenomena of supercompensation occur. If a new strain is introduced before full recovery, the fatigue becomes greater, and the overall performance goes down. To get the best results out of any constructive training, a new exercise should follow only after full recovery, at the peak of supercompensation.

We want to extend this model of supercompensation to cover the development of individual and collective skills. The development occurs over time, step by step, through consecutive exercises. As long as each exercise is followed by a proper recovery stage, the development of skills will be constructive. How much or how little time is needed is a subjective judgment. You may wait until you feel ready or set specific intervals for yourself and the team. A weekend may be enough for a transition between stages in a larger engagement, and several weeks may be needed after a long arduous journey.

(*continued*)

(continued)

To enhance this recovery process, a team (or in some cases just selected individuals) can look back at the previous journey and identify points of success and improvement. This action learning helps individuals bring their performance to a higher level than before, after which they are better equipped for a new journey. As a general rule of thumb, individuals and teams are ready for the next "exertion" once they have taken time for reflection and identified how they will modify their efforts in the next iteration.

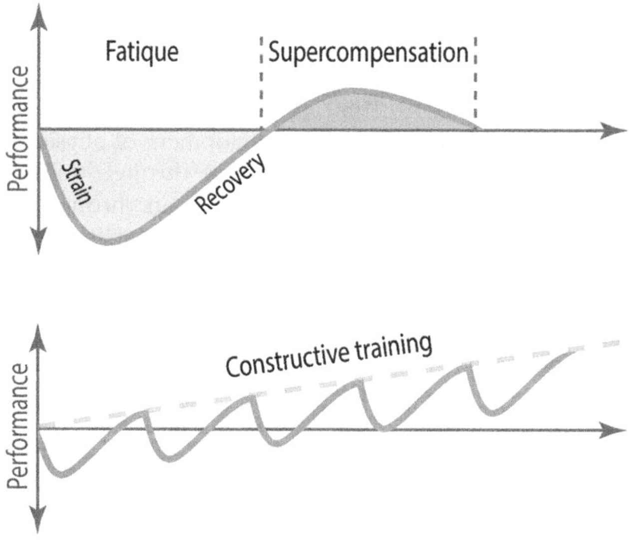

Fig. 7.1 Nikolai Yakovlev's supercompensation theory

Supercompensation is a mechanism for capacity building, which translates into more productive teams and greater potential for creative breakthroughs. Rest and reflection in-between activities triggers supercompensation, restores energy levels, and makes you better prepared for the program. If you take this time for yourself and the team, you will perform better in the marathon to come.

Packing the Backpack

The choices we make begin with a challenge or spark of an idea that establishes the need for co-creation. The ACME story begins with one such moment.

April 14th

The idea had been discussed many times over the past few years, but until now nobody had taken the initiative to proceed with the thought. ACME Ltd was already an established player in the field of children's toys, and for many it was a natural step forward, even though it was a recognized fact that the organization lacked in some key areas of expertise required for stepping into this new field. Baby monitors were produced and sold in millions by numerous other companies, and ACME was now ready and willing to grab its share of this market. So, on a sunny Monday afternoon in February, the head of R&D got her request approved by the executive board. The journey for baby monitors was on.

Since ACME was new to the field of baby monitoring, the first steps to take were to create a comprehensive understanding of the field and to acquire the capacities necessary for developing a well functioning baby monitor. As ACME already had world-class expertise related to the expected use context of these devices, and to the needs of the end-users, this area was considered to be well covered. However, the company had only very superficial understanding of radio-frequency communication, and of relevant monitoring systems. For this reason ACME decided to recruit a seasoned professional from the field of telecommunications to provide their organization the type of expertise they were currently lacking.

Setting the Direction

Many things need to be decided and set into place before a creative journey begins. If all has gone well in the lead-up to a program, the *Xd* has already worked closely with the client and/or stakeholders to understand the needs and context. It is good practice to then crystallize the objectives into a creative brief.

The most important element is making sure that the overall goal is clear enough, since everything else follows that. A mission statement is a good way to clarify the objectives in a way that helps all stakeholders understand the essence of the project. Ideally the mission statement also creates engagement. For this reason, it is sometimes a good practice to let the team draft the mission statement—perhaps as their first task as a team—based on the creative brief. Formulating the mission statement could be a co-creation exercise itself, and it can be created, for example, in collaboration with the corporate executives and/or key stakeholders. This approach would help in engaging the team, as well as building commitment to the project throughout the participating community. We will explain how to facilitate this exercise in the next chapter.

As detailed in Part I, engagement begins with a compelling needs story, a breakthrough question, or challenge that *draws* people to it. The rest of the brief frames the project and helps the team know what is expected of them. Expectations derive initially from stakeholder interviews, but these can change once a team is formed around the challenge. In co-creation we often invite participants to help set expectations and create a social contract for how we will work together. Because this is a "we"-centered approach, expectations set prior to a program are best kept loose, or "fuzzy," so that they can be reshaped.

Fuzzy Goals

The text *Gamestorming: A Playbook for Innovators, Rulebreakers, and Changemakers* defines fuzzy goals as emotional, sensory, and progressive, explaining[1]:

Emotional: Fuzzy goals must be aligned with people's passion and energy for the project. It's this passion and energy that gives creative projects their momentum; therefore, fuzzy goals must have a compelling emotional component.

Sensory: The more tangible you can make a goal, the easier it is to share it with others. Sketches and crude physical models help to bring form to ideas that might otherwise be too vague to grasp. You may be able to visualize the goal itself, or you may be able to visualize an effect of the goal, such as a customer experience. Either way, before a goal can be shared it needs to be made explicit in some way.

Progressive: Fuzzy goals are not static; they change over time. This is because, when you begin to move toward a fuzzy goal, you don't know what you don't know. The process of moving toward the goal is also a learning process, sometimes called successive approximation. As the team learns, the goals may change, so it's important to stop every once in awhile and look around. Fuzzy goals must be adjusted (and sometimes, completely changed) based on what you learn as you go.

The advantage of fuzzy goals is twofold. First, they allow for iterations on expectations, thus enabling the *Xd* more space in a program to flex.

Second, it opens the doors for true creativity. Programs that have preset expectations, such as deliverables, hinder creativity by constraining the team to work in the Known. Yet because creativity comes from the Unknown, the space of potential, it is impossible for any *Xd* to say with confidence what will come out of a co-creative program. Fuzzy goals help to meet the needs of the client by giving them some idea of what might happen, but do not constrain the team to meet those outcomes.

The ability to set fuzzy goals depends on the "givens" of any program. In some cases, the expectations are clearly fixed by leadership going in. In other cases, especially in internal control scenarios, there may be no expectations set ahead of time, and you begin a program with little more than a mission statement. The ACME creative brief illustrates a well-crafted creative brief.

ACME Creative Brief

Background

ACME Ltd is a leading manufacturer of children's toys, specializing in products with educational functions under the general slogan "Toys with a Purpose." ACME is a trendsetting pioneer that has always put a lot of effort into making sure that its products will surpass even the toughest safety standards while offering a wide range of building blocks for a stable and inspiring childhood. ACME excels in giving a physical form to the many explicit and implicit needs of parents and daycare professionals that aim to provide a happy, healthy, and safe growing environment for their children.

Project Goals

ACME wants to expand its current line of products by establishing a set of technical devices that will help parents in their continuous journey to supervise, monitor, and raise their children. As a first step in this direction, the primary goal of this project is (1) *to produce a baby monitor* that matches the general requirements of ACME products; they will need to be safe to use for both children and parents, they will need to be 100% reliable in use, and they will need to provide something more than the standard products in the market currently offer.

(*continued*)

(continued)

As a longer-term goal, ACME wants to become an expert in automatic monitoring of infants and toddlers. In order to reach this goal, ACME needs to develop and expand its knowledge so that it will cover all the areas required to master this field. In order to get to this point, the secondary goal of this project is (2) *to acquire and develop an internal base of knowledge* that will be used to develop further products for this category.

Mission Statement

We will design and introduce a new approach to supervising babies in their daily lives. This solution will reduce parents' constant burden of watching over their babies and offer them a completely new dimension to the interaction between them and their babies.

Resources and Budget

The project core team will consist of eight people, two of which are new recruits. Project manager, marketing and sales specialist, business specialist *(new)*, production engineer, design engineer, telecommunications expert *(new)*, industrial designer, and a psychologist. The budget is set at $2,200,000, including personnel costs.

Schedule

This product should be developed, tested, and launched within a *period of 18 months.* The first functional prototype should be test ready in six to eight months, after which there will be a testing and validation period of six months. Product evaluation and approval takes place at the end of this period.

If the final product is approved for production, the team will also need to lay out a detailed roadmap for two to six additional products that will be launched within this new product line for ACME. This product roadmap needs to be finished along with the marketing plan for the baby monitor by the end of the 18-month period.

As we can see, the ACME creative brief contains all of the core elements. It also contains a mission statement, a good start that the team may recraft into a more evocative statement as they work on the project. Finally, ACME felt the need to inform participants of the background of the company, the team composition, and a timeline. These details are plenty to frame the co-creative process to come. Yet there remain decisions to be made.

Deciding on Leadership

In addition to crafting the creative brief, an equally important decision to make early on is the form of leadership. A co-creative team needs good leadership in order to achieve its goals. This does not necessarily mean that the team would need a designated "leader." There can be many roles within the team, in which a certain level of leadership should be demonstrated, but none of these roles should be considered mandatory. More important is to achieve a good balance between creativity and productivity. Every team member can be expected to display some form of leadership during the journey, and anyone can assume an informal leading role that helps the team toward its goals. This is why in Part I we made the point that the catalyst can be anyone, and it is our job as *Xd* to design opportunities for others to take on that role. In the following chapters, we will share some tools and tips that may help any leader to guide their team as a coach, coordinator, mentor, facilitator, manager, or in any role that they feel suitable for a co-creative journey.

Many people assume that co-creation requires a very soft style of leadership. This assumption is easy to relate to, as both creativity and collaboration are commonly characterized by loose constraints, empathy, and benevolence. However, even though soft leadership has been successful in many co-creative projects, there is no reason why teams could not be equally successful when operating under tough leaders. As the former CEO of KONE Ltd Matti Alahuhta once said, the essential extremes are not soft and hard leadership, but good and bad leadership. Bad leaders fail regardless of their leadership style, while good leaders prevail—also regardless of their leadership style. So the question concerning leadership styles is ultimately a matter of choice, which depends on many factors such as the context of the challenge and your own capacities as a creative leader.

A key leadership decision is the management style for the mission. In order to achieve goals, it is important to make sure that the team stays on track at all times of their journey. There are two opposite approaches to managing the journey—the responsive and empowering styles. Responsive management sees the creative team as a probing crew, which is expected to communicate efficiently with decision-makers who are not participating in the journey themselves. This form of management is used to harness the collective knowledge of the team, without necessarily asking or expecting the team to act upon the insights generated. Empowering management, by contrast, gives fully autonomous teams internal control of their journey, and they are expected to plan and execute their decisions somewhat independently. The ability to take control in their own hands depends on the level of collective intelligence of the team—their capacity to exploit their own collective knowledge.[2]

It is worth noting that both forms of management produce results, and these results are of different quality and scale. In many cases co-creation is a process used to produce collective knowledge. Using co-creation in this way is valuable because it can be considered to be an investment that increases the knowledge capital possessed by the organization. As long as this knowledge remains within the organization, and can be accessed by the executives, the investment into collective knowledge can be considered worthwhile. Which brings us to the important questions of *what the executives expect to achieve* through this collective knowledge, and *how do they intend to access it?* If they expect their organization to answer questions or to solve problems presented by the heads of the corporation, then chances are that this is exactly what they will get: answers and solutions. Co-creation helps ensure they are of very high quality.

The problem in the responsive style of management is that the quality of the answers and solutions will always be constrained by the quality of the original question or problem presented. If the original task is based on wrong information or misunderstandings, then it is obvious that the outcomes will reflect those flaws as well. If the management instead chooses to rely on the greater collective capabilities of their organization, they may decide to take the road of empowering their organization instead of just squeezing juice out of them. The alternative, *empowering style of management* taps into the *collective intelligence* of the organization. The main difference between these two styles is that the latter encourages the team to take greater liberties in pursuing their goals, which enables them to make changes in the project course if they discover something that challenges the original direction.

In reality, it is difficult—if not impossible—to draw a line between these two approaches, since it is quite rare to encounter cases that would represent one extreme or the other. Even autonomous teams will need to stay in constant touch with their home base, keeping their organization informed of the progress and discoveries of the assignment. And even a tightly controlled team can change their course, as long as they can justify it and get a permission from their superiors.

Collective knowledge might be ambitious enough as a goal, and your organization might be able to get what you want just by reaching that level. However, there are clear benefits to collective intelligence that might justify reaching for this higher level of intellect. First of all, the collective decision-making mechanism enables the team to make very quick field decisions that are based on their recent discoveries and their collective insight. This allows the team to study some spin-off topics based on their collective intuition, or experiment with some dark horse ideas that might increase their overall understanding of the greater assignment. Many of these trails might turn out to be dead ends, which as such would be difficult to justify for any outsiders, but which might jointly provide clarity to the more general topic at hand and therefore help the team to reach something that could not have been anticipated beforehand. Achieving this level of collective intelligence will also enable the team to be proactive when planning and preparing next steps after the project has been completed. This way the new discoveries and positive outcomes of the co-creative journey can extend way beyond this individual project.

To summarize, if you want your project to reach for the higher level of collective intelligence, then you will need to consider how to structure the project, how to form the assignment for the team, how to build control mechanisms for it, how to select individuals for the team, how to assign roles for them, and so on. If collective knowledge is good enough, then you can be more strict with your assignment and management style. Then again, if your task doesn't require any type of collective performance, but rather depends on top-down control and task distribution, then co-creation might not be the approach you are looking for.

It is most likely that you will decide (or be told) which management style is to be implemented in or from stakeholder interviews. This decision is relevant because it helps determine how you place yourself and other facilitators in relationship to the co-creative process. Will you be acting as part of the team? As an outside consultant or facilitator independent of the organization? Or as a design lead in your own studio? Each of these scenarios is a different style of leadership that affects how you design and lead the experience.

Team Selection

Team composition has two poles. At one end of the spectrum, teams are predetermined by the client and/or design studio. At the other end, they need to be built from scratch. *Xd* are often faced with a mix of these, with some participants predetermined and others to be selected. You may not always have choice in this matter, but even in contexts where the team is predetermined, it is possible to "shuffle the deck"—creating groups with the characteristics you need.

If the composition of the co-creation team is already fixed, then there are issues that still need to be decided. For one, the leadership and management styles should be chosen deliberately according to the mission objective and individual capabilities (as above). If the team size and composition have not been fixed, they should be built to fit the goals.

Having a creative brief, or at least a mission statement, in hand and the leadership style decided makes it much easier to choose who best suits the needs of the process. The creative brief is a good guide for selecting an optimal composition for the co-creation team. As soon as there are team members assigned for the team, they can be involved in further defining the brief, which will help them take the goals for their own. The next phase of the ACME story illustrates what team selection can look like.

June 1st

Barely a month ago, Dorothy had been invited for an interview, which went quite well for her, and now she was doing interviews herself as the newly assigned project manager. She would only have two months until the project was about to start, and she would have to go through a long list of candidates, who all seemed more than qualified for her team. The one thing she tried to keep in her mind was the instruction she received from her old friend and mentor just before he retired. An innovative and effective team should be small in size, and wide in diversity. This way the internal communication would be simple, team dynamics would not become too complicated to manage, and the team would collectively have a very wide perspective over the subject. She wanted to build a winning team, and she was not afraid of disagreements, which both meant that the team would most likely be heading for quite a rollercoaster.

In this story Dorothy is choosing her team based on the guidelines we explained in the Team Dynamics section of Chap. 2. Just as she has, we must think about how to create a team that is:

- Small in size, wide in diversity
- Diverse in personalities and operating styles, to avoid groupthink
- Diverse in skills and experience to add dimensions to the solution space

If a team is built to meet these guidelines, you are creating a group of people whom are quite different in skill sets and personality. While this is advantageous for co-creation, it's worth considering the common fact that the team members themselves may have different perspectives of the composition. Our ACME team formation illustrates how someone might feel.

August 1st

Out of the newly established team of six, Tina had only met Allen and Dorothy before, so she was quite anxious to meet the rest of her teammates and learn to know them. At the same time, she was a bit worried about how things would go, since she had heard some rumors about the new team. Her biggest concerns were about David, who had worked at the sales department for more than fifteen years, and who had a reputation outside his department as a stubborn number-pusher who only cared about money and who did not seem to get along with people very well. At the same time, she had full confidence in Dorothy, who she had worked with previously on several occasions. Dorothy was an experienced project manager, whose tolerance for pressure was simply incredible, and who had many times proven that she could handle challenging situations as well as deal with difficult people. There was no doubt in Tina's mind that Dorothy could handle the team and guide them to their goals in time.

As we can see from this story, Tina's perspective is one that is both hesitant about other members and confident in Dorothy's leadership. She, Dorothy, and every other team member will walk into the program with preconceived ideas of the roles and relations they will be working with. It is your job to make sure they can come into the process as smoothly and confidently as possible.

The creative brief goes a long way in providing the structure for the team, and there are other small acts that can also help. If possible, meet with each participant and have a dialogue about the project and their roles within it. Ask them of their questions and concerns, providing them with the clarity and reassurance they seek. Excite them with the possibilities, and again make it clear the value of their contribution. If you do not have the opportunity to meet, or even know, all of the participants beforehand, then the creative brief must be good enough to do this job for you. This is why a compelling, engaging issue is so important. If you can create a pull, a desire within participants to be part of something, then they will walk in more open minded. If you fail to create the drive, then be prepared to meet with a variety of attitudes from enthusiastic to downright skeptical. For an optimal team engagement, it might be a good idea to give the team members an opportunity to contribute to the final appearance of the mission statement, or even to the entire creative brief. The following story shows how *not to* do this.

Relay Does Not Equal Co-creation

Redesign of ACAN Website

The head of marketing at ACAN had noticed that the company website had not been updated since the 2000s, and it was outdated in both content and structure. She decided it was time to take some action and create a new site by utilizing the collective expertise within the company. The first thing to do was to prepare a list of individuals whose input would be valuable for this process. These people would then be asked if they would be willing to participate in the process. Finally, a professional web design team would create the website according to the instructions from these internal experts, making sure that each one of them would get a chance to make their contribution to the website. And so the journey began.

To get the process started, the web design team had studied the old website and extracted certain key elements out of it, such as the taxonomy of information that the website was trying to convey, and the visual identity that the website had chosen. Based on these elements, the team created their first draft of the website, which they would then pass around to the selected internal contributors.

(*continued*)

(continued)

The first person to address the new website draft was the CEO of the company. She did not have much time to study the draft and did not feel it was her place to make decisions about their website in the first place. Since she wanted to show her support and respect toward the marketing division, she felt she should at least give them something. So, based on what she had seen, she made two delicate suggestions: the website should reflect their corporate values, and it would be nice if the pages were so easy to use that even her grandmother could go through them without any trouble. However, as she tried to put it, she was not an expert of websites and did not feel very strongly about either of these issues. They were just the two first thoughts that came to her mind.

So, the web team made some changes to the layout, bringing the company's vision, mission, and values to the front page, just as the CEO had suggested, and tried to simplify the interface by removing most of the drop-down menus. This second draft was as good a match to the CEO's desires as they could make, and they were ready to move forward with it.

The second person to view the draft was the head of human resources department. She immediately had a strong reaction to the corporate values on the front page. These official value statements did not reflect the true values of the workers, and publishing them in this way might be interpreted as disrespect toward all the hardworking employees. Instead, she suggested, they could publish some of the anonymous value statements they had collected from the employees during their annual work atmosphere survey. She provided a list of 25 suitable value statements for the web team to use in the front page and felt relieved that she had been able to stop this tremendous mistake from taking place.

The web team made a third draft based on these instructions, and the development rounds went on. As one might already guess, by the time the draft had reached its seventh round, there was nothing left of the original idea they had generated based on the previous website. It took indeed a lot of time from the web design team to

(*continued*)

(continued)

produce these new drafts, but they were already very satisfied with the results so far. After all, the company wanted to replace the old website, and at this point there was nothing left of it anymore!

What the design team did not understand was that at this point, there was nothing left of the second, third, or fourth draft either. So even though many people had contributed to the design, they all had participated individually, not collectively, which meant that in many cases their contribution was neglected by another person, without any consideration or acknowledgment of the reasons to introduce them in the first place. The head of marketing was happy, though, as she had given everyone a chance to contribute to the process.

The ACAN story illustrates the fact that many leaders make the mistake of confusing participation with collaboration or co-creation. As the example above shows, the outcome of sequentially divided participation might be just about the exact opposite of co-creation, even though on the surface these methods might seem very similar. First of all, in the ACAN form of participation, the contributors were separated from each other. They were not aware of the content of the previous contributions, much less understanding what reasons there might have been behind them. Without a mutual understanding, they were unintentionally disregarding much of the previous work and starting their own efforts from scratch. And even though the people might have felt *during* their participation that they were leaving their mark on the project, chances are that afterward they felt disrespected or ignored because the final outcome did not reflect their contribution in any ways at all.

Co-creating a brief or mission statement follows the same rules as the rest of the co-creative process. People need to be in the same space, physically or virtually, creating a shared knowledge base and working from that foundation together. Serial contributions, as well intentioned as they are, do not meet these criteria. In the ACAN case, it would have been much better for them to start off with a brief from the head of marketing inviting the team to co-design the new website. Even if the brief was just a rough draft with a few initial ideas, that would be enough to get the right people involved and hammer out the details together.

Different Backpacks

The stories in this chapter represent only two possible scenarios among many. As design projects, ACAN and ACME have certain characteristics, roles, and contexts that help us design the co-creative process specifically to them. Organizational development, education, non-profits... these all have different cultures and strategies that must be considered in the preparation stage. One of the reasons why we refer to co-creation as an art rather than a science is that there is no one "Way," or formulaic method, to follow. Like an art, although we may be using the same medium (e.g. paint on canvas), each expression is different from the last. And like painting, packing the backpack requires careful consideration of context to select which elements (and guidelines) to implement. This is an important caveat to keep in mind as we move into the last part of this chapter.

We want to offer some roadmaps that you can use as a starting place, or as models to look at as you reflect on programs that you have designed and led in the past. Both lenses have value. When we first began, I searched desperately for things like these to help me structure creative programs. Perhaps it was the musical producer in me—but I needed to see the whole before I could understand the parts. Some readers will relate to that. Others have a mature philosophy already, and their interest may lie in specific tools to be used in their own approaches. We do our best to meet that need by making detailed references to our colleagues who work in the related fields of design, organizational change, and leadership development. Be sure to explore the chapter endnotes, where we place "For more information see ..." commentaries. If you pursue the links there, you will find a great treasure house of techniques to use in co-creation and many other processes.

For readers who skipped straight to Part II, it is worth reiterating the point that our objective is not to explain in detail the techniques we use. To do that would require several more books, and these resources are readily available for the majority of tools we use. We make reference to these sources to help you explore them and also to save space for our arguments.

The main foci of this book are (1) to reveal the underlying architecture for collective creativity—the Space Between and Co-Creative Journey models—and (2) to offer guidelines for designing and leading a co-creative journey. Together, the guidelines and models can help you harness the full creative potential of teams. Throughout the text we seek to answer a few basic questions:

1. What is co-creation and why is it valuable?
2. What issues should you consider when designing a co-creative experience?
3. How should you plan your facilitation steps so that the flow of techniques nurtures co-creation?

As scholar practitioners, we are also attempting to advance design thinking with a shift in focus to experience design, for it is from experiences—not processes—that creative breakthroughs manifest. If our arguments, guidelines, and roadmaps help unleash collective creativity, then we have accomplished our goals. May they serve you well.

Experience Design Roadmaps

The Co-Creative Journey is the underlying grammar, or process architecture, for the experience design roadmaps provided. The use of the term "roadmap" is meant to connote both a sense of the past and a possible future. The examples offered derive from real application, so in one sense they are a description of past programs. However, like a map, they can also be used to chart out or inform future process designs. Each of these loosely corresponds to what IDEO calls an "experience blueprint," explaining that[3]:

> The blueprint reveals on a single page both the general plan and the specific detail, the final objective and the practical means of implementation. Just as a product begins with an engineering blueprint and a building with an architectural blueprint, an experience blueprint provides the framework for working out the details of a human interaction.
>
> The difference is that unlike the plans for an office building or a table lamp, an experience blueprint also describes the emotive elements. It captures how people travel through an experience in time. Rather than trying to choreograph that journey, however, its function is to identify the most meaningful points and turn them into opportunities.

We appreciate this explanation because it highlights the need for both pragmatic and experiential goals, which we consider to be the starting point for any co-creative experience design. It also refers to the "touchpoints" of the journey—those moments where important shifts occur and breakthroughs can happen. Identifying and catalyzing these moments is a large part of the art of co-creation that we attend here in Part II. But we don't just wait for them to occur and hope that we have the right instincts to act accordingly. We *design* these moments.

Roadmaps

What follows are three experience design roadmaps derived from real applications. The first is from a design context and the latter two from organizational development. We begin with a roadmap from product design to illustrate how close design thinking is to co-creation while also illuminating some key points of contrast. As you will see, in design the primary focus has been on the user journey rather than the designer journey, even though the design thinking process has brought attention to the designers' experience of the process without explicitly saying that.

In design, "co-creation" makes the user an equal contributor in the process, but the focus remains on "how to complete the process efficiently" rather than "how to make your team perform better." Interpersonal aspects, team composition, and creative tension have been mentioned and discussed in quite a few books. Emotions not so much. Teresa Amabile and a few others have touched the subject by addressing, for example, motivation, but this has been considered only on the level of process prerequisites, rather than the emotional rollercoaster that the Journey is.[4]

The second roadmap is a one-and-a-half-day co-creation workshop focused on helping workers in a large organization unleash their creative potential. This type of workshop is highly valuable as a form of annual training or team building and can generate insights that have the potential to change organizational culture.

Our final roadmap is a three-day visioning process. This experience design is comprehensive, carefully weaving all aspects of the co-creative journey together to build the highs and lows that foster bonding and breakthroughs. In an organizational context, this three-day program might be the beginning of a larger change initiative.

How to Read the Roadmaps

The roadmaps are a simplified version of the worksheets many consultants actually use. A typical worksheet is created in Pages (OSX) or in Excel (OSX/Windows). The header bar looks like this (Fig. 7.2, next page):

Time is the time of day and/or date when the activity begins.

Duration is the time length of the activity.

Time	Duration	Activity/ Topic	Who's Responsible	Goal/ Result	Process	Resources	Comments

Fig. 7.2 Facilitation worksheet

Activity/topic is the name of what we will be doing. This is what you out in flow of the day charts or visuals.

Who's responsible is the person in charge of leading that activity.

Goal/result is what you would like to accomplish. We list pragmatic and experiential goals here.

Process is a set of shorthand explanations and/or reminders to yourself and the facilitating team on how to lead the activity.

Resources are the materials/supplies/environment needed for the activity.

Comments are whatever else you need to note for the activity/stage of the process. We often put key quotes to refer to here or leave it blank so that we can write in comments as we go. Comments are also where we add in notes that arise in the pre- and post-team meets.

In our experience, this format is fairly standard among consultants and facilitators. Although it is not particularly remarkable, it does the job. What it does not do is reveal the underlying process architecture, which can make a process design difficult to interpret. We spent two years continually asking our colleagues "Why are you doing this?", "Why is it here and not there?", and "What happens if this doesn't work?" to develop the capacity to see beyond the sequences laid out on the page and grasp the underlying structure and flow.

Approaches such as the Double Diamond, Theory U, nowhere's creative rollercoaster, the Bridge Fellowship, and our own Co-Creation Journey have visuals that illustrate a process architecture. The following examples apply this architecture to roadmaps with a slightly different layout and a set of visual codes that indicate what aspect of the journey the activity/technique affects.

Given the space constraints of a book, our simplified version cuts columns focused on logistics or process. Here we also refrain from descriptions of the activities. As we progress through the next chapters, we will provide these details and references to the developers of each method in the endnotes. Some of these you will recognize. Other activity titles may be unfamiliar. In such cases look at the goal/result and other columns to see why it is used there. The activities listed reflect our own personal styles, and we encourage you to fill in these spaces with your own toolkit rather than attempting to use something you may not be comfortable with.

The space created by these omissions makes it possible for us to mark other features of each activity. There is a key at the top of each roadmap, with colored/shaded circles that indicate what aspect(s) of the creative journey the activity emphasizes.[5] Because many activities affect all three aspects, the size of the circle is indicative of the relative focus. A larger circle = more focus. In addition to the three aspects, we have included a fourth (yellow/lightest shading) circle to indicate program pieces that are designed to cultivate capacities beneficial to co-creation. These are gross measures, surely, but they do help illustrate our emphasis on designing for all aspects of the creative journey. Let's look at brainstorming as an example (Fig. 7.3).

KEY: Aspects of Creative Journey		Knowledge ●			
		Emotions ●			
		Team Dynamics ●			
		Capacity ○			
Act I: The Climb					
Activity/ Topic	Goal/ Result	Aspect			
Brainstorming	Generate Lots of Ideas	●	●	●	○

Fig. 7.3 Roadmap guide

In this example, we can see that brainstorming is useful for generating lots of ideas. Brainstorming is also good for team dynamics. The facilitator can encourage people to build upon other's ideas, a skill they will use time and time again. Finally, brainstorming is a good way to kick up the energy of the group. These characteristics of brainstorming are why we put it in Act I: The Climb, for it is in this stage that we are trying to get the team enthused, bonding, and building a collective knowledge base.

Before we move on, there is one caveat to reinforce. *The map is not the territory*. Co-creation, like design, is not as linear as it might seem. Many people have made the mistake of taking templates such as these literally.

They are nice visuals, but the implied linearity is misleading. If we were to draw out what a design journey actually looks like, you might end up with a visual of a spaghetti ball or knotted rope (Fig. 7.4).

Fig. 7.4 Design spaghetti

In addition to co-creation being nonlinear, it would be a mistake to believe that we actually follow these roadmaps as they are initially designed. Each of the following examples went through several iterations as conditions changed. What you see below is the final version with a few post-program tweaks that we felt could have improved the process. Yet even these versions would need to be adapted to the specific context of the next usage, and surely we would make shifts on the fly as we navigated the balance between guiding and following the energy of the group.

In many cases our designs include complementary coaching and mentoring activities. The challenge is finding the balance between capacity and skill development and the needs and flow of a creative process. The best types of coaching and mentoring are very catalytic, and they should take place within an actual design/development process. This way the lessons are directly connected to a natural context, and there is no gap between theory and practice. If a coaching drill might disturb the creative process critically, then a good alternative would be to arrange the exercise in parallel with the process. This way the drill would not interfere directly with the process, but the participants would still have an immediate context to apply their new knowledge and skills.

Less effective options for coaching and mentoring are methods that would interrupt the process flow completely while having no direct connection to the process context. In some situations, these types of strong interventions might be required to wake up or shake up the team, of course, but they should never be pre-planned as a part of the journey. The roadmaps need to tie coaching and mentoring to specific stages of the co-creation process. Other types of exercises, which could interfere with the flow of the project, should only take place before the project is launched or after it has been finished.

Adaptive Use

Co-creation is iterative and at times chaotic, meaning that at any point in time you may need to jump from one point in the process to another. You may, for example, come up with a great idea, only to find out that it is not original. Alternatively, you can develop what the executive board feels to be a brilliant strategy, only to have realization fail due to budget cuts or internal fighting. We have seen both happen. At these points, you must evaluate and step into the creative space that is needed in the moment. Our point is to *use these templates adaptively*, flexing as needed without fear of what might happen to the sense of linear flow.

Product Development Project (PdP)

The first template illustrates a process of a Product Development Project (PdP) as it has been taught at the Aalto-Tongji Design Factory in Shanghai, China. PdP is an eight-month industry project course, originating from Aalto University where it has been taught in its current form since 1997. Project BioHao was one of the three student projects that took place in Shanghai during the academic year 2012/2013, and it was sponsored by a foreign company that was planning to enter the Chinese market. The project was led and executed by a team of university students, who had a fixed budget and a fixed deadline allocated for the project (Table 7.1).

The original brief for this project was "To design a solution related to Home Composting and Gardening in China," which was narrowed down to *Home Gardening in China* as the journey shifted to Act II. The team was very efficient in increasing their understanding of their target market and their possible solution models during Act I and Act II, to the point where a perfect solution just emerged during rigorous concept development. The final solution—a stackable flower tower with integrated watering system provided by a wicking string—had its roots in many corners of the knowledge that had accumulated during the journey, so it would be difficult to pinpoint an exact moment where this specific idea got started. The team had played with tower-shaped flower stands already quite early in their process, but these ideas were abandoned until they came back to mind at the critical moment. The wicking string was studied and discussed a lot, but it did not connect to a sensible concept until a particular flower-pot shape was introduced. Soon after that moment, pieces began to fall in place quite rapidly, and the team managed to design and build their final, fully functional prototype in a matter of few weeks.

Table 7.1 Product Development Project (PdP)

Experience design roadmap			
Program title		*Duration*	
Product Development Project BioHao		8 months	Knowledge Emotions Team dynamics Capacity
Act I: The Climb			
Date	**Activity/topic**	**Goal/result**	**Aspect**
Oct 11	Kick-off meeting		
	Introducing the project brief	Getting on the same page about the project	
	Team introduction	Getting to know each other	
	Brief analysis	Need to *recruit a designer* for the team	
Oct 18	Sponsor meeting 2	**→ Recruit 2–3 Chinese team members**	
		Getting to know the sponsor	
		Hearing sponsor's mission and story	
		Understanding sponsor's situation: no market, no customers, no products	
		Specifying the theme: home composting and gardening in China	
Oct 19	Debrief	Debrief of sponsor meeting	
	Mind map	Mind map of home gardening in China	
	Idea map	Idea map based on mind map	

(*continued*)

Table 7.1 (continued)

Experience design roadmap		
Program title		*Duration*
Oct 22	TMPDI 2: foresight	Tools and methods of product design and innovation
	PESTE	Analysis of Chinese market situation with regard to brief
	Scenarios	Scenarios of Chinese market in the future
Oct 23	TMPDI 3 and 4: idea generation + concept selection	Tools and methods of product design and innovation
	6-3-5 idea generation Brainstorming	Testing idea generation techniques, full team working all the time, team building, get a good start to the project → **"Poop-your-flower"**
	Idea clustering	Clustering the ideas generated with the two methods
Oct 24	TMPDI 5 and 6: idea generation + concept analysis	Tools and methods of product design and innovation
	Concept screening and selection	Screening and selecting the concepts
	Morphological matrix	Improving the concepts and generating new ones
	Post-it brainstorming	Generating a name for the team instead of doing the TRIZ exercise (since it was so boring and unproductive) → **BioHao/Bio好**
Oct 25	TMPDI 7: concept development	Tools and methods of product design and innovation
	Ishikawa diagram	Customer need analysis
Oct 26	TMPDI 8: understanding customer needs	Tools and methods of product design and innovation
	CPM method	Collaborative physical modeling of the customer needs → **Breakdown of Poop-your-flower**

(*continued*)

Table 7.1 (continued)

Experience design roadmap		
Program title		*Duration*
Oct 27	TMPDI 9: PD7	Tools and methods of product design and innovation
	Product Development Project in 6 hours	Re-did all the previous methods and stages, built a physical model of **flower tower** (concept was still flower wall)
Act II: The Dive		
Oct 29	User research begins	Surveying the needs of the user group
Nov 8	Check-point meeting	First check-point meeting of PdP • Review: project plan, schedule, budget • Introduction of project brochure • Introduction of project poster • **Focus narrowed to gardening**
Nov 15	Analysis team meeting	Stakeholder analysis
Nov 16	Engineering team meeting	Technical documentation
Nov 22	Marketing meeting	
Nov 23	Sponsor meeting 3	→ **Focus on watering system**
Nov 28	Visualization of 3 concepts	3D renderings finished of the 3 concepts
Dec 18	Marketing meeting 3	
Dec 26	User research photos	→ All balconies face South!
Jan 4	Mid-term presentations	• Solution concept freeze: (1) plug it, (2) grow it, (3) eat it • Mock-up of flower tower
Jan 6	Team time	Dinner and foot massage
2-month break		
Mar 8	Project re-start	Kick-off with new team members
	6-3-5 idea generation	Team building and idea generation

(*continued*)

Table 7.1 (continued)

Experience design roadmap			
Program title		*Duration*	
Mar 15	Sponsor meeting 4	• Presenting "Modular Honey Comb" • Presenting service/business model • Focus on watering: wicking or roots in fabric	
Apr 4	Concept development	**Stackable container introduced**	
Act III: The Rise			
Apr 16	Functional prototype	Pot proto with wicking string	
Apr 23	3D modeling	3D models of the flower tower	
Apr 24	Technical modeling	Technical model finished	
Apr 26	3D modeling	Almost finished appearance	
May 3	Technical testing	Technical testing of the model	
May 15	Wicking test May 15–21	Testing of wicking materials	
May 24	Prototyping	Glass fiber + epoxy experiment → **no-go**	
May 25	Prototyping	Milling first proto out of plastic	
May 29	Prototyping	Final proto arrives	
May 30	Final gala	Presentation of finished product	
Jun 4	Feedback session	Project debrief	

In this project, the key discoveries and essential shifts of turn took place during the Dive. The project deadline was approaching and the team still had a million ideas in their heads. It was just that most of these ideas didn't even work, and out of the ones that did work, none were really able to capture their vision of a simple, modern, and inspiring home gardening product. Being close to running out of time, the team just decided to pull together whatever pieces they had at hand and create something very simple and elegant out of them. Suddenly it all started to make more and more sense. They started with a plastic water container that happened to have a handle attached to one side of it. This handle made the container suitable for attaching it to a wall that would have matching holes in it—and so the final concept for a flowerpot was there! The journey took its turn to begin the Rise, and small details began to fall into their places, one by one. The handle happened to have a groove in it, which offered a perfect location to place a wicking string. And since the string looked pretty ugly from inside the groove, they decided to cover it and made the handle hollow. They still needed to create an elegant water container to act as a base for the flowerpots, which brought them back to an older idea of a flower tower that they decided to use instead of building a wall. And then the water pump, and testing the wicking mechanism, and choosing the manufacturing methods, and the materials, and… In just a few weeks the final prototype was ready.

The key moments of this journey were not planned. They took place because the time was right, because the team was there, and because they had discovered and generated enough knowledge between themselves to make the last steps feel simple and easy. All of the idea generation sessions, the surveys and interviews, the prototypes, and meetings with the sponsor took them forward as a team, leading them closer to the point where they would be able to co-create something very simple and great.

Organizational Change

Experience designs for organizational change can take on a number of forms, and these are often constrained by much shorter timelines that design projects. It is not uncommon for a co-creative process to be only one part of the overall change initiative. This is especially true for large-scale changes such as developing new strategies or shaping culture. In other contexts, such as ideation workshops, the co-creative process can be truncated into one- to three-day programs. It is possible to take a team through a co-creative journey in one day, although as we noted in Part I, you must be willing to accept the trade-off between quality and quantity. One day will not afford any deep exploration of issues and, at most, can generate arenas of action to be further pursued.

In our experience, three contact days is a minimum, with one day dedicated to each Act of the journey. Additionally, we have found that the shorter the journey, the more time should be given to the preparation and the follow-up. Every day that we spend in person co-creating with organizations requires an equal and often greater amount of time in pre- and post-activities. These are the constraints of the organizational context, demanding careful planning and thorough follow-up to ensure the most bang for the buck.

Given this diversity of programs possible in organizations, the templates we present represent one of each: a one-and-a-half-day program and a three-day co-creative visioning initiative. You will find that these processes do not have an "ending." This reflects the fact that co-creation is an iterative process, with the outputs of one program becoming the inputs to the next cycle.[6] In large-scale change initiatives, short co-creative programs such as these can be used whenever collective ideation and empowerment are needed.

Co-creation Workshop

Creativity workshops are an excellent way to introduce co-creation. They can be stand-alone events or one piece in a larger engagement. This roadmap is from a 1.5-day workshop aimed at helping individuals, teams, and the organization identify ways to unleash their creativity.

Background

The challenge brought to us was siloing, resulting in communication problems and redundancy across divisions of a large family-owned corporation. Over several months of stakeholder dialogues, the executive board asked us to help the teams work better across divisions (the silos) and be more creative. Our answer was to design a large group engagement with teams comprised of members that in normal working life never collaborate directly. We framed the engagement around the breakthrough question of "How do we unlock our creative potential to make a difference"? Our first pragmatic goal was to answer this for each individual, their teams, and the overall organization. Our second goal, both experimental and pragmatic, was to improve understanding and communication across silos through the act of co-creating answers to the breakthrough question (Table 7.2).

In this program the breakthrough moment came in the mark making exercise toward the end. As teams marked the emotional contours of the journey, one young man from the technical division shared how difficult and uncomfortable it was for him to open up. His authenticity in that moment caused the breakthrough, a sudden shift in the emotional landscape. He was followed by several heartfelt expressions, and comments began to surface from the group such as "We have never bonded like this before." The breakthrough was not the answers to the breakthrough question, but rather the transformation of relationships among peers. That is what co-creation can do, and we are confident that the change in relationships translated into improvements in organizational communication that the client sought us out for.

Table 7.2 Co-creation workshop

Experience design roadmap		
Program title	*Duration*	
Co-creation workshop	1.5 days	Knowledge ● Emotions ● Team dynamics ● Capacity ○
Act I: The Climb		
Activity/topic	**Goal/result**	**Aspect**
Welcome and intros	Motivational/set expectations	●
ESP cards	Socializing/styles empathy	● ● ○
Organizational timeline	Create shared understanding of past to show what they are building on	● ● ●
Dinner	Socializing/bonding	●
Fireside chat	Helicopter view (by CEO) on company creativity	●
Closing	End of day one	
Welcome—set scene	Integrate organizations inputs into flow	●
Input I (by Chairwoman)	Give orientation and direction	●
Reveal breakthrough question	Focus creative energy—give direction	● ●
Stillness exercise	Bring into present—calm awareness	● ○
Input II: making a difference	Open thinking process	●
Journaling	Reflect and digest input on 3 levels (Me, We, It)	● ● ○
Act II: The Dive		
Activity/topic	**Goal/result**	**Aspect**
Y-III intuition walk	Deepen knowledge, intuition of subject	● ● ○
Break	Allow individual processing	
Group art exercise	Use art to represent what is emerging/taking shape	● ● ●

(*continued*)

Table 7.2 (continued)

Experience design roadmap		
Program title	*Duration*	
Lunch	Socializing/bonding	
Present "Art Pieces" in plenum	Create shared understanding of insights/mutual empowerment	
Past–present–future maps	Creating a shared understanding on the core forces affecting ability to make a difference (subgroups)	
Macro areas of attention	Identify arenas of action (subgroups)	
Present MAOA in plenum	Build collective knowledge	
Presencing	Apply awareness to sense potential	
Break		
Act III: The Rise		
Activity/topic	**Goal/result**	**Aspect**
MAOA group formation	Self-selecting work groups—collect ideas on how to progress from here (post workshop)	
Mark making	Reflection and sharing of emotional journey	
Checkout	Bring awareness to energy	
Closing comments	Sense of completion and what's next	

Insights Creative Rollercoaster

Co-creation is often at its best when used for visioning. Creating a field of collective intelligence and then tapping into that superpower can lead to strategic innovations. A creative rollercoaster (CRC) is exactly what the name implies, a journey of ups and downs in pursuit of the elusive breakthrough idea.

Background

This design was for a group of friends who wanted to explore what they might build together that could harness their diverse talents into one or a set of closely related initiatives. It was a collective visioning process, with pragmatic goals of co-creating a vision and an action plan. The experiential goals were to explore different ways of knowing and transform relationships from friendship to a leadership team.

This example is applicable in team start-up contexts and in larger organizations when a leadership team is formed to envision the next... Unlike the previous examples, this design specifically attempted to facilitate resonant co-creation, transforming the field of collective knowledge into collective intelligence (Table 7.3).

Table 7.3 Insights Creative Rollercoaster

Experience design roadmap		
Program title	*Duration*	
Insights creative rollercoaster	3 days	Knowledge Emotions Team dynamics Capacity
	Day I (half day)	
Act I: The Climb		
Activity/topic	**Goal/result**	**Aspect**
Welcome and introduction	Introduce approach—multiple ways of knowing and space between	
Tuning in and stilling	Begin to tune awareness	
Talking circle	Share expectations Introduce rules of dialogue Set the personal container	
Input: the creative rollercoaster	Purpose, objectives, outcomes, outputs Set the process container Introduce resonance	
Push hands	Learn to work with energy of others	
Sharing: exploring the need	Pairs deep listening dialogue	
Break		
Input: the power of questions	Introduce breakthrough questions	
Holding a question	Practice for coming visioning session "What is my Unique gift?"	
Pair share	Deepen social connection	

(*continued*)

Table 7.3 (continued)

Experience design roadmap		
Program title	*Duration*	
Group share	Introduce power of subconscious mind	
Dinner		
Personal shields	Chart what brought us here to see what we are building on	
Group share	Bond team closer	
Checkout circle	Close the day	
	Day II	
Optional morning practice: meditation	Cultivate presence	
Community breakfast	Bonding/review flow of the day	
Generative dialogue: BTQ	Co-create the breakthrough question	
Asset mapping	Create visual inventory to demonstrate wealth of resources	
Lunch		
Group adventure	Give team time to digest and have fun = renew energy before going into dive	
Act II: The Dive		
Activity/topic	**Goal/result**	**Aspect**
Prime the senses	Preparation for exploration	
Guided visualization	Imagine what the future might look like	
Marking the future	Silently brainstorm key features of vision	
Theme analysis and dialogue	Explore emerging themes as a group	
STEMS	Rebalance team dynamic	
Dinner		
Possible human banner	Create visual artifacts of each person at their best	
Group share	Reinforce positive contribution to vision	
Checkout circle	Close the day	

(*continued*)

Table 7.3 (continued)

Experience design roadmap		
Program title	*Duration*	
	Day III	
Act III: The Rise		
Activity/topic	**Goal/result**	**Aspect**
Optional morning practice: yoga	Start off the day relaxed and loose	
Community breakfast	Bonding/review flow of the day	
"I like, I wish, what if" dialogue	Process review, check in with what is needed, make sure voices are heard	
Input: convergence	Bring group to sense of place in process. Generate energy for the rise	
The social contract	Co-design principles to be applied in coming work	
The creative brief	In pairs then group shape the brief. Bring clarity to purpose, objectives, outcomes	
Lunch		
Zip Zap Zop	Fun stoker	
Participatory action planning	Co-create strategy	
Dinner		
Checkout circle	Close the day	
	Day IV (morning only)	
Community breakfast	Review flow of the day	
Trim tab	Identify key levers	
Decision council	Create 100-day plan	
Break		
Doorway	Review what has been learned and what each person will do	
Closing dialogue	Reflect on CRC, validate the journey	
Checkouts	Close the day	
Departure		

The Insights Creative Rollercoaster was successful in meeting both the pragmatic and experiential goals. For one, the process validated how closely aligned their personal and professional interests were. The collective vision manifested with almost no debate. Everyone built on each other's ideas, and in a few short hours the group had sketched out what their future retreat center could look like. Moreover, what started off as major differences in ability transformed into a large resource pool where everyone could see the value the others brought. Perhaps most important, each person acknowledged what they would have to let go of in order to make this vision a reality. While this three-day visioning was only the first step on a long road, it ended with focused energy and intention.

An experience design such as this will, at times, meet with initial resistance. In this case, during the first stages of the process, a couple of the group expressed impatience. They wanted to jump straight to action planning, feeling that as friends they had already made clear a vision. I held them back, asking for patience while guiding them into spaces to explore each other before working on the vision. Fortunately, they trusted me enough to go along with my process, and as it turned out the vision did need to transform from one or two people's ideas to a collective one. We accomplished this. In the closing dialogue, we discussed the co-creative journey, specifically the value of the "soft skills" capacity building and interpersonal exercises. In a reversal of the initial stance, the "doubters" expressed how pleased they were that we spent so much time bonding and exploring different ways to tap into intuition. It was those processes that set a strong container and aligned the group. As a result, in the Dive the collective vision emerged without difficulty. This is a sign of resonance. The lesson is that it is worth taking the time to slow down, deepening relationships and establishing a collective intelligence, if you really want to create a compelling vision.

Conclusions

Preparing for co-creation parallels the athletic training processes. It begins with the people, training, and resting needed to continually improve upon yours and your team's capacity for co-creation. An action learning approach will help improve your skills as an *Xd*, facilitator, and leader. When a team also has the opportunity to learn by doing, reflecting, and resting, their capacities to perform when it is needed will also improve.

The question is, what kind of team do you want to have? If you want to win the World Cup, then you need to learn to work together with near-perfect synchrony. At the same time you need diversity of skills and strong leadership. These qualities make for a great co-creative team. When possible, work with clients, stakeholders designers, and members of the community to put together the *right* team for the task, not just any team.

Team formation is closely linked to leadership style, and before you begin any co-creative process, it is wise to decide on what management style to use and how that choice will impact the process. Is the program led by one person, or is leadership rotated? How will you support the emergence of catalysts throughout the process? Are you "tuned" correctly for the process you are about to facilitate?

Other preparatory considerations include: Will you provide them with a detailed creative brief beforehand, or can you ask the team to co-create the mission statement and other details? How much control do you have over the environment, and what preparations can you make to set the container before a program begins? And finally, what does your experience design look like? Is it fully fleshed out, or just a skeleton frame? What are your pragmatic and experiential goals, and how does your process meet those ends? These are among the important decisions that we benefit from making before we ever set foot in a room with a group. The answers help us design co-creative processes bespoke to the situation at hand, meeting needs and delivering results.

With design in hand, you are now ready to begin the Climb. In the next chapter we move into facilitation of the co-creative journey. As we travel this road, we continue to weave theoretical points with explanation and illustrations. Given that the majority of guidelines were explained in Part I, you will find few new guidelines in what follows. Our focus now is on *How* to enact those guidelines. The presentation follows the flow of the journey, explaining key touchpoints and techniques as they might occur in a process. Enjoy the ride.

Notes

1. Gray et al., *Gamestorming*, 8.
2. Capacity here refers to a level of collective insight on ***how to*** exploit collective knowledge.
3. Brown, *Change by Design*, 126.

4. Amabile, *How to kill creativity.*
5. The color-coded key is available in the digital print version of this text.
6. We will have more to say on the iterative cycle in Chap. 11: Follow-Up.

References

Amabile, Teresa M. "How to Kill Creativity." *Harvard Business Review* 76, no. 5 (1998): 76–87.

Brown, Tim, and Barry Katz. *Change by Design: How Design Thinking Transforms Organizations and Inspires Innovation.* Adobe Digital Edition ed. New York: Harper Collins e-books, 2009.

Gray, David, Sunni Brown, and Macanufo. *Gamestorming: A Playbook for Innovators, Rulebreakers, and Changemakers.* Sebastopol, CA: O'Reilly, 2010.

CHAPTER 8

Act I: The Climb

September 3rd

Eventually the big day arrived, and the entire team was ready to get started with their project. Many of the team members already had the opportunity of taking a jump-start to the project. Simon had even dug up some of his old school books to make sure that he was up to the challenge, since he expected his role within the team to be much more challenging that in any of his previous assignments. Roberta had contacted her former colleague to catch up on the latest details in child safety standards and related legislation. Despite all the efforts and preparations that had already been done, this was the day of official kick-off for the project. The intensity of the moment was dense, and you could almost smell the anticipation in the air, as the team met for the first time. Some people seemed very nervous, while others appeared calm or excited.

The preparations have been made. The backpack is packed. It's time to start the climb. A co-creative journey normally begins with exploration of the Known, familiar territory. The participants need to share their knowledge and relevant experiences with each other, which can be started with some sort of brainstorm or ideation workshop. Along with providing starting points for the journey in the form of diverse ideas, this type of loosely organized collective sessions will help the team members to understand more about each other's perspectives and knowledge regarding their co-creation challenge. A joint workshop will also help to focus team members' minds on the given task and tune them to the collective modus operandi. During the idea generation stage, the team members are sharing

B. R. Rill, M. M. Hämäläinen, *The Art of Co-Creation*,
https://doi.org/10.1007/978-981-10-8500-0_8

their knowledge about different aspects of the topic and begin to search for more information. Through the practice of sharing and synthesizing, a new layer of collective knowledge is generated on top of the preexisting individual bits and pieces.

The Known is where people are most comfortable, as they are working well within the limits of their personal comfort zones. The biggest challenges of this stage are related to different issues of team dynamics rather than individual progress. The work in this stage is based on their experience and guided by their field-specific expertise. It is in this space that many preliminary "solutions" first arise. Often in creative processes people jump straight from brainstorming or other idea-generating exercises into these "solutions," following what seems at that time to the best idea that someone has. This, we argue, is not very creative, but rather a mandatory stage that needs to be completed swiftly. If we act from what we know, we are never developing anything new, which lies at the core of creativity. True newness comes from what we don't know.

Metaphorically the climb is intended to take the team to the highest possible peak of the Known world, so that they can get proper speed for their deep dive into the Unknown. The general atmosphere during this stage is positive, and as the eyes of the participants open wider and wider, the excitement increases until the imminent dive must begin. Until that point, the team must learn to know each other, to trust each other, and to discover the most efficient ways for them to work together.

The main task of the *Xd* in this stage is to ensure that the team is bonding and all team members are preparing themselves for facing forthcoming challenges and obstacles together. The *Xd* must pay close attention to the team chemistry, and he or she should plan and assign collective tasks for individual team members or sub-teams in order to test, evaluate, and train their collective performance. In this chapter, we describe how the process of knowledge sharing and generation can be led and how to facilitate team building.

The Social Dimension of Knowledge

Establishing collective knowledge requires a *social connection*, which dictates how and when this collective knowledge can be applied. The Chinese term *Guanxi* (关系) describes such a connection within a pragmatic social network, which is based on loyalty, reciprocity, and trust. Collective knowledge requires this social component; otherwise the identified, existing knowledge cannot be applied for shared goals, and the bits of knowledge remain scattered. This means that in addition to maximizing the awareness of all the combined personal knowledge within the team, the team needs to develop ways to utilize this knowledge collectively. Once this collective knowledge base is built, the direction of the journey will shift from knowledge assembly to exploration.

The insight we share here is that, in the context of collective creativity, knowledge is useless without strong interpersonal connections and ways of relating to one another that facilitate the sharing of it. In other terms, what is needed is a strong container.

How Do You Set the Container?

Imagine yourself arriving to a conference room on an early Monday morning, intending to participate in a co-creation workshop, just to notice that half of the participants have not arrived on time, and the other half have come completely unprepared. People feel hungry and confused, having skipped their breakfasts in hope for a cup of coffee and a sandwich as a reward for their earlier-than-usual start for a week. Every new participant who arrives late disturbs all the other participants and interrupts the flow of the workshop, forcing the facilitators to restart the session every half-an-hour or so. Some people disrupt the workshop with questions that seem silly or inappropriate, while others have lost their focus completely. This is how a poorly prepared workshop often begins, and indeed most of us have similar experiences from such events.

The beginning of a co-creative journey can seem quite chaotic. Even with a creative brief, at first there may be no clear understanding of what to expect. Yet people are still using a lot of energy to get their voices heard and to push things forward. If you find yourself in this situation, here are a few tips of what to do to get your journey moving forward.

First, it is good to remember that this is just the *beginning*, which means that things will have time to evolve and change many times before the journey even reaches full speed. The beginning is a perfect time to get an understanding of what's going on and to decide where to move from there (what to do next).

It is safe to assume that at this point there is some friction and turbulence in the air. In fact, if things are going really well between all team members, it should raise some concerns, since smooth team chemistry at this point might be a symptom worth watching. For one, it could be a sign that the team members are not committed to their joint task, and for that reason they do not care that much if somebody disagrees with them. Another issue that might lead to an overly smooth start of a project is a situation where the team members already know each other well and have perhaps worked together before on several occasions. This type of situation might lead to groupthink or NIH syndrome, common social phenomena associated with well-established teams. In both cases, the cohesion of the team has developed to a level in which it is beginning to have negative consequences on the team performance. Groupthink typically occurs when the team members value harmony within the team over the quality of their work. The team begins to suppress or ignore any opinions that would conflict with their consensus, resulting in a limited perspective on the subject (a.k.a. "tunnel vision"), and eventually poor decision-making. NIH is short for *Not Invented Here*, and refers to situations where the team becomes so self-assured that it begins to undermine any ideas or opinions that originate from outside the team. The team refuses to see value in alternative solutions and hence is incapable of acquiring new knowledge or insights from them. If you sense that you might be facing either of these situations—NIH or groupthink—then this would be a good time to dig a bit deeper and find out if there are reasons for concern. Small changes at this point will be still quite easy to make. For example, introducing new members to the team might shake things up in such a way that the team would be able to accept new perspectives through these new individuals—provided that the team is willing to accept them as part of the team even though they come from outside. More tips for steering away from these situations are provided in Chap. 10: The Rise, which is another time when we need to avoid these pitfalls.

If things look more like the situation in Fig. 8.1 (next page), then your team might in fact be off to a good start. You can feel the intensity and anxiousness to get things rolling, as people have been waiting for this project to begin—and finally the journey is on its way! For the *Xd*, it is very important to keep in mind that from now on the journey should proceed along multiple dimensions at the same time. Even though the primary goal of this stage is to get a comprehensive understanding of the task at hand (= reach the edge/peak of existing knowledge), at this point it is still much more

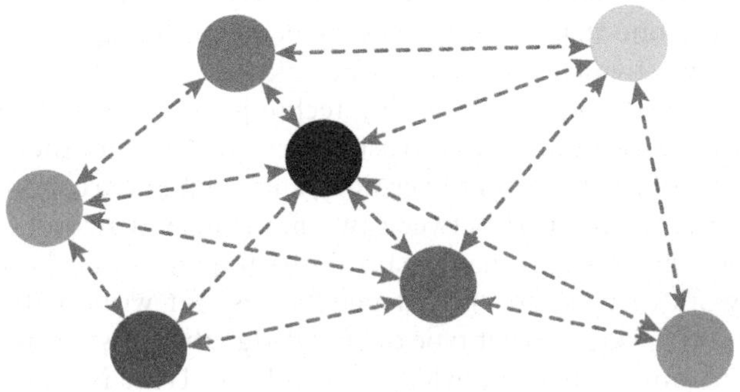

Fig. 8.1 Interpersonal communication at the beginning of a journey

important to make sure the team develops the basic characteristics required for co-creation. Simply put, they must have developed a shared framework of knowledge (collective knowledge base), and they must be able to work as a team. Without these characteristics, the team will not be able to co-create.

Onboarding

A good container is characterized by community (togetherness), trust, safety, engagement, and clarity (clear expectations). Our job in this stage is to convince people to feel safe with and trust our process while at the same time bonding them together and raising excitement.

Setting this container begins by establishing trust. In order to reach a high level of collective knowledge, team members must learn to trust each other—as a team. They need to learn about each other's capabilities, such as their knowledge and skills, to the extent where they will be able to depend on these collective capabilities.

Key to establishing such mutual understanding, and the trust that evolves with it, is authenticity. Authenticity is an attitude *within* people is that cultivates trust *between* people, and this attitude can be nurtured. As such, our choice of activities for onboarding the team is constrained by the fact that we *must* establish authentic interactions. Fortunately, the sense of authenticity is one that we can create by being authentic ourselves, complemented by activities that we describe below.

Before we move on to onboarding techniques and guidelines, we caution against the assumption that trust comes quickly from these methods. Deeper levels of trust are built over time, and complete trust only exists in utopia. In reality, the trust between two individuals is a constantly evolving variable, which means that a team always functions based on a complicated network of trust and interdependencies. Yet without trust people will not let others know what type of knowledge they possess, nor will they be prone to utilize their knowledge for others. Trust is a necessity that needs to be built between the team members before the team can be expected to start performing collectively. For this reason, we often follow what Napoleon once said to his army, "Slow down! I am in a hurry." If the team members—or at least the majority of the team members—are strangers to each other, trust building needs to be started from scratch and continually reinforced throughout the Climb.

To use the container metaphor, trust is one of the raw ingredients that make a container possible. Without it the container will be structurally unsound, and participants within it will likely withhold their full potential out of fear of what might happen. If people are suspicious of each other or the motivations behind the process, there is little chance they will open up and be authentic, nor feel safe enough to explore. Trust creates the safety net to stretch boundaries.

Manage Perceived Risk

A guideline especially salient to the climb is to manage perceived risk—the sense of safety among participants.

Less perceived risk = more open dialogue.
More perceived risk = less open dialogue.

This is a guideline that we always take into consideration when onboarding. Personalities have a lot to do with how much or little an individual contributes to a dialogue, and it is all too easy for us to label someone as "shy" or "extroverted" based on their activity. These may or may not be accurate impressions. Less noticeable is how risk affects engagement. A normally outspoken person may say very little when they perceive risk, and vice versa. This was an especially important consideration in our work in Asia, where the thought of shame (losing face) often put a stop on a group's willingness to engage in the types of dialogues we need for co-creation. In Asia and elsewhere, the perception of risk decreases by giving permissions to speak freely about anything, not just the topic. But alone this can be insufficient. Trust and familiarity are the real answer. When people get past platitudes and the desire to appear socially harmonious, they open up and begin authentic dialogues. They begin to act with courage, one of the pillars of co-creation. Yes, this can lead to heated debates, but that is a creative tension we need. Without energy there is little to harness.

We put this guideline up front because it influences all our other choices. Preparations and onboarding should manage perceived risk as we build the bonds between people. If the safety net is woven tightly, the team will be much more willing to make the leaps you will ask of them.

Techniques and Guidelines

Ideally much has been done to set the container early on in the co-creative process, before entering the group engagement. To Recap Part I:

1. Through stakeholder dialogues and interviews, you have gained the client and team's trust in the lead-up to a program. They believe in you, giving you the creative freedom to design and lead a co-creative process.
2. The creative brief, initially co-designed with the stakeholders, brings clarity and sets expectations with a clear program description, rationale, and other relevant information. It also generates energy and engagement by illustrating the integration of needs.
3. The environment (physical and symbolic) is designed to help establish a conducive atmosphere for co-creation. Knowing that space they walk into will have a major impact on the team's perceptions and workflow, you have created or rearranged the tangible environment to disrupt normal working modes. The physical spatial design is complemented with semiotic primers and culture hubs to facilitate socialization and play.

4. The process design is built upon the architecture of the Co-Creative Journey, using techniques that create an oscillation between the Known and the Unknown in search of the New. You have chosen activities that touch on all three aspects of the journey to harness the most potential from your team.
5. You have shown up internally prepared to be the tuning fork for the process, with the requisite awareness to see and move with the energy of the group. You are ready to flex and flow as needed to tap into the team's potential and guide it toward creative outcomes.

If you can check off these five preparatory steps, then you have already set an initial container with the right qualities. Once in the space with the team, it is time to finalize setting the container by bonding the group to the process and to each other. There are many ways to approach this issue, and most of these activities could be commonly categorized as *Team Building*. There are a few simple steps that should be taken, in one form or another, when trying to weld a group of strangers into an effective team—learning to know each other, sharing experiences with each other, showing emotions to one another, creating something common, or reaching a common goal together. In design, these activities are often woven together in a dress rehearsal.

Dress Rehearsal

Many product design project courses have taken it as a common practice to start their student projects with a more or less structured team building activity. In Stanford University course Global Design Innovation (ME310), the format has been known as Paper Bike, a two-week long team challenge during which each team builds a 'Paper Bike' using only paper or cardboard as their material. This exercise ends in a tournament in which the teams compete against each other with these paper bikes. The challenge forces the teams to go through a full yet rapid cycle of product design, during which they face common team building challenges under a strict schedule. Similarly, Aalto University course Product Development Project (PdP) kicks off with a PD6 Workshop, short for "Product Design Process in 6 hours." During this exercise, the student teams collaborate with their industry sponsors to complete a rapid product design challenge. Again, the team members face many typical challenges related to team dynamics, and due to the time pressure caused by the extremely tight schedule, the teams are forced to find ways to overcome any issues that might be causing them friction.

These examples, and many similar programs in other schools, have been built to create a first round of shared experience for fresh teams, along with teaching some practical product design and development skills, methods, and practices. According to the previously introduced *supercompensation theory*, skills development takes place during the recovery period after an exercise. The recovery from the first exercise round in this case could be enhanced and sped up by a simple, reflective wrap-up session. During such a session, the team is guided to relive the key stages of their exercise, then to analyze it, and finally to identify and point out any lessons learned that will need to be considered for the following stages of co-creation.[1]

After such an exercise, even when done as quick, superficial session, the teams will be better prepared. They have a deeper understanding of the challenges—both internal and external—that they might be facing during their co-creation project. Internal challenges are issues related to how well the team works together, and external challenges are issues outside the team's direct control, such as activities of competitors, changes in legislation, and shifts in global economy.

Dress rehearsals meet several early process needs. They are the first stages of team building, giving everyone a sense of their colleagues and how they act under pressure. In these contexts the first interpersonal bonds are formed, and in many programs much effort is spent helping participants understand leadership and good teamwork. The dress rehearsal is also the time to introduce the overall process and relevant skills needed. While these are often abbreviated versions of what will come, the introductions help to establish the collective intelligence needed to innovate. Finally, dress rehearsals set expectations and generate deeper engagement with each other and the process—both vital to setting the container.

The Wider Toolkit

Design, education, and business each present their own challenges. Different contexts and constraints require additional techniques to choose from. Our toolkit consists of a wide array of possible tools, derived from the fields of design, organizational change, leadership, psychology, and consciousness studies. It would be a daunting task to try and list all of these. Extending the metaphor of packing a backpack, here we make a selection and present what we consider to be fundamentals. They are fundamental in that they are field-tested methods—reliably doing what they set out to do. Moreover, these techniques and guidelines help to establish PACE, special qualities of a container that support resonance and creative breakthroughs. There are many more tools out there that may do the job as well as or even better than the ones we list here, but these are the ones we know to be effective. We invite you to add to these as you build your own signature toolkit.

Co-creation often begins with a memorable opening to galvanize the energy and commitment of the group, followed by team building activities that help people get to know each other, set and manage expectations, and establish a social contract on how they will work together.

Evocative Inputs

We can strengthen the container by bringing in powerful inputs at the right times in a program. In the roadmaps offered in the last chapter, each program began with an evocative input. In the workshop focused on unlocking creativity to make a difference, the program began with an impassioned speech by the founder about the organizational values and commitment to excellence. The Insights Creative Rollercoaster began with short videos on creative leadership and the space between.

An evocative opening speech or impactful media help to set the stage for the actors (your team), reminding them of why they are there and aligning their attention to that task. In some cases the opening will be the first time they have actually paid attention, or even been informed, of what they are doing. In many other cases, even with thorough preparations people show up not fully comprehending the scope of the process or challenge. For these reasons it is key that you clearly communicate the essence of the creative brief up front.

It can help if you bring in a guest speaker to frame the issue. Guest speakers are given a special consideration, and they may need to play a more directive role than you want to. A good speaker can not only set the direction and generate energy toward it, but also serve to validate the process you are asking people to trust you with. This is often why we have keynotes, inspirational individuals that people will believe just because of who they are or what they have done. When Steve Jobs came out and gave an evocative speech, you can bet people listened. Once the energy is kicked up and everyone is on the same page, you can then move into activities to bond the team and build collective knowledge.

Getting to Know You

Socialization activities are common tools to help people learn about each other, their work styles, and their expectations. Even if an *Xd* knows a lot about their participants, the team must be given the opportunity to share that information with each other. Socialization activities are when people build the bonds of trust. We facilitate this with activities that encourage authentic sharing information about each other, collaboratively working on tasks, and play.

One of the most valuable activities you can do in this early stage is share expectations with each other. Asking participants about their expectations helps the facilitator know what forces are at play and adjust accordingly to give a valuable experience. Moreover, by asking you are giving permission for people to be authentic. This helps set the container by "thickening" the social space—strengthening interpersonal bonds. Populating the field of information with people's real feelings vs. telling them what their expectations should be is part of establishing an authentic and empathic social space.

One means to establish authenticity is through shared vulnerability. In her TED talk, Barbara Brown argues that vulnerability is essential for a good container.[2] Sharing our fears and weaknesses alongside our strengths and expectations rapidly thickens the social space by deepening the mutual knowing of one another. It humanizes the connection, which in turn cultivates empathy and trust.

We agree that vulnerability is a wonderful tool. It is not, however, easy to use in all contexts. Trying to get Asian students to explore personal vulnerabilities in a group setting can be tricky, and it might have the effect of damaging rather than building the container. We must take caution with the techniques we use, nuancing them to the cultures in which we work. Vulnerability can work in Asian contexts if you make it a group expression rather than a solo one. The trick is to shift the expression of deep feelings from how "I" feel to how "we" feel, thus reducing the possibility of any individual losing face. When you accomplish this, it creates a special "we" container, wherein permissions have been set for anyone in the group to have the full range of feelings expressed in the group share.

Socialization activities also allows for people to decide how they "show up"—what face they want to display for the engagement. Most people are social chameleons to some extent, meaning that they have a variety of dispositions and roles that they can play. There may be times when a person needs to be a leader, and other times a supporter. Some days they might show up with a lot of energy, and others less so. During socialization people make choices on how they want to show up and gauge how other people do the same. These are the moments in which team dynamics begin to take shape, and it is important for the *Xd* to pay careful attention while also allowing the team to find its own comfort zone.

There are times when you need to be directive about team formation, and there is also great value in facilitating self-organization. A common pattern in nature, self-organization is when a system organizes itself without external control. With people, self-organization can be used to help groups form based on common interest, and the result is usually a much more engaged and productive team. Open Space Technology (OST), initially developed by Harrison Owen, is an excellent example of self-organizing systems.[3] OST can be used at multiple points throughout a creative process, or it can be a format for an entire collective ideation process. OST is highly co-creative in that it purposefully creates an egalitarian social space where the participants come up with the issues to discuss and the solutions. OST has very few rules of engagement, and they are put into place only to provide a skeleton framework of engagement and set permissions for people to move about based on interest rather than loyalty, friendship, or any other social guideline. The beauty of OST is that it encourages emergence—self-organization at work. It is also a great socialization tool. Open Space engagements, because they are so unstructured, open a space (hence the name) for people to fill with their own ways of working. In any OST engagement, people will learn a lot about each other's styles and personalities, as well as the ideas they bring into dialogue.

What you must watch out for is group formation based on familiarity or politeness rather than real interest. Co-workers, friends, and cultures will cluster together into teams because of comfort. We are all more comfortable with people whom we perceive to be members of the same social or cultural groups. Given the fact that we often work with established social groupings, in the beginning it can be useful to direct people into teams that disrupt existing comfort zones. After the team has shared and become a micro-community where everyone is part of the "we," then self-organization is more effective.

Open Spaces, as wonderful as it is, takes a lot of time. Card games are a more structured exercise that can be done in a much tighter time window. Cards can be used in a variety of ways, including styles mapping, creative ideation, and even strategic planning. *Getting to Know You* cards are those that facilitate personality and style sharing. Examples we use include the Values Cards, ESP cards, Thinkpak, and Dixit. There are a host of other decks available on the MethodKit website, and you can even design your own for them to print.[4]

We use cards because they bring an element of surprise and enjoyment to socialization. They can also add an unexpected depth to sharing activities. Cards, although initially perceived as "just games," are incredibly powerful tools for mapping out many unspoken dimensions of people. As an example, when we used value cards to help our students get to know each other before forming design teams, what emerged were very different worldviews and styles of leadership. In one group a heated yet respectful debate ensued between students whom had never before even hinted that they held such strong views. Notably, each became a leader of a team.

Let's take a closer look at how to use a card game. Our colleague from Brains on the Beach developed the ESP cards, which is an ingeniously fun way of improving team chemistry through styles mapping.[5] ESP (empathy, style, preference) cards are grouped into four styles (Fig. 8.2, next page):

As with many card games, people are asked to choose from a table full of cards which ones represent them. They then share these cards in small groups with the options to trade—ultimately trying to have a "hand" with three or four cards that depict their style. From this point there are a few different options available, depending on how much time you have and what you want to do. The cards can be used to create diverse teams, each comprised of individuals with different dominant color suits (e.g. mostly blues). They can be used as tools in a longer dialogue about styles in teams. Or they can be used in another activity such as Six Thinking Hats, which has people play one of six different roles to develop empathy and new ways of thinking about a subject. The possibilities go on, but common to all of them is an active learning approach that impacts all three aspects of the creative journey. By having fun you can build dynamic teams, raise the energy and excitement of the group, and form the initial collective knowledge base.

We complement card games with related activities such as personal maps, personal shields or totems, asset inventories, and other style maps. Each of these is a self-assessment that allows, as we have noted above, for people to decide how they show up and share that with others. One thing that we have noticed is that people will invariably create a different representation of themselves each time you ask them to do this. The reason for this is that the essentialized Western notion of Self is simply not true. How

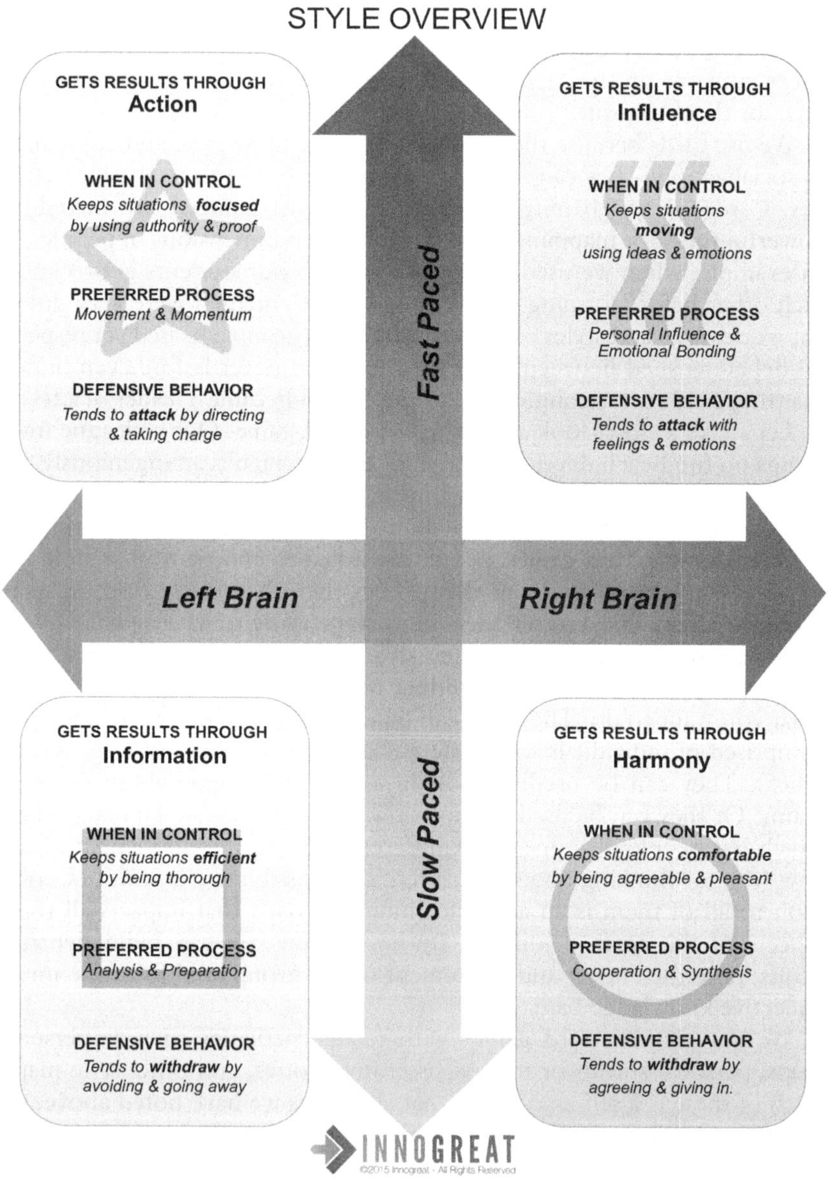

Fig. 8.2 InnoGreat ESP cards

humans construct the Self is a discussion too long for this book, but the stance we take is that identity (the Self) is a strategic assertion at any point in time. We *are* whatever we present our Self to be and what others perceive us to be. It is all perception, which is why socialization activities are so important. They forge the perceptions that everyone is going to act on. And because we are sensitive to context and a host of other influences, most people will present a slightly different Self depending on how they feel that day and their perceptions of the environment (physical and social). For us, it doesn't matter who a person is in their other roles. It matters who they show up as, and that is what we need to share.

Socialization consists of more than just words and diagrams. We communicate a great deal of information about one another through our clothing, our choice of food and beverage, and especially paralinguistic communication. Paralinguistics are all the acts of communicating we do without words or text, such as a body language. We encourage tapping into such additional forms of engagement, rounding out our socialization toolkit with bodily interactions. Somatic exercises get people out of their heads and into closer interpersonal spaces. A favorite, from tai chi, is push hands. This is a basic yet profoundly impactful exercise. Push hands requires two people to face one another and touch palms gently. One person leads in moving, while the other does their best to mirror with their own body. The roles then shift, and sometimes the pair loses sense of who is leading and who is following. That is the ideal state, for synchronized movement is a perfect expression of co-creation.

We cannot explain why, but somatic exercises like push hands thicken the social space just as effectively as vulnerability. When people touch one another, a unique bond is formed. Perhaps it is because it requires trust and surrender to let go of thinking and feel your way into things. Perhaps it is because we so rarely allow ourselves to be that close to our colleagues. Whatever the reason, engaging with our bodies is an effective tool to test the edges of comfort zones and deepen bonds. Somatic activities thus nicely complement other socialization techniques.

Rules of Engagement

Co-creation works best when the team decides on how they will work together. Creating a social contract is often the very first co-creative act, and it is an important one. Just as we take on different roles and behaviors in a game, we do a similar thing in a co-creative process. By taking on roles and adopting different behaviors, we can achieve something different from our default way of working. And just like a game, those roles and behaviors are temporary. We agree to them for a particular space and time, and at the end of the process we may or may not choose to continue to abide by them.

Giving permission for a team to decide **How** it will work is empowering. It also lays out rules that, by virtue of the fact that the team actually wrote them, they are much more likely to stick to. The *Xd* is part of this process, and he or she can make the case for certain procedural rules and/or introduce the "givens"—guidelines and constraints defined through stakeholder dialogues.

This is a point where constraints benefit the creative process. Creativity without constraints can easily lead to non-realistic blue-sky thinking. While at times we need this, people tend to work better when they have a basic framework to work within. Introducing timelines, commitments, deliverables desired, and resources are a few of the givens you can introduce to frame the engagement. The social contract can then be built together around this frame.

Time together is a valuable resource, so it is not necessary to spend a lot of time here. The main point is to give the group a chance early in the process to declare the manner in which they want to work together. Throughout the process you can draw the group's attention to how they are operating out of this agreement or challenge the group if they are slipping into behaviors not in alignment with what was agreed to.

Finally, a word of caution. Allowing a team to co-create their own social contract can be incredibly empowering, but it can also have the opposite effect if not managed properly. We must take different personalities into account when giving permission for such an open-ended process. The space created can easily be filled by dominant egos and/or well-presented ideas, neglecting the shy or less vocal team members. It is paramount to ensure that everyone feels their value. Even if roles shift throughout the creative journey (which they will), making agreements about how these roles will come about and be shared increases engagement and creates the feeling of mutual empowerment we need.

To clarify this point, let's consider two scenarios. Scenario 1 is a design team whose composition was carefully selected based on the skills each person brings. In Scenario 1 participants have a clearly defined value up front, but leadership has yet to be determined. The team decides to work on the creative brief first, laying out what they want to accomplish before deciding how to approach it. Once this is done, they then decide that rotating leadership will suit their needs best. At some points throughout the journey, each person will be asked to lead part of the process. Anyone who needs help can ask for an assist from other team members, ensuring that each person has the opportunity to lead and the resources available to do so.

Scenario 2 is the formation of an executive leadership team for an organizational change initiative. The CEO and *Xd* have invited a small group of people from leadership positions throughout the organization to make up this team. The mission of team is to co-create the change initiative and how to implement it. In this scenario, the CEO has agreed to hold the space for emergent leadership. There are no pre-assigned roles coming into the process, and she is not going to tell anyone what to do or how to do it. In the initial gathering, the team, with the CEO's encouragement, also agrees to refrain from assigning roles. These will be decided throughout the journey as it becomes apparent who is best suited for each part.

In these scenarios the teams made their own decisions about leadership and roles. Even though they chose two different approaches, both were co-creative in that the entire team was involved in the process. Ensuring that everyone has had the opportunity to participate and be heard in this early stage of co-creation sets the standard for activities to come.

Co-creating the Mission Statement

The creative brief can take on several forms, from a one-sentence breakthrough question to a detailed design document. Allowing the team to create from scratch, or even fill in, a creative brief has similar effects to co-creating the social contract. Both acts empower the team while binding it to the commitments it lays out. The social contract is *How* they will work together. The creative brief and mission statement contextualize and further develop the *How* with the *Why*, *What*, *When*, and *Where*.

In our last chapter we stated that co-creating the mission statement allows the team to determine their own focal point. This is like giving a group a sailboat and then asking, "Where do you want to go?" What you are really asking is how they envision meeting the challenge. The *Where* (the focus point) may be defined by the objectives of the project, but like navigation there are many possible courses we chart to get there. This is an early opportunity to allow for emergent leadership in your team. It may not be always useful, but see what happens when you present the creative brief and ask the team "How do you want to get there?"

What we don't want in a mission statement is a burning bridge approach. Propositions, such as "We have communication issues that are ruining our productivity," "We need to be more innovative or we are going out of business," or "This is a shitty design," all followed by "Fix it" are not constructive. A project may begin due to problems like these, but just stating the need to solve it is not a very good mission statement. What is needed is a reframing of the problem into a challenge. A resolution-centered approach can transform the energy around an issue from pessimism to enthusiasm. Bert Hellinger, one of the founders of the Constellations methodology, said the following about evoking creativity.

> The creative force doesn't work in relation to problems, but only in relation to resolutions. When I confront a person with a problem or describe it to that person, I'm in a one-up position, but we search for a resolution together as equals.[6]

This quote highlights a key part of forming a co-creative mission statement. The attitude is not pessimistic (Fix it or else!), nor a service mindset (What I can do for you?), but rather "What can we do together?" Problem statements draw one form of energy. When restated as something that invites resolution, the needs story or question draws energy to it, igniting the creative fire.

A simple but effective tool to help here, or when a team needs to move from a basic creative brief into generative dialogue or brainstorming, is point-of-view (POV) exercises. The Stanford University d.school has three POV tools: the Madlib, Analogy, and Wanted Ad.

The d.school's "bootcamp bootleg" method cards are a set of tools commonly used in participatory design. Each method card explains "Why use…" and "How to use…" for the tool described. The "Why use a POV analogy," for example, reads:

> A point-of-view (POV) is your reframing of a design challenge into an actionable problem statement that will launch you into generative ideation. A POV Analogy can be a concise and compelling way to capture how you define the design challenge (your POV!). A good analogy will yield a strong directive of how you go about designing the final solution.[7]

"How to use a POV analogy" begins with,

> Use concise analogies to distill ideas. Metaphors and similes can encapsulate your insights in a rich picture. Discover metaphors from the work you do in synthesizing information, and looking at analogies between your user's situation and other areas.

The classic example from industry that the POV method card refers to is "Personal music player as jewelry," the analogy that led to the iPod. An analogy common to luxury goods is "Beverage X (usually expensive liquors) as high social class." A spin on that is "Coca Cola as fun," which is an underlying analogy for the recent coke advertisements. All of these open up new creative spaces and engage the team by challenging them to think differently about the product or service they are designing. They *create* energy, the goal in developing a mission statement that evokes the creative force.

Co-creating the creative brief and mission statement sets the container by involving the team in the creative process from the very beginning. Rather than being told what to do, they are co-determining their own path. Yes, that path has goals and constraints, but giving permission to collectively decide how they will work within that framework is incredibly empowering. Permission and aid in this process are perhaps the most valuable gifts you can give a creative team early on. Not only will they value and contribute to the process more, but their perspective of you will shift from "controller" or "guide" to "enabler." You *become* the midwife, a welcome and necessary part of their delivery.

Rituals

In Chap. 4 we dedicated a section to the power of rituals, explaining that rituals are the central mechanism through which culture is created and conveyed. They are the vehicle for creating and transmitting the mythology of a group. We argued for the need to designing rituals in which the people themselves create meaning, and then displaying the artifacts of that creation in the environment to give it culture. The guidelines we describe above—evocative inputs, socialization, and co-creating the social contract and mission statement—are the means to this end. As described in Part I, an optimal process flow uses the outputs from one activity as inputs for another. Social contracts and team symbols, two such outputs, can be used as the foundation of the team culture. Put them up on the walls so that everyone can see. These artifacts become a common reference point—tangible manifestations of shared experiences and expressions. These objects, physical and symbolic, remind teams of where they come from (e.g. group identity work) and what they have made.

We also stated that rituals encourage "stepping into" different modes of interaction and behavior, increase group solidarity, convey key information or rules of behavior, and encourage designed behaviors. For co-creation, we want people to step into what the Center for Courage & Renewal calls "Circles of Trust."[8] A circle of trust is a good initial container, a "magic circle" wherein group dynamics are different from the norm. They are situated realities in which people who know one another are encouraged to suspend their everyday relationships and try out something new. In the context of a diverse team with no shared history, we take advantage of the fact that people do not know each other and avoid external roles and statuses that could interfere with the situated reality. To do this we must create an internally coherent situated identity—a temporal culture for the duration of the co-creative journey.

From an anthropological perspective, these circles are very similar to a tribal council. A tribal council, or at least the romanticized version of one, consists of a group of elders (leaders in that form of society) who gather regularly for festivals, decision-making, and sharing. Their social contract is one that emphasizes mutual respect, open dialogue, and collective decision-making. The chief may have the final say on some matters, but he or she places great value in the ideas of others and often makes decisions collectively with the council. Our fictional, co-creative tribe is one that values balanced power and seeks to ensure that everyone's voice is heard. Their social contract serves to support this culture, and so too does their way of interacting. What can we do to establish our own tribal council?

The answer is to follow the same ritual logic that tribes use to create and maintain their cultural system. We design rituals that establish an environment characterized by the following:

1. Separation (as in rites of passage): Separation is necessary to deconstruct the normal social relations/roles that people occupy.
2. Authenticity: Authentic interactions create trust, without which the container is unstable.

3. Connection: We must bond the group together and connect them with the wider issues at stake.
4. Engagement: The team must have a buy-in, either in the form of a collective goal or a problem to solve. This is the initial energy required to start the reaction.

How do we do that? Part of it, as alluded to above, lies in the environment design. Something as simple as a sign that reads "Say what you mean, and Mean what you say" can have a profound impact on how people perceive the space they are entering into. For readers that skipped straight to Part II, we recommend going back to Part I for guidelines on how to set the stage for co-creation. Complementing the environment are ritual engagements.[9] We like to begin with a very basic ritual: the check-in.

A check-in, where people sit in a circle of chairs and share briefly how they are feeling, is a highly symbolic act that can be used to open the space for activities and set the container for the day. It helps people come fully into the space and be present within it, rather than sitting quietly thinking of a million other things. The talking circle emphasizes the discipline of being present by drawing people's attention to their ability to focus fully on the other people as opposed to their own thoughts. It is a micro practice of deep listening, a skill that we use extensively.

Checkouts at the end of the day are equally useful. In checkouts, people again briefly state how they are feeling, but the content can be quite different from the morning. Checkouts differ in that the expressions are usually directly related to how a person feels about the process they have just gone through. Checkouts are thus a very good gauge for how well your process is going, helping the *Xd* make adjustments while showing empathy toward how everyone feels.

Checkouts also validate the experience of the day. This is especially powerful when acknowledging the emotional highs and lows. When people realize that they are all natural feelings that everyone goes through, they gain courage. The only feeling you need to watch out for is boredom. That is an indication that someone has disengaged the process, and adjustments may be warranted to re-engage that person and whoever else silently agrees with them.

Check-ins, checkouts, and other group dialogues are great ways to express membership, simply by virtue of being in them with others. We ritualize these by making them an established part of every opening and closing. In short time, they become a routine cultural act that people rely on to become present, authentically share, and give feedback on their journey.

Another possibility is to hold a formal opening ritual. A ritual opening takes more time and planning, but it can pay dividends for setting the container and establishing a uniqueness to your program. The story in Chap. 4 of a hotel ballroom setup with a giant teepee in the middle and no chairs is one example. When the 300 participants came in for their co-creative workshop, they were astounded and surprised. Immediately, the catalysts achieved separation. This entry, followed by activities parallel to those described here, set a very strong container for that process.

An opening ritual can take a "shock and awe" approach, establishing separation through radical difference from norms. An alternate technique is to make separation an intentional act. There are many approaches that value the power of intention, from Native American purpose quests to the popular Law of Attraction. Intention is powerful not only because it sets a direction but also because it can help us step into new roles and develop courage. Take, for example, the following ritual opening:

Step One: Relax into stillness (mindfulness exercise).
Step Two: Focus on your intention for the day/week (visioning).
Step Three: Cross ritual threshold (rite of passage).
Step Four: Hold the intention (transition into new attitude/role).

This opening begins with presence to eliminate distractions from the past or future, neither of which are in the room. Next is crystallizing awareness to a focal point (the intention), followed by creating a symbolic space for people to step into whatever role and attitude is necessary to enact their vision. This threshold space can be internal and imaginary, but it is better if give a physical presence. A simple piece of cloth for them to step over or a doorway to walk through can serve this purpose.

People are extraordinarily good actors, even those who feel they don't have an acting bone in their body. This opening ritual sets the context for and facilitates stepping into another role, which might otherwise be very difficult for someone to do. Once in a new role, people develop courage quickly. This is partly since the role they are playing is not their normal Self, and they feel more free to do things that they might otherwise avoid. Yet another reason is because they have already been courageous enough just to cross the threshold. That may have been perceived to be a big risk, and after that it gets easier to take initiative. Developing courage is a subtle art, but setting the container as a safe place to test one's edges, knowing that they will have permissions and support, is a good start.

Weaving Three into One

Setting a strong container is an essential step in the co-creative journey. The activities in this stage work best when they weave together all three aspects of the journey. A rule of thumb you can use to select activities that affect all three aspects is head, heart, hand. Any activity that asks people to think about, feel into, and physically act with others engages multiple intelligences and the interactional field with the rest of the team.

A tight (successful) weave creates and harnesses positive energy, forges a team dynamic characterized by trust and authentic interactions, and lays the foundation of a collective knowledge base. Together these elements are the ingredients for a container that can survive and thrive in the Unknown.

It may appear that team building and setting the container occur prior to knowledge creation and sharing, but in actuality these processes can co-occur. It is really up to the *Xd* to decide what flow works for them and their client. Brainstorming is one example of an activity that gives you maximum bang for the buck (weaves all three aspects).

While the most common goal of brainstorming is to generate a large quantity of ideas to be further examined, the activity is also an opportunity for a team to practice listening and building on each other's ideas. Brainstorming generates knowledge by leveraging the collective thinking of a group, intentionally turning up the generative part of the brain and turning down the evaluative part.[10] It can be used any time in a creative journey any time you need to come up with ideas.

Like a dress rehearsal, Brainstorming can be an excellent opening activity in that it gives everyone a taste of what it is like to work with the rest of the team. The energy is usually high and mood positive. Throughout the activity people will reveal aspects of their personality and the roles they like to play. Brainstorms also draw attention to key dynamics of teamwork, such as the ability to listen, lead, and follow. In the CCI Dialogue Sessions, for example, we used brainstorming as a way of shedding light on six types of roles that people typically play: leader, follower, builder, antagonist, mediator, and observer. After the first 30-minute session, we sat in a circle and discussed who played what part in the brainstorm. Through this reflective addition to brainstorming, the students gained an awareness into roles that allowed them to take ownership of their dominant role and develop empathy for other roles. Because the point of the Dialogue Sessions was to improve upon dialogical skills, we would then have a second brainstorm where students had to play different roles, much like Six Thinking Hats. This deepened their empathy and made the students receptive to the ensuing training, in which they learned techniques for working with different roles. Not only did they learn how to communicate and work better together, their ideas also improved once they learned how to step into the space of others. This, we shall see, is another vital skill in co-creation that can be cultivated early on.

In that brainstorming can be a first step for the team working together, the ideas generated may be less important than what the interactions among team members teach us. That does not mean throw out the ideas generated! To the contrary, this is an opportunity to see what intrigues or excites people. Keep the ideas with the most energy behind them, ignoring for the moment feasibility. With any brainstorm you want to preserve a breadth of ideas without settling for a safe or easy solution. In doing so you establish a more robust field of collective knowledge.

Building Collective Knowledge

Early on we used the analogy of a safari expedition to explain the value of a good container. The container is your Jeep or Land Rover, the vehicle that carries you onward and keeps you feeling safe in the vast wilderness. You don't want to be in cheap sedan when there are lions lurking in the bush. A strong container gives us the ability and confidence to explore what we know and what we don't know. That exploration begins by creating a shared understanding of the territory.

Metaphorically, the primary objective of the climb is to reach the peak of existing knowledge. In practice this means that the team members will share their relevant preexisting knowledge with each other while simultaneously looking into what others have discovered about the topic before. Through this process of sharing and acquiring, the team will build a collective base of knowledge that will act as the foundation for the rest of their journey (Fig. 8.3, next page).

This gradually advancing stage leads the team first through a territory that is already well known and familiar to at least some members of the team. Since somebody in the team has good enough knowledge about these areas, the path is quite predictable, and hence this part rarely contains

Fig. 8.3 Bridging more and more knowledge between team members during the Climb

any big surprises. During this part, the more experienced participants share their previous knowledge and experiences so that everyone within the team can grasp their understanding of how to deal with the obstacles that might still lie ahead.

After the well-known areas are left behind, the stage continues through territories that are less familiar to the team, but which still have been explored and charted by somebody else before them. Even though the team doesn't have experience in these parts, they still know for sure that there is a safe passage available, as long as they can find it. The destination is clear, even though it might still be unclear *how* exactly this destination could be reached. The team has to keep pushing forward on their course and use their prior experiences to get past any obstacles on their way.

Through the practice of sharing and synthesizing, bridges will be built between previously isolated instances of information. Over time, a network of knowledge bridges will be generated, acting as a web that binds many smaller bits of knowledge into collective knowledge. The network can then be used to utilize knowledge within the team. We can visualize the types of knowledge bridges formed as follows (Fig. 8.4):

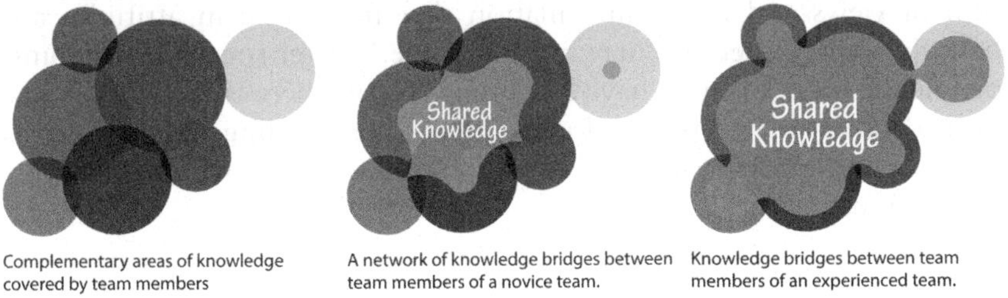

Fig. 8.4 Knowledge bridges

In design, a project room may be a powerful tool for bridging knowledge within the team during the research phase, when the team is sent out to observe user behaviors or a new context for a product or service. The team takes pictures, makes notes of observations, and may even collect artifacts from the study. They then begin to bridge and share their knowledge with the other by posting their notes, photos, and other visual information on the walls of their space while simultaneously explaining the relevance of this information to their teammates. While at first look everything seems like a jumbled mess, by looking at the data inputs together, the team begins to identify points of value for their design. Regrouping content, using string to connect data points, just glazing through the material at until a flash of insight comes ... all are equally good ways to look at a wall of information and begin to weave it into something meaningful. By doing this process as a team, the group forms shared understandings and models of what they are working with.

From walls full of sticky notes to mind maps and elegant diagrams, collective knowledge can be harnessed and shared through a variety of techniques. Affinity diagrams, asset maps, mood boards, spectrums, and LEGO® SERIOUS PLAY® are all ways to visualize and analyze knowledge. Some of these describe a scenario. For example, breaking down the experience of a hotel front desk interaction. Descriptive maps, like the organizational timelines, culture boards, and user journey maps, aim to represent and share what we can observe. Descriptive maps help us see the Known and identify the edges that need to be explored.

Other knowledge maps aim to bring coherence to, organize, or evaluate ideas. These can take on many forms depending on how you want to slice the pie—what variables are chosen to classify and determine relationships between units of data (information), as well as what lenses you use to look at the information. Among the tools we use, spectrum maps are helpful in that they visually lay out the diversity of perspectives team members have on a particular issue. They allow for anonymous expression of views and reveal information that has a role in attitudes and behaviors that otherwise may not be visible.[11] After spectrum mapping, people are more likely to have a holistic view of where they stand in relation to other perspectives, all without anyone standing out. This technique is particularly valued in contexts where saving face or shame is a motivational factor.

Complementing these are affinity maps, a categorical tool. Affinity maps have value after a brainstorming session when you need to create meaning from all of generative ideas presented. An affinity map reveals and can help us break embedded patterns and/or mental models by sorting information into relationships. Put into diagrams, affinity maps become mind maps, where relationships are indicated by lines, colors, shapes, and distance.

We can further examine and sort relationships by changing the constraints of the dialogue. Designers like to introduce constraints as levers to focus or reframe the field of knowledge. "How would Apple do it?," "It needs to be made from vinyl," or "We need to do this with no money," and "On a train, this would..." are all examples. Imposing constraints is a fantastic tool that can be used at any stage of the creative process. A tool we use derives from Theme-Centered Interaction, a method introduced earlier as a means to build ecosystem awareness. We ask the group to look at ideas on the levels of "Me, We, and It." This produces a unique knowledge map that can be used in conjunction with other methods to flush out how an idea might impact different stakeholders in the value chain.

We can even be more adventurous by adding the element of theater. As Brown explains in *Change by Design*, acting can be a very useful design skill.

> Learning to feel comfortable acting out potential ideas is obviously important for anyone contemplating an experiential approach to prototyping—Mattel's Ivy Ross went so far as to teach new recruits to the Platypus program how to use improvisational acting techniques in the first couple of weeks of the session. Knowing some of the basics, such as how to build on the ideas of one's fellow actors and being willing to defer judgment of them, increases the likelihood that collaborative, real-time prototyping will be successful. The amateur theatrics of an experiential prototype can look foolish. It takes a certain confidence for individuals to loosen their ties, slip off their heels, and explore an idea through improvisation.[12]

The passage points to fundamental co-creative skills, from building on ideas to deferring judgment and encouraging play. Yet theater provides us with far more than just capacity building. It can create unique knowledge maps of each other, which is great for team building and also understanding the world of our teammates/end users/stakeholders. As an example, let's consider a common co-creative team, what IDEO calls the "unfocus group."

> One of the techniques we have developed at IDEO to keep the consumer-designer involved in the creation, evaluation, and development of ideas is the "unfocus group," where we bring an array of consumers and experts together in a workshop format to explore new concepts around a particular topic. Whereas traditional focus groups assemble a random group of "average" people who are observed, literally or figuratively, from behind a one-way mirror, the unfocus group identifies unique individuals and invites them to participate in an active, collaborative design exercise.[13]

Diversity comes with the price of unfamiliarity. The people in an unfocus group have little knowledge about the everyday world that the others live in, and that diverse life experience is precisely what we want to bring into the space between to develop collective knowledge. We can use theater as a fun method to share different lived realities. In one of our projects at CCI, we used a theatrical variation of the game called "Welcome to My World" to help two very different groups come together as one design team. Welcome to My World is based on the proposition that:

> Many of us make the mistaken assumption that others see what we see and know what we know. No one in the world shares your internal system map of reality. The best way to compare notes, so to speak, is to actually draw an external representation of what you think is happening.[14]

In the game people pair up with someone from a different background or organizational role and try to draw out how they envision their partner's everyday reality or a specific situation. Afterward they have a dialogue about the similarities and differences between what the person drawing depicted and reality. In our version at CCI, we skipped the drawing and had teams from each organizational background come up with a miniature play. They could do all the acting themselves, or they could recruit members of the "audience" in and have them improvise a role. We left it up to each team how they would use the space, what objects they would bring in, and even the script. The goal was to show the other group what a day in the life of a ___ was like. Each team had 30 minutes for their "play."

The next day we dedicated two hours to each "world," beginning with the play and then having dialogues to further understand one another. In the process, one group created user journey maps, and the other a composite character profile. These are important artifacts in design, knowledge maps that help clarify a target audience and their needs. In our case, these maps helped everyone capture each other's lived realities, resulting in much greater empathy, richer conversations, and budding friendships. For all the knowledge work we did, the theater was the most fondly remembered activity. It was a "win-win-win" in that it strengthened the container, bonded the team, and built valued collective knowledge.

These are just a few of the techniques to render knowledge in a collective space. Knowledge mapping techniques populate the informational field, establishing the space between with which the team can work. We want the space between to be rich with information from multiple sources. For this reason, we do our best to fill it not only with conceptual knowledge but also with embodied, metaphorical, and intuitive ways of knowing. The space between is the field where all forms of knowing, as well as the emotions and interpersonal dynamics of the team, come together. The more raw "stuff" we have in it, the more potential there is for novel intersections—our source of creative insights.

The Road to Discovery

Dorothy was now ready to set her team on their way, and she sent them out on their first mission. During this first part of the climb, new knowledge was to be produced through two parallel processes—the internal search and the external search. In an internal search, new ideas are generated in-house through brainstormings and similar, more or less systematic methods. In an external search, ideas are collected from outside the home organization. Inspiration and ideas are extracted from existing products and existing solutions so that everyone can get a deeper understanding of all aspects of the problem they are solving, and of the solutions that already exist. In ACME's case, this meant that Dorothy sent her teammates out of the office with their cameras, recorders, and notepads to start digging into what their competitors are doing, what their potential users have used to solve their challenges in this field before, and what researchers have recently discovered about baby monitoring.

The team was able to get good information from their survey of existing solutions with a simple Google search, and the most interesting ones were chosen for a more in-depth examination. Simultaneously, Tim and Allen had started to look into the latest research on biometric sleep monitoring and on sleep behavior of infants, while Tina and David were looking at various parenting support communities for expert insights and lead-users. And as soon as new information started to pour in, the team began to generate and share ideas about their own solution. A docking station for plugging in the baby monitor, an x-ray monitor and an ultrasound for monitoring the insides of a baby, and many more sketches were drawn just within the first two days. The climb was definitely on its way.

Collective knowledge relies not only on what people know coming into a process, but also on what they discover during it. As we start making the climb, where can we look to expand the knowledge base? The ACME illustration (above) sheds light on two parallel pathways, the internal and external search. Internal methods are those that tap into the existing knowledge of the team, using dialogical and related methodologies. External searches are research.

Design research includes ethnographic and other methods. Ethnography is used to understand potential users and the way they interact with the world. The methods, derived largely from anthropology and marketing, observe and participate with people in their natural settings. Ethnography is a minimally intrusive method to see life "as it is." Insights from such research serve to illuminate things they may not have previously seen, opening up space for innovation to meet or create needs.[15] For example, Dr. House says "Everybody lies." The observation that people lie is why we cannot let interview or survey answers dictate what we will design for people. Ethnographic observation gives us another perspective—peoples' actual behavior. People believe what they believe, even if their behavior tells something else. So we have to look beyond what they say and watch what they do. The sweet spot is where these two sources of information intercept.

Design research also includes more controlled environments to cultivate empathy or test specific aspects of a design idea. Prototyping for empathy entails the construction of a mock-up environment. The design team then role-plays the lived reality of the environment they have recreated to get a more direct, experiential understanding of users and their needs. The empathy developed through the exercise helps the design team see from users' perspective—an invaluable lesson.

Built environments can also serve as a way of testing out design ideas. We often use mock-ups and models to test assumptions and prototypes in the Rise, and these same methods can be applied during the Climb. As the ultimate goal of design ethnography is to produce a commercially viable solution that improves the quality of life for a target group, the research focuses on observing the changes that can be generated by introducing something new to the normal routines of test subjects. In order to make the testing setup as valid as possible, the research should be conducted in an authentic environment. A simple setup could consist of two sets of observation, of which the first one would be an unaffected control study, and the second one would be affected by a testable solution. Observations and interviews would be made for both setups, and particular emphasis is given to understanding how the test subjects behaved during the study and why they did so. A secondary objective can be to identify what types of impacts occurred after the testable solution was introduced and applied.

Complementing ethnographic and other user research, a lot of information can be found from books, scientific journals, and other forms of publications. Using a search engine to make a survey of these might be a good investment of time and would help you understand the extent of the problems and solutions that you are dealing with. Finding an expert could provide a valuable shortcut. Interviews of experts can give valuable insights, as these can react and build on the specific case you are working on—unlike passive information that you can collect from databases. But where and how would you look for these people? Finding a person who could help solve all your problems might not be a simple task, so most people won't even bother to try. It might help to understand that you don't need to find the right people immediately, but you can make a plan to locate them gradually instead. As long as you have a good idea of which direction to go first, chances are that your first step will help to determine the next one, which again will lead to the third one, and so on. This way, you will only need to (1) plan your first step and (2) prepare to follow wherever that leads.

Finally, in addition to looking for processed information from your own field, you might also want to look at your competitors and perhaps identify some parallel fields that could have solved similar problems in ways that could be utilized in your own context as well. For example, devices intended to speed up the recovery process for athletes or surgery patients may include some functions that could help relax an infant before or during its sleep. Looking into the research and the existing products within these parallel fields could provide some testable ideas for solutions while increasing the general understanding of the problems and opportunities related to the topic.

Internal and external searches are two pathways to build collective knowledge. But how do we go about these? Does everybody work on the same thing? Do we all sit in the same dialogue circles? Are these efficient means? The answer is no. Co-creation is collective creativity in that everyone is working toward the same set of goals, but it is not always collaborative. Sometimes the best approach is to divide into groups, or individuals, that pursue different pathways.

Working as a Team

Even with a detailed recipe, it is next to impossible to prepare a perfect soufflé if you have never seen and tasted one. And even if you have, it would still be very difficult to do if you are not familiar with the techniques required, such as separating eggs, beating egg whites to a soft peak, or folding dough. It is equally impossible to run a co-creative process if you have never experienced true *teamwork*—a joint effort in which team members are collectively working on the same task. You will need this kind of experience to understand the relationship between the two complementary forms of collaboration, ***task sharing*** and ***task distribution***.

The difference between these two complementary forms of teamwork can be illustrated by how a team completes a task. If the task is broken down into subtasks, which are distributed and solved individually, the dominating collaboration style is task distribution. If all team members are simultaneously contributing to creating the solution, the dominating style is task sharing. A well-balanced co-creation process can be seen as a delicate dance between these two styles of working. Neither style dominates, and all team members are contributing to the process through their individual efforts and through participating in shared tasks (Fig. 8.5, next page).

To ensure that everyone knows and understands the difference between shared and distributed tasks, it might be a good idea to organize an exercise during which these two forms of working are demonstrated. The first part of the exercise could be a distributable task such as collecting some specific information (their main product groups, their personnel in numbers, their official vision and mission, etc.) about your four main competitors. This task can be broken down to subtasks and distributed between team members in several ways. You could assign each person to focus on a specific company, or alternatively each person could be in charge of collecting a specific set of information from all companies. After the first part has been completed, you could assign a shared task, which preferably

Fig. 8.5 Distributed vs. shared tasks

would be based on the output from the previous task. The shared task could start by sharing and combining the previously collected information within the team and then jointly building a roadmap for your own organization to get past these competitors in all fields and numbers. Once it has been explained to the team, this demonstrative exercise should help the participants to understand the two ways of working.

The value of shifting among complementary forms of work comes from combining the strengths of both forms. Task distribution makes it possible to advance multiple tasks at the same time, while task sharing enables the team to focus all their collective capabilities on a single task for a short period of time. In many organizations, it is still a matter of preferring and choosing one form over the other, rather than trying to take advantage of both approaches. From a management perspective this might make sense, as the two forms require very different styles of leadership. If the prevailing organizational culture favors one form at the expense of the other, it might be difficult to find managers or experts who would have sufficient experience in working with the complementary form as well. In many ways, co-creation as a management approach is about appreciating both forms of collaboration and knowing how to make smooth transitions between them in an effortless way in order to get the maximum benefit of both.

Leading the Climb

The main goal for a leader in this stage is to foster optimal conditions for collective intelligence to emerge. This takes place, as we have discussed, through different forms of team building and knowledge sharing. What else can we do to support the team? How can we be the "midwife," helping the delivery rather than having the baby ourselves?

Whether leadership be internally generated, rotated, or assigned, there are special considerations for this role. These considerations are meant to complement the discussion of creative leadership in Part I. There we focused on the capacities for creative leadership. Here we build upon that foundation, illustrating how these capacities can be put into practice.

Supporting the Team

A co-creative team needs to have balance, and to build or maintain balance you can put into practice the following guidelines.

Recognize the Unique Complexity of Each Person

Everyone has value in a program, whether you selected them or not. By recognizing that value and encouraging it to be expressed, you get the best out of people.

The Wisdom of the Group Is Always Greater Than That of the Facilitator

Co-creation is a process that cultivates collective knowledge and potential. We value collective wisdom over individual expertise. This is true not only with respect to knowledge but also to the energy of the group. There may be times when the group wants to do something that deviates from the program. As long as they feel that it relates to or meets a need in the overall process, let them.

Trust the Team

Acknowledging the wisdom of the group that is greater than one's own ideas is a matter of trusting the team. Trust leads to (1) emergence of things that you could not have anticipated and (2) personal growth for the participants (even if it is painful at times). Like a good coach, we can offer support, but ultimately we must be able to let our teams play, make mistakes, and learn from them. Sometimes they will surprise you, if you let them take ownership of the process.

Allow for Fluctuations in Engagement (Set Permissions Up Front)
People cannot be in flow all the time. Allow for people to contribute when they feel they can, and not to when they don't want to. If you give this freedom up front, it becomes easier to ask for peak performance at crucial junctions.

Encourage and Balance Different Perspectives
Diversity is a core element of collective creativity. With this comes the challenge of conflicting egos. Use shifting group formations and dynamics to manage egos rather than risk confrontation.

Maintain Creative Tension
Although we strive to minimize direct conflicts, we must also avoid group-think and premature compromise or consensus. Creative tension purposefully holds contrasting forces/ideas in tension. Creativity often emerges out of the tension between opportunity and constraints, so it is constructive for us to manufacture such tensions. These must be held with care if the tension lies between individuals in order to avoid a transformation of the tension into a potentially destructive situation. A strong container can hold such tensions, but the leader must stay alert and maintain the trust.

Team Spirit and the Importance of Having Fun

When Frederick Winslow Taylor published his *Principles of Scientific Management* in 1919,[16] he was set on a mission to harness the power of human motivation. Taylor had noticed that people seemed to spend tremendous amounts of energy while playing some sports, but for some reason they lost all this energy when they were expected to perform in their jobs. His conclusion was that people needed clear goals matched with appealing incentives to be productive at their jobs. Since the beginning of Taylorism, this has been a dominant form of management.

The irony of Taylorism is that, while on a mission to incorporate people's innate motivation into their work, Taylor made sure that nearly for a century people have been managed through fear, control, and authority rather than being allowed to enjoy their jobs, develop their capabilities, and bloom at the top of their game. Even though Taylor's approach to motivation was shredded to pieces by the 1950s and 1960s,[17] his practices dominated the field of management for most part of the twentieth century. Today, the connection between intrinsic motivation and the ability to create is more clear than ever, but the practices that run our organizations still largely refuse to recognize the importance of enjoying your work and having fun.

Co-creation breaks this mold. We build motivated teams (in line with Taylor's original mission) combined with environments and practices that tap into and harness creative potential rather than stifling it with authoritarian controls. Part of designing and facilitating these experiences is being sensitive to team spirit and fun. The creative process is a series of ups and downs, iterative loops, and moments of profound frustration followed by insights and potentially breakthroughs. And like a rollercoaster it can be quite enjoyable. We best support our teams by balancing good performance, skills development, and play. It is a holistic approach that begins with setting up a container that provides a safe, supporting, and enjoyable environment for the co-creation process.

Having said that, it is worth noting that in the majority of circumstances, the container should not be mistaken as an objective of the journey. For any knowledge-creating organization, it should be clear that the container is a means to an end. Even though it has a good chance of producing positive side effects in the long run, it should be regarded as a powerful tool that can help the organization to take its performance level through the roof. Hence while co-creation integrates team building into its process, we must not lose sight of the larger goals.

Tuning and Tracking

An essential practice to stay on target with goals is monitoring the team. At every moment of the journey, you will need to know exactly where you are, where you are headed, and where you should be headed. As trivial as it may sound, being able to spot an error in the direction of a co-creation team is the most critical and the most delicate skill that a leader can possess. Lacking this skill would be somewhat equal to a chef working without taste buds. You need to be tuned to monitor the team on several different levels. We will cover here three significant levels of monitoring co-creation.

The easiest level to monitor is the *level of activities*, which enables you to track the progress of the co-creation process. By looking at *what* people are doing at any given time, along with the tasks they have already completed, you will be able to estimate whether the teamwork is proceeding as planned. This is usually the type of information that project managers will be collecting and reporting to their superiors, as it is easy to observe and measure objectively. For a co-creation *Xd*, in addition to keeping track of *what* the people are doing, it is equally or perhaps even more important to pay attention to *how* they are approaching and completing their tasks. Have they divided the tasks between individuals, or are they working in sub-teams? Are they sharing their discoveries and insights with the rest of the team, or are they only focusing on their own tasks?

This second level of monitoring is the *level of team dynamics*, and it focuses on the interpersonal aspects of the process. The co-creative journey could be proceeding very smoothly on the level of activities, yet under the surface there might be a big turbulence brewing in the relationships between the team members. Quite often these problems will begin to surface only during the later stages of the journey, in which case it might already be too late to change the course. A co-creative team may be able to produce decent or even good outcomes even while major turbulence and friction are hindering the team's performance, but if you want to make sure that your team can reach the highest possible level of performance, then they need to be functioning well *as a team*. We influence the development of team dynamics from the very beginning of the project (i.e. setting the container and team building), and we must continually monitor the strength of the container. This is especially important in the Dive, when team dynamics can make or break the process.

Beyond team dynamics lays a thin, almost unobservable layer that has a strong, immediate impact on the real-time performance of the team. This *level of emotions* is the third and final level we will discuss here, and it is by far the most difficult one to monitor and observe. Tuning oneself to be sensitive toward emotions is virtually impossible to learn through conventional management training programs, as it requires highly developed awareness and empathy. These capacities are quite difficult to acquire without some form of contextual, tacit learning.

The level of emotions is where there can be a lot of fluctuation within the team, especially in the beginning of a new project and at the turning points of a process. This is also the level where a good catalyst can have a huge impact with a minimal effort. The four levers we discussed in Chap. 5: The Intangibles of Experience Design—Time, Space, Information, and Energy—are tools that profoundly impact the emotional experience. Empathic leaders are very good at sensing how others feel and manipulating their energy with these and other tools.

It is crucial to find a balance between being sensitive to emotions and remaining objective in decision-making. We recognize the fact that all so-called rational decision-making is both emotional and objective, and we cannot fully separate one from the other. The skill required is to recognize the reactive (emotional) and objective elements of any dialogue or decision and then make informed decisions from that place of awareness. A seasoned leader might be able to tune into their own and others' emotions while staying grounded in objectivity, but for a less experienced or for more emotion-driven leaders, it might be challenging to make this distinction. A good idea to build balance is splitting these two tasks with someone else within the team. Having someone assigned as the designated sensor/rationalizer could help create a balance between these functions and release some pressure from the shoulders of the team leader or catalyst.

Making Adjustments

Tuning into and tracking the team are practices that help us identify where we might need to make adjustments and bring balance. If your course is correct—people are doing what they are supposed to be doing—then you can sit back, relax, and enjoy the ride. If not, then some adjustments may be required. But before doing anything hasty, it is always good to take a step back and get on top of the situation. Only after an analysis of the situation should you take action. And after you are done, you will still need to make sure that your action had the impact you desired so that you can attempt to manage any possible side affects you may have caused.

Let's look at an analogy. If you ask people about how they drive their car, most would describe how they steer the wheel, shift the gears, and push the pedals in different situations. From these descriptions, it would be easy to assume that all it takes to become a skillful driver is to train your hands and feet for these repetitive small operations, and that arms and legs are the most important assets for a good driver. As the focus is on the car, not many people would even acknowledge the importance of using their eyes and ears for observing the environment, their sense of touch to locate the shift stick, or their sense of balance to feel how hard the car is accelerating or decelerating. But the more you think about it, the more obvious it becomes that in fact you drive your car with your senses rather than with your hands and feet.

Similarly, a co-creation catalyst and a team leader need to develop their senses for identifying various nuances of team spirit, atmosphere, interpersonal tension, emotions, and many other issues within their team and then combine this information into an overall understanding of the state of the team. They will also need a good sense of where the team is at in respect to their goals. Only after they have reached a clear understanding of the state of the team and the situation they are in will it become useful to apply facilitation skills to make adjustments.

Many accidents have occurred when inexperienced drivers have hit the accelerator instead of the break when they have found themselves in a difficult situation. Even more accidents have occurred inside organizations when team leaders have decided to "just do something" after they have realized that everything is not right within their projects. Often this "just doing something" has brought good results, but probably an equal number of times the consequences have been disastrous for the team and the project. In the failed cases, it is easy to put the blame on the creative workshop, declaring that it was not suitable for the organization instead of evaluating whether it was the right tool for the situation to begin with. Hindsight is always easier than staying on the road when the going gets tough, and this is why skillful drivers (*Xd*) are so valuable for any organization. With all that being said, here are a few tips that might come in handy if you find yourself in any of the following difficult situations.

Maintaining Good Team Dynamics

First of all, team leaders and catalysts of a co-creative team should always do their best to stay on the inside of their team. This is true even when their positions will make it difficult, as they might hold more formal authority than their teammates and have closer connections with the higher authorities within their organization. Getting and staying on the inside might be crucial for the success of the co-creative process because it is extremely difficult to sense any changes in the atmosphere, or to spot interpersonal tension that can be slowly building up among team members, without experiencing these issues from the same position as the rest of your team. Sometimes team spirit becomes negative because of some very small issues that could have been avoided if they had been spotted sooner. Being part of the team, as an insider, makes it easier to make changes to the team, organize an intervention, and deal with the issues at hand. This way you will know whether you will need to encourage an individual member of the team who just needs a push, or to slow down a team that is wasting its energy on a wild goose chase.

Dealing with Emotions

Just like any other rollercoaster, a co-creative process will come with its own set of emotional highs and lows. It can be said almost certainly that an intensive project will bring up strong emotions in the participants, and some of these will be positive while others are going to be negative. Emotions come and go, and they never last for very long. And while our first reaction to any strong emotions might be to hold them in until we calm down, they might also present an opportunity to build stronger interpersonal connection within the team if some room is given to expressing and dealing with them. For example, positive emotions can be very contagious, so expressing them may be able to pump up the team spirit and give a positive boost of energy for the entire team. Naturally this requires some sensitivity toward those teammates who might not be in the mood for any cheering or do not feel comfortable with physical expressions such as hugs or high fives. But generally, it is a good idea to share any positive emotions with the team as they emerge.

Dealing with negative emotions is more challenging, which is why we have an even stronger tendency of hiding them. However, the appearance of negative emotions can be used to build trust within the team if the emotional incident is dealt with appropriately. In these cases, it is very important to first give enough space to the person who is experiencing the negative emotions and let the moment pass. Once the incident is over, it should be dealt with in a respectful and understanding way. If the entire team can send a signal saying "it is okay to feel bad, we will still be there for you," there is a good chance that these negative incidents can be turned into a source of power for the team.

As many of us are not very good at handling or post-processing emotional situations, these might be the types of situations in which an experienced and well-trained catalyst can show his or her worth to the team. This may or may not be the *Xd*. A catalyst is an agent of transformation, and any member of the team can find themselves being the catalyst for an emotional breakthrough. Our colleague Nic, who has decades of experience holding spaces for emotional breakdowns and breakthroughs, advised us to keep it in the group. If you take a person aside every time they have an issue, it violates the trust of the group. Why, after all, should certain individuals get all the attention? There may be times when a side intervention is necessary, but in general it is better to encourage all expressions take place in the group. A strong container will hold even the worst breakdowns, building even greater trust and authenticity by making it safe to expose vulnerabilities and responding to these with compassion.

Reaching the Peak

October 1st

At the beginning of the third week, the team completed a very simple but exhausting brainstorming program, during which they were able to produce 138 solid ideas, categorize them into 9 clusters, and eventually produce 12 reasonable concepts for the baby monitor. The next two days were used to further develop and polish these concepts to the point where they could be used as the starting points for the rest of the product design and development process, and then the team broke apart for the weekend. On the following Monday, part of the team started their first long stretch, to analyze and break down the concepts, while others were assigned to continue benchmarking relevant existing products, and to survey possible technologies that could be used to realize these concepts.

The Climb ends at a climax, a critical mass of shared knowledge. The ACME story above illustrates a good outcome from the climb, a team that has produced many ideas and narrowed these down to set to further explore. The result is both thorough and efficient, and ideal combination. Also, at this point the team has identified some of what it does *not* know. Identifying the need to explore is what provides impetus into the Unknown.

Even though the objective of the brainstorming workshop described above might be stated as producing relevant ideas and concepts for the baby monitor, there are more important goals lying beneath the surface—even if these goals are not understood or discussed publicly. These include:

- Bringing everyone on the same page
- Aligning efforts
- Mapping/sharing knowledge
- Building interpersonal relationships
- Building internal communication skills
- Developing a shared framework of knowledge

In other words, what the story does not tell us are the emotional and interpersonal aspects of the journey. Throughout this chapter we have emphasized the need to balance all three aspects of the journey. Those who focus solely on building collective knowledge do so at their own peril. In Act I it is especially important to build the relationships and communication required to endure the challenges of what comes next.

In an ideal world, this is a time of great enthusiasm paired with a certain degree of exhaustion. A team that has been thorough has worked hard to get everything they know out into the field of play, and in so doing they have spent their emotional, energetic, and knowledge resources. They likely feel either that they need a serious break, or they are ready to jump to prototyping solutions. It is human nature to get excited about ideas, so it should come as no surprise that teams will attempt to jump straight to prototyping. Here is where it becomes critical to slow things down, even force the team into a deeper exploration of the ideas they have developed. It is time to shift them from the comfort of the Known into the uncertainty of the Unknown. It is time for the Dive.

Notes

1. A static human resources strategy sees the people as steady sources of labor. This type of strategy is built to make sure that the people can continuously work at their maximum performance level. A more dynamic HR strategy parallels co-creation in that it sees the people as constantly evolving sources of work. This type of strategy focuses on constantly increasing the capacities of the people.
2. https://www.ted.com/talks/brene_brown_on_vulnerability?utm_campaign=tedspread--a&utm_medium=referral&utm_source=tedcomshare. Accessed July 10th, 2017.
3. Owen, *Open Space Technology.*
4. Tools available at https://methodkit.com, www.creativethinking.net.
5. Jimbo Clark. InnoGreat. www.innogreat.com.
6. Hellinger et al., *Love's Hidden Symmetry*, 221.
7. The work is licensed under the Creative Commons Attribution-NonCommercial-ShareAlike 3.0 Unported License. To view, visit http://creativecommons.org/licenses/by-nc-sa/3.0/.
8. www.couragerenewal.org/approach.
9. It is actually not that complicated, which is surprising given how much organizations state the need for a good container and don't know how to set one.

10. d.school bootcamp bootleg. Brainstorming method card.
11. Gray et al., *Gamestorming.*
12. Brown, *Change by Design*, 97.
13. Ibid., 60–61.
14. Gray et al., *Gamestorming*, 134.
15. Chipchase and Steinhardt. *Hidden in Plain Sight.*
16. Taylor, *The principles of scientific management*, 80.
17. Maslow, "A theory of human motivation," 370–396. Herzberg, "One more time: How do you motivate employees," 53–62.

References

Allee, V. "Value Network Analysis and Value Conversion of Tangible and Intangible Assets." *Journal of Intellectual Capital* 9, no. 1 (2008): 5–24.

Brown, Tim, and Barry Katz. *Change by Design: How Design Thinking Transforms Organizations and Inspires Innovation.* Adobe Digital Edition ed. New York: Harper Collins e-books, 2009.

Chipchase, Jan, and Simon Steinhardt. *Hidden in Plain Sight: How to Create Extraordinary Products for Tomorrow's Customers.* New York: HarperCollins Publishers Inc., 2013.

Gray, David, Sunni Brown, and Macanufo. *Gamestorming: A Playbook for Innovators, Rulebreakers, and Changemakers.* Sebastopol, CA: O'Reilly 2010.

Hellinger, Bert, Gunthard Weber, and Hunter Beaumont. *Love's Hidden Symmetry: What Makes Love Work in Relationships.* Phoenix, AZ: Zeig, Tucker & Co., 1998.

Herzberg, Frederick. *One More Time: How Do You Motivate Employees.* Harvard Business Review Boston, 1968.

Maslow, A. H. "A Theory of Human Motivation." *Psychological Review* 50, no. 4 (1943): 370–396.

Mootee, Idris. *Design Thinking for Strategic Innovation: What They Can't Teach You at Business or Design School.* New Jersey: John Wiley & Sons, Inc., 2013.

Ogilvie, Tim, and Jeann Liedtka. *Designing for Growth: A Design Thinking Toolkit for Managers.* Columbia Business School Publishing. Kindle Edition: Columbia University Press, 2011.

Owen, Harrison. *Open Space Technology: A User's Guide.* 2nd ed. San Francisco, CA: Berrett-Koehler Publishers, 1997.

Porter, M. E., and V. E. Millar. "How Information Gives You Competitive Advantage." *Harvard business review* 63, no. 4 (1985): 149–160.

Taylor, Frederick Winslow. *The Principles of Scientific Management.* New York: Harper Brothers, 1911.

CHAPTER 9

Act II: The Dive

The Dive is when we focus on experimentation and producing new knowledge. A passage from *Designing for Growth* captures this transition,

> Having synthesized the data and identified emerging patterns, ideas begin to pop into our heads of their own volition. We start to consider new possibilities, trends, and uncertainties. Even without consciously trying, we are beginning to develop hypotheses about what a desirable future might look like. And so it is time to move from the data-based exploratory What is stage to the more creativity-focused question, What if?[1]

Driven by a need to break through preconceptions and reframe initial insights, this exploration is often the most unpleasant part of the co-creative journey. It begins when the team has reached its highest possible level of existing knowledge and is ready to start heading toward something new. All the simple solutions have already been identified, and the leader needs to shift the focus and mentality of the team from knowledge collecting to knowledge generating. The team will need to start exploring and testing new possibilities, trying to discover something that no one else has discovered before. They will need to study new territories and experiment with the Unknown, stretching their old boundaries, until they begin to feel comfortable with it.

At this point, all the roles and tasks need to be clearly defined within the team, so that everyone knows exactly what is expected of them. Since everyone has already become quite familiar with their teammates, they can

B. R. Rill, M. M. Hämäläinen, *The Art of Co-Creation*,
https://doi.org/10.1007/978-981-10-8500-0_9

Fig. 9.1 Expanding knowledge base through exploration

work independently from each other and still keep the team informed of any discoveries that could be relevant for someone else as well. Collaborative work is not required at all times. Instead, we emphasize the value of good coordination and management. Towards the end of the Dive, the individual streams of knowledge need to be intertwined so that collective insight can emerge (Fig. 9.1).

The leader should encourage the team to look for new questions and problems rather than seeking simple answers and solutions. They should look for outside-the-box ideas through a process of constructive destruction, where old, existing models are broken apart and used as building blocks for novel solutions. They will need to drill toward a critical question and a critical problem that needs to be identified and solved. More often than not, once the critical problem has been identified, a previous solution might turn out to be quite trivial. This is why, in design, we spend as much time in the problem space as we do in the solution space.

In this chapter we will highlight the significance of suitable leadership skills for a successful journey. In the Dive people are leaving their comfort zones, followed by clearly observable changes in their behavior. Team dynamics are strained, testing the character of the team members and leadership abilities. On an emotional level, the team balances between states of curiosity and fear, which might lead to frustration. On an interpersonal level, the team members depend on each other, and this dependence might create discomfort and anxiety at one end of the experiential spectrum while nurturing positive feelings like comfort of belonging and safety at the other end. It is in this space where keen observation of subtle movements in energy or focus, the ability to relate to the emotional states of the participants, and letting go of process designs are so important. The Unknown can be just as uncertain for the leader as it is for the other participants; thus he or she must be experienced and skilled enough to guide the team through it all.

We conclude by explaining two key observations of the Dive, which together indicate when the team is ready to move into to the final stage of the journey. First is emergence, the phenomenon where creativity pops up from seemingly nowhere. This is the fundamental quality of the space between we strive for. Second is the energy that comes with new ideas. This energy eventually catalyzes an emotional shift, the curve of the journey turns upward, and we are propelled into Act III: The Rise.

The Unknown

October 12th

At this point everyone's faces were getting serious, as there began to be so many open questions and contradictions in the air that they seemed simply overwhelming. Dorothy realized that they had reached the point where people were being pushed outside of their comfort zones, and as a sign of this, their behavior was changing quite radically. The people who normally had been open, relaxed, and always smiling, were now barely talking at all, and seemed overly critical and sensitive towards other people's thoughts and ideas. The general atmosphere was becoming hostile, so she would have to act fast before it was too late.

Warm-up is over, and it's time to roll up the sleeves and get to work. At this point, the co-creative journey leaves the well-known, familiar path and begins a long dive through uncharted territories. Even though in reality there are no signs saying "leaving the safe path, you're on your own now!" there are signals that will indicate when you are leaving the Known and entering the uncharted grounds. First, you will begin to notice a lot of "we already tried that" and "somebody else has done that" replies, when trying to come up with new directions to pursue. This will lead to frustration, as almost nothing seems to take the project forward anymore. Because of this, progress is getting slower and slower, people are spending less time together, and the general energy is beginning to decline. These are all symptoms of reaching the point where there is no more knowledge to share, and no more existing knowledge to find. This is the periphery/

fringe of existing knowledge, which means that the direction of the journey must shift from sharing (existing) knowledge to exploring and producing new knowledge.

This is the moment that the experienced leaders have been waiting for, as they knew that until this point the journey has been merely a warm-up for the next stage. As far as the pragmatic goals are concerned, even though the first stage plays a critical role in developing team performance, Act I is usually quite insignificant in terms of creating or producing something new. On a co-creative journey, the ultimate success is measured in terms of creative output, and so far in this regard only marginal development has occurred. For leaders, the Dive is the point where the journey of discovery really begins. The goal of reaching the edge of existing knowledge is left behind, and the journey takes a shift in direction by beginning to push the boundaries through different forms of exploration.

Constructive Destruction

In the last chapter, we discussed the use of ethnography and other design research methods to chart the Known. Observations help us understand our target audience, whether that be users of a product or service, or stakeholders within our organization. At first, our observations tend to focus on confirming assumptions or filling in gaps to existing knowledge bases. Yet in the process we often encounter things that don't fit into our preconceived models, things that stand out as "odd" or "surprising." These exceptions, or anomalies, are indicators that there is more to things than meets the eye. They are clues that can lead us into the Unknown.

If we record these anomalies, the knowledge maps created in Act I illuminate the Known while also drawing attention to what is not known, thus opening up space for innovation to meet or create needs. Further exploration requires a shift in the role of ethnography to a process of discovery. This is where the Dive often begins.

Dr. Bruce Grindal, an anthropology professor at Florida State University, used an elegant model to explain ethnography as discovery. When we first explore another culture, we notice many things that seem out of the ordinary and apparently random. The fact that bullet trains in Japan are so quiet and that Japanese homeless people take off their shoes before sleeping on their cardboard boxes are two examples. When you ask people why they do these things, they will give you "secondary explanations." These are surface explanations, such as "because it is rude to talk loudly in public," or "because we don't want to get the cardboard dirty." Most observers use secondary answers to describe other cultures, highlighting the features that make them different from our own. That might make for interesting table talk, but such understandings lack depth. Secondary explanations are insufficient for explaining *why* a particular behavior exists.

What is needed are primary explanations, root causes that explain a wide array of observable behaviors. Primary explanations take time to discover. Like so many insights in design and ethnographic research, primary explanations emerge from combing through a mass of data for patterns and connections that make sense of it all. Primary explanations are not visible on the surface because most often they are unconscious, or taken-for-granted, aspects of culture. Pierre Bourdieu, a French sociologist, called this "habitus." In the examples above, the primary explanation for quietness on trains is the cultural emphasis of harmony, the value of which is written in as a pillar of the Japanese constitution. The desire for social harmony affects many aspects of Japanese society, from public behavior to language forms and bento box design. The reason the Japanese homeless take off their shoes is due to a desire for cleanliness, but the "dirt" they are referring to is not dirt in a physical sense. It is spiritual dirt (*hitogomi*), which people pick up any time they go out of their home. The aversion to spiritual dirt explains not only why the Japanese take off their shoes, but also their insistence on purification in ritual and other contexts. Discovering a primary explanation is an "ah ha" moment that suddenly makes sense of the jumble of observations gathered. Primary, not secondary, explanations are what we are really striving for. Ethnography is at its best when it is process of discovery. It bridges the Known and the Unknown, making it the perfect tool for the transition between the two stages.

Sensing Journeys

Otto Scharmer calls this exploratory work "sensing journeys." According to Scharmer, in the 15 years of using Theory U, sensing journeys have consistently been cited as one of the most impactful experiences for participants.[2] Why is that? Sensing journeys take people from the Known and move them into the new social realities. It helps them:

- See with new eyes
- Generate new ideas

- Build relationships with others (whom could be part of prototyping and testing)
- Produce a mindset shift in the sensing team that is more profound than what can happen in a workshop space

Of the many resources on how to do design ethnography well, we find Scharmer's instructions for sensing journeys to be among the most efficient, especially for those who are not trained as anthropologists. His explanation, delivered in a video from the Theory U course in Shanghai, is as follows:

How to Do a Sensing Journey

1. Select the right sites, according to two criteria:
    (a) Is it relevant for what you are trying to do?
    (b) Is it a place you know very little about?
2. Prepare for the journey:
    (a) Clarify your questions. Ask, "What are we wanting to explore?"
    (b) Write down your key assumptions. Ask, "What do we expect to see on the sensing journey?" This reveals your mental model, which allows you to later return to it and identify what you have learned. Any deviation from what was expected to sheds light on the New.
3. During the journey:
    (a) Deep listening.
    (b) Access your ignorance[3] (i.e. lean into the Unknown).
    (c) Ask powerful questions.
    (d) Go with the flow (follow what is emerging).
4. Follow up:
    (a) Journaling: Key observations, What stood out? What surprised you? What did you notice about the system? About yourself?
    (b) Connect with your own passion/inspiration.

These instructions enable a creative team to condense the ethnographic process, which can take weeks or months, into a set of short site visits. We would rather take more time and reach deeper insights, of course, but sometimes a single visit to a new environment can be enough to trigger profound insights.

In addition to Scharmer's work, the text *Hidden in Plain Sight: How to Create Extraordinary Products for Tomorrow's Customers* by Jan Chipchase and Simon Steinhardt is an excellent resource for design ethnography. Their work distills decades of design research experience for many of the world's largest companies, drawing attention to how consumers think and behave as well as the methods to understand them. Equally valuable is the fact that the text is an easy read, which helps people develop a degree of fluency with ethnographic methods without years of academic training.

Techniques and Guidelines

The Dive is when we experiment, not only with ideas, but also with techniques. There are two overall objectives to constructive destruction. First is to take Known things or ideas apart, critically evaluate them, and try to see them from new perspectives. A common design technique, Seeing as Pieces, deconstructs an object into the elements that create what we see. A bottle, for example, is nothing more than lines and colors that we interpret as a bottle. Seeing as Pieces breaks the object down into its constituent parts so that we can reimagine them. Several of the techniques in the Dive serve this same purpose, breaking down ideas so that we can reframe them and explore novel recombinations of the constituent elements.

The second objective is to discover the New. In co-creation we are striving for innovation, using any and all techniques to tap into and unleash our creativity toward that end. To do that we need to leave the familiar comfort of the Known far behind and dive into the dark and murky waters of the Unknown. This too has its methods.

Both objectives require techniques and guidelines that focus not only on knowledge, but also on emotions and managing team dynamics. Some of these may be familiar, others less so. Tools for the Dive draw from a wide palette, ranging across the disciplines of design, leadership, facilitation, psychology, and human potential.

For the sake of presentation, we have arranged this chapter so that the knowledge aspect of the journey comes first, but in reality the order is fluid. The *Xd* must have the requisite awareness and flexibility to shift the process as needed, especially in the Dive when things are so uncertain. Remember this credo:

> ***Process is the driver, but team dynamics is the engine, and emotions power the engine.***

If emotions and team dynamics are not managed well, the knowledge aspect will suffer. Moreover, collective intelligence is impossible without a synergy between all three aspects. Many programs have fallen apart simply due to the neglect of the humanistic dimensions of creativity. Don't make that mistake. Having said that, let's dive into knowledge creation.

Creating New Practical Knowledge

In contrast to science, the ultimate objective of a co-creative process in product/service design or organizational development is not to produce new knowledge, but to create impact and results. This is not to say that knowledge creation is not important in co-creation. This just states that knowledge is a means to an end, and as such it doesn't always have to be very accurate or even true. For example, let's think about a company that operates within the fashion industry and specializes in women's clothes. This company has always produced only red clothes, because they know for a fact that all women love the color red. Over the years, they have remained very successful in comparison to their competitors, and they know that the reason behind this success has been their devotion to the red color. In fact, they have been so certain of their superiority that they have been confident to market their products very aggressively with a slogan "All you need is red." It is quite possible for a company to be successful with this type of a strategy, but it is much less likely that they are successful because all women love the color red. Yet, for the company it doesn't matter *why* they succeed, as long as they do.

For the same reason, the validation process in a real context can also differ from scientific validation. Where science aims for general and comprehensive validity, for practitioners a case-based validation is most often more than enough. Ideas are validated through simple experimentation, and if an experiment is successful, then it can be repeated and turned into a successful practice. This type of approach encourages jumping to conclusions way ahead of time, and relying on intuition and determination when making decisions. Any failures can be seen as learning opportunities that will help us identify problems and weaknesses, and these increase our understanding of the issues we need to be dealing with. *Fail early, fail often* is a product design mantra that reminds us about the importance of continuous experimentation without being afraid of failures. Any mistakes are almost certainly easier (and usually much cheaper) to fix if you spot them early on in the process—before they have accumulated into big problems. For this reason, it makes sense to devote the first part of a co-creation process to discovering, identifying, and fixing these issues that might otherwise lead into serious problems later on.

Since all problems cannot be avoided, nor can all mistakes be prevented, it is essential to identify the areas that are most critical for the success of a co-creative project and to make sure that at least these areas have been explored and understood. First, the team should look into their mission brief and list all of the problems, questions, and conflicts that could be connected to their main objective. The list can then be clustered according to associations between individual items, and clear connections can be indicated by drawing a line or an arrow between the items. This clustered map can be further developed by, for example, indicating potential consequences of these listed issues or by adding relevant stakeholders to it. Once this visualization of pitfalls and traps has been completed, it can be used as a map to navigate through the Unknown. The visualization can also help in analyzing which questions, problems, or conflicts are critical for the success of the journey. These critical issues can then be used as beacons that will help in identifying the critical functions or operations that are required to create a final solution, and to lead the journey out of the Dive.

Active vs. Receptive Approaches

In his text *Leading from the Emerging Future*, Scharmer summarizes the techniques used in many design and change initiatives as follows[4]:

> The best practices in human interaction and systems thinking were tapped into and brought into the design. The entire process was a mix of plenary conversations, small-group discussions, and individual moments of reflection. To maximize the creativity of the participants, various tools and techniques in creative processes, such sculpting, drawing, painting, systems games, and journaling, among others, were used.

Theory U combines what we might call "active" and "receptive" approaches. Most facilitation and design methods are active approaches, seeking and actively reframing knowledge. These have a particular energy to them, a feeling that insights can be found if we seek them diligently. Active design methods include Mind Mapping, 2 × 2 Matrixes, Powers of Ten, "How might we ..." Brainstorms, Cultural Probes, Assumption Testing, Guided Visualizations, User Journey Mapping, and more.[5] Complementing these are many other tools, such as MethodKit Card Games, Iceberg Analysis, Image Interpretation, World Cafe, Six Hats, Case Clinics, Theme-Centered Interaction, Focused Conversations, and Bodystorming.[6]

These methods constructively deconstruct knowledge while at the same time building the collective knowledge base as the team explores and experiments. An underlying assumption is that insights lie in the informational field, the space between, created by these exchanges. Our job is to populate that field with as much information as possible to facilitate the novel intersections from which insights arise.

But how do we recognize an insight when we see, or feel, one? How can we, as Scharmer says, lean into the emerging future? There will be times when an insight "pops up," and these "ah ha" moments are easily recognizable. Yet there are other times when emergence is much subtler. It is in these moments that the capacities we have been arguing for (i.e. PACE) bear fruit. Creative leadership skills such as presence, empathy, and the ability to hold a space and wait find their best application in receptive approaches. Receptive approaches operate on a somewhat different understanding of creativity than active approaches. Although the scope of that argument is far beyond this text, a simplified version can help us understand why these two approaches are perfect complements to each other.

The predominant theoretical model posits that creativity is a cognitive process, closely related to logic and problem solving capacities in the brain.[7] The notion that divergent thinking benefits creativity derives from this paradigm, and many of the techniques above facilitate a movement between divergent and convergent thinking. Stanford's "Double Diamond" and the three stages of Gamestorming (divergence, emergence, convergence) are processes based on this model.

Contrasting the cognitive model is what we might call the "inspirational" model. Artists throughout history have claimed that their ideas were divinely inspired. What does that mean? In modern terminology, we might rename divine inspiration as "tapping into" a broader collective consciousness. In her text "The Field," Lynne McTaggart argues that theoretical physics is now confirming what spiritual traditions have been saying for millennia—that there is a unified field we all are interconnected with.[8] The theory has matured greatly since her writing, and among physicists it is no longer a question. We are all entangled together in some complex weave that we cannot perceive directly. The Field, superconsciousness, or whatever you want to call it, is the interconnected reality we all live in. Human beings can tune themselves in to this field like an FM stereo picking up radio waves. That "tuning" results in inspiration from the greater whole.

We do not claim to be authorities on the validity (scientific or otherwise) of the inspirational model, but we can discuss the receptive approach and what that means for creativity. Receptive approaches come in two forms. One is based on the cognitive model of creativity, specifically the fact that insights often occur when the brain relaxes from cognitive tasks. When we are actively thinking, our mental space is filled up. When we calm the cognitive forebrain (the "thinking" part), we create a space for ideas to "bubble up" to the surface. Attention Restoration Therapy, intuition walks, and "cave time" (isolation periods) are a few ways to encourage this gestation.

Receptive approaches can also be means to tap into the Field, connecting with larger wholes that provide sources of inspiration. This is what Scharmer means by "co-presencing," waiting in stillness for insights to emerge from the field of potentials (the Unknown). The space between, from this perspective, is much more than the informational field created through techniques to create and share collective knowledge. The space between is a that ***plus*** the wider interconnected systems that we are all part of. Receptive approaches invite and wait for that field to answer—which come in the form of insights "showing up" from seemingly nowhere.

Receptive approaches are not "doing nothing and waiting." They are active in that attention is focused on potentials. When skilled teams "sense" potentials, they can then act in an instant on them. Such teams do not exist without careful development, a reason why we have argued for complementary processes to cultivate these capacities. A skilled creative leader can recognize and guide a team through receptive approaches, but a whole team with such talent is more likely to come up with truly breakthrough ideas.

Our position on creativity does not require one paradigm being more "right" than the other. We advocate what works, and we have seen both active and receptive approaches used to drive innovation. What "works" is whatever you and your team are comfortable with that benefits the creative process. Begin with dialogical techniques, for we cannot build or reframe collective knowledge without skilled communication. Dialogue alone may be sufficient if the goal of the creative process is to share existing knowledge and act from that base. When there is a need to lean into the Unknown in search of the New, additional techniques may be required. In these circumstances, we invite you to play with more experimental approaches that tap into different ways of knowing. Human beings, after all, are incredibly complex creatures. Our cognitive, rational mind is only one among many "intelligences" that we have. In what follows we will introduce some of our methods, beginning with dialogical techniques and then stepping outside the box to look at methods that derive from other ways of knowing.

On Dialogue

Dialogue is not about the physical act of talking, it is about minds unfolding.
—Bettye Pruitt and Philip Thomas

Techniques for building, exploring, and reframing collective knowledge rely heavily upon dialogical practices, by virtue of the fact that we use language to communicate with one another. Yet dialogue itself is taken for granted, as if everyone knows how to do it well. We disagree, strongly. Dialogue is a complex art form, and without understanding its subtleties, co-creation has little chance of success. People need to be able to communicate with authenticity and empathy if they are to have dialogues—talking ***with*** each other. Everything else is not dialogue, but rather people talking ***at*** each other.

Our conception of dialogue is best illustrated by the quote above. Stemming from David Bohm's seminal work *On Dialogue*,[9] we see dialogue as an exploration between two or more people. Dialogue is not telling (talking at one another) or defending entrenched positions. It is also different from negotiation, where two parties have to come to an agreement even if there is no deepening of mutual understanding. The two parties might negotiate the end to a war but still remain bitter enemies and misunderstand each other. Krishnamurti, an Indian educator and philosopher, said it well in *Talks and Dialogues* (1970)[10]:

> If we try to listen we find it extraordinarily difficult, because we are always projecting our opinions and ideas, our prejudices, our background, our inclinations, our impulses. When they dominate, we hardly listen at all. One

> listens and therefore learns, only in a state of attention, a state of silence, in which this whole background is in abeyance, is quiet. Then, it seems to me, it is possible to communicate.

To illustrate this point, let us consider an ACME moment.

> ***September 6th***
> *Roberta was really pissed off at David, since she felt that he was completely ignoring everything she was trying to explain to him, and kept on pushing his own numbers about market sizes and break-even points. Sure, all that data would probably have some use when the team started to think about the advertisement campaigns, but at this point when the design process hadn't even started... She was furious! At first, she thought that David was just not aware of the legal aspects and safety standards related to baby monitors, so she was trying her best to bring up and introduce these topics to him—along with the rest of the team—emphasizing the critical nature of safety standards. Since her words didn't seem to have much of an impact on David, she was now beginning to feel that there was maybe something else behind his objections. Could it have something to do with her age, or her gender? Or maybe a bit of both? Even though she was young and rather inexperienced, she had graduated at the top of her class, in addition to which she had been tested and hired to her position at ACME out of hundreds of talented applicants. Maybe if she brought up these characteristics of hers, Simon would start to acknowledge her. She decided to give him one more shot.*

When we engage in dialogue with our attention focused inward, specifically on our own filters, it becomes a tool for delving deep into the structures that underlie our thoughts and behaviors. Bohm explains how, through dialogue, we can get past the predicament we see in the ACME story:

> Dialogue is a way of observing, collectively, how hidden values and intentions can control our behavior, and how unnoticed cultural differences can clash without our realizing what is occurring. It can display how power is assumed or given away and how pervasive are the generally unnoticed rules of the system that constitutes our culture. But it is most deeply concerned with understanding the dynamics of how thought conceives such connections.[11]

Revealing hidden values and assumptions is essential for working with interpersonal tensions such as those we see in the ACME story. Like breaking a habit, the first step is awareness. Awareness brings in the element of choice, but it does not automatically lead to change. The reason for this, as Bohm notes, is that we tend to like our mental models of the world.

> Owing to their internally coherent nature, confirmatory bias and selective perception, mental models are relatively stable and persistent over time and within communities-of-practice. Ample disconfirmatory evidence and a crisis are often required before existing mental models are challenged and critically examined.

The good news is that dialogue brings internal mental models to light in conversation and makes it possible to create new mental models. "By rendering visible the taken-for-granted causal linkages, the managers' understandings can be mapped out and understood to explore alternative perspectives, relationships, opportunities, threats and actions."[12]

When entering into dialogue, it is prudent to remember that every person's worldview is internally coherent. No matter how at odds another person's perspective is from our own, to them it makes sense. Often their worldview and the behaviors that stem from it are the very basis of their success, and challenging that foundation can be perceived as a personal attack. "I'm right" and/or "You are wrong" statements indicate an unwillingness to enter into a true dialogue. Good dialogue is relativistic, accepting that *all* of our perspectives are conditionally based on our life experience and the groups we are members of. There are no absolute rights or wrongs, but rather what is defined as right or wrong by the social systems that we are part of.[13]

In creative teams, what matters most is what best meets a challenge, so we must be willing to let go of individual positions to pursue what is best for the whole. We must strive to separate ego from ideas and throw our ideas into the space between without being attached to what happens to them. This is an act of surrender that challenges each and every person to let go of the need to be right. Naturally, this is not easy to do. So can we facilitate good dialogue? And do we really need to go this deep?

The short answer to both questions is **yes**. Dialogue is a cornerstone to nearly all techniques used throughout the co-creative process, and the ability to critically evaluate assumptions and explore different viewpoints is particularly salient to the Dive.

It is no wonder then that the cornerstones for the Center of Trust and Renewal are dialogical principles. Or that one of the most popular masterclasses offered at the Ashoka Exchange, a summit for innovation in higher education, was on dialogue. What struck us the most at the Exchange were the tales of how dialogue circles are transforming university landscapes. People are finally beginning to talk *with* each other, entering into co-creative relationships and collectively addressing challenges. And yet, for all the inspiring tales, it is often left unsaid how to cultivate the capacity for good dialogues. Some facilitators create circular environments and semiotically prime the participants by posting the rules of dialogue, or they have a short group's discussion in which they lay out these rules as a social contract in the situated reality of the task at hand. Unfortunately, in our experience, you can't just post the rules of good dialogue and expect people to be able to follow them. You need to show them.

Teaching Dialogue

One of the Co-Creation Initiatives at the Hong Kong Polytechnic University was the Dialogue Sessions, a six-week experiment with a group of design students who volunteered to participate. We met weekly for three hours, each session experiencing and exploring different aspects of dialogue. Working with students for whom English is a second or third language posed a particular challenge, in that there was no way we could ask them to read and understand Bohm or any other scholastic sources. We had to teach the art of dialogue entirely through practices and reflection. As it turned out, this constraint led us to develop some effective methods to show, rather than tell, the characteristics of good dialogue.

We organized the sessions to explore dialogue one "layer" at a time, starting with easily observable factors that influence communication. The first session began by organizing the 20+ students into groups of five to six members and asking them to answer the question, "What is Design?" We gave them 30 minutes to have a discussion and come up with a one- or two-sentence answer. We then sat back and watched it unfold. As expected, the teams struggled to come up with an answer to what was an entirely unfair question. Ask any designer and they will tell you that there are many different perspectives on design, and that question almost inevitably leads to a long discourse.

For the first 20 minutes or so, the teams communicated very politely, taking turns speaking and inviting all to contribute. Everything changed when we told them they had ten minutes left. Suddenly the team dynamics shifted, with some people taking charge, others opposing, and others checking out. When we called "Time!" several groups were visibly disappointed. Most had not come up with an answer. We drew everyone back in to a large group circle and asked, "What happened?" At first the answers focused on the ability, or not, to answer the question. We listened patiently, then asked again, "What happened?" Upon receiving confused looks, we added "Between you and your peers." The dialogue then shifted from *what* happened to *how* it happened, shedding light on the roles that people adopted. We asked the students to identify and write on the whiteboard what roles they encountered and to mark what felt most natural to them. This, in turn, created an opportunity for us to introduce the concept of role-playing and engage students in a dialogue as to what roles they play and how they respond to other roles. We then had them make a second attempt at answering the question, but this time playing a different role in the team. In our second reflective dialogue, we asked them how it felt to play roles that felt different or unnatural and how that affected their communication with others. The students impressed us with their answers, cautiously at first but getting more authentic over time sharing their sentiments. By this point our lesson had been conveyed, without saying much at all. We facilitated the experience while the students, with a little guidance, taught themselves the lesson—how roles affect communication.

Let's zoom out for a moment here to consider the design of this experience. Given the constraints of no reading or preparation ahead of time, we decided on an experiential approach. We would "teach" each lesson by having students experience the content and then draw out the important points in group reflective dialogues. We never told them that the answer to "What is design?" was irrelevant. In the activity, we used one of the four levers we explained in Part I—time. The time constraint, specifically running out of it, catalyzed the shift in team dynamics that we wanted to draw out. As experience designers, we manipulated the dynamic to draw out predisposed roles. When it came to group reflection, rather than telling the students about roles, we asked the simple two-word question "What happened?" This is a particularly powerful question with dialogue circles, and the answers get quite deep as the group digs deeper and deeper into the forces that affect communication. In summary, our approach was to facilitate, not lecture about, greater awareness and comprehension of dialogue.

The remaining weeks followed a similar format, each one peeling back a different layer. Through experiential learning, the students collectively explored how roles, culture, gender, spatial design, and positioning affect communication. One of their favorite moments was when I led the group reflection lying on the floor while they stood on chairs. None of them could take me seriously, until I reversed the positions. It's amazing how subtle things like relative height have such a profound impact.

At week 4 we shifted gears, making the transition from physical and sociocultural factors to internal filters and mental models. We taught the students how to meditate and focus attention on quietly observing the inner experience. We brought in our colleague Jimbo Clark to facilitate his "In and Out of the Box" workshop, a gamified approach to raising awareness and cultivating empathy. Each week we put students into dialogues or shared tasks that required communication and coordination, while subtly playing with the different levers to manipulate team dynamics. Each time when we asked, "What happened?" the dialogues got deeper.

In the closing Dialogue Session, we brought the groups together and asked them to identify the ingredients for good dialogue. Here is the list they came up with, without any input from their design professors (us).

- Empathy
- Respect
- Active listening
- Participation
- Non-attachment to "right"
- Courage
- Patience
- Leadership

The parallel between these "ingredients," the qualities of strong container, and principles of good dialogue as articulated by ourselves and other leadership programs is no coincidence. All that we have done is codify the wisdom that is inherent when any group of people takes the time to explore the dialogical space within and between themselves. A problem is that very rarely do people or organizations dedicate the time and resource to cultivate this knowledge and capacity. In the contemporary world, where no one has the time to slow down, lack of dialogue has become a serious challenge.

> Once a society loses this capacity [to dialogue], all that is left is a cacophony of voices battling it out to see who wins and who loses. There is no capacity to go deeper, to find a deeper meaning that transcends individual views and self interest. It seems reasonable to ask whether many of our deeper prob-

> lems in governing ourselves today, the so-called "gridlock" and loss of mutual respect and caring might not stem from this lost capacity to talk with one another, to think together as part of a larger community.[14]

The CCI Dialogue Sessions were one method to meet this challenge. Many of the students in those sessions became leaders of their design teams, and those that did not want to lead were highly sought after. They had learned how to communicate and work in teams much more effectively than their peers who had not participated. The sessions demonstrated, to us at least, the clear connection between dialogue skills, leadership, and being a good team member.

Levels of Conversation

We can operationalize dialogue to meet different needs by defining levels of conversation. The CCI Dialogue Sessions, inspired by the traditional Bohmian approach, were effective but time consuming. We don't often have the luxury of six weeks to develop our team's capacity for dialogue. Today there are derivatives of the Bohmian approach, many of which contain efficient means to cultivate dialogical skills. Among these, Theory U has developed a very practical model. We have seen this adopted by many different organizational change consultants because it makes it easy to identify different forms of dialogue and then shift from one to another. In the process of making such shifts, people unconsciously adopt the principles of good dialogue.

Theory U defines Four Levels of Conversation, based on the observation that conversations have patterns. These are relatively stable but can be shifted to another mode of interaction. Each level has its benefits and drawbacks. Each also has indicators that can aid us in self-monitoring the level at which we are operating.[15]

***Downloading**, or Talking Nice*

This level is characterized by politeness at the expense of authenticity. It is speaking from what others want to hear instead of saying what you think. The benefits of downloading are that it maintains social harmony and is a skillful way of playing defense when trust has not yet been established. The drawbacks are that it creates challenges to building authentic relationships, and it is dysfunctional for organizational learning and change.

How can we know whether we have been operating on level one?

> When you come out of a conversation, and everything that you expected to see actually did happen, that's a good indicator that you have been downloading, that you have been part of a conversation where nothing new really happened. Everything that did happen was fitting into your old frameworks--your old expectations.

***Debate**, or Talking Tough*

This level is characterized by divergent perspectives. People say what they think and often argue about which perspective is better or worse. Personal ego and ideas are closely attached (i.e. "I am my point of view"). Due to this attachment, it is difficult for people to get past their own perspective. The benefit of debate is that it can reveal a person's worldview, which once identified makes it easier to work with them. Debate is also a crucible for ideas. When done well, debate can uncover the source of ideas, the values attached to them, and their merit in a particular situation.

How can we know whether we have been operating on level two?

> When you come out of conversation that resulted in some new aspects, some new data points, some new viewpoints that you weren't aware of before, that is challenging some of your own assumptions, that's a good indicator for having been in a good debate, in a good conversation that is exposing you to some new realities outside there that you weren't aware of, and that are challenging some of your own assumptions.

***Dialogue**, or Reflective Inquiry*

This level is characterized by a movement from defense to inquiry into different viewpoints. It is a shift from Me to We (i.e. "I am my jacket" to "I have a jacket and I can take it off"). In dialogue, people see how they are part of a larger whole and speak from that relative position. They connect with others and reflect on how they contribute. This level of conversation is where we ended up in the CCI Dialogue Sessions. The benefits of dialogue we have already made clear. The shift of conversation from level two to three is at the heart of change management because it opens up an authentic space to see and address the root causes of issues.

Yet, like the other levels, it also has drawbacks. First, dialogue exposes vulnerabilities that can be taken advantage of by process hijackers or otherwise manipulative people. It is crucial to set the container before asking people to reveal their weaknesses. Dialogue also establishes new or brings to light existing relationships. These relationships affect the creative process in positive or negative ways depending on the degree of trust and respect, as well as the how skillfully the leader or facilitator can manage personal conflicts toward productive outcomes. At times, there is a benefit to not knowing the other people on your team closely, in that people might feel freer to be creative without concern for relationships.

How can we know whether we have been operating on level three?

> When you come out of a conversation that not only is exposing you to new data that is challenging your assumptions, but that really allows you to see reality through another perspective, through another pair of eyes, and to begin to see yourself through the eyes of another, through the eyes through the experience of another stakeholder. Level three is achieved when you come out of a conversation with a new perspective, not just with new data points.

***Collective Creativity**, or Generative Flow*

This level is characterized by generative dialogues, which Theory U describes as "speaking from what is flowing through." This is the Holy Grail of creativity, the conversations in which the team explores the space between to collectively feel for the New. It is what Scharmer calls "leaning into the emerging future," which is an exploration of potentials that are waiting to be realized. Generative dialogues are when presence and surrender are most vital. Highly attentive stillness (presence) enables us to see the potentials as they first manifest. If we are stuck in our own thoughts, we will miss opportunities. Surrender is necessary to go with the flow of what emerges.

The benefits of generative dialogues are twofold. One, the creative ideas that come forth from them are the seeds of innovation. Second, generative dialogues are transformative for the people in them. Whenever I ask people to recall an experience of breakthrough creativity, it is these moments that they remember best. They are empowering, catalyzing the energy to move into the Rise.

There are two drawbacks to generative dialogues. First, they take a lot of time and are messy. By messy, we mean that such conversations can meander off topic easily and sometimes lead to a host of other issues that have nothing to do with the challenge at hand. It takes skill for the *Xd* to navigate these waters and gently steer the team back on course. Second, generative dialogues are hard to maintain. It is all too easy to slip back into routine ways of doing and being, back to the comfort of the Known. It takes a special effort by all parties to stay in the Unknown, holding the space between and all the ambiguity and uncertainty that comes with it. This is the most difficult aspect of the co-creative journey, and an important differentiator. The more a team has the capacity to stay in the Unknown and hold generative dialogues, the greater chance they have of breakthrough innovations.

How can we know whether we have been operating on level four?

> There are a few key indicators. One is energy. Your energy is way up, your level of inspiration is much higher. A level four conversation also means that's something that wasn't quite there before is in the process of being born. It has to do with profound innovation, which often feels like a birthing process.
>
> Finally, if you leave that conversation and you're still the same person that entered it two or three hours before, then you have not been part of a level four conversation. What this means is that you are different in terms of you, you are more your authentic self. You are more closely connected to your purpose and to your emerging self, rather than to the person that entered the conversation who was more formed or informed by your journey of the past.

While the peak of our journey may focus on collective creativity, we actually operate on all four levels. High-performance teams move across the spectrum of all four levels as needed. Low-performance teams are stuck on one or two. So when do we use each level? The answer to that is not as straightforward as it might seem. Obviously, we don't jump into generative dialogues on the first day. One of the objectives in Act I is to build a strong enough container for these, and to do that we need to progress from levels one through three.

Using the convention of levels is advantageous in that we can use the framework to point out how we are collectively operating at any point throughout the co-creative journey. It is a monitoring tool that can create valuable touchpoints for us. If, for example, the team is supposed to be having a generative dialogue and it slips back into a debate, the *Xd* can draw attention to this. At that point the team can try to reset and re-engage generative dialogue, or they may need to take a step back and look at what underlies their perspectives. Perhaps the generative dialogue has brought to light previously hidden assumptions that need to be evaluated. Perhaps the dialogue has uncovered a false assumption in the problem statement, and the team realizes a need for a downloading session to better understand the challenge before they can ideate on solutions.

Complementing the value of the monitoring process, levels of conversation help us to monitor ourselves. It would be wonderful if, after helping people understand the principles of good dialogue, they could enact those principles at will and with skill. Most of us, authors included, struggle with this. No matter how good a person is at dialogue, or facilitating it, we are all equally human. We are all somewhat attached to our ideas, and when they are challenged it is difficult to not take it personally. The only way we can step outside our ego and enter into authentic and generative dialogues is to check in with *how* we are contributing. It all comes back to awareness, particularly self-awareness. Tools like the levels of conversation are instruments with which we can make quick measurements and adjust as needed.

Levels of conversation, dialogue circles, and other methods to build capacity for collective creativity are integral to the co-creative process. They can take on the form of complementary workshops, professional development trainings, or be woven into program pieces. All are good means to learn how to dialogue with the proficiency needed for co-creation.

Dialogue in Practice

Communication and interpersonal skills pay dividends in creative processes, especially when trying to fully understand or reframe an issue, or hold a generative "what if…?" exploratory dialogue. Among the approaches we discuss, 2 × 2 matrixes, Powers of Ten, Brainstorming, MethodKit Card Games, Six Hats, World Cafe, POV exercises, Why-How laddering, fishbowl, spectrum and affinity maps, and focused conversation are all dialogical tools. There are many more, but common to all of them is the reliance on dialogue as the primary means through which exploration and sharing takes place. Let's look at how we might apply dialogue in the Dive.

A technique that applies the principles of good dialogue to problem solving is the focused conversation, a dialogical tool developed by the Institute for Cultural Affairs.[16] It is one of many methods used to challenge and explore concepts. Focused conversations, or variants of them, are how we identify the critical problems introduced above in the section, "Creating New Practical Knowledge." It is through such dialogues that we create visualizations of critical problems and opportunities, which in turn help the team navigate through the Unknown.

As an example, when the conversation brings up a problem, a good practice is to first identify whether it can be solved or not. If it cannot be solved, then it is not a problem but a fact—because by definition all problems can be solved. And in the case of a fact of any kind, the only logical step to take would be to adjust to the situation. If it can be solved, you can prepare a list of all the effects that are caused by it and identify what impact these effects have. It is good to also evaluate the chain of consequences that would follow from solving the problem. If the problem seems to be the cause of many more problems, a solution would also get rid of these. In such cases, we would label the problem as a critical one and treat it accordingly.

Focused conversations separate objective "facts" of a situation from people's emotional responses and the underlying thought patterns that create the "symptoms" we observe as a problem. For example, as a group we can delve deeply into the trail of contradictions and conflicts that will lead the team to the underlying root causes from which the derived problems emerge. The Iceberg, a system thinking model, illustrates this process (Fig. 9.2).

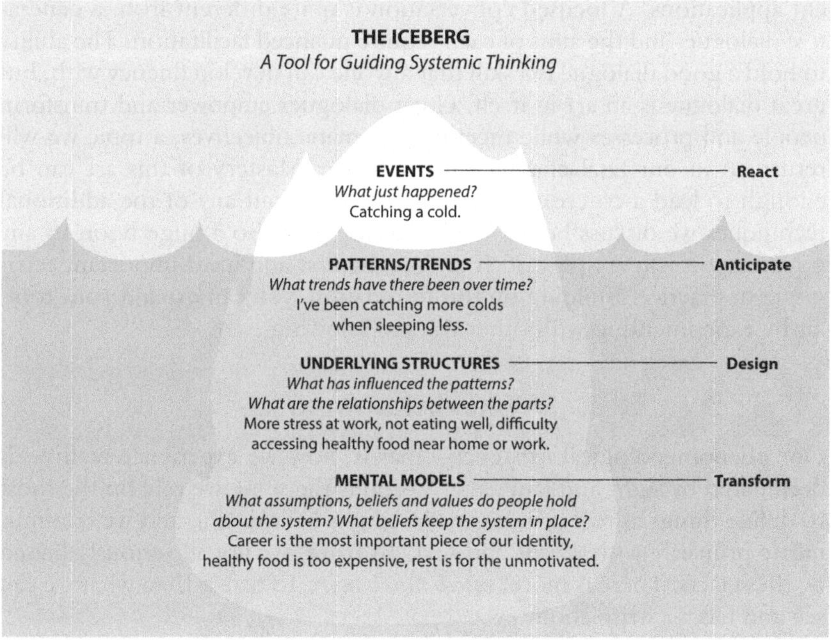

Fig. 9.2 Iceberg model[17]

To use the Iceberg metaphor, the conflicts we encounter are only the part of an iceberg that sticks up out of the water. They are symptoms. On this miniature Dive we look under the surface to discover the systems and thought patterns that create the symptoms. We continue this process until the team has reached the bottom of the issue. Only after uncovering and honoring the root causes will the conflicts begin to unravel.

The point of this exercise is for the team to understand the complex connections between source (mental models), system (structures), and symptom (patterns/events). Based on this understanding, they can identify the problems or contradictions that are most essential and critical in terms of impact. These critical problems can be used as pivot points to create an impactful solution, in that solving an essential problem can lead to chain reaction that resolves many other problems.

Dialogue is perhaps the best tool we have in our toolbox. It is a multi-use tool, a jack of all trades that can do everything from identifying critical problems and opportunities to solving interpersonal conflicts. Dialogue is also our main tool for the exploration of "what if?" We advise browsing through the range of dialogical techniques available and practicing different applications. A focused conversation is quite different from a generative dialogue, and the aims of each require nuanced facilitation. The ability to hold a good dialogue is a skill that anyone can develop fluency with, but great dialogue is an art in itself. Great dialogues empower and transform people and processes while meeting pragmatic objectives, a topic we will return to in our final chapter on resonance. Mastery of this art can be enough to lead a co-creative process, even without any of the additional techniques we discuss below. Skilled dialogue is also a huge boon to any organization you are part of. It is thus the first and most important technique to practice. Building on this foundation, you can expand your toolkit by experimenting with other ways of knowing.

Ways of Knowing

Our phenomenological existence—that is, how we experience reality—is dominated by sight and language. Vision is the sense we rely on the most to define things as real or not (i.e. "seeing is believing"), and we communicate primarily with words and text. In truth, we are all seriously biased by these facts. There is more, *much much more*, to reality than what we can see and talk or write about.

In co-creation we want to fill the space between with as much information as possible, from all possible sources. The more populated this field is, the more novel intersections occur—hence the more latent potential to be acted upon. Dialogical tools are the most common means to fill the space between, and they are effective. But we can do better. We can bring in information from other ways of sensing and knowing.

The subject of consciousness is trending right now, especially the capacity we have to cultivate and master more effective modalities from which we can operate. Humans have been trying to enhance their capabilities for millennia, and consciousness is the new frontier for this endeavor. As but one example, Mihaly Csikszentmihalyi's study of flow states has inspired books like *Stealing Fire: How Silicon Valley, the Navy SEALs, and Maverick Scientists Are Revolutionizing the Way We Live and Work* by Steven Kotler and Jamie Wheal. A spin-off from this is the Flow Genome Project, a research center dedicated entirely to understanding flow states.[18] Their "Flow Dojo" is a specialized retreat programs where, for around $5000, people can develop their capacity for flow.

What they are doing at the Flow Dojo is not new, but how they are selling it is. The new consciousness trend is a rebranding of the human potential movement that started in the 1960s. Centers like Esalen and Naropa University have been helping people master themselves for decades, and their work is now backed with a substantial amount of credible scientific research.[19] The Flow Dojo has jumped on that research to create their programs, framing techniques that have been used for millennia in new language. As advocates of human potential, we also have practices that help us harness our full potential, and we create opportunities for others to grow as well.[20]

Leadership development and creative retreats focus on capacity building and skills that apply those new capacities. Throughout this text we have continually stressed a similar capacity development, what we have called "creative leadership." Here we focus on techniques that help teams tap into other ways of knowing, simultaneously developing and applying our skills.

Models of Consciousness

To successfully harness the benefits of other ways of knowing, we need a model of consciousness that defines what it is we are tapping into. Part of the genius of the nowhere group lies in their codification of four ways of being present in the moment and then offering techniques to master each. The four ways of being present are phenomenologically, emotionally, intuitively, and intellectually.[21] These are complemented by four "qualities of consciousness" (presence, intention, interconnection, and energy) that amplify creative potential. The nowhere group has been operating behind the scenes of major corporations for years, using this framework to catalyze innovation. To us, the fact that nowhere and other consulting groups are finding success in consciousness-based approaches is proof that these methods are both relevant and effective.

If we look closely at the nowhere framework, examining what lies behind the clever branding, we find that the four ways of being present in the moment are actually ways of knowing. Using more commonly known terms, we could restate them as cognition, emotional intelligence, somatic (body) intelligence, and intuition. Recast in these terms, we can see the parallels with the more widely known theory of multiple intelligences. In 1983 Dr. Howard Gardner, a Harvard University professor of education, suggested that the traditional model of intelligence was limited. He proposed eight different intelligences to account for a broader range of human potential.[22] These are:

- Linguistic intelligence ("word smart")
- Logical-mathematical intelligence ("number/reasoning smart")
- Spatial intelligence ("picture smart")
- Bodily kinesthetic intelligence ("body smart")
- Musical intelligence ("music smart")
- Interpersonal intelligence ("people smart")
- Intrapersonal intelligence ("self-smart")
- Naturalist intelligence ("nature smart")

The map is never the territory, so while these eight "intelligences" might not be a perfect model of human capacities, they are a good start for helping us get past traditional forms of learning.[23] Each intelligence, which may be better called "aptitude," suggests a different modality for learning. The American Institute for Learning and Development suggests[24]:

- words (linguistic intelligence)
- numbers or logic (logical-mathematical intelligence)
- pictures (spatial intelligence)
- music (musical intelligence)

- self-reflection (intrapersonal intelligence)
- a physical experience (bodily-kinesthetic intelligence)
- a social experience (interpersonal intelligence), and/or
- an experience in the natural world (naturalist intelligence)

Gardner's list does not include intuition, but it could be argued that intuition is simply being receptive to information from all eight forms of knowing. Recalling our earlier point, insights often arise when we relax the cognitive forebrain and allow for information from other sources to come forth. If it were our list, we might make a couple changes, notably adding "field-knowing" (awareness of larger wholes) and "imagination"—which we feel is a unique power that could be considered a form of intelligence. Walt Disney certainly agreed, codifying it as "Imagineering."[25]

Whatever models we use, the fact is that human beings are capable of multiple ways of knowing, and that for each there are techniques to access and further develop that aptitude. Equipped with this broader perspective, we can more readily identify the link between specific techniques and the ways of knowing they access. Bodystorming, for example, accesses somatic and social emotional intelligence. So does Social Presencing Theatre, a Presencing Institute and U.Lab technique. Intuition walks, particularly those done in natural settings, access natural intelligence. Sculpting, drawing, and painting tap into our intuition and imagination, helping us relax our rational minds while also working with our hands. Most designers encourage such acts of "doing" as ways of thinking, and indeed there is a close link between physical tasks and creativity.[26] This is one reason why prototyping can be used early and often in a creative process. It, like dialogical and other tools, is a way of "thinking around" a subject.

Practices

While at the School of Design in the Hong Kong Polytechnic University, one of the courses we taught was the "Psychology of Creativity." My co-instructor, Dr. David Williams, came from a background in psychology and favored the cognitive model of creativity. I, coming from a background in anthropology and consciousness studies, liked to explore a wide variety of techniques from across diverse cultural traditions. We had a productive creative tension, offering students a palette of possible techniques to invoke their creativity and allow them to decide which, if any, paradigm to adopt. Our classroom approach preceded ours here: whatever works is what you should use. We introduced students to techniques ranging from gestalt and divergent thinking exercises to lucid dreaming and meditation. What we found is instructive. Every approach we practiced works equally well. Naturally students had their preferences, but we found that anyone who dedicated themselves to expanding their personal toolkit perceived some improvement in their creative efforts. That, and the fact that leading design and creative enterprises are using these tools, are further evidence to support the notion that tapping into different ways of knowing is beneficial to the creative process.

As we provide illustrations, we should note that it is quite difficult to state with any certainty exactly what modality or modalities any one method is accessing. Our understanding is not that precise, and some of these are entirely unscientific. Yet they work, and that makes them valuable techniques to put in your toolkit.

Just as a musician or elite athlete must train regularly, so too do people who wish to maximize their creativity. Practicing these tools helps us harness creative potential in ourselves and our teams. They are means through which we develop fluency working with the Unknown. Here are short descriptions of several techniques that we enjoy using. Following the convention used throughout this text, we direct readers to source materials in the chapter endnotes.

Thinkpak[27]

Thinkpak is a brainstorming card deck designed by Michael Michalko, author of the book *Thinkertoys*. The deck contains stimulating cards to help think about or reframe an issue. Thinkpak is helpful in identifying critical problems, reframing the parameters of ideation (i.e. shifting constraints), and evaluation. Tools like Thinkpak and other card games provide easy-to-follow guidelines and sample questions, making them particularly valuable for those new to critical exploration and evaluation of concepts.

Lego Serious Play[28]

The LEGO® SERIOUS PLAY® (LSP) Method is a co-creative process that uses questions to probe an issue, followed by responses that require building a 3D Lego model to answer the guiding questions. Despite the common misunderstanding of LSP as a game, it is a powerful technique for everything from creative discussions to problem solving and decision-making. LSP embodies the design emphasis on working with the hands, creating physical prototypes to think with and explore new possibilities. In our experience, LSP can also reveal many of the underlying assumptions and thought patterns that dialogue strives to draw out. For example, asking two individuals or teams to build a bridge and then connect the two will uncover hidden assumptions about bridges and force the team to make decisions on communication and leadership styles. LSP is thus useful in both Act I and II, and it impacts all three aspects of the creative journey.

Medíts[29]

Medíts are quick meditation practices that develop the capacity for presencing. These are meant for people who do not have time for, or wish to complement, more disciplined practices such as daily sitting meditation. Short meditations are effective for capacity building, as well as bringing presence into daily activity where its benefits can be realized.

One is Image Interpretation, an exercise used by Joanna Ziegler in her classes at Holy Cross College. She had students travel to a museum and look at the same art piece weekly for an entire term. Each time she asked, "What is actually there? What are you bringing to it?" She then read students' answers, noting how every one of them was different. By looking repeatedly at the same image while exploring within to identify what was affecting the interpretation, students learned how their own conditioned judgments affected perception. Image Interpretation is a nice complement to Seeing as Pieces, deconstructing not only what is seen but how it is seen.

A second Medít is Listening Out. In this exercise you have a group of people train their attention to different sound fields. Sitting quietly, the first tuning is to the sounds within the body. You then ask them to listen out to the next field, the sounds between people in the space. The next field is the sounds of the environment, such as air conditioners and people walking by in the halls. The final field is the world outside the room. To conclude, you ask them to try to hold all of these levels in attention at the same time, which for most people is challenging. The point is obvious … we cannot possibly perceive everything that is occurring within and around us. Our perceptions are always limited by capacity and what we focus attention on.

These Medíts are just two of many techniques to train attention, which lies at the heart of presence. Focusing attention on something external is the easiest way to begin capacity building, and it has additional benefits. Image Interpretation and Listening Out reveal just how much our perceptions, which themselves are conditioned, construct "reality." Once a person experiences this truth first hand, it is very hard to maintain a position that their view is the "right" one. Medíts are thus quite valuable in the early stages of the Dive to help separate peoples' ideas from their egos, which helps us constructively deconstruct ideas without the feeling of being personally attacked. At the same time, they build the capacity for presencing, which we will use to sense for new potentials.

We recommend what might be called a "layered approach" to building the capacity for presencing. You can't start off expecting people to be able to sit quietly for 30 minutes and allow for insights to emerge. That skill, if it is needed, takes time to develop. A layered approach is one that introduces people to presence with short, easy-to-master exercises like Medíts. In contemplative practices we can observe a similar approach, starting off with focusing attention on the physical senses. It is easy to identify the breath and observe it without judgment. It is much more difficult to stay equanimeous in the observation of one's own thoughts, or in the midst of a discussion. Practice, whether through short five-minute meditations, sitting quietly, or long walks in nature, will develop the skill so long as one focuses their intention and attention on it.

Prime the Senses[30]

Priming the senses is one of several techniques from Social Artistry, a framework for personal development created by Jean Houston. The Social Artists Field book states,

> Social artistry training facilitates the development of skills and potentials in both individuals and groups in ways that enhance their societal awareness, liberate their inventiveness, increase their ability to work cooperatively with others, and raise their levels of self-esteem.

Social Artistry offers its own model of consciousness that identifies four "realms" of awareness: physical/sensory, psychological/historic, mythic/symbolic, and unitive/integral. Mastering each realm is both liberating and empowering, a reason why we find it valuable for creative leaders and teams.

Priming the senses is a technique for mastery of the physical/sensory realm. It is a guided practice wherein you invite your partner to experience each of their senses. The act of doing this "primes" all of the senses, which helps people move away from vision as the predominant sense and use all of their faculties. Priming the senses is a warm-up for the next two techniques and can be used at the beginning of any creative process where you want people to tap into body intelligence.

Self as an Instrument[31]

Self as an instrument is a technique based on the fact that a large part of communication is non-verbal. Any expression contains not only tone, energy, and content but also a tremendous amount of more subtle information. We can apply our body intelligence, tapping into subtle informational fields, by treating the body and its senses as an instrument.

In this exercise, you must come present into the moment, turning attention inward and attending to what the body is "telling" you. You invite data from the body as it reacts to what you are thinking about or listening to. A few questions you might ask are "Does this feel 'right'? How am I reacting? What in me is reacting?" and "What does this evoke?" As fluency develops you will be able to notice different energy states, which can be very helpful in decision-making. In one application, for example, you visualize the impact of different decisions, holding each scenario in your imagination and being receptive to how that feels in the body. Scenarios with positive or calm energy indicate an internal alignment around that decision. Scenarios that feel "off" or odd in some way indicate a misalignment, perhaps stemming from neglect of something important. In such cases, the exercise points to a need for further examination of that decision.

Guided Visualizations

Imagination is one of the most powerful creative faculties we have. Guided visualizations are one way of tapping into this aptitude, and they take on a variety of forms. The *Gamestorming* text offers "Cover Story"—a game that uses the format of a magazine or newspaper cover as the canvas upon which people lay out their ideal future.[32] Cover stories are inclusive of headlines, key quotes, images, and other specifics that flush out the details of the envisioned future. Details facilitate the transition from very broad, idealistic visions to more actionable ones with elements that can be set as goals to strive for.

Social Artistry uses an imaginary exercise called "Stepping into the Future." In it, one person is guided by a partner down an imaginary path into the future, using all of the senses to make it more real. The guide must balance very detailed descriptions of the pathway with an openness that allows for the participant to fill in their vision and the important milestones along the way to achieving it. Like Cover Story, this exercise asks the participant to fill in concrete details of their vision. It adds a sense of the journey and what incremental steps are necessary.

Guided visualizations like these can start in the present or past and work their way forward, or in the future and work backward. Both approaches have value, with the quality of results relying on the skill of the guide and the imaginal capacities of the listeners.

Journaling

Sometimes all it takes to step into the future is a journal and good questions. Coaching questions such as "What do you want to create and what are you creating now?" are another form of guided visualization.

Journaling can be used to imagine the future, evaluate the present, and reflect on the past. The U.Lab workbook contains a series of poignant questions for a self-reflective process that guides a person from their past into the future, facilitating a "helicopter" view that provides fresh perspective.[33]

Journaling can also be an inner expedition. According to Scharmer, the purpose of journaling is to connect to a deeper level of self-knowing and to begin acting from that place. Its outcomes are:

- A heightened level of self-knowing.
- A shift in the state of attention (consciousness) of the group to a deeper level.
- A new awareness and new questions about who I am and what I want do with the rest of my life.

A disciplined journaling practice is an invaluable tool for action learning. It connects people to their purpose and can also be an important indicator of change in oneself and one's ideas. The ability to see change over time makes journaling a valuable measure of personal growth.

Intuition Walks and Holding Questions

Questions, as we have seen, can be used in a variety of active approaches. They are equally powerful in receptive approaches. The nowhere group often begins their creative journeys with a "breakthrough question," an evocative form of a compelling needs story or mission statement. Breakthrough questions, they argue:

> [A]re like keys to doors. They are essential for unlocking our personal creativity. For creativity rarely begins with an answer. As soon as we discover an answer, learning tends to slow down and curiosity diminishes. By reframing an initial insight, intuition or notion as a breakthrough question, we are able to trigger our curiosity. Curiosity creates vitality, and together they generate enough energy to start and sustain the creative process. Breakthrough questions should therefore lead us into the unknown. They should create a sense of excitement, enthusiasm and momentum, yet at the same time generate a sense of trepidation and fear. They are designed to reveal their magic over time as we learn to 'hold' as opposed to answer them.[34]

Holding the question—consciously trying to *not* come up with solutions—is a receptive approach that invites information from other ways of knowing. As simple as this sounds, holding a question is much harder than you might think. We all want to jump straight into solutions, most of the time with the best of intentions. Pressing "pause" on ourselves is not easy to do, and yet it is exactly what we must do if we are to successfully tap into other ways of knowing. Pausing creates a space within and between us for emergence.

We can facilitate holding questions with other activities that help us pause our thinking processes. A favorite is intuition walks, preferably done in natural settings with minimal human impact. Based on the Native American medicine walk, an intuition walk is a long walk in nature holding a question. For young Native Americans, their question was often, "What is my purpose?" The answer to that helped them understand their role in society as the adult they were becoming. Intuition walks in nature tap into what Gardner called "natural intelligence." Nature acts as a mirror to our questions, reflecting back to us information that helps us reframe our perspective on it. Nature does not speak in human language, however. It uses symbols, metaphor, pattern, and coincidence instead. Ask yourself this, "Why is it that you notice the things you do when out on a walk?" What we notice may be somewhat random, but we would argue that some of it is also related to the intention you are holding. If you are holding a question, for example, you will notice things that have some relevance to that question.

On an intuition walk you ask people to bring a journal and capture what occurs, especially the random or striking things they notice. Have them write and also draw or take pictures. They then share their notes with peers who took the walk with them, who help them see patterns, repetitions, and other unique aspects of their experience. The listener must be careful not to interpret what they hear or give advice. It is not their journey, and the role they play is that of mirroring back to the speaker only what might shed new light on their question.

In the dozens of times we have used intuition walks, we have consistently observed that people who go on an intuition walk come back with a fresh or deeper perspective on their question. Perhaps it is natural intelligence. Perhaps it is just the fact that they have taken a bit of time to deeply reflect on an important question. At the very least it helps quiet the rational mind so that people can listen more fully to their intuition. Who knows? It works, and in our experience people cite intuition walks as one of their favorite moments.

Case Clinics

Case clinic, a peer coaching technique from the U.Lab, uses metaphor and symbol to augment peer interactions. The method integrates multiple ways of knowing as input streams by inviting the coaches to listen to the case giver with an open mind, open heart, and open will. After listening, the coaches mirror back what they have heard by sharing images/metaphors, feelings, and gestures that arose for them while listening. Like an intuition walk, the coaches are allowing other "voices," or sources of intuition, to be expressed. Having listened to all the coaches, the case giver then reflects back what they have heard, followed by a generative dialogue on how these observations can offer new perspective. The tone of the entire case clinic is one of service to the case giver, without a pressure to resolve or fix the issue.

CCI hosted the Hong Kong "hub"—a peer learning group—for the first two years of the U.Lab course. We ran case clinics weekly for the course and continued them afterward in our own CCI Sessions. We learned two valuable points. First, case clinics require a lot of practice. They require holding questions and pressing "pause" on the desire to find solutions, an aptitude that does not come easily. It also takes time to develop fluency with consciously tapping into intuition and capturing the signals sent. Most of the time we captured these in metaphor or drawings, which leads to our second observation. In nearly all cases, discussion of our intuitions led to profound perspective shifts.[35] Discussions without these supported or helped reframe the issue, but rarely led to major change.

We cannot offer any scientific explanation for this, but the fact is that it worked in our group. Part of it was likely due to the fact that we had a very strong container, with sufficient trust to share openly without fear of our inputs being perceived as strange. We also maintained the service attitude, rotating the weekly case clinics so that every person had the support of the whole group on their issue. With practice, we got over the need to offer solutions and were able to hold purely exploratory dialogues. Finally, there was the mysterious power of intuition. Case clinics provide a structured format to tap into other ways of knowing. When we create this space within and between people, we are often given insights that can and do facilitate perspective shifts.

Art Explorations

Art is a language that invites and expresses far more than what we can convey in words. Consider the saying, "A picture is worth a thousand words." Images show us what we may or may not ever be able to describe. Similarly, music evokes and conveys powerful emotions and memories of times and places we are far removed from. Paintings are often said to capture the soul of the artist, and we study them to get a glimpse into their world. Theater can share entire life experiences, both real and imaginary.

Art explorations are the use of artistic medium to explore and express ideas. The use of art is limited only by your imagination. In one of our events, for example, we worked with a company that produces clothing, from growing the cotton to making yarn and designing shirts. We asked teams to create collaborative art pieces using the artifacts of their industry: buttons, strings, pins, measuring tapes, and cloth. They found great joy in expressing their vision of the future through art, and the energy of the sharing session was off the charts.

Social Artistry uses watercolor painting as a way to tap into the unitive/integral realm of awareness. Participants are asked to explore with colors, water saturation, and brush strokes on paper without any sense of purpose. By refraining from goals and judgments, they tune their attention to what is emerging. Only after a time do they begin to give form to their work. The aim is to work with a sense of intuition and "unfolding," with process rather than outcome. Through the exercise they are learning to play with emergence itself. This is a skill that transfers to the co-creative process, cultivating the capacity to sense for potentials—the New.

Theater is powerful in a number of scenarios. The U.Lab technique "Social Presencing Theatre" combines presence with dance to restore the natural synchronicity between the body and mind.[36] It slows people down and brings them into the present, resulting in greater emotional intelligence and heartfelt listening. It is a great technique to use prior to or in the middle of intense brainstorming, resetting, and grounding the team.

Story Bridge, the folk theater program developed by Richard Geer, is an incredible one-day workshop that empowers and bonds communities in a journey of self and group discovery.[37] Story Bridge takes untrained actors and has them both write and perform short scenes related to a theme. Similarly, IDEO at one point had a design team train in improvisational theater to help them role-play different users and scenarios. Theater brings to life many dimensions of life that cannot be expressed in any other way. It is incredibly valuable in cultivating empathy for others while exploring, creating shared expressions, and empowering groups.

Butterfly Test (IDEO)[38]

The butterfly test is tool to extract the intuition of the group. We quote here at length to preserve the quality of Tim Brown's description.

> Invented by Bill Moggridge, design thinker extraordinaire and one of the pioneers of Silicon Valley design, the butterfly test is a thoroughly unscientific but amazingly effective process for extracting a few key insights from a mass of data. Let's imagine that by the end of a deep research phase, numerous brainstorming sessions, and endless prototypes, an entire wall of the project room has been covered with promising ideas. Each participant is then given a small number of small Post-it "ballots" to attach to the ideas they think should move forward. Members of the team flutter about the room inspecting the tableau of ideas, and before long it is clear which ones have attracted the most "butterflies." Of course, all kinds of issues come into play, including politics and personalities, but that is what reaching consensus is all about. Give and take. Compromise and creative combination. All these and more play a part in reaching the end result. The process is not about democracy, it is about maximizing the capacities of teams to converge on the best solutions. It's chaotic, but it works surprisingly well and can be adapted to the peculiarities of many organizations.

The butterfly test is one of many forms of "voting" on ideas. Voting has two major benefits. First, it is a measure of where the energy lies. "Winners" may or may not be the "best" idea, but they are the ones that the majority of people are willing to take forward. They have the highest engagement and commitment, which increases the likelihood of successful implementation. Other ideas may be brilliant, and these should be kept as backups for future creative efforts. Yet for co-creation we need collective engagement, and voting helps us put a finger on where that momentum lies.

As discussed in Chap. 6, voting—in the form of marketplaces—is also an effective leveling device. People may be forced to listen to a particularly powerful ego for a time, but when it comes time to decide what to take forward, voting allows for anonymous feedback. If that person or team's idea was poor, or if they are not liked, their plan might die in the marketplace.

Adventures

Our technique guidelines would not be complete without including adventures. Group adventures are perhaps the best way to create a miniature creative rollercoaster, giving the team a taste of the entire journey as well as helping them come to terms with the process and all its contours. An adventure is a collective Hero's journey. Joseph Campbell, a famous mythologist, created a model of the Hero's journey that is widely applicable in life. It is particularly appropriate for visualizing creative adventures (Fig. 9.3).

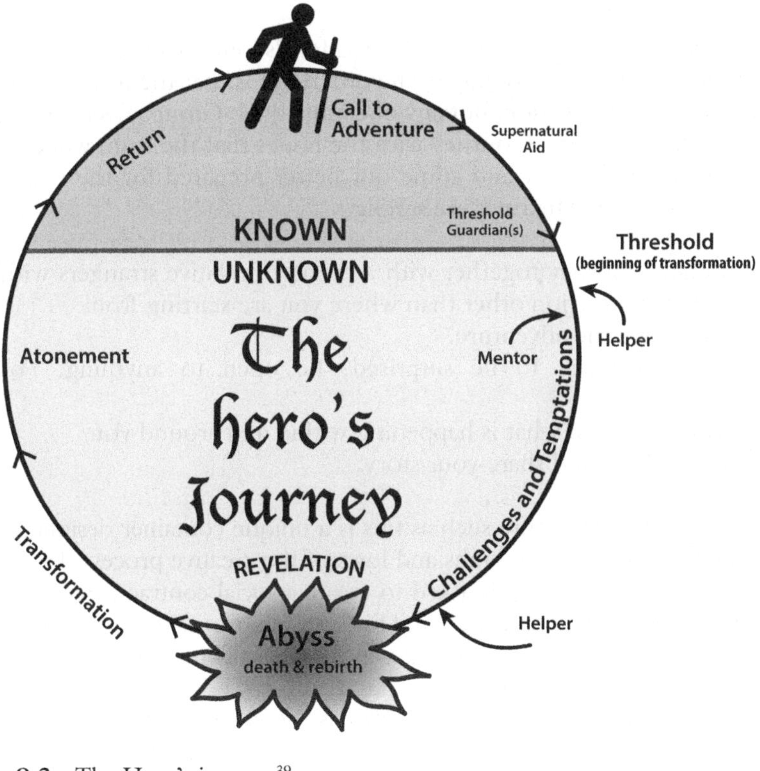

Fig. 9.3 The Hero's journey[39]

Campbell's Hero's journey is familiar because it is the template for many video games and movies such as Harry Potter, the Matrix, and most Disney movies. The Hero is given some call to adventure, which at first they resist, and something happens that compels them to take on the quest. They are given some form of supernatural aid, in the form of special powers or helpers, which they must learn to master to become the Hero. In our context, these are creative leadership capacities (e.g. PACE) and skills (holding space, presencing).

The journey takes the budding Hero from the familiar, Known world into the unfamiliar and dangerous Unknown. In myths this is the dark forest or another strange world. In co-creation this is the Dive. In the Unknown the Hero faces trials to master their newfound abilities, which they must pass or perish (project failure). The old self dies and is reborn as the Hero in the Abyss, the place of greatest fear and uncertainty. If they survive this, they emerge transformed and bring their new powers back to society as gifts (Innovation).

The co-creative journey parallels the Hero's journey in many ways, and it can be equally transformative. The difference is that the team *as a whole* is the Hero in co-creation, not any one individual. Group adventures facilitate a collective Hero's journey with the hopes that the team will explore the Unknown together and come out better prepared for the real journey—co-creation. The rules are simple:

- Begin a journey together with a group of relative strangers with no sense of direction other than where you are starting from.
- Co-create the adventure.
- Allow yourself to be surprised. Be open to anything. Follow emergence.
- Take notice of what is happening within and around you.
- Come back and share your story.

An open-ended adventure such as this is a unique container designed specifically to encourage the highs and lows of the creative process. From the very beginning the group is asked to create a social contract, step into the Unknown, sense for emergence, and figure things out as they go. Given that they are strangers, you can expect things to start off with politeness and then get messy as ideas and attitudes begin to conflict. They will learn a lot about each other's personalities and capacities as they take on the journey. They can also practice new skills along the way, such as being present and following flow. If they stick to the rules and allow for emergence, the adventure will undoubtedly have some interesting twists and turns. How they reacted to these (individually and as a group) is instructive for how they will act in the creative process. Finally, asking them to bring along a journal and reflect on their inner and outer experience is a valuable growth tool.

When the groups return, it is helpful to contextualize their experience in light of a creative rollercoaster. The nowhere group does this beautifully, with one rendition laying out the contrasting forces that everyone must deal with (Fig. 9.4).[40]

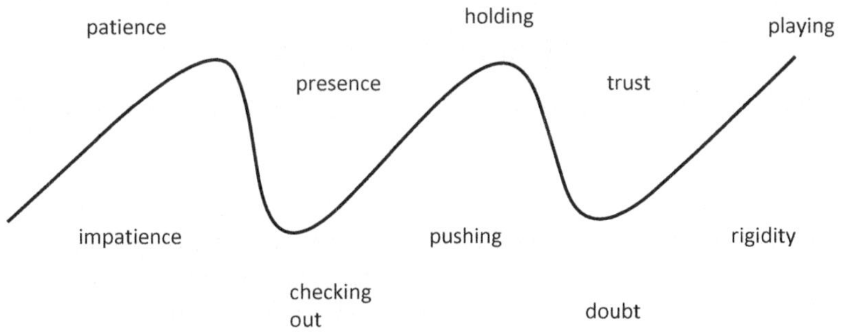

Fig. 9.4 Contours and contrasting forces

Visualizing the contours of the experience validates all three aspects of the journey, as well as the emotions, tensions, and breakthroughs that come with them. It gives the team an experiential model for the larger co-creative journey that they are going through, which helps them accept the process. Finally, by revealing opposing forces and the tensions these create, it helps people manage the Unknown. If I know, for example, that I am must check in with my own feelings and any doubts that I have, then I will do so with awareness. That gives me the ability to intervene with those forces and channel my energies to where they are needed.

This section on techniques contains methods that we have seen work well and adopted into our own practice. It is not a complete list of possibilities, and there are many different toolkits that you can use. We are not trying to be the authority, but rather one voice complementing several solid approaches to which we refer to throughout the text. What differs here is perhaps how we categorize techniques and the value we place on multiple ways of knowing. If you find value in these, use them. If not, either adopt a toolkit more suited to your style or be creative and make up your own. The tools are just tools, and there will always be more than one way to get the job done. If you can guide the team into and through the Unknown, testing and reframing the collective knowledge base while exploring for the New, then you are doing what is needed for the knowledge aspect of the journey.

Next comes the question of how we can support the emotional and interpersonal aspects of the journey. There are a variety of complementary processes that we can employ to build capacities in our teams and help them navigate the uncertain waters of the Unknown. We begin with what is perhaps most important—managing uncertainty.

Managing Uncertainty

Process is the driver, but team dynamics is the engine, and emotions power the engine.

In our illustration of the three aspects of the creative journey, a "Red Curve Transition" is a key emotional touchpoint in the overall process. It indicates a point in the exploration when team members need to come together and start relying on each other to be able to stand up to the challenge. How will this collective shift of approach take place? There are probably as many alternative ways to achieve this as there are different types of teams. What works well for one team might have disastrous effects on another. To find an approach that works, one should be well tuned for what is taking place underneath the surface/façade of the team (Fig. 9.5).

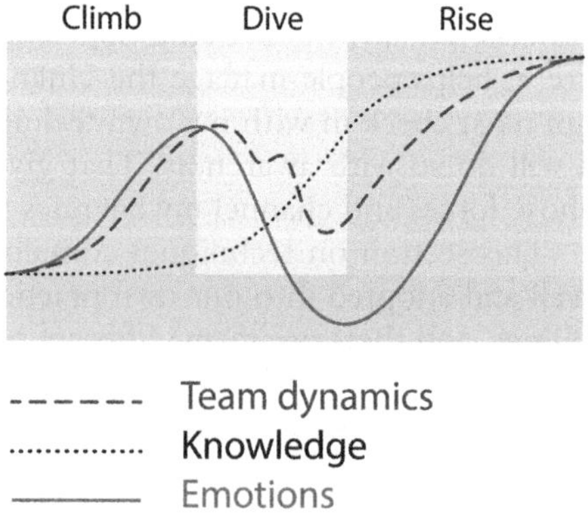

Fig. 9.5 Aspects of the co-creative journey

First, a leader and a catalyst should understand that there are consequences to pushing the boundaries of the Known, and these consequences stem from the elements of ***uncertainty*** and ***ambiguity***. People will react very differently to these elements based on their personalities, their relationship to the topic, their fields of expertise, and of course their level of experience in these types of situations. These reactions may cause them to behave in a more or less irrational, yet usually quite predictable manner. Some people might feel that they are losing control of the process, as they are leaving their comfort zones, while others feel that they are finally arriving at the spot where they are no longer inferiors to "the experts," and that they can finally start to apply and show their strengths. These emotions might drive some people to isolating themselves from everyone else, while others might react in the exactly opposite way by seeking comfort from their tribe. The diversity of these feelings and reactions will create barriers between team members, which might lead to major problems in internal communication and coordination unless the underlying issues are addressed and handled appropriately.

Harmony or Apathy

Solving a conflict at ACAN

The team had already worked for a few months, when it became clear to everyone that Laura and Jim could not continue behaving the way they did. Already during the first team meeting, Theresa had sensed some friction between them, but at the time she had decided to ignore it and see how their situation would evolve. To her, it was quite understandable that Laura and Jim were not getting along very well, since they came from two different worlds. Laura had received her MBA at the top of the class just few years ago, yet she had been promoted to a senior position at ACAN because of her skills and ambition. Jim on the other hand had been working for the company for more than 20 years, and during that time he had seen these brown-nosers come and go, so he didn't give much value to her presence in the team. So nobody expected them to become best friends with each other, but everyone assumed that they would be able to work in the same team.

However, now that the team was getting ready to dive deeper into exploration, the situation had become unbearable for everyone. Theresa took control of the situation and decided that one of them would have to

(*continued*)

(continued)

leave the team. She talked with all team members separately to find out which one was to be blamed for the problems. Most agreed that it was Laura's strong opinions that had made Jim so uncomfortable to begin with, and many of the teammates admitted that they didn't always agree with Laura either. Since the entire team was already very emotional about the situation, Theresa also asked her colleagues outside the team for help. They did not know any details about what had happened between Laura and Jim, but for them that was no reason to restrain from sharing their opinions with her. Some were criticizing Jim for stubbornness, while others were blaming Laura for being too pushy and naïve. Between these interviews and opinions, Theresa decided that Laura would have to take the fall since she had less experience in ACAN than Jim.

Laura was kicked out, and Theresa apologized to her team for not reacting any sooner. The team went on with their journey, and everyone was happy that peace had returned to their team. Team spirit was high again, and everyone was happy that nobody was continuously and arrogantly questioning the team's choices. And when the project came to a conclusion, everyone was happy even though they were not quite able to reach any of their objectives. Most likely that was Laura's fault, too.

Right and Wrong Kinds of Conflicts

As the ACAN story demonstrates, once strong emotions emerge and start to take over, the chance of conflicts between individual team members increases rapidly. Any conflicts that began to emerge at the end of the first stage will start to gather like dark clouds above the team, acting as a source of negative atmosphere and interpersonal tension. This dense atmosphere will become even thicker and more dominant as new conflicts emerge during the Dive. On their way down, the unity of the team is continually tested, which puts a lot of pressure on the leaders and requires persistence from the team members.

Despite all the negativity associated with these conflicts, these contradictions are in fact the types of discoveries that the team needs as clues to lead them forward. If neglected or mistreated, conflicts can lead the team to lose all their momentum and ultimately end up in a complete standstill. However, if utilized appropriately, these conflicts can act as powerful thrusters that spark the team to take giant leaps in conquering the Unknown. For this reason, it is crucial that the team knows not to hide such conflicts, but to embrace them and share them with the team. Successful teams are not afraid of conflicts or problems. A strong leader's reaction to the first conflict would be something like: "Great, we have a problem! Now how do we solve it?"

Dealing with Diversity and Conflict

It has been said that personal growth can only take place outside of one's own comfort zone. When a contradiction between two perspectives appears, the conflicting team members need to be encouraged to step outside of their comfort zones and start reforming their views. Once they can find common ground for their perspectives, they can start resolving the conflict and align their efforts toward discovering solutions. As long as there is trust between the conflicting individuals and willingness to resolve the issue, the conflict will lead the team forward in their quest. Without trust, respect, and common commitment, it is difficult to expand the common ground or to look beyond one's own perspectives.

If a tension evolves into a conflict, we must determine whether it is an affective or substantive conflict. Affective, or interpersonal, conflicts stem from personality clashes or different communication styles. Substantive conflicts stem from performance, management, or different domain expertise, and often relate to project or organizational goals. Both types of conflict can have positive or negative effects on the creative process.

Conflict management techniques come in many forms, yet underlying most of these are good dialogue and feedback mechanisms in a safe container. If a person feels that they can be authentic and share their true feelings, then sometimes all you need to do is create space for them to share their frustrations. A good part of effective therapy is deep listening, complemented by advice that is in service to the person you are listening to. You don't have to be a psychotherapist to manage conflict, all you need is the right attitude (trust, empathy, authenticity, service) and a few tools.

One simple feedback exercise, useful at many points throughout the creative journey, is asking people what is good about what is happening, what is difficult, and what they might do differently. By asking what is good first, it creates an overall positive tone to a feedback session. Inviting feedback at regular intervals also deepens relationships, which can deflate tensions before they become conflicts.

We can attempt to resolve affective conflicts with peer-to-peer or group relational councils, a tool best used to explore a behavior that conflicts with your values. Relational councils combine active listening with the focused conversation method to tease apart observable facts of a situation from emotional reactions. Revealing emotional, conditioned responses is the first step. Acknowledging and honoring them is the second. When a team holds the space for such authentic exchanges, it can resolve tensions and catalyze emotional breakthroughs. Even if the conflict is not resolved, at the very least there's a new awareness of the facts of the situation and how people react to them. A skilled leader can then choose to redirect people's efforts or restructure teams as they see necessary to manage the conflict.

Individual coaching may also be needed in some contexts. Coaching helps someone develop or improve upon their capacities and/or skills. While most often used in leadership contexts, everyone can benefit from coaching. GROW is one non-directive coaching model that is simple and effective for many situations.[41] GROW is an acronym for G (goals), R (current reality), O (options), and W (will do). In a coaching session you guide the other person through a thought process that connects them to their purpose and helps them chart a path forward to their goals, including specific actions they will take. We have found success using GROW when an individual is either disengaged or being detrimental to the creative process (e.g. "hijackers"). For the disengaged, it is a miniature strategic visioning session that can help realign their actions with their interests, kicking up their energy and engagement. For hijackers, it is a reality check. If their goals are aligned with the co-creative process, GROW will reveal what behaviors are inconsistent with realizing those goals—which are typically the same behaviors that are causing conflict. If goals are misaligned, then steps can be taken to either (1) bring them into alignment or (2) do something different with that person.

It is wise for an *Xd* to have relational councils, peer counseling, GROW, and other coaching techniques in their toolkit.[42] Co-creation, by virtue of the need for diverse teams, will almost always have affective conflicts. We have seen what happens when a facilitator tries to avoid conflicts. The container ruptures, losing the energy and creative tension we need. If we don't deal with interpersonal tensions, they will fester and potentially grow into harmful conflicts. A better stance is to come in expecting and prepared for conflict, defusing the bomb before it explodes.

Substantive conflicts are a different challenge, and like all challenges, they can be opportunities. Per the Lumen course "Boundless Management,"

> Substantive conflicts can affect performance for the better by removing barriers caused by different assumptions or misunderstandings about a team's tasks, strategy, or goals. Conflict can be constructive when it creates broader awareness about how team members are experiencing their work and thus leads to changes that improve members' productivity. Conflict can also lead to process improvements, such as when it reveals a deficiency in how the team communicates, which can then be corrected. Clashes of ideas can lead to more creative solutions or otherwise provide perspectives that persuade the team to take a different approach that is more likely to lead to success.[43]

In co-creation, substantive conflicts are best managed in group dialogues that create transparency, shared understanding, and alignment. Focused conversation and similar tools (discussed above) tease out the underlying reasons for substantive conflicts. When done in the group context, these dialogues expand collective knowledge while simultaneously enhancing the team's capacity to constructively work with difference. While a dialogue may or may not resolve a substantive conflict, it will at least give voice to every person's perspective and identify the critical problems and opportunities to be addressed. In this way, the team can move forward with mutual respect for their differences, yet remain aligned toward the program goals.

Holding Creative Tension

The tricky thing about conflict is that it might not always be a good idea to release the tension, if the tension acts as the push needed to take the team forward. Peter Senge, author of *The Fifth Discipline*, talks about the difference between *creative tension* and *emotional tension*, saying that these two should not be confused with each other.[44] Creative tension comes from the difference between our current reality and our visions. It is the force created by the gap between possibility and constraint. This distance can make a vision seem unrealistic or unachievable, resulting in feelings of pessimism or hopelessness. This is emotional tension, the negative emotions related to creative tension such as anxiety, discouragement, hopelessness, sadness, and worry, which will keep us away from pursuing our visions.

Managing creative tension lies mostly in the perspective we have toward it. By making the distinction between creative and emotional tension, we are able to separate the two and see the positive value in the former. As Senge writes, "… the gap between vision and current reality is also a source of energy. If there was no gap, there would be no need for any action to move toward the vision. Indeed, the gap is the source of creative energy."[45]

There are two ways to relieve creative tension. One pathway is to lower the ambition of visions, settling for comfortable mediocrity. Another path is to step outside comfort zones and pursue the vision, reducing the gap between current reality and the potential future. It is our role as leaders or catalysts to help the team step forward rather than backward. We must help them unlearn fear and return to a state of curiosity.

> We allow our goals to erode when we are unwilling to live with emotional tension. On the other hand, when we understand creative tension and allow it to operate by not lowering our vision, vision becomes an active force. Robert Fritz says, "It's not what the vision is, it's what the vision does." Truly creative people use the gap between vision and current reality to generate energy for change.[46]

It is through mastery of creative tension that we learn to deal with failure. We have the potential to learn far more from failures that we do from success. Failure, in Senge's perspective, is "evidence of the gap between vision and current reality. Failure is an opportunity for learning—about inaccurate pictures of current reality, about strategies that didn't work as expected, about the clarity of the vision."[47] This is why designers often recite the mantra, "fail faster." The sooner we fail, the faster we learn and move on to the next, and better, iteration. In our experience, one of the best ways to help a team grow more comfortable with creative tension is to encourage failure early on. A "Bad Idea Jam"—a game where the team ideates on the worst possible solutions to the challenge and then tries to identify the good elements—is one quick method. This game is a miniature version of a more vital process—stepping back from a failure to reflect on what can be learned from it. Action learning, as this group reflection is known, should begin early on and continue throughout the co-creative process. Every time you recast a failure as a learning opportunity, you transform it into a partial success. And that builds confidence in the team, helping them replace fear with curiosity and courage.

Creative Team Dynamics

Highly productive and creative teams are rarely nice, nor calm, nor harmonious. Or like Kathleen Eisenhardt put it, "the absence of conflict is not harmony, it's apathy."[48] Instead of showing smiley faces all day long, successful teams tend to have a continuous pool of disagreements and conflicts. For outsiders, these type of teams might seem to be on a path of failure, because disagreements and conflicts are considered to be signs of a poor functions and failed internal communications. Many times this might be the case, and teams that are not able to handle these conflicts will obviously not be able to collaborate efficiently. However, if the team is prepared for internal conflicts, and they are able to turn those into a source of inspiration—rather than taking them as a solely negative burden—they will be able to build on each other's strengths and collectively work on a level they would not be able to reach as individuals.

How can this level of teamwork be achieved? There are no cheap tricks or shortcuts that lead to this type of success. A well-functioning co-creation team has a solid foundation of the right individuals, based on a suitable mixture of diversity with enough common ground in between, as described in our discussion of team dynamics in Chap. 3. This team then has to learn to operate together in highly stressful situations, where internal conflicts are trying to rip the team apart. This requires a bond of unbreakable trust between the team members. It will be virtually impossible to continue the journey if the team has not been able to build sufficient trust between each other, or if they for some other reason are not able to face their challenges collectively—as a team (Fig. 9.6).

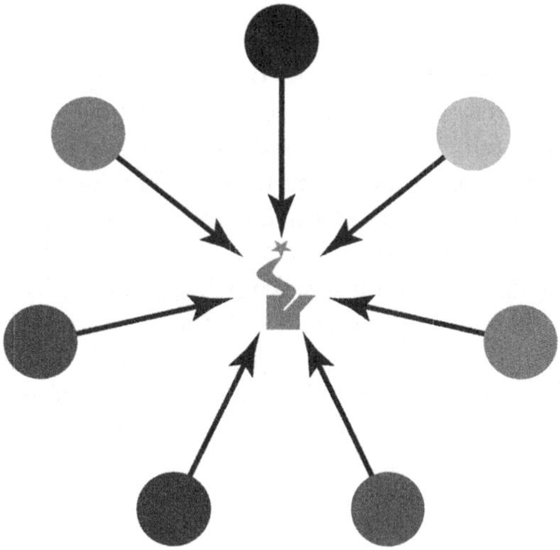

Fig. 9.6 Aligning efforts

Resilient yet flexible teams capable of handling uncertainty are not easy to create. When given the opportunity, the *Xd* designs their teams ahead of time based on information from stakeholder dialogues and the creative brief. In such circumstances, it is possible to carefully think about team dynamics and existing relationships to pick the right people for the task. In other circumstances, we might be given a team to work with or even come into a room having no knowledge of the participants. In such contexts, the *Xd* must put extra effort into setting a strong container in Act I, ensuring that that the team has the trust and interpersonal bonds needed.

Having a dynamic team and strong container goes a long way in mitigating uncertainty. In some instances, this is all you need. If you trust your team and process, you can be surprised at what they do in the Unknown. Some teams take the initiative and self-direct. These are teams with collective intelligence, the capacity to explore the Unknown with confidence. Other teams might charge the Unknown as if it were a great adventure, meeting fear with courage. They may or may not be prepared for what they encounter. Still other teams need careful guidance, even prodding, to get them to step off the ledge of the Known into unfamiliar and uncomfortable territory. Working with different team characteristics requires careful monitoring and responding to challenges that arise with the right form of leadership.

Leadership Through Hardship

The strongest steel is forged in the hottest fire, and the strongest teams are strengthened through difficulties and struggles. The Dive is our blacksmith's anvil, a shift from building to testing/forging/tempering. It is a mentally and emotionally tough stage that is initially dominated by ambiguity, uncertainty, and tension. This stage of the journey calls for extensive experience and adaptive leadership skills.

The *Xd*'s role is to lead or catalyze the collective performance of the team, producing new knowledge and unlocking the capacity of the whole (collective intelligence). Creative leadership is not about knowing the right answers or solving problems. It is about knowing how to inspire, how to ask the right questions, handling the inevitable ambiguity and uncertainty to hold the space between long enough for potentials to manifest into innovative ideas.

Situational Choice Making

At the two big shifts (Act 1->2 and Act 2->3), the *Xd* needs to make some choices, based on the prevailing situation. The choices we must make can be thought of as process control. We must never forget that co-creation, like design, is not a linear process. It is iterative, which means that we may need to loop back and forth between stages several times. "We'll need to improve the team spirit" or "the team is not trying hard enough" will lead to choosing a certain first step over another. Given this fact, we must acknowledge several alternative curve patterns for this stage that all lead to positive results. They can be visualized as follows (Fig. 9.7):

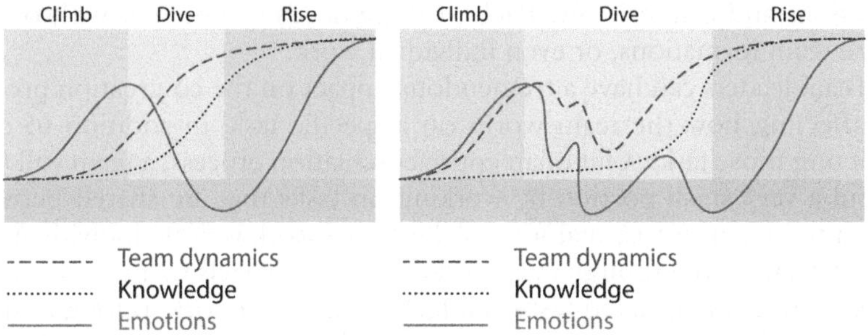

Fig. 9.7 Two alternative process curves, lift-off and vortex

In addition to moving activities around within one stage, it may also be the case that we need to iterate between the larger Acts themselves, moving back and forth between the Known and the Unknown. This is why we stressed flex and flow as an experience design principle in Part I. The *Xd* comes in with a program "roadmap" that at first glance seems progressive, but anyone with experience knows that this is a fiction. The map is not the territory, and skillful facilitation requires knowing when to throw the roadmap in the bin. Situational choice making is about awareness, sensing when to push on, when to adapt or intervene, and when to pull the plug. This last decision is perhaps the most difficult. We all want our teams to succeed. But sometimes they don't. Sometimes co-creation fails. We have to let go of owning results, doing as we ask our teams to do and learning from our failures. What we do own is our process, and in that regard we can offer several guidelines for leading through hardship.

Varying Team Size

One of the most important situational choices for leaders is team formations. The guiding question is, "What needs to be done and what is the optimal team arrangement to achieve it?" In Chap. 3 we discussed team design and four different forms of work. This is where these come into play. Our goals are multiple, including processing information, creating subgroups to work independently on tasks, developing new relationships and networks, learning and talent development groups, and formulating questions and action items. Each of these needs can be met with one or more team formations, or even individual work.

Team leaders can have a tremendous impact on the co-creation process by affecting how the team works on a specific task, in addition to constructing those tasks. Out of an entire co-creation process, a team will only spend a very small portion by working on tasks that are shared between the entire team. A vast majority of the actual work is done individually or in sub-teams, even though in a good team it rarely feels that way. Even the most boring and isolated tasks can feel like a team effort, as long as there is a collective feeling that all of the work is done for the team. A good leader knows how to build and maintain this kind of a feeling within the team by building smooth transitions between different work forms and team formations. For example, there might be a period within a process, during which the skills of some team members are not needed at all, while some others can have their hands full with their own tasks. In this situation, an experienced leader could come up with some parallel assignments that are not necessarily so important for the process, but could be extremely important for maintaining a good team spirit. By preventing one part of the team from idling while others are neck-deep in work, the leader can help maintain unity and balance within the team.

Team formations are often decided by task, but they may also need to be structured according to emotions and/or interpersonal dynamics. In Part I we discussed "hijackers," which we can all be guilty of being. Strong egos and passions can be managed effectively through team formation, but there are no hard and fast rules for this. You may want to have only one Type A personality in each team, or you may compose a team entirely of them in order to raise the creative tension. Team formation is all situational choice making, with the core criterion being what best serves the whole. The *Xd*'s role is to respond to the energy of the group as it occurs in the moment. If people begin to lose energy, change the form of the group to revitalize it.

In our experience, playing with team arrangements is one of the more enjoyable aspects of co-creation. Participants will have mixed reactions. Some want to stick with their initial groups because of the bonds created. Others want to escape their group as soon as possible, either due to a lack of energy or conflicts. In either case we have two guidelines. First, whenever creating new groups give them time and activities to socially bond. Each team needs to set its own container within the larger one defined by the overall process. Second, do not shift groups at the first sign of conflict. Difficulties, per se, are not a reason to split up groups. As we have seen, both affective and substantive conflicts can be transformed into positive energy. Breakdowns can and do lead to breakthroughs. It is the loss of energy that we must be wary of.

Gandalfing

A completely different approach is named after Gandalf, a wizard from the Lord of the Rings trilogy by J.R.R. Tolkien. Our colleague Todd Peterson from Southern Utah University uses "Gandalfing" to describe when a leader holding the space retreats into the background to let the participants take ownership of the process. In the Tolkien stories, Gandalf starts an adventure and then disappears, leaving the Hobbits to figure things out themselves. He is giving them personal accountability for their successes or failures, intervening only when he must to give direction or prevent disaster. When applied to collective creativity, what begins as **the** process becomes **their** process, which can be an important shift.

Gandalfing requires trust, in both the team and their capacity to succeed without your guidance. In other terms, it requires collective intelligence—the ability to act on collective knowledge and evolve. We might think of this as the capacity for self-organizing systems to grow with minimal external influence. Gandalfing works with motivated people. This is true even when it might seem that the team does not demonstrate the collective intelligence you wish they had. It is *through* such experiences that many teams develop collective intelligence. If they fail, so what? They can learn from that and do better the next time.

The choice to use Gandalfing depends on how much faith you have in your team, the tolerance for failure, and to some extent whether you believe in self-organizing systems of not. Try it first in a low-consequence project and see what happens. With practice you can develop fluency at the fine art of subtle intervention at just the right moments.

Principles of Creative Leadership

What we do as leaders is one aspect of our role. *How* we do it is another. In this final consideration of leadership, we summarize principles that we have discussed in different places throughout the text. These applications of inner creative leadership capacities help us maintain the container and space between that we have worked so hard to create. They engender the shift from command and control to co-creative leadership.

Hold the Space of Uncertainty

- People will normally jump to the first seemingly viable solution. Get people out of their comfort zones and keep them there to reach deeper insights.

Invite Moments of Stillness

- Enthusiasm and engagement tend to keep people running in high gear. While this is valuable, so too are moments to slow down mental and emotional processes.
- Most insights emerge from down times when the mind is relaxed, not the brainstorming sessions themselves.

Questions over Statements

- Use coaching tactics to guide processes. Questions are not threatening to people's egos. Statements can be.
- Questions invite people to dig deeper into their understanding. Asking questions that reveal the emotional as well as rational aspects of a decision can catalyze reframing and new insights.

Encourage Generative Dialogue

- A generative dialogue senses for possibility with the spirit of open mind, open heart, and open will.
- Generative dialogue is one in which there is a separation of ego from concept, allowing critical exploration of issues without a sense of personal attacks or defenses.

Disruption (Entropy)

- Disruption can be a good catalyst, but that does not mean disruption = good. Entropy has its place in creativity, but it cannot be allowed to take over. The key is to make space for disruption in a way that serves the group instead of purely self-interest.

Trust

- Trust the team's growing collective intelligence, encouraging them to take ownership of their process.
- Trust the co-creative process you have designed. The whole is greater than the sum of its parts.

Support the Team

- Co-creation relies on strong containers and a "thick" space between. Maintaining trusting and authentic relationships is the bedrock for both.
- Be there for the team, holding them through the emotional contours of the journey.
- Offer coaching and/or mentoring to continuously develop their collective intelligence.
- Actively listen to both what is being said and what is not.

Active Learning

- For a team to reach their full potential, the focus on performance needs to be complemented by a desire to learn.
- Celebrate failure early and often, giving time and space for reflection and growth.

Intentionality and Presence

- Creative leadership relies on cultivating inner capacities. The quality of your own consciousness will have a significant effect on the team. Tend it carefully and diligently.
- Tune yourself to the flex and flow of energy and emotions through heightened awareness. This is the foundation of adaptive leadership.

Acknowledge Culture

- Culture—the "informal organization"—is the context in which all creativity and change occurs. Process, leadership, and culture must mutually support each other for optimal productivity.
- The situated reality of the co-creative process is a miniature culture. Give it power with symbols and artifacts.

Shift Attitude from Ego to Eco (Systems Thinking)

- Tapping into collective potential requires a decentering of ideas from any one person's position (ego) to seeing from the perspective of the whole (eco). The whole is the ecosystem in which the challenge resides, from individuals to the group and the world (consumer base, organization, planet). In other terms, this is a shift in perspective from "I" and "my" to "we" and "it."

Integrate Needs

- Co-creation does not exist in a vacuum. The needs of the process must integrate with those of the larger systems of which it is part. Continually ask, "How does this serve the whole value chain?"
- People need to see a path. Stay connected to purpose, allowing freedom while maintaining alignment with the parameters of the creative brief.

Co-creative leaders embody and enact these principles in everything they do. This is more than skill set. It is a set of personal practices that transcend specific techniques or stages of the process. Being as they are practices, one cannot expect fluency to come from reading this or any other book. Mastery is a tacit knowledge that comes from doing and being rather than reading and thinking. Get out there and do it.

Emergence

As the individual elements of new knowledge begin to find a balance between each other, these elements merge into organizational knowledge. Little by little, the chaotic spectrum of overlapping perspectives is first forged into complementary pieces of partially shared knowledge and then finally tempered into *collective insight*. This insight is the core element required for co-creative solutions to emerge, and as it surfaces, the team proceeds to the final part of their journey.

There are two indicators of emergence, which we observe as shifts in emotions and energy. Sometimes our indicator of energy comes from techniques such as IDEO's butterfly test. We allow for the whole to "vote" on what they feel is the best idea and are willing to commit themselves to. Clear majorities indicate a moderate consensus, which we can then take forward to further develop. A lack of majority, by contrast, indicates a need to spend more time in the Unknown. The collective has not yet come to a place where they can coalesce their energies and commit to acting on one or a few possibilities.

At other times an insight might seem to manifest out of thin air, and the collective intuitively feels that this is the direction to pursue. In such cases voting is unnecessary because there is an energy around that insight. That energy is one that, like an engaging breakthrough question, compels us forward. Sudden insights are an indicator of the quality of the space between. When these occur, we know we have done a good job. It is not time to pat yourself on the back yet, but such indicators validate the process and lend confidence to the decision to move forward.

The energy of emergence catalyzes an emotional shift in the team, an almost tangible felt sense of clarity and growing excitement. On the journey thus far, the team has been acquiring new knowledge and developing their team working skills preparing them for what to do when the Rise begins. But now something is changing. People start to smile again and may grow restless as the team slowly begins to understand that they are about to cross a line. This is the point where the team has the collective knowledge and capacity to actually start creating something New together. They need to act. Suddenly all the curves (knowledge, emotions, team dynamics) take a shift and begin the upward climb out of the Unknown. The energy and generally positive emotions propel us forward into Act III: The Rise.

Notes

1. Ogilvie and Liedtka, *Designing for Growth*, Kindle Locations 615–622.
2. Theory U Course, Week 2: Shanghai Sensing Journey Video.
3. A phrase Ed Schein uses in his consulting work.
4. Scharmer and Kaufer, *Leading from the Emerging Future*.
5. Sources include d.school bootcamp bootleg, *Designing for Growth*, and Cultural Probes (http://infodesign.com.au/usabilityresources/culturalprobes/).
6. Sources include MethodKit (https://methodkit.com); U.Lab: Transforming Business, Society, and Self (http://www.ottoscharmer.com/programs/ulab); the Ruth Cohn Institute for TCI international (http://www.ruth-cohn-institute.org/home.html), Six Thinking Hats (http://www.debonogroup.com/six_thinking_hats.php), World Cafe (http://www.theworldcafe.com), and the Institute for Cultural Affairs (http://www.ica-usa.org).
7. See, for example, Weisberg, *Creativity*.
8. McTaggart, *The Field*.
9. Bohm, *On Dialogue*.
10. Krishnamurti, *Talks and Dialogues*.
11. Bohm 1991, 3.
12. Ibid.
13. Bert Hellinger's text *Love's Hidden Symmetry: What Makes Love Work in Relationships* is an excellent, if controversial, thesis on how relational systems define our notions of right and wrong, guilt, and conscience.
14. Peter M. Senge, in "A New View of Institutional Leadership" in *Reflections on Leadership*.
15. We transcribed the answers to "How do you know if you are operating at level X?" content with little editing from the Theory U edX online course.
16. www.ica-international.org.
17. Image adapted from https://www.nwei.org/iceberg/. Accessed November 28, 2017.
18. http://www.flowgenomeproject.com/train/flow-dojo/.
19. We will look more closely at the historical origins of these methods in our final chapter on resonant co-creation.
20. For more information, see the Eliad Group (www.eliadgroup.com) and Insight Quests (www.insightquests.com).
21. The nowhere model derives from the Native American concept of the four directions, each with its own energy: creativity (E), nurturing (W), adventure (S), action (N). See *The Way of nowhere*.
22. http://www.institute4learning.com/resources/articles/multiple-intelligences/.

23. Gardner's model receives criticism from cognitive neuroscience and psychology, on grounds of lack of falsifiability and an incorrect understanding of how brain structures operate. See Waterhouse, "Multiple Intelligences, the Mozart Effect, and Emotional Intelligence: A critical review." While this is a good criticism for why the term "intelligence" may not be a the best choice, his theory has merit in illustrating the different modes of knowing we discuss here.
24. http://www.institute4learning.com/resources/articles/multiple-intelligences/.
25. https://disneyimaginations.com/about-imaginations/about-imagineering/.
26. Weisberg, *Creativity.*
27. http://creativethinking.net.
28. https://www.lego.com/en-us/seriousplay/the-method.
29. Our term, not a translation from the original Hungarian. Individual practices come from a variety of sources, such as the Center for Contemplative Mind in Society (http://www.contemplativemind.org).
30. International Institute for Social Artistry and the Jean Houston Foundation.
31. The nowhere group ltd. (www.now-here.com).
32. Gray et al., *Gamestorming*, 89.
33. This work is licensed by the Presencing Institute—Otto Scharmer—www.presencing.com/permissions.
34. Turner and Udall, *The Way of nowhere.*
35. Many times these shifts occurred within the session and then deepened by later reflection on the journal captures.
36. This work is licensed by the Presencing Institute—Otto Scharmer—www.presencing.com/permissions.
37. Geer, *Story Bridge.*
38. Brown, *Change by Design*, 83.
39. Image adapted from http://mrskirksscholars.weebly.com. Accessed November 27, 2017.
40. Drawing from Riding the Creative Rollercoaster Intensive, 2013. Austria.
41. Learn more at http://www.thegrowmodel.com.
42. Co-Active Coaching (http://www.coactive.com), the Center for Creative Leadership (https://www.ccl.org), and the Institute for Cultural Affairs (http://www.ica-usa.org) all have excellent resources and training available.
43. https://courses.lumenlearning.com/boundless-management/chapter/managing-conflict/. Accessed November 28, 2017.
44. Senge, *The Fifth Discipline.*

45. Ibid., Kindle Location 2274.
46. Ibid., Kindle Locations 2314–2317.
47. Ibid., Kindle Locations 2328–2330.
48. Eisenhardt et al., "How management teams can have a good fight," 77–85.

References

Bohm, David. *On Dialogue*. London: Routledge Classics, 2004.

Brown, Tim, and Barry Katz. *Change by Design: How Design Thinking Transforms Organizations and Inspires Innovation*. Adobe Digital Edition ed. New York: Harper Collins e-books, 2009.

Eisenhardt, K. M., J. L. Kahwajy, and L. J. Bourgeois. "How Management Teams Can Have a Good Fight." *Harvard Business Review* 75, no. 4 (1997): 77–85.

Geer, Richard. *Story Bridge: From Alienation to Community Action*. Community Performance Inc., 2012.

Kotler, Steven, and Jamie Wheal. *Stealing Fire: How Silicon Valley, the Navy Seals, and Maverick Scientists Are Revolutionizing the Way We Live and Work*. Dey Street Books, 2017.

Krishnamurti, J. *Talks and Dialogues*. Servire, 1970.

McTaggart, Lynne. *The Field: The Quest for the Secret Force of the Universe*. Element Books, 2003.

Ogilvie, Tim, and Jeanne Liedtka. Designing for Growth: A Design Thinking Toolkit for Managers (Columbia Business School Publishing) (Kindle Locations 615–622). Columbia University Press. Kindle Edition.

Scharmer, Otto, and Katrin Kaufer. *Leading from the Emerging Future from Ego-System to Eco-System Economies*. San Francisco, CA: Berrett-Koehler Publishers, Inc., 2013.

Senge, Peter M. *The Fifth Discipline: The Art and Practice of the Learning Organization*. New York, NY: Doubleday, 1994.

Spears, Larry, ed. *Reflections on Leadership: How Robert K. Greenleaf's Theory of Servant-Leadership Influenced Today's Top Management Thinkers*. USA: John Wiley & Sons, 1995.

Turner, N., and Udall, N. *The Way of Nowhere: Eight Questions to Release Our Creative Potential*. Harper-Collins E-Books, 2008.

Waterhouse, Lynn. "Multiple Intelligences, the Mozart Effect, and Emotional Intelligence: A Critical Review." *Educational Psychologist* 41, no. 4 (Fall 2006): 207–225.

Weisberg, Robert W. *Creativity: Understanding Innovation in Problem Solving, Science, Invention, and the Arts*. Hoboken, NJ: John Wiley & Sons, 2006.

CHAPTER 10

Act III: The Rise

We have some great seeds of potential. Now what are we going to do with them?

Act III: The Rise is when we perform. To continue the artistic metaphor, the stage is set. The actors have trained and rehearsed. The theater seats are filled by an audience and the lights are up. Now it is time for the show. To use another metaphor, the Rise is like the playoffs in sports. There are no more practice or drills, no more unproductive activities. At this stage, every action needs to have a clear and immediate impact on the process, taking the team one step closer to the finishing line.

The third stage of our journey is fundamentally about harvesting the seeds that were planted during the previous two stages. One way to look at this transition is a movement from "what if" generative mode to "what wows" strategic mode. With product and service design, our goal is to identify opportunities that "pack a potential 'wow,' that hit the sweet spot where the chance of a significant upside in customer value meets attractive profit potential. This is the 'wow' zone."[1] Change and educational initiatives have a broader range of goals, but they share the desire for creating something that has positive impact (adding value) with enough "wow" for people to adopt it.

Rising up from the Unknown, this rewarding part of the journey brings to surface the novel outcomes of the co-creative process. At this stage, the team possesses collective knowledge that did not exist before. All team members are empowered by having a meaningful role in the process and

B. R. Rill, M. M. Hämäläinen, *The Art of Co-Creation*,
https://doi.org/10.1007/978-981-10-8500-0_10

they are reaching for a common goal. The team must utilize this knowledge, refocus their intent, and create something novel that satisfies the project constraints.

Signaling the Shift

January 20th to 23rd

Finally, there was light at the end of the tunnel. The whole group had teamed up for the entire week, just to go through all their relevant ideas and discoveries. By Thursday evening, the concept had become obvious, but it was only after Roberta put it into words that the team understood what they had to do. In the end, it was quite simple—combining the two-way radio function of a conventional baby monitor with the biometric surveillance functions of a sensor blanket. ACME would be able to deliver a product that was simple to use and familiar to their target group, while offering them some additional benefits in the form of biometric monitoring.

Despite this realization, the journey was far from being over. Dorothy asked everyone to take the next day off, enjoy an extended weekend, and come back on Monday, ready for a new challenge. The team would now have to put all this down into a clear concept so that they could get a final approval for the product from the executive team, and start preparing a detailed plan for the home stretch of their journey.

The second Red Curve Transition—a major shift in emotions and energy—takes place after the team has reached the point at which they can generate something innovative based on the new knowledge they have produced. This shift is perhaps not as dramatic and clear as the first one, but the entire team needs to understand and follow it if they intend to achieve their goals and produce good results. Sometimes the final discovery emerges out of the blue, after the team has acquired enough knowledge and insight into the topic—just like in the ACME example above. On other occasions, the discovery needs to be squeezed out of the team. Regardless of how the team has reached this point, from now on they are expected to produce results—and fast!

This is where the team can—and should—feel a big change in course of the journey. The direction has shifted from digging for new knowledge to producing results. Ultimately it's up to the *Xd* to make sure that the team makes this mental shift, changes into the next gear, and begins to push toward the end line. In most cases the shift of stage is so obvious that the team doesn't need a separate signal to tell that they have crossed a critical milestone, as the team begins to prepare their final prototypes, tests, and pilots. However, in some cases the final threshold might be crossed more gradually, which means that the team will need a clear indication to make the mental shift. This signal can be very subtle, perhaps just inviting everyone for a nice dinner during which an announcement could be made. Or it could be as Dorothy did—calling for an extra day off to celebrate the end of a stage. This is enough to create a small disruption for everyone, helping them clear their heads and transition their thoughts to the final stage.

Sometimes a subtle gesture is not enough to send a clear signal to the team. This could be the case in situations where the intensity of the teamwork has been so high that the team members are in a "flow state"—deeply committed to their specific task at hand—from which they might need to be shaken away so that they can see the change in the big picture. Or perhaps the team has been working so dispersedly on separate topics that they need to be pulled back together before a collective mental transition can take place. In these cases, a more powerful signal needs to be generated. For example, the team could shift their base of operations to a different location—perhaps somewhere closer to the manufacturing or testing site, or just to a higher floor to symbolize "moving on to a new level." If a change of location doesn't make sense, a ritual transition could be arranged, where all the old and obsolete schedules, drafts, to-do lists, and so on, could be ripped down from the walls. Replace these with a new schedule, a simple draft of the final concept, or something else that helps the team to shift their minds away from the "old chaos" and start focusing on their new, explicit goal.

Regardless of how the shift is made, the direction that follows should be very clear to everyone. The team needs to start applying their knowledge and creative insights. From the organizational perspective, the goals at this point are (1) to harvest the *collective knowledge* and (2) harness the *collective intelligence*.

Harvesting the Seeds

Let's step back for a moment and take another look at the final stages of Act II: the Dive. At that point, if all has gone according to the plan, the team has reached a peak of their performance. This progress has taken place along two complementary dimensions, as illustrated in Fig. 10.1 (next page). In the vertical scale, the team has expanded its body of knowledge through

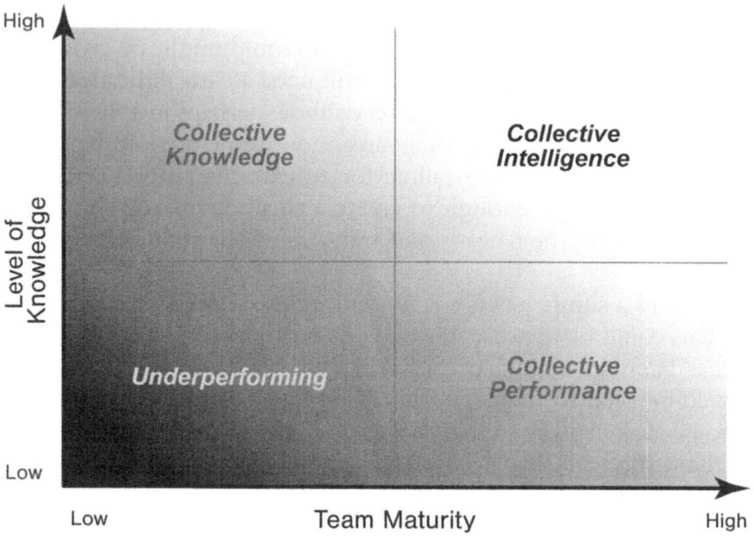

Fig. 10.1 Dimensions of co-creation

internal sharing and external exploration and forged this knowledge into a *collective form*. During the quest for new knowledge, the team has also evolved in the horizontal scale, as the team members have become familiar with each other's skills and capabilities well enough to use them *collectively*, as extensions of their own abilities. The shared body of knowledge, combined with collective performance skills, has brought the team to the highest level of co-creation. They have reached the state of *collective intelligence*, where they can use their insight collectively to analyze problems and then generate new, innovative solutions to the challenges at hand.

Collective Intelligence

Figure 10.2 (next page) further illustrates the two target zones for a co-creation team's development. If the team has been successful in exploring the Unknown, it means that they have produced some *New Knowledge*—the raw material they need for creating a breakthrough. If team members have learned each other's capabilities and honed their working skills to a collective flow, their performance can be described as *resonant co-creation*.

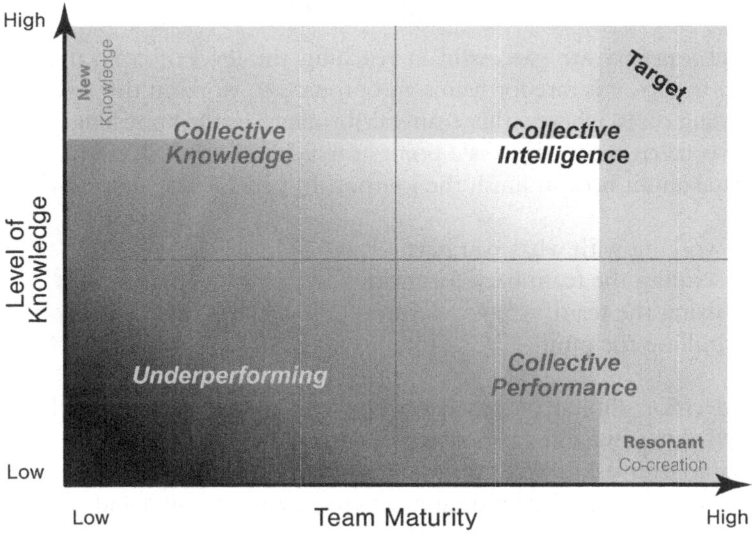

Fig. 10.2 Target zones for collective intelligence

Breakthroughs occur when the blue target zone of New Knowledge intersects with the red target zone of Resonant Co-creation at the top-right corner of the image. At this point the team is feeling almighty, and for a good reason. They have unleashed their full potential. This situation, however, produces a new dilemma. How should this new superpower be used so that it will bring maximum benefits to the organization? In the optimal case, where the team is performing well and has developed a wide understanding of their topic, the natural choice would be to *release the team* to complete the task that needs to be accomplished. Their combined skills cannot be transferred, nor could anybody else apply their knowledge as efficiently as they can, so it would be make perfect sense to let them do the job themselves.

We recognize the ambition of our ideal state of co-creation, but it is important to set high goals for ourselves. If we don't aim high, we will never experience collective intelligence. We will be far less likely to ever be part of a truly breakthrough innovation. Great rewards require significant investments of time and resources, as well as skilled design and leadership. In the next section, we discuss the decision-making and leadership aspects of a successful team on the Rise—one that has a measure of collective intelligence. But before we can move on, we must consider what happens when we have problems.

Tough Decisions

Not all journeys are successful in reaching the level of collective intelligence. In fact, it is rare for teams and projects to work on this level. In the remaining cases, where either team performance or the knowledge exploration has fallen short, there is a point at which a difficult decision needs to be made about how to finish the journey. In general, the alternatives are:

1. working with what you have
2. sending the team back for more
3. fixing the team
4. pulling the plug

This decision should be based on how the co-creative process has progressed along two dimensions—the maturity of the team and the amount of the collective knowledge they possess. The illustration (Fig. 10.1) is intended to help understanding where the team is located and what could be done to improve the situation.

If the team is performing well, but they have not been able to make any relevant discoveries, then the team has drifted to bottom-right section of the diagram. There are several good reasons that may have led the team to fail in producing new knowledge, including lack of resources, time constraints, and more. If any of these reasons fall under the category "bad luck," the team might still have potential for success with their *collective performance*. Since well-functioning teams are rare to find and difficult to develop, they should be valued as they are. It would make sense to find alternative ways to utilize them. So, if the team has failed in their mission due to unavoidable reasons, they could be simply sent out for a new mission. As the team members already know how to work together, they would have a good head start compared to new teams. Given that they would not need to use their time and energy on team building, they could move quickly through the Known and into the next Dive.

Alternatively, if a mature team has failed due to a relevant gap in their base of expertise, they could be reinforced with an expert from a suitable field and sent back to their original mission. Having stated that, there is a right way and a wrong way to bring in outside expertise. Consider the following ACAN story…

Paper Cannot Replace a Person

Half-Page Summary of Expertise

The ACAN board was considering expanding their business to China. One of the board members, Lisa, remembered that their outsourcing manager Kimberly had lived in Shenzhen, China, for eight years, and her perspective and understanding of China could be a valuable source of expertise for the board. So Lisa approached Kimberly, arranged a private lunch meeting with her, and at the lunch brought up the topic.

After an extended lunch talk, Lisa was convinced of Kimberly's expertise on the topic. Even during that short talk, she had learned a lot about China that she was not aware of before, and she was really glad that they had been in contact. Lisa realized that she should present many of the issues mentioned by Kimberly to the corporate board, so that they could also realize the many things she had just understood herself.

Lisa also realized that she would not be able to explain these issues as well as Kimberly just did. Since they were not simple matters at all, the board would need a lot of time to discuss all the possible implications this might have on their China initiative. She knew that they would need at least a ten-page description to explain this complicated topic, but since she would only have a few minutes to address the issue, she would have to summarize everything. So she asked if Kimberly could write a half-page summary of their previous discussion, which she could then present to the board in their next meeting.

Kimberly took this request to heart, and even though it seemed like mission impossible—to explain China in 300 words—she was willing to accept the challenge. Since she knew that she would not be there at the board meeting to clarify any of points that were unclear, it meant that she had to make every word count. She decided to exaggerate many of the issues they had previously discussed. This exaggeration was to make sure that her words would be acknowledged and taken seriously, which had been Lisa's wish as well.

Later that week, Lisa presented Kimberly's summary to the board, describing many of the challenges they should be aware of before taking on China. The words were strong, and as a result the board decided to postpone their China initiative and start their expansion in Asia from South Korea instead. When Kimberly heard about this afterward, she

(*continued*)

(continued)

felt really bad, because she had no idea that the board was also considering alternatives for China. Had she known about the South Korea alternative, she would have been able to tell them that most of the same issues exist there as well. At this point it was already too late, and thanks to Kimberly's words, the board was now under the impression that the company should avoid China at all costs. Without the contextual awareness and participation in the actual decision-making, her words had misled the board toward a direction she would have recommended against, had she been there herself.

The ACAN story is a great example of how expertise should *not* be used within any organization. It illustrates our argument that knowledge cannot be fully captured or stored. Even though it is quite easy to produce snapshots of knowledge—just like Kimberly did—these isolated fragments cannot replace the original. Many professionals can easily relate to this situation, where they have been requested to produce expert statements for situations that clearly require active participation of an expert rather than a just shallow string of words.

Active participation of people who can collectively cover the entire range of expertise required for a task is a foundation of co-creation. When bringing in new expertise to a team, our first guideline is to bring the whole person in, not just their ideas in a summary statement. Second, bringing in a new person requires attention to the container and team dynamics. They need to feel the same sense of community, safety, and trust that the rest of the team shares. Finally, before an underperforming team is sent back to action, one should check to make sure that the team has not fallen into any of the traps mentioned in previous chapters.[2] These pitfalls could be the real reason behind their poor performance, which means that they would be preventing the team from getting anywhere in the future as well. If this seems to be the case, then the team should be either led through a new round of team building exercises[3] or broken apart completely. If the team has worked together for a long time, it might be especially difficult to steer them away from the characteristic problems associated with old teams. Splitting the team apart might be the only solution that can spark their flames up again—as a part of new teams.

It is quite common for a team to have experienced unresolved incidents during their journey. These may have caused so many interpersonal conflicts and tension that the team is not able to demonstrate the teamwork required for a collective performance. If the team is *not* working particularly well together, but have made relevant discoveries together and produced a good body of shared knowledge, then there are still ways to utilize this team. The focus in these situations shifts away from performance to taking advantage of the team's *collective knowledge*. Even though this approach may be less effective than the autonomous application of collective intelligence, it can still lead to acceptable outcomes.

When team performance breaks down, there are alternatives to consider. First, there are many ways to *harvest the knowledge* from the team,[4] which might make sense whether your intention is to terminate the project or not. Based on this explicated knowledge, you can then decide what would be the best course of action. If you decide to give them one more shot, perhaps the easiest way to help the team reach their goals would be to put them on a short leash with external guidance for the rest of their journey. Although this form of working would be far from collective intelligence, it would still give the team a chance to capitalize on their discoveries and finish what they started. In practice this would mean that the team is stripped of autonomy, and they would have to report back to their supervisors on a frequent schedule. Alternatively, a new project manager could be assigned to the team, after which they could then continue their journey under strict internal command. As the new project manager would not be familiar with the collective knowledge they share, this form of management would have to rely on predetermined steps rather than collective insight of the team.

In our experience, it is highly unlikely that the general atmosphere within the team improves significantly in either of these two cases, even if these changes help the team reach their objectives. This should be taken into consideration when making a decision to either continue the journey or to terminate the mission and count the casualties. In best-case scenarios, the team responds positively to new leadership and more strict controls. They might successfully capture their collective knowledge, creating new resources and opportunities for leadership or future teams. They might deliver on the project goals with professionalism, if not fondness, for one another. In worst-case scenarios, a continuously negative team spirit could lead some members of the team to resign from the organization. Losing talented people, or destroying their motivations, could turn out to be the ultimate cost for finishing a project. The choice to carry on or pull the plug is best not taken lightly, and we recommend that it be made in dialogue with the senior stakeholders.

Finally, if the team is underperforming in a way that has prevented them from producing any relevant knowledge, the only reasonable choice is to *retire the team* and proceed to the follow-up activities described in the next chapter. The failure should be analyzed appropriately to understand what went wrong, so that the same mistakes are not repeated in another project.

The Final Stretch

For teams with enough collective intelligence to carry on, the Rise is an exciting time. There is particular energy—that of inspiration—that needs to be acted upon. Whether it arises naturally or needs to be guided, the energy must focus now on doing, or making. In the language of an Experiential Learning Cycle, the Rise is when we clarify our concepts and test the implications of these in new situations.[5] This begins by crystallizing our intent.

> Crystallizing intent requires being open to the larger intention and imaginatively translating the intuitions that arise into concrete images and visions that guide action.[6]

Those familiar with strategic visioning will recognize this focusing act as connecting to purpose. It is intuitively recognizing what needs to be done and the *Why* behind it. From this point, it then becomes possible to link together the past, present, and future to chart ways forward. In organizational development, we might call these "strategic change" or "culture building" initiatives. Co-creation is one among several valuable approaches for implementation.[7]

Crystallizing intent enables us to take our first steps with our new superpower—collective intelligence. Our aim is to create something New by building, testing, piloting, prototyping, and communicating. We are also collectively learning as the process proceeds, further increasing our potential to innovate. The outcomes of this stage have different names. In design, the language centers on prototypes, with the objective being a testable product or service. In organizations, the language is that of initiatives or projects, and the goal is to have a pilot ready for launch.

This process carries with it a few novel considerations. First among these is introducing the element of assessment. As the goal is now in sight, at this point it should be easy to evaluate whether some act is taking the team forward or not. During the Rise, we can use benchmarks and evaluative measures to keep the team on track with a tight timeline.

The shift in focus for the Rise also means that some of the old rules don't apply in the same way as they did before. The principles of the co-creation process remain—of course—but at this stage there is much more freedom for making exceptions and breaking the rules. After all, the rules are made for the team, not vice versa. As long as everyone is performing for the team, nothing else really matters.

Another consideration is that during the first two stages there have most likely been interpersonal incidents that have required guidance or even intervention from the *Xd* or project leader. These incidents, and particularly the corrective actions that followed, have hence had an impact on what is considered acceptable behavior for this particular team. These new norms are rarely written down in any explicit form, yet they act as a strong binding force that unites the team and defines how they should do their work as they are trying to complete their tasks.

These considerations, among others, help us move into the first phase of the Rise—planning. For ACME, their Rise began as follows:

January 27th

Monday morning came, and there was no need for pep talks. Everyone had arrived early at the Team Room. They were sitting quietly with their coffee mugs or herbal drinks, waiting to hear from Dorothy on how they should proceed now that they had passed one of the critical milestones. This was the beginning of the final design phase, and the fact that they had made it to this stage was enough to show how far they had come from their first team meeting in September. In September, there was a lot of tension in the air, but now everyone was fundamentally calm and prepared to take the next step. And at this moment, everyone was looking at Dorothy.

During the weekend, Dorothy had received several ideas, questions, and suggestions from her teammates. For her, that was a good sign, even though she had replied to most of them with a short "Let's wait until Monday, and discuss this then." It was clear that the team was pumped-up and ready for their next challenge.

"Listen up" she said, just to get started, even though everybody's eyes and ears were already on her. "This is the end-game, and now it's time to get very real. There are two more tasks that we will need to accomplish, in a relatively short

time, and those two tasks cannot be separated from each other. We will all have to stay on track with both of them from now until the job is done."

"The first task is to build a market-ready Bionic Baby Monitor with all the necessary components, software, manuals, and packaging. And before we can get there, we will have to demonstrate that this thing can actually work as we have described, so that ACME can make the go/no-go decision. In the next three weeks, I want us to build a proof-of-concept model of a complete product. This needs to be ready on Thursday the 13th, and we will review and test it on Friday the 14th. To make sure that the product concept passes our company requirements, I will personally do my best to rip this thing apart during these three weeks. If—and only if—it survives this internal test of ours, we will present it by the end of February to the corporate executives for their final approval."

"The second task is to build a roadmap for the additional products in this new Bionic Baby Monitor line. The first draft of these products needs to be ready by the time we present the Proof-of-concept, so there is not much time for this task either."

"To get things off to a fast start, I purchased a Beddit™ sleep monitor for everyone in the team so that you can get familiar with the possibilities offered to adults by this type of technology. I want you to use it yourselves and study how it works. Do the first round on your own, so that you will understand what normal people go through when they are starting to use this product. After you have tested it yourselves, please talk with Tim, who has been getting familiar with Beddit™ since November. He knows the tech side of it by heart, and will share the essentials with everyone later this week."

Planning for Success

Given the changing conditions of the Rise, it is valuable to begin with a planning or directive session. The ACME story above illustrates a typical process, where the project lead clearly denotes the shift to the Rise and offers direction to the team. This is one style of leadership that works quite well in many circumstances. Another style is to continue co-creating with the team, tapping into the collective intelligence to determine the next steps. Design and organizational change use different methodologies at this point. Yet, as we illustrate below, there are common features to both.

Design Methods

Once a design team has a clear vision of what they need to develop, the next step is to set the design specifications and strategies that are called "design principles."

> Design principles are strategies to solve a design challenge independent of a specific solution. You, as the designer, articulate these principles, translating your findings—such as needs and insights—into design directives. These principles give you a format to capture abstracted, but actionable, guidelines for solutions, and communicate your design intentions to others.[8]

Design principles are a set of internal guidelines for your team's creative process. They provide structure and direction for the creative process—parameters that make it possible to focus the energy and insights gained thus far. They describe *how* the design process should be conducted, complementing the design specifications that define *what* needs to be designed. These principles differ from the social contract created in Act I. The social contract was a way of working for the creative team. Design principles, by contrast, focus on design solutions. They are abstract guidelines derived from understanding of the design space and users. In other terms, they are a set of "maker" guidelines based on everything you have figured out thus far. These guidelines are independent of specific implementation, which gives the team creative freedom within the parameters set. Here is how the d.school creates design principles:

> You develop design principles in a number of ways. You can translate your point of view, needs, and insights into design principles by stating your findings in terms of solutions rather than the user, while maintaining the focus on the user-centered needs and insights you discovered. For example, a user's "need to feel instrumental in creating a gift" could become a design directive that the solution should "involve the user in creating the final gift outcome." You can also back out design principles from potential solutions that you and users find compelling. Ask yourself what aspects of the solution resonated with users, and those aspects may be abstracted and formed into design principles.

At first glance, design principles may appear to be identical to the creative brief. This may be true. In some cases, the design principles and specifications are already defined in the creative brief. That we would label as a "fixed brief," which is often used in conventional design processes, such as designing improvements and revisions to existing products. An "open brief" follows the design thinking process, which means that the design specifications are set only later in the process—in our case, at the beginning of Rise. An open brief is required when a team is acting on new knowledge. How, after all, could we set design principles and specifications before ever exploring the Unknown? If we had, the result of the creative process would be at best incremental innovation—an improvement on the Known. Perhaps for some teams that is enough. But if you want to create something radically new, then new guidelines are needed.

Developing design principles is a time when you can change the rules. It is at this point that you reconsider accepted models of behavior and established workflows. "Are these the right models to continue with? Or do we need something different?" are fair questions to ask. Making new rules, and breaking them, is perfectly acceptable so long as the behaviors and actions serve the larger goals. For example, once we get into the act of creating, we might want to purposefully invite entropy back the mix. Controlled chaos is part of the recipe for success at IDEO and Google, so why not try it? The trick is to make sure that the container is strong and all acts are done in service of the larger whole. As long as the team maintains its trust and ecosystem awareness, rules can be bent or broken without catastrophic consequences. In fact, we *need* play, conflict, and flights of fancy in the Rise. Sometimes the greatest inventions come simply from tinkering with things, and it usually benefits the process by encouraging such learning by doing. Whatever you come up with, your design principles need to unleash creativity while simultaneously giving it some structure. It is the balance of these two that harness inspirations into innovation.

Concept development and assumption testing are additional tools that balance creativity with pragmatism.[9] Concept development brings together innovative building blocks into coherent possibilities or solutions that can be explored and evaluated. It is the translation of insights and/or inspirations into form, a process that begins early and continues throughout the Rise.

Assumption testing isolates and tests key assumptions of a concept that will drive its success or failure. When we advised teams in the School of Design at PolyU, for example, a common issue was the assumption that people would like their design simply because they had identified a need for it in their research phase—or so they said. In many cases, careful questioning revealed the fact that one or two people on the team had begun the project with a creative inspiration and sold it to their teammates. Their "research" suffered from confirmation bias, and when challenged most teams could not offer any evidence of their assertions. Did some of these projects go on to commercial success? Yes. There will always be cases where inspiration alone is enough for entrepreneurial success. But these are few and far between, and when designing for other stakeholders, they will need to be convinced.

Assumption testing is a powerful tool because it helps us make better choices in the face of uncertainty. At this stage, we don't actually know whether our ideas are good or not. Even though inference can help us analyze the ideas, the only way to know for sure whether they are good or bad is by testing them. A lot can be learned from even simple tests, and for this reason it is important to create different types of models and prototypes throughout the concept development process for testing and validating different aspects of the ideas. Any tool that can help us screen our concepts brings value to the journey by advancing the process. Questions such as "Under what circumstances does our concept work?" and "What is needed for this concept to bring business value?" reveal conditions that we assume to be correct. We can then test to see if these conditions (our assumptions) are true or not, hence building the argument for or against a particular concept. We provide examples in the coming section on prototyping, particularly "Other Conceptual Models."

When it comes to planning, it's worth noting that designers are likely operating from a very different worldview than their business world counterparts. Concept development and assumption testing, for example, may start at the beginning of the Rise or while prototyping. Nothing is fixed in design at this point. Because design is an iterative process, we "loop back" to continuously refine our concepts and assumptions as we go. The text *Designing for Growth* offers a good comparison of mindset between business and design.

> All design is essentially hypothesis driven, which, in the design world, is shorthand for saying that the solutions generated are the outcome of an iterative rather than a linear process. That is, design starts with a tentative solution and expects to improve it through experimentation… Design favors trying over extensive planning and is overwhelmingly experimental in its approach. Designers expect to iterate their way to increasingly "better" answers.[10]

The design journey is one of learning, even while they are doing. By contrast,

> Business thinking assumes rationality and objectivity. Its decision driver is cold, clean, economic logic. Reality is precise and quantifiable. There is "truth"—and answers are "right" or "wrong." Business thinking favors analytical approaches; decision-making processes demand "proof" that we have arrived at the "correct" answer. So the MBAs make their case with ROIs and PowerPoints.[11]

This contrast in worldview profoundly impacts how teams in different organizational domains approach creativity and planning. The authors of *Designing for Growth* argue, and we agree, that both are needed in innovative organizations. There is a time and place for design thinking and for business thinking. However, for co-creation, even in business contexts, it is important that we retain the design thinking orientation to planning. This is no small act, especially for business teams that excel at strategic planning. They will, if left to their own devices, slip back into the default analytical operating mode. We need to maintain a participatory and learning-oriented approach to planning. Fortunately, there are good techniques for this.

Organizational Change

Earlier in the text we introduced the Institute for Cultural Affairs (ICA) and told a bit of their story. The ICA, founded in community development, has been working creatively with communities all over the world for decades. Over the years they codified a facilitation framework called the Technology of Participation, and in this toolkit they offer a simple yet elegant method for co-creative planning in organizations. The ICA calls it "Participatory Action Planning" (PAP), one possible decision-making technique that can be used here. Action planning comes in many forms, and can scale from a couple of hours to days or weeks of work. We introduce it here as a planning tool used at the beginning of this stage, but it can also be a more encompassing framework that structures the entire Rise.

Participatory Action Planning

PAP is co-creative in that the methodology is based on the active participation of everyone present in the decision-making process. Each person has an equally valued role, their voices are given space to be heard, and ownership of tasks is self-selected. Skillful facilitation of PAP maintains engagement and the sense of mutual empowerment, significantly impacting how people come out of the planning process. Imagine the difference between work teams comprised of individuals who are passionate about their task(s) vs. teams whose composition is assigned by someone else. Both may be productive, but the self-selected team is far more likely to excel.

PAP begins much like the co-creative processes, with a provocative question or mission statement and an opening agreement (the social contract). It is a time to reflect on what has been done up to this point and decide on how to move forward. Sub-teams then develop what they envision to be a victory scenario. These are then brought into the whole group context to evaluate and develop a shared vision. The group as a whole decides what core components are needed for the vision to become reality. This parallels the process in design of revising or making new design principles.

Next the team steps back into the current reality, using SWOT to analyze the situation and align the group's resources with its task. As a whole, they discuss the potential benefits and dangers that would result from succeeding with the action plan. In organizational change initiatives, this is a very good point to reflect upon integration of needs and stakeholders, both obvious and hidden. Given that any change initiative has "winners" and "losers," it is wise to consider what forces will act to support or resist change—no matter how beneficial and/or innovative the overall change might be. Force Field analyses and "Me, We, It" dialogues are additional tools that can bring value to this "reality check" moment.

The team can then make commitments, defining and articulating exactly what the group aims to accomplish. As the final part of the visioning stage in action planning, the team holds a "measures of success" dialogue in which they co-determine evaluation standards. It is critical for the group to decide on success measures *before* developing specific actions. Doing so creates alignment and reduces the blue sky thinking of the victory scenario(s) into more concrete outcomes. Only after grounding idealism in realism should the team move into the second stage—planning.

The planning stage is comprised of three parts: brainstorming detailed actions, discerning work groups, and organizing the forces. Depending on the overall group composition and the number of objectives to be pursued, you can have either one team or sub-teams take on these tasks. Planning defines the concrete actions that need to be taken to meet a vision within the constraints agreed upon and the necessary conditions of reality. Once everyone knows these details, the planning stage concludes by assigning or selecting task and work groups. It is often wise to first ask if a particular person is *needed* for a specific task. They get assigned to that task by necessity. Allowing everyone else to self-select helps assure engagement.

In our ACME story, Dorothy made these decisions on her own as the project lead. She decided what steps needed to be taken and who was to work on them. Dorothy's expertise and familiarity with the team enabled her to make choices for them. This is perfectly acceptable, but note that the decisions made rely on only one person's intelligence—Dorothy. By contrast, PAP relies on the collective intelligence throughout all decision-making. This is a point where the *Xd* or project lead must make a judgment call. If you trust the collective intelligence of the team, then you can rely on the fact that a group's wisdom will almost always supersede that of the leader. Letting go of control at this point, when there are clear timelines and deadlines, may be challenging, but it is essential to retain the qualities of creative leadership—holding the container rather than controlling it.

Once teams are decided, these subgroups then need to align and develop their own internal measures of success, specific actions, and resource estimates. From there everyone moves into the orchestrating stage, first creating subgroup timelines and then integrating these into the larger project timeline. PAP seeks efficiency by doing this in a whole group context, visually laying out individual timelines next to one another to identify points of overlap and redundant work. This helps save costs and time.

PAP closes with a final consensus dialogue. The main aim of the consensus dialogue is alignment, not just an understanding of what needs to be done, but also energetic and emotionally. Similar to a check-in or checkout, it helps to begin by inviting people to state in a few words how they feel. This is a good time to reflect on the overall journey, taking stock of memorable moments, the surprises, the disappointments, the breakthroughs, and the personal significance for each individual. After a long period of planning, it helps to reconnect people's individual *Why* with the larger *Why*.

In the closing moments of planning it also helps to motivate the team. They are about to embark on the last major stage of the creative journey, the climb to the peak of the mountain that they can finally see. Channeling that momentum can begin with something as simple as a catchy title or visual, complemented with short discussion on the next step or two to take. For each subgroup, you can simply ask "What are you going to do tomorrow?" "How will you document your progress?" These specifics help reduce the complexity of the whole action plan down to much more manageable steps. In the coming section, we will be discussing how to continue leading the Rise. For this point in the journey, however, we have come to a critical touchpoint. It is time to celebrate!

Strategic Planning

In essence, these sessions and/or workshops are strategy exercises. The aim is to lay out the *Why, What, Where, When*, and *How* for the final co-creative act—giving form to the New. They are focused, taking advantage of collective knowledge and collective intelligence to streamline the process of *making*. Co-creation is perfect for strategy sessions among such highly aligned teams. It is not, however, recommended in all strategic contexts. Consider the following ACAN story…

Chaos Doesn't Equal Creativity

Strategy Workshop for ACAN

The chairman of ACAN board had just read this book about the virtues of co-creation, so she decided to give it a shot by arranging a creative workshop. ACAN was in the process of renewing its strategy, and many of the board members had suggested that they should use a participative approach to building this strategy. They wanted to ensure that the company employees would adopt this strategy as their own. Her idea was to invite as many people as possible from all corners of the company to a massive one-day workshop, during which they intended to frame the new strategy. Since their head of Human Resources had often mentioned how ACAN's strongly hierarchical, top-down culture was eating up motivation from the employees, they also decided to make sure that each participant would have an equal voice in the workshop. In order to achieve this, the participants were going to be placed in a circle, where nobody could hide behind the others, and everyone was expected to state their opinion on all of the issues.

The workshop got off to a great start after the chairman expressed her gratitude to all participants for showing up. People were clearly excited to make contributions to the ACME strategy. The organizers had reserved the morning for going through their old strategy and identifying the parts that would require improvement. Based on this analysis, the afternoon would then be used for co-creating a new strategy.

The first round of review went smoothly, as most people still hesitated to state their opinions in front of so many unfamiliar faces. After some encouragement from the workshop facilitators, even the more shy participants started to feel comfortable in speaking up. Most of the participants

(*continued*)

(continued)

were not familiar at all with the previous strategy, so there were many details that had to be broken down and explained to them. This ended up disturbing the flow of the workshop. Many of the managers and other senior members of the ACAN community pulled out their cell phones or laptops and started tapping those every time there was a new explanation of some detail requested by one of the participants. Thanks to the stated workshop principles, some people realized that this was their opportunity to be heard by the managers. They took it upon themselves to make strong comments on every issue that was being discussed, even when they knew that they didn't fully understand what the discussion was about. There was a lot of talk. Numerous opinions were expressed by the participants and documented by the facilitators. Eventually the senior staff members began to withdraw from the conversation, because they felt that their expert opinions were completely neglected by the facilitators. The discussion continued to be dominated by the numerous layman opinions.

By the time they were able to finish the morning session, so many conflicting points of improvement had been stated and documented that it would have been virtually impossible to go through all of them in the afternoon, much less use them as the foundation for renewing the strategy. Instead, since the old strategy had been introduced quite thoroughly during the morning, the facilitators decided to start building a new strategy from scratch in the afternoon. However, when they came back from the lunch break and tried organizing the afternoon session, they soon realized that it would be impossible to make any agreements between the participants about even the smallest details. Everyone was holding on to their own opinions, and nobody even wanted to listen to others.

At the end of the day, the only thing there was clear consensus over was that co-creation was clearly not suitable for ACAN, and these hippie methods should never be used again inside the company.

The point of this story is that co-creation is not meant to be democratic. Nor does everybody need to be actively involved in the process of co-creation. There are other ways to let people participate or contribute to the process than being part of the co-creative team. Instead, a co-creative team should include only whom it needs to for the process at hand, and each person should have a clear, significant role within that process. It is then up to internal communication to make sure that other members of the organization or community are kept in the loop and perhaps given a possibility to participate some other way.

There are numerous approaches that fall under the general category of participatory problem solving or participatory design. Co-creation is one of them, but not the only one, and not one that is suitable for every situation. Throughout this book we have emphasized the critical nature of establishing a safe container around the co-creation team, making sure that everybody can trust each other and feel safe before they get to work. Establishing a container is a process that takes time, and if this process is skipped or not completed, then there is a good chance that the foundation for co-creation is too thin to carry the team. This means that the bond between teammates could easily break during the first point of conflict, just like it shattered during the morning session of our ACAN example above.

Strategic planning requires contextual awareness—choosing the most appropriate approach based on an honest assessment of what you have, what is needed, and the available energy. Although you have worked hard to build momentum throughout the program to reach breakthroughs, it is vital to work with what you have instead of what you designed for. Co-creative outcomes are not always desired or ideal. Nor is consensus always required. You must adapt the program to where the group needs to go and where there is energy, even if that means revising or at times abandoning initial goals. Such considerations return our attention to the leadership required in this stage.

Leading the Rise

The specific constraints of the Rise mandate that leadership tasks change a bit from previous stages. In a way, the change is quite radical, even though it might not appear so on the surface. Until now the focus of the interpersonal aspect of the creative journey has been in *team building*. Our techniques have been aimed at improving the collective performance skills of the team. But now the team building is finished. The team has reached the level where it was expected to be—where the team members can function and perform well together. With no more team building, it's time to break them loose and let them do what they were built to do! This means that in many ways the *Xd* will need to switch from *coaching the team* to *leading the team*. In practice this shift has a few immediate implications:

1. The short-term achievement goals will take priority over the long-term development goals, even though the tools for leading the team will remain pretty much the same as they were before.
2. Leadership needs to make sure that the team stays on track, as they can easily get sidetracked in all the excitement.
3. Leadership must also avoid tunnel vision and immunity to critical thoughts or comments.
4. As the energy converts to speed, it is necessary to pay special attention to routine details, such as documentation and decision-making, so that speed blindness does not turn into sloppiness.

Empowerment or Control

As the nature of activities changes from exploring to constructing, the performance requirements of the team become critical to the success of the mission. This means that the leader's role will be to make sure that the team is performing well at all times. There are many ways to achieve this, and the spectrum of alternatives ranges from the "whip and scream" methods of tough leaders to softer "encourage and observe" approaches (Fig. 10.3).

Fig. 10.3
Closed vs. open leadership

Closed		Open
Control	⇔	Trust
Demand	⇔	Support
Require	⇔	Allow
Coordinate	⇔	Collaborate
Group	⇔	Team
Me	⇔	Us
Teaching	⇔	Learning
Pride	⇔	Respect
Follow	⇔	Explore
Respond	⇔	Initiate
Order	⇔	Encourage
Plan	⇔	Prepare
Supervise	⇔	Empower

Co-creation tends to favor open approaches, but not to the exclusion of closed leadership. Team empowerment will enable the shift from collective knowledge to collective intelligence, but how that is led is more a matter of personal style and skill than any mandate that we could offer. Maintaining PACE helps creative leaders learn through experience what works for them. As a reminder, this entails:

- Being present to your internal states and external actions—taking notice of the effects.
- Being authentic with yourself and others—accept your strengths and weaknesses for what they are.
- Having the courage to change—take personal responsibility and celebrate failure.
- Thinking of the whole and how you can best serve.

Creative leaders who act from this internal worldview will continually improve themselves and their ability to lead. By embodying the pillars of co-creation, they find their own way while continuing to serve as the tuning fork for the team, which helps others maintain a co-creative mindset. Creative leadership, as we see it, is rooted in states of *being*. A leader's inner state conditions their outer actions, which is why closed, open, or a mix of the two approaches can be equally effective. Co-creative leadership is contextual and follows our process design guidelines. There are no "rights" or "wrongs." Rather, there are "better" or "worse" approaches, and we make situational choices that "better" our team's efforts. It may be the case that in the Rise leadership needs to shift from an open approach to a more closed one, being directive and imposing controls to ensure achievement goals are met. The opposite may also be true, letting the team run loose while gently holding the container.

Staying on Track

Regardless of the leadership style chosen, a key to performing well lies in successful monitoring of the team, as described in *Chap. 8—Tuning and Tracking*. By Act III, it is assumed that the team has found its own ways of working and formed stable interpersonal dynamics, which they can regulate on their own. Given this, it's not very important to monitor team dynamics anymore. It will be what it is, for better or worse. Additionally, as long as the team has agreed on its objectives, it can also monitor its activities. Benchmarks and evaluative measures to keep the team on track were decided in the planning at the onset of the Rise. With these in place, it is fairly easy to monitor progress toward pragmatic goals.

The only thing left to be carefully monitored are emotions and the energy of the general atmosphere. These might change very quickly and have a great impact on team dynamics and therefore on the process itself. For the *Xd*, it is now more important than ever to make sure that the team stays on track with their mission. A team might feel that they can accomplish anything, but they need to be kept on point. The million other great ideas can wait.

As explained in Part I, a well-performing team is also at risk of slipping into one of the many pitfalls awaiting nearby—tunnel vision, groupthink, NIH syndrome, just to name a few of them.[12] To avoid these, leaders needs to look after the team more than coach them. Most of us all too easily slip back into our boxes, our comfort zones. When the energy is high and people are excited to do something, they tend to lose the ability to slow down and deeply consider novel possibilities or conflicting information. Especially at this point of the journey, the team might be very reluctant to receive any new information that might jeopardize their efforts. They might ignore relevant messages or constructive criticism. Thus, while it is important to stay on track, the *Xd* also needs to make sure that the team stays open to any new cues or signals that could benefit the process.

Maintaining the "Co" in Co-creation

Slow down. I am in a hurry—Napoleon

Although timelines are tight in this stage, everything still needs to be documented and shared. And even though the goal is in sight, all decisions need to be shared and approved per the team rules. Finally, while the team will be tempted—and maybe even encouraged—to take shortcuts to speed up the process, it is critically important to hold on to the same shared mechanisms and practices that brought the team to this point. Otherwise there is a big risk that one small mistake may go unnoticed and push a snowball in motion under the radar. Once this snowball surfaces, it might be too late to react to it. So even though the time might be tight, there should not be excuses for rushing things through without a deliberate reason. Here is what can happen when you do…

Rushing Only Leads to Fumbling

Breaking Your Own Rules

Lisa and Rick had been put in charge of making the proof-of-concept prototype for ACAN. Lisa was an obvious choice for this task, since she was more than familiar with their manufacturing facilities and personnel. She had been teamed up with Rick, who was an expert in rapid prototyping. They both were well aware of the fact that they had a ridiculously tight deadline—the prototype was supposed to be ready for testing in two-and-half weeks. Luckily they also understood that they did not have to consider most of the requirements that would affect the actual mass production. Everybody knew that this was only built as a quick, glued-together demonstration model.

After a brief survey of their alternatives, Lisa and Rick decided to build the prototype around a third-party microcontroller that was suitable for mass production. Rick had used the same controller in one of his previous projects, so he knew that it was already in use in many commercial products, and therefore it was of high enough quality to be used in their final product as well. Based on this knowledge, he labeled the part as "suitable for production" without any hesitation, even though they probably would not be involved in designing the actual production model. They already knew that Frank, their Senior Design Engineer, was in charge of the pre-production models. He would eventually verify the components they would use for the later Alpha and Beta prototypes. Therefore it would be totally up to him to pick and choose the components they would use in the actual production.

As the responsibilities of Lisa and Rick were limited to the PoC model, they didn't see any need to document or share any details about their preliminary decisions related to the controller. It later turned out that this particular controller was in its end-of-life and had already been replaced by its manufacturer with a newer model. So even though they were successfully able to use it in their proof-of-concept model, as an obsolete component it was not suitable for mass production. They also realized that the obsolete controller model did not have enough output channels for all the accessories that needed them, so it did not even fit all of the basic requirements set for the final product. Alice, the outsourcing lady, could've spotted these issues straight away, but nobody asked her during the process. The team was in big trouble, very big, from a small mistake.

The ACAN example illustrates how even a small deviation from established routines may be enough to cause a chain reaction that leads to severe harm or even a complete disaster. Rushing of things has a tendency of increasing the number and size of blind spots. The worst part about this speed blindness is that you won't be able to sense or realize yourself that your vision has become limited.

The best way to avoid this type of tunnel vision is by sticking to the daily and weekly quality assurance routines that were introduced to the team during the Climb—and hopefully perfected during the Dive. These include many small and simple routines, such as making sure that everyone in the team knows about any changes to previous assumptions or agreements, and about any new decisions or new discoveries made during the process.

If an exception needs to be made—and at this point there might be several justified reasons for making one—it needs to be very cautious and deliberate. It should also be communicated clearly to everyone who might be impacted by it. The person who makes this exception will also need to take responsibility of following up on the consequences.

In the ACAN example above, the trouble could have been avoided by very small acts. If Lisa and Rick had told others about their decision to add an unsuitable component to the list of prototype components, there is a good chance that Alice or Frank would have paid attention to the quality mismatch. They could have suggested replacing the component with a better one, or at least acknowledged that the component was not suitable for mass production and made a mental note to address this issue later on in the process. Alternatively, if Lisa and Rick had acknowledged their responsibility for following up on the issue, they would have ensured that everyone was aware of what they had done, and what influences their decision might have on other tasks. Either way would have been enough to prevent a chain of wrong assumptions from causing a snowball effect with disastrous consequences.

Maintaining the "co" in co-creation will help to ensure that all the unique considerations of the Rise are met. As long as the team has a measure of collective intelligence, you can trust them to move on in the process of making with a high degree of autonomy. The primary tasks for the *Xd* are to structure the workflow, keep the team on track, and be mindful of the pitfalls common to this stage. You must balance order with chaos, imagination with constraints, and the multiple personalities whom are all integral components of collective creativity. Teams will need varying degrees of direction, support, and controls. In all things communication is paramount, ensuring that it is the collective "we" moving forward.

Prototyping

I have an Idea. How do I build it?[13]

After avoiding the pitfalls at the beginning of Rise, there will be a rather long and steady period of "just doing"—or performing. The goal of the co-creative journey has been to get the team to this point, where they have created a winning concept that they can realize. Now it's time to enjoy the ride. If all has gone well, the team has reached a state of *collective flow*. We observe flow often as total absorption in tasks, and when there is sufficient collective intelligence, the team performs with little need for explaining things to one another. They become immersed in the creative act with passion and focus. This state is very rare, and it will give such satisfaction to the participants that many will get hooked on the feeling, wanting to experience it again and again.

Co-creative performance during the Rise is centered on prototyping. Many people define *prototyping* as the *final stage* of a product design process, during which a functional model of the product is created. In organizational change, prototyping may be related to a product. Or it could be the translation of an idea into experimental actions—a pilot for a new service or change initiative. This is a very short and accurate description of that final stage, which is probably the reason why most people assume that this is the whole truth about prototyping. However, prototyping is also a term used to describe the *process* that tries to model certain features or functions of a product concept for various purposes. There can be numerous different reasons and objectives for prototyping during a co-creative process, but we can divide these into two general categories—communication and learning. If one picture can tell more than a thousand words, we could add that a prototype can tell more than a thousand pictures. Whether we are talking about internal or external communication, having a prototype will add credibility and accuracy to most forms of communication. This makes it much easier to give specific feedback on different aspects of the concept. The greatest advantage of prototyping, however, comes through different forms of learning. The prototyping process itself helps to understand what can or cannot be done and improves understanding of how to realize the concept. It also enables different forms of testing, starting from aesthetic evaluations and ending in mechanical simulations, crash tests, and concept validations. What is common between all these purposes is that each prototype will help the team to understand more, which in turn takes the process one step closer to a final solution.

While the prototyping stage is reasonably linear, predictable, and straightforward, one could say that the prototyping process is just about the opposite. Prototyping as a process is experimentation, testing, and refinement of concepts.[14] As Brown argues in *Change by Design*[15]:

> Prototyping is always inspirational—not in the sense of a perfected artwork but just the opposite: because it inspires new ideas. Prototyping should start early in the life of a project, and we expect them to be numerous, quickly executed, and pretty ugly. Each one is intended to develop an idea "just enough" to allow the team to learn something and move on. At this relatively low level of resolution, it's almost always best for the team members to make their own prototypes and not outsource them to others.

Only after several build → test → break → and start over cycles do teams reach clear definitions and models worth taking out into the world. Prototyping process includes prototyping to think and other forms of learning and exploring through making. We have seen these techniques in the first two Acts of our journey, and they take on a central role in the Rise.

Prototyping Process

Prototyping begins with conceptual design, the phase of the creative process in which inspiration is translated into a broad outline of function and form. As we have noted, this can occur as early on as the creative brief, or in the beginning of the Rise by setting or revising design specifications. Conceptual design is a description of the proposed product or service that conveys what it should do, behave and look like in a way that is understandable for users. It includes the design of potential interactions, experiences, processes, and strategies. A tool that we find helpful for conceptual design is a prototyping worksheet in the U.Lab Source Book.[16] The questions, presented in brief here, help bring clarity.

- **Is it relevant?** Does it matter to all the key stakeholders?
- **Is it right?** Does it have the right size and scope? Does the microsystem you are focused on reflect the whole (ecosystem) you are dealing with?
- **Is it revolutionary?** Is it new? Can it change the game?
- **Is it rapid?** Can you do it quickly, getting feedback and adapting?
- **Is it rough?** Can you do it on a small scale, locally, with basic resources?
- **Is it relatively effective?** Does it leverage the strengths, competencies, and possibilities of the existing networks and communities at hand? Does it "mostly" work?
- **Is it replicable?** Can you scale it?

Key to creating a successful product or service lies in understanding what the customer wants and what the customer needs. Providing something that a customer wants is vital to getting a new customer. Filling an actual need will ensure that the customer is satisfied. A satisfied customer will come back for seconds and make recommendations to his or her friends. A good conceptual design is one in which the relationship between *Promise* and *Delivery* is clearly articulated through concept sketches, storyboards, mock-ups, and models. It tells a "compelling story that makes sense and makes the idea feel real to your collaborators."[17] In co-creation, conceptual design begins early, and there are several stages in which prototyping has value.[18] The following presents these uses in the order they often occur.

Prototypes as Shared Models for Communication

In the very beginning of the journey, prototyping can play a crucial role in building effective communication, shared understanding, and even a foundation for trust within the team. When the members of a newly formed team are starting their climb, and trying to find their own roles within the team, there is usually a lot of turbulence, friction, and confusion in the air. At this point, the prototyping process can be used as a powerful tool to bring the team to the same side of the table and align their efforts toward solving a common problem—rather than arguing over their differences in perspectives and opinions. In this context, a prototype functions mainly as a ***shared model*** that enables the team members to debate and share their perspectives in a constructive way. Once a prototype has been created, and once it has been accepted as a shared model between the individuals, the team can start improving it by making additions, exclusions, alterations, and so on to the model—just as long as it stays as the one shared model. The team members have to justify their proposals to the rest of the team, which will help them understand each other's perspectives. By forcing people to articulate their views to others, this process improves the internal communication within the team, increases the shared base of knowledge, and encourages people to trust each other.

Prototyping as Experimentation

As the journey proceeds, the role and objectives of the prototyping processes will also evolve. Once the team begins to understand each other's strengths and personalities, prototyping might not be needed as a communication tool anymore. Instead, prototyping can be used as an ***experimentation method***, which is aimed at increasing their understanding and producing new knowledge in the Unknown.

In the Dive we introduced prototyping as one of our "thinking" tools, emphasizing the value of learning by doing and working with the hands. Drawing is one method to help us conceptualize.[19] Words and numbers are fine, but only drawing can simultaneously reveal both the functional characteristics of an idea and its emotional content. To draw an idea accurately, decisions have to be made that can be avoided by even the most precise language; aesthetic issues have to be addressed that cannot be resolved by the most elegant mathematical calculation. Whether the task at hand is a hair dryer, a weekend retreat in the country, or an annual report, drawing forces decisions.

The same can be said for sculpting and other forms of crafting. A different medium allows us to express and perceive with all of our senses, tapping into the many ways of knowing and intuiting.

Famous Silicon Valley mantras encourage this type of prototyping by telling everyone to "Fail early and fail often," or simply to "Fail forward." These mantras seem to capture the essence of ***experimental prototyping*** quite well. Such prototyping welcomes new discoveries of what ***doesn't*** work and what ***not*** to do, as well as the more expected results of identifying solutions or opportunities. Both outcomes bring clarity into a previously unclear issue and hence take the team forward.

Finding Form Through Mock-Ups

At some point of the journey, there might be a need to see and feel the product in real life, even though the concept is still just an abstract idea in someone's head. Mock-ups are used to bring physical form to a product idea or a concept. Quick 'n dirty prototypes function as such, trying to capture the essence of a form without putting a lot of time or energy into producing it. These types of mock-ups can be made of very simple materials, such as cardboard, sticks, paper clips, modeling clay, straws, and paper cups, but they might still succeed in conveying the physical form of a product—usually with the help of a bit of imagination. Higher-quality mock-ups can be made, for example, by cutting and carving out of blue foam, by CNC machines out of wood or plastics, or by heat forming out of moldable plastic sheets. Even though these mock-ups are just visual and tangible models, they can be made to a very authentic form and appearance, and as such they can be used to get valuable feedback from experts or from potential users.

Physical mock-ups are valuable not only for bringing form to ideas, but also as a communication tool. LEGO® SERIOUS PLAY®, for example, quickly reveals differences in worldview when people are asked to build their concept and share it with others. At CCI we used a variation on this theme, asking a group to build a 3D model of their vision from poster stands, string, and post-it notes. While at first they found this challenging, the introduction of 3D objects and space created tangible reference points for their ongoing dialogues. At several points in time, teams used their models to advance or clarify their ideas.

Testing Conceptual Models

During conceptual design, there is a constant need to test and validate the latest concepts. There are many ways to get feedback about a concept even before building a functional prototype. An example of this would be so-called *Wizard of Oz* prototypes that try to imitate the functions of the concept through low-tech approaches. For example, a technical operator could be changing images on a screen or making sounds behind a wall, to give an impression that a dumb device is responding to the commands from a test user. If this test user shows an image on her cell phone to a screen attached to a wall, the technical operator could take a photo of that image on her camera, then upload the image on her computer, and finally display it on the screen in front of the test user, with a small square added to the screen saying "PRINT." If the user then presses this "PRINT" button on the screen, the technical operator would print the image on glossy paper and push the printed image to the test user through a slot underneath the screen. This way the test user would get an impression of a machine that could capture and print an image that was shown to it, even though the operations were not conducted by the machine but rather by a Wizard of Oz.

Digital technology enables us to make more complicated models that can be used for simulations or realistic visualizations of what the concept would look like in an actual context, or how it would behave in expected use. Sometimes these digital models can be used for marketing purposes before the actual product is available, and in some cases, they remain in the marketing materials even after a product has been completed.

If only things were so easy in organizations! Whenever people and cultures are involved, concept testing becomes much more challenging. It would be nice if we could create an AutoCAD[20] walk-through of a change initiative, giving us a virtual tour of what our design would look like in implementation. Organizations have different tools for concept testing, including focus groups, empirical tests in semi-controlled or natural environments, action learning initiatives, and more. While the methodologies differ, they share the need to test and validate ideas before investing significant resources in them.

At the final stage of conceptual design, there is a need to validate the concept with a prototype. These validation prototypes have many names, for example, demo-or-die prototypes, proof-of-concept models, critical function prototype, or minimum viable products. Regardless of their title, they all serve the same purpose. They should validate the concept at the end of conceptual design and get an approval for moving forward. Otherwise they die and it's time to move on to another concept.

Prototyping Stage

Once the conceptual design is complete and the team knows what they need, it is time to start building the actual product, service, or pilot. This is the prototyping stage, which has only one goal—to build it. The prototyping stage begins by further refining the design into specifications, plans, and resource estimates. Designers call this the "Detailed" or "Final" design. In our discussion of PAP, this is the "planning" stage that comes after success criteria (e.g. design standards) are set and the team is ready to move into specific actions. What comes next varies greatly, depending on the experiential and pragmatic goals of the co-creative process. A prototype can be anything really, from new wine opener to a pilot for a massive change initiative. For many of these, but not all, there remain two more steps in the Rise before we cross the finish line.

Alpha's and Beta's

Before the big conveyor belts can be switched on, all the components need to be designed, manufactured, assembled, tested, and approved for production. The first complete, fully functional prototypes are usually called the Alpha's, and the more advanced, almost-ready-for-production models are Beta's. Both Alpha's and Beta's will go through several rounds of rigorous testing, which usually lead to improvements in individual components or even the entire layout.

Another terminology is that of versioning, with a 0.8 version being equivalent to the Alpha. A 0.8 version is something that is "ready enough" for testing, but not complete by any means.

> Prototypes should command only as much time, effort, and investment as is necessary to generate useful feedback and drive an idea forward. The greater the complexity and expense, the more "finished" it is likely to seem and the less likely its creators will be to profit from constructive feedback—or even to listen to it. The goal of prototyping is not to create a working model. It is to give form to an idea to learn about its strengths and weaknesses and to identify new directions for the next generation of more detailed, more refined prototypes.[21]

In the School of Design, for example, our MSc students had less than a year to come up with a creative idea, form a design team, and then build and test it. Their deliverable was an Alpha, or 0.8 version. None of these were ready for market, but they all had been sufficient to rigorously test the designs and identify what changes were needed for a Beta.

Organizational consultants are often expected to perform miracles, delivering the equivalent of a Beta with minimal fiscal and time resources. In today's climate, for example, consultants are hard pressed to get an organization to dedicate three days or more to a co-creative process. Whenever resources are restricted, quality is sacrificed, and thus the best outcome in such cases is an Alpha. Some consultants refer to these as "Areas of Attention" or "Arenas of Action" to be further considered.

They might be two or three possible trajectories, which the leadership then vets and assigns task teams to implement. For reasons stated earlier in this chapter, ideally team that developed the concept continues to work on it, applying the collective intelligence they have developed. But this may not be the only, or best, option. In some organizations the co-creative team serves as a "think tank," coming up with ideas designed for others to develop. In any of these scenarios, before making any final decisions it is wise to involve the stakeholders/users and learn though testing.

Co-design

In an ideal world, stakeholders from across the value chain have been intimately involved in the co-creative process. This is co-design, one end of the stakeholder involvement spectrum.[22] At the other end users/stakeholders are observed, interviewed, and brought in to test an Alpha or Beta, but otherwise they had no active role in the co-creative process. In the middle lies participatory design approaches that involve users/stakeholders to various degrees. Co-creation strongly favors co-design, but that is up to you and your client. All that we can do here is reiterate the value of diversity in collective creativity. The decision, from our perspective, should not be about whether or not to include diverse stakeholders. Rather, it is concerned with *when* to include them.

Anyone familiar with design, or more specifically, designers, knows that there are many successful lone wolfs (solo designers). Asking a designer to co-design with users might not get the best reaction. And yet almost every designer acknowledges the value of stakeholder engagement. Most designers will involve stakeholders in the prototyping stage, soliciting feedback to help them modify an existing concept. Stanford's d.school calls this creating a "user-driven prototype." The method card explains[23]:

> Whenever you engage a user with a prototype, you are trying to better understand him and perhaps his reaction to your solution-in-progress. Often with prototypes, you ask the user to experience something you created, and you gain insight by observing their reaction and by talking to them about the experience. The intention with a user-driven prototype is to gain understanding by watching the user create something, rather than try something that you developed.
>
> The value of a user-driven prototype is that different assumptions and desires are revealed when the user is asked to create aspects of the design, rather than just evaluate or experience the prototype. The goal is not to take

what they made and integrate it into your design, but rather to understand their thinking and perhaps reveal needs and features that you may not have thought of.

Like designers, an *Xd* may bring in outside stakeholders at specific points in the co-creative process. Evocative inputs in Act I are one example. Expert consultation may benefit the process at several points. Even disruption, planned or unplanned, has value if it shakes up and advances the process. None of these needs require that the agent (whomever or whatever it is) be present throughout the entire process. Who, how, and when are decisions the project lead must situationally make. However, for co-creation the one time that stakeholders *must* be involved is during prototyping. Given that co-creation strives to integrate needs across the value chain, it is simply impossible to be co-creative without investing the time and resources to engage a range of stakeholders. Not only will your ideas suffer from lack of diverse perspectives, but you lose the collective empowerment and ownership that come with co-designing. The tremendous success of value co-creation—a major trend in product design and marketing—rests on high levels of engagement with users who feel empowered by their ability to affect the marketplace and the products they consume. The same phenomenon is true of change initiatives that authentically engage employees across levels of the organization. They are *much* more effective than top-down approaches, no matter how noble the vision of leadership. The bottom line is simple … engage stakeholders early and often. Create the space and resource to bring them into your process, but leave an option to expand or shrink the size of the team as needed. Co-design is great when stakeholder involvement is beneficial, but that is not all the time. That balance will vary by project, so the best thing you can do is build in flexibility.

Learning Launches

The Rise concludes with evaluation. Having a working prototype in hand doesn't mean that we are finished. It means that we have something to show people and learn from. Before we invest tremendous resources to release our great new idea, product, or service, we have an opportunity to solicit feedback one last time. *Designing for Growth* calls these "Learning Launches: creating an affordable experiment that lets customers experience the new solution over an extended period, to test key assumptions with market data."[24]

The first component of a launch is user testing. UX (user experience) testing can be as rigorous as the initial design research, and the aim is to make sure your ideas are valid before allocating further resources. The best way to do this is to put your Alpha prototype in use and solicit feedback. It is vital to look for disconfirming data—things that will prove your assumptions false. Confirmation bias (when we think our ideas are "right") makes it easy to overlook contradictions, but these are the gems you need. To find them, collectively determine what disconfirming data would look like. Then, as a team, run your tests. With more than one set of eyes, you are much more likely to notice these potentially project saving details.

Designing your launch also requires considering how you will get people to try it—the "on-ramp."[25] Until you sell the idea enough for others to want it, it will remain just an idea, an unrealized seed of potential. In organizations, this might be as simple as the leadership informing employees that they will be adopting or piloting a new initiative. Initiatives may or may not be incentivized to encourage engagement. If your position is that of a consultant or an HR professional, perhaps you need to sell an idea to the leadership. In either scenario, it is helpful to look back to Chap. 3: Working with People, the section on stakeholder dialogues. Your launch will be more successful if it has a compelling needs story to engage the stakeholders you wish to reach. Even better is when the initiative aligns culture and strategy in a mutually reinforcing feedback loop.

For product and service design, the on-ramp must get the attention of potential consumers. How will you build awareness? Are you meeting an exciting need or defining a new one? If manufacturing desires, how do you convince people? What else might be going on that could affect your campaign? These are a few key questions to ask to situate your message and launch. With those answers, you can move on delivery and other logistics, such as marketing channels, resources, and timelines.

Learning launches are an *active* learning process. Throughout, it helps to maintain the design mindset of iterating toward better and better solutions. *Designing for Growth* offers some useful principles[26]:

> Work in fast feedback cycles. Minimize the cost of conducting your experiments. Fail early to succeed sooner. Test for key trade-offs and assumptions early. Most important, play with the prototypes in the field instead of defending them.

Adding to that, for organizational initiatives we would advise working in expanding circles of influence. Begin with a small team who can best create and communicate the first iterations of the prototype. Use this team to test and address critical questions or issues that arise. Then, in broader circles, invite in others who need to experience the prototype to evaluate it. Help the core team revise as needed and then re-test with the broader circles. When possible, co-create between circles to improve the prototype. After several iterations, the prototype will evolve into a pilot.

Prototyping at ACME

To conclude our discussion of prototyping, let's look at how ACME built their new baby monitor. We begin with concept design.

February 10th–14th

The name B-Beam came along as soon as they had started using BBM as the acronym for Biometric Baby Monitor, and Dorothy picked it up right away as the working title for the product. At this point, there were still eight product concept left as candidates for the product family, but the bottom three were quickly ruled out as "technology oriented gadgets," which were not a good match with ACME values. Roberta and David had teamed up to define the marketing promise for B-Beam, and they had ended up with a simple "Baby monitor that can predict the waking-up of a baby by understanding the physiological elements of sleep". All other features would bring additional value for the user, at least from the marketing perspective.

Product Family Candidates

B-Beam Standard*—Robust unit intended for permanent installation, plugs to wall, wireless connection, carries audio and video signals*

B-Beam Lite*—Portable, battery operated, completely wireless, no camera*

B-Beam App*—Mobile app for iPhone + Android; the user interface for B-Beam; includes an open interface for developer communities*

B-Beam Display*—Real-time display of data + video in the background, including ambient temperature, humidity, luminosity, noise level, sleep state graph*

B-Beam Camera*—Wireless camera for Lite. Possible addition to the family*

~~***B-Beam Rocker****—Rocking device for helping baby fall asleep. Possible addition to the family*~~

~~***B-Beam Massage****—Morning massage mattress. Possible addition to the family*~~

~~***B-Beam Dock****—"Docking station" for a baby. Possible addition to the family*~~

After deciding on the best product concept, the next step was to get a green light for it from the management team. For this, the team had to demonstrate that the concept was feasible and that it would be able to deliver what they had promised to the users. This would be done by building a suitable proof-of-concept prototype and creating a demonstration.

The team was expected to build a demonstration device, so the first question to answer was that of what to demonstrate. Based on their original concept, the team had decided to build a demonstration of the biometric monitoring, presented as a graph on the screen of a mobile phone, with a time displayed on screen as the prediction of how long until the baby would wake up. On Thursday the Proof-of-Concept was ready for testing, and on Friday it was put in use by the team for the first time. The technical tests went well, the team cleared the prototype to be suitable for the required demonstration. They were done with the first task.

At this point of the journey, the team has been in the high-performance mode for a while. The only problem was that they used up 90% of their time and the deadline for the presentation was approaching fast. Because of the time pressure, combined with the facts that the team was working rapidly and autonomously, there was now a real risk of making mistakes that could jeopardize the entire project. These are the moments that call for good judgment and strong intuition from the team leaders, because nobody from outside can tell how the team should proceed. In some cases, it might be a good idea to slow things down, but in other cases this could take the momentum away from the team. One option would be to tighten the control of the team, but that could confuse the team and impact their motivation. As a general guideline, it would be good if the team leader and *Xd* could stay close to the team, keeping their eyes and ears open and reminding the team to stick to their old routines while trying to stay out of their way.

The task list was still very long, and all the tasks were equally critical, if the team wanted to make their deadline. The proof-of-concept prototype was ready, but nothing else was done. They still needed to build a convincing presentation, and somehow incorporate a demonstration with the prototype. They also had to prepare a detailed plan for producing the two products—

B-Beam Standard and B-Beam lite—including an accurate schedule, resource allocation plan, and a budget. In addition, they were expected to present a comprehensive roadmap for the rest of the product family, describing which products will be later added to the family, and when would they be introduced to ACME and to the public. They had less than two weeks to put this all together.

Preparation for the corporate presentation and demo was a point at which the ACME process could have derailed. With a tight deadline and so much to do, it would have been easier to delegate tasks and have each person report back once finished. Dorothy, however, was mindful of speed blindness and the lurking dangers of breaking from routine. She insisted on daily check-ins, careful reporting, and time to continue aligning ideas with each other. The days were longer, but the result was a presentation that everyone was proud of.

Demo Day

Finally, the Demo Day had arrived. This was a big day for ACME, and there was a lot of anticipation in the air. The entire management team had come down to the R&D auditorium to evaluate their results. The management team was accompanied by the head of human resources, and they had also brought two outside experts with them to consult in areas they were not familiar with. This day was expected to introduce a new chapter to ACME's product portfolio, so the expectations for the demonstration were set quite high. And so the demonstration began…

During the demonstration, everyone was looking at the front row where the executives were sitting together with their reinforcements. No visible reactions were expressed, until the CEO looked at the others and nodded while saying "Okay, let's do it!" After a brief discussion, they invited Dorothy and David to join them for a short meeting. During this meeting, they expressed their concerns about the proposal to introduce B-Beam Lite as the first product. Even though Lite was predicted to be much easier to manufacture, and also a less risky alternative due to having fewer components, the CEO was worried that they would send a wrong message to the market if they introduced a simplified version first, instead of the full product. After getting support for this argument from David's market survey, they made a decision in favors of Plan B. This meant that the Standard model would be published first, followed soon by Lite, while the additional products were to be introduced later on according to the roadmap. A budget was allocated for them according to the plan, and a new leaf was to be turned in the dynasty of ACME.

With the concept now tested, validated, and approved, the team could move on to building a fully functional prototype. The concept had been co-created by the team, so everyone in the team knew quite well what would be expected from them during the final stage. Although the final prototype might be quite simple to complete, it could also end up being a difficult and demanding part of the journey. After all, had the team truly challenged themselves when creating the concept, this task could be at the far end of their collective capabilities. Yet what could be more rewarding than challenging yourself with the plan that you just created with your teammates? The final part of the journey applies the collective knowledge, one task at a time, until the team crosses the finish line.

Monday morning came, and there was one more goal left for the team—to build the final Alpha prototype. They had the permission and the resources they needed, so it was time to finish. The team had gone through some rough times to get to this point, and finally they had a chance to start doing what they do best. Start designing the Alpha, start designing the App, finish the system design for Lite, Display, and Camera. Start involving actual users in design process. All this was simple and enjoyable for the team. They were at the top of their game.

Over the next weeks, the ACME team worked with tremendous focus and flow, successfully creating Alpha prototypes for the main products in the new line, B-Beam Standard and B-Beam Lite. They decided to outsource the App development to a partner company, and that the display and camera add-ons could wait until after the main products were launched.

We have reached *The End* of our ACME journey. To finish the project, Dorothy served champagne for her team on the day of B-Beam unveiling. She told the team to take the rest of the week off and come back to a local hotel for a debrief on the next Thursday. Dorothy wanted to give the team one last chance to meet and share their memories before the project was concluded and the team broken apart. This was her way of closing the curtain for the final act.

Crossing the Line

From an organizational perspective, a co-creative process is fundamentally cyclic, with the outputs of one process becoming the inputs for another. It is not uncommon to launch an initiative, have it fail or succeed, and then start a new co-creative process for the next challenge or opportunity. Change is constant, and all organizations need reevaluation and renewal if they are to survive. If an organization chooses to tackle their challenges collectively, there will always be a place for co-creation.

The Rise is not the end for design projects either. After the team has completed their co-creative journey and created a successful line of product, there are a series of follow-up activities. The design process continues, as the rest of the product family needs to be designed. The learning process continues, as the team needs to debrief and wrap-up the journey. And the organization continues to start new journeys. Some people move on to other projects, while others continue to develop the current one. Our point is that there is not necessarily a clear end to the journey here. However, this is a point at which a celebration should take place with the team, to commemorate a successful completion of the Rise. The team finally has something to show for their efforts. It has passed the tests necessary to please the project sponsors, and it is time for implementation.

While the actual implementation is part of the follow-up, the Rise concludes by planning for it. In some cases this planning may be exhaustive, with detailed cost predictions, timelines, and action plans that stretch out over the next months or year. PAP, when used as framework for the entire Rise, concludes with an "orchestration" phase that focuses on these considerations. In other cases a co-creative program ends with a small set of possibilities to further pursue in specialized task forces. If it is called for, you can assist the transition from prototyping to implementation with tools that help people make decisions and chart their path forward.

The sheer amount that needs to be done can be daunting at times, and teams may get stuck in analysis paralysis. "Where do we start?" is a question you can help them find answers to with exercises like trim tab.[27] A trim tab is the small rudder inside a large rudder on ships. It acts as a lever to initiate a larger movement. Applied to decision-making, we ask "What are the smallest actions that can make the greatest impact?" The objective is to identify the actions with the greatest impact for the least effort. These are much easier to implement than trying to move the whole rudder at once.

A strategic agenda may also be useful at this point. A strategic agenda identifies critical pillars, or levels of activity, that will manifest a strategic intent. Each pillar has its own set of priorities, objectives, resources, success measures, and timeline. These coordinate action on what is most important, rather than the long list of possible activities in any day. Strategic agendas are valuable in cutting through organizational inertia, bringing focus and clarity to actions.

A final tool is the roadmap. Introduced in Chap. 7, roadmaps capture both where you have been and how you might get to your destination. The map is not the territory, but it is a valuable frame of reference to align efforts or look at when you get lost. One type of implementation roadmap is the organizational backbone, a nowhere group tool.[28] The backbone is a visual metaphor that connects an organization's story, brand, purpose and values, strategy, and ambition together in a unified framework. It connects past, present, and future together while also aligning purpose, strategy, and actions. Organizational change usually has several moving parts worked on at different times and locations. Change may begin with an organizational purpose quest, for example, followed by the assignment of a transformation team whose task is to co-create a strategy and its implementation. Another team may be tasked with internal and external communication. The organizational backbone brings these different engagements together into a larger picture—a roadmap that helps everyone see the value (staying connected to the *Why*) of their contributions.

The Final Checkout

As teams cross the finish line, the *creative* aspect of co-creation comes to a conclusion. While there remain steps to be taken in the follow-up, this is a significant moment for the team that is best not ignored. They have been through an incredible journey full of moments of tension and flow, emotional highs and lows, frustrations, and breakthroughs. This is a time to take a step back and honor all aspects of the journey. Earlier in the text we introduced checkouts as a valuable tool for setting the container, acknowledging how people feel, and maintaining alignment. Checkouts give people voice and perspective, and in our experience, it is often in closing circles that emotions and gratitude pour out. It is almost as if the closing moments are the only time when people can see the magnitude of what they just went through, and it hits them all at once. As experience designers, we honor everyone's journey by holding a space for expression. It is the least we can do for our hardworking team, and often it is these moments that persist as memories of the time spent together. Make it count.

Notes

1. Ogilvie and Liedtka, *Designing for Growth*, Kindle Locations 663–666.
2. Chapter 2 (Team Dynamics) and Chap. 8 (How Do You Set the Container?).
3. As described in Chap. 8—How Do You Set the Container?
4. The process of knowledge harvesting will be described in detail in Chap. 11.
5. Kolb, A., Kolb, D. (2005, May 15) The Kolb Learning Style Inventory—Version 3.1 2005 Technical Specifications. Retrieved from http://learningfromexperience.com/media/2010/08/tech_spec_lsi.pdf.
6. Senge et al., *Presence*, Kindle Locations 1864–1866.
7. There are several sources beyond the scope of this text. See, for example, the Journal of Organizational Change Management or Kotter, *Leading Change*.
8. d.school. Design Principles method card. This work is licensed under the Creative Commons Attribution-NonCommercial-ShareAlike 3.0 Unported License. To view a copy of this license, visit http://creativecommons.org/licenses/by-nc-sa/3.0/.
9. See *Designing for Growth*.
10. Ogilvie and Liedtka, *Designing for Growth*, Kindle Locations 684–686, 306–309.
11. Ogilvie and Liedtka, *Designing for Growth*, Kindle Locations 290–294.
12. Chapter 2 (Team Dynamics) and Chap. 8 (How Do You Set the Container?).
13. Design Thinking for Educators (2011). IDEO. Retrieved from http://designthinkingforeducators.com.
14. See, for example, Aspelund, *The Design Process*.
15. Brown, *Change by Design*, 106.
16. This work is licensed by the Presencing Institute—Otto Scharmer—www.presencing.com/permissions.
17. Ogilvie and Liedtka, *Designing for Growth*, Kindle Locations 700–701.
18. For succinct instructions on prototyping, see the d.school bootcamp bootleg Method Cards.
19. Brown, *Change by Design*, 80.
20. AutoCAD is a commercial computer-aided design and drafting software application.
21. Brown, *Change by Design*, 91.

22. Chapter 2 contains a more a detailed discussion of this spectrum.
23. d.school bootcamp bootleg. Creative Commons Attribution-NonCommercial-ShareAlike 3.0 Unported License. Visit http://creativecommons.org/licenses/by-nc-sa/3.0/.
24. Ogilvie and Liedtka, *Designing for Growth*, Kindle Locations 557–563.
25. Ibid., Kindle Locations 717–722.
26. Ibid.
27. Trim tab is a technique from Social Artistry to identify key levers for moving forward.
28. Visit www.now-here.com or see *The Way of nowhere*.

References

Aspelund, Karl. *The Design Process*. Fairchild, 2010.

Brown, Tim, and Barry Katz. *Change by Design: How Design Thinking Transforms Organizations and Inspires Innovation*. Adobe Digital Edition ed. New York: Harper Collins e-books, 2009.

Kotter, John P. *Leading Change*. Boston: Harvard Business School Press, 1996.

Ogilvie, Tim, and Jeann Liedtka. *Designing for Growth: A Design Thinking Toolkit for Managers*. Columbia Business School Publishing. Kindle Edition: Columbia University Press, 2011.

Senge, Peter M., Claus Otto Scharmer, Joseph Jaworski, and Betty Sue Flowers. *Presence: Exploring Profound Change in People, Organizations, and Society*. Kindle Edition ed.: The Crown Publishing Group, 2005.

Turner, N., and N. Udall. *The Way of Nowhere: Eight Questions to Release Our Creative Potential*. Harper-Collins E-Books, 2008.

CHAPTER 11

Follow-Up

June 26th

Two weeks after the Unveiling, Dorothy invited the team members to a full day debrief session. She wanted this event to be very focused, which would not be easy since the team still had their heads in the clouds after a hard-earned victory. At the same time, she was hoping that two weeks was enough time to bring some emotional distance to the intensive final stretch of the project. This would ensure that the team could look back at the project objectively, without being blinded by the celebratory team spirit.

In previous projects, Dorothy had experienced several problems that she later figured were associated with a lack of focus due to the many distractions that were constantly lurking around the team at the office. For this reason, she thought it might be a good idea to invite the team to a nearby hotel just outside of the town. The team members could take a complete break from their daily routines and have some time and space for themselves. And so the team was invited to the hotel on the evening before the de-briefing.

The evening turned out to be a perfect tool for starting the process of reflection within the team. It gave them an opportunity to celebrate their success and look back at their previous achievements together, as a team. During the conversations with their teammates, everyone brought details about the journey back into their minds. When the next morning came, everyone was up and ready for the debriefing.

The journey is now over, but life still goes on, so it's time to wrap things up and move on to the next challenge. Follow-up activities have parallel

B. R. Rill, M. M. Hämäläinen, *The Art of Co-Creation*,
https://doi.org/10.1007/978-981-10-8500-0_11

objectives that need to be considered during the process. The first objective, the *harvesting of knowledge*, is most often the primary goal. Knowledge harvesting aims at making sure that all the discoveries and results that took place during the journey have been properly documented and analyzed. The second objective, the *refinement of the shared experience*, is an aspect of team and culture building. This is conducted to ensure that the team can build on their collective effort, maximizing the development of their co-creative skills and innovative capacities. Even though it is quite often considered to be a mere by-product of the process rather than an explicit goal, we emphasize the value of this second objective as essential in building a culture of innovation within an organization.

While there is no prescriptive recipe for follow-up, there is a need for a sense of continuity between a co-creative journey and the return to everyday work. If a program is seen as a "one off," the outcomes are ignored, or if the outcomes are kept behind closed doors, participants lose the sense of empowerment. In these cases, when the "co"—or collective—is lost, creative energy dissipates and the program can be mistaken as simply another team building exercise. Preventing these mistakes lies in good follow-up that integrates co-creation within the larger picture.

Unfortunately, in many cases these follow-up activities never take place, in which case a huge part of the knowledge generated during the journey can go untapped. When this happens, people can become skeptical of any creative program, feeling that their valuable time and efforts were wasted. To prevent this from happening, follow-up activities should become a routine part of any co-creation project, with their value for the organization understood explicitly.

Most of the issues we discuss in this chapter are common to many types of collaborative projects, while some of them are specific to—or at least more relevant for—co-creation. In this chapter, we go through steps that we recommend following after every co-creation process. The basic steps are quite simple and clear, regardless of how the process ended or what the outcomes were produced. But before we move into those steps, let's look at what outcomes are possible.

Outcomes

There are two types of outcomes expected from a co-creative journey. The most obvious results are the *tangible outcomes*, such as the new products or solutions produced by the team, which are the fruits of the project.

These "fruits" are the substantive results of meeting the pragmatic and experiential goals of the project. Tangible outcomes produce the required return on investment for the project owner, and they are the primary measure of success for a co-creation project.

The other form of outcome that we will consider here are the *intangibles*, the implicit revelations and insights developed by the team during their journey.[1] Intangibles also include growth in capacity—individually and collectively—such as creative leadership and collective intelligence. Intangible outcomes are potentially transformative changes within the organization or design team. These outcomes are the seeds for the next journey and/or culture change in an organization. If they are harvested and treated appropriately, they will carry on to forthcoming projects, spreading successful practices and improving performance all around the organization. While the fruits are direct results that need to be picked up for immediate and easily measurable outcomes, the seeds can have a more powerful long-term impact on the organizations. They will accumulate over successful projects; hence they should always be harvested and utilized with respect to the next season.

When preparing a program, it is necessary to define how to measure these outcomes, and in the follow-up the measures need to be enacted. For example, a review of a co-creative program aimed at organizational development can be conducted in the form of a simple debrief. The team reviews the project and provides feedback for both the project arrangements (external feedback) and their own performance (internal feedback). This feedback is collected for improving the organizational process for the next round of development.

As we mentioned in Chap. 10, there are many ways that a co-creative journey can come to an end, and unfortunately not all of these are very pleasant for the participants. Contrasting successful projects, there will be those that did not meet their experiential or pragmatic goals. This is a natural course of action, deriving from the fact that all ambitious projects incorporate a risk of failure. The higher the bar is raised, the greater the chance that something will go wrong, and the project will crumble. On the other hand, even in successful journeys there are often elements that did not go very well, and these need to be acknowledged and responded to in order to improve the process in the future. We will address these two types of cases—successfully finished and prematurely terminated ones—as we move through the follow-up steps.

Follow-Up Steps: Overview

If the journey was a success, then there is a chance that at least part of the team will continue working on the project while the rest of the team moves on to new projects. In some cases the entire team continues, but there is still need for an end to the journey. In all cases, the project needs to be closed while there is still a team. Otherwise the ending will not be controlled, and there is a good chance that some of the unresolved issues will come back to haunt later projects.

Follow-up activities usually begin with a quick *debrief* of the team, followed by a *wrap-up* to conclude the journey for the team. The wrap-up offers a channel for constructive feedback, helping them build on the successes of the journey and learn from their mistakes. Paired with this is a *follow-through process* to ensure that the organization learns something from the journey. The objective of a debrief is to share experiences and evaluate journey, forming a comprehensive understanding of what took place, what was good, and what could be improved. After this knowledge has been harvested, there should be a deliberate effort to connect the knowledge and shared experiences to future projects in order to ensure that the good practices have a chance to spread, and the mistakes are not repeated. This follow-through process is aimed at building continuity between projects and at strengthening the culture of innovation within the larger organization.

Evaluation and feedback, which occur throughout the follow-up, take place on three levels: individual, team, and organization. We focus on individuals and team in the debrief and wrap-up, then shift emphasis to the organization in the follow-through.

Personal evaluation and feedback are highly valuable for individual development, if conducted appropriately. As we have done throughout our journey, we recommend a coaching approach that focuses on growth. In such light, assessment can be a good thing.

Teams can also be evaluated in terms of capacity and growth, but evaluation must take into consideration the fact that team composition may change with respect to organizational goals. To clarify, individuals live on even though their position and role might change. Teams might continue their existence, but usually there are at least some changes made to its roster. This raises some interesting considerations for evaluation and feedback. As one example, with new members will it be the same team anymore? And even if the composition stays intact, what does the fact that everyone has grown during the journey do to evaluation standards? In Wizard of Oz,[2] the lion developed courage, the scarecrow grew a brain, and the tin man discovered a heart. They changed as individuals as well as a team. In our case, there is no going back to Kansas after a journey is over. It is wise to situate evaluations in light of potential changes in membership and the collective intelligence that the team has developed (or not).

On the organizational level, feedback and evaluation concern organizational functions such as project preparation, team assembling, decision-making, and internal communications. For this reason, higher authorities need to be involved. If co-creation is new to the organization, it will be particularly good to organize a thorough review of the co-creative process. Because the co-creative process has to adapt to the prevailing organizational culture, co-creation is always bespoke. Its tailored practices deserve a special focus of attention, to ensure that forthcoming projects are better prepared to take advantage of the capacities developed in each iteration. A thorough review is also instrumental in efforts to spread best practices across the organization.

Debrief

Follow-up begins with a debriefing, which is typically a short, intensive session intended for producing a snapshot of what took place and what was experienced during the past journey. A debrief aims to be objective, yet that objectivity is not cold rationality. Rather, it is an authentic reflection on the entire creative journey, including the knowledge, interpersonal, and emotional aspects in addition to the process itself.

If we were to compare the checkout circle at the end of the Rise to the debrief, the former is "hot" while the latter is "cool." They have distinctly different feels, but both can have a huge impact on implementation, peer relationships, and personal growth.

Timing Is Important

As the ACME story at the opening of this chapter indicates, a debrief takes place shortly after the project concludes. There should be enough time for the individuals to establish an emotional distance from the project. They need time to cool off and process the intense checkout that concludes the Rise, enabling a more objective process review in the debrief. The timing requires extra care in cases where the project has been terminated without reaching its goals. Too short a time, and there is not enough separation to establish distance and objectivity. Too long, and events are no longer in fresh memory. In our experience, one to three weeks that includes downtime for people to reflect on their own is usually a good interval. Waiting any longer can be detrimental. Closure is needed to help move on, both as individuals and as a team.

During a debrief, it should become clear which issues need to be further investigated or addressed within the team, which issues might need special attention from leadership or HR, and which issues should be wrapped up and concluded. To tease these issues out, it is good to arrange two separate debriefs. One is held for the whole team and another held for each of the team members separately. These sessions can take place in either order, but there are some rules of thumb to suggest which order would be most suitable for different situations. For example, if the team will be broken apart, then it would make sense to debrief the whole team first and then build a conclusion to their journey by symbolically separating the team for the individual debriefs. This way, the team debrief can double as a wrap-up for the journey and a closure for the team. If the team has performed poorly, and there have been unresolved conflicts within the team, the opposite order could facilitate a road to recovery for the team. In this case, individual debriefs could be used to build a common ground for a therapeutic team debrief, which would be used to release some of the tension within the team before breaking them apart.

Harvesting the Seeds of Success

After a successful journey, it is good to start and end a debrief with a clear and sincere “Great job, everyone! Great job!!!” Even though the focus will be on positive experiences—the good practices that made the success possible—there can also be a place for a more critical reflection on issues that could be further improved. In most cases, the team spirit is still very high at this point, in which case there is no point in bringing this spirit down, even during the critical parts of the review. In the few remaining cases, where the project results have been satisfactory but have come at the expense of good team spirit and atmosphere, you might consider opting for the reverse debriefing order described below (Dealing with the One That Got Away).

In the team debrief, the focus lies in compiling a comprehensive map of the journey, identifying the key incidents and decisions that guided the team through the Climb, Dive, and Rise. Comprehensive in this context means that the map includes the knowledge, interpersonal, and emotional dimensions of the journey in addition to the recorded events of the process. In our experience, it is helpful to draw the Co-Creative Journey illustration on a large whiteboard and then capture specific points where they occurred in the journey. In essence, what we are doing is creating a journey map of our own collective experience—visualizing the process that the team went through.

This process is a narrative device that can help the team to identify touchpoints where the team experienced their most important shifts during the journey. These shifts could have taken place along any of the various dimensions—knowledge, interpersonal, or emotional aspects. In addition to the major shifts, the incidents noted could also include the moments when the team just barely avoided making a wrong turn, but for some reason decided to stay on course. These touchpoints and decisions are worth identifying and documenting, to be used as a positive reference in the future. Part of an action learning strategy, these notes are the building blocks for continuous improvement.

As described in the previous chapters, some of these shifts and key moments derive from disruptions in the atmosphere and team dynamics, while others come from changes in the process. These changes could have originated from either inside or outside of the team. Disruptions in the team atmosphere could result from something as simple as an unresolved interpersonal conflict, or from more deliberate acts such as adjustments to team roles or adding new members. The act itself could have been very small, but if it triggered a chain of constructive (or destructive) events, then it should be pinpointed and picked up for further analysis.

Changes in the process direction could have taken place in the form of expanding, narrowing down, or completely changing the focus of the journey. During a debrief, it is enough to identify the points at which these key turns took place and to make a note about the individuals who were involved in making them happen. Strong teams will stand united at this point, which means that the team members will not stab each other in the back, nor will they be keen to reveal anything that might make any of their teammates look bad. For this reason, it will be very important to pick up even the small cues and signals that could reveal issues that deserve a second, more critical look.

Once the team debrief is concluded, it is time to move on to the more detailed, personal debriefs. These individual debriefs should cover everyone within the team, even those team members who dropped out of the team at some point of the journey for one reason or another. They can bring light to issues that call for special attention or improvement of the co-creative process. A simple way to continue the reflection that began during the team debrief would be to re-introduce some issues that could need special attention. Leading the conversation toward these topics can be done quite delicately, for example, by something like "This morning, Roberta mentioned something that I didn't quite understand. Could you explain what she might have meant by this?" Since this type of question might give an impression of an interrogation rather than a friendly debrief, it is also good to clarify the motives behind them. After all, the goal is not to accuse or judge people, but rather to identify points of further improvement for individuals, the team, and for the larger organization.

Dealing with the One That Got Away

The End of ACAN

The word came out that the boss had decided to pull the plug on the project, just three months before they were supposed to be finished with the first prototype. The last two months had been tough for the team. They had put a tremendous effort into the process, working late nights and making personal sacrifices to get the project back on track, but apparently it was not enough for the company. And to be honest, there was so much tension and so many unresolved conflicts within the team, that it was a small miracle that the team had even made it this far in the process. But now it was time to face the facts and drop the ball.

Ambitious projects come with a high risk of failure. As many coaches have said, if you have never failed, that probably just means that you have not tried hard enough. Successful co-creation projects usually have one common denominator—they put all the pieces together. Their journey began by building a capable team, then developing collective knowledge, and finally applying their superpower (collective intelligence) to co-create something new according to their original mission statement or task. If any of these pieces failed, then the chances are that the project collapsed and failed as well.

In failure cases, it is usually easy to indicate what went wrong or to identify the mistakes that could not be corrected during the process. What is more challenging is to dig a bit deeper behind the superficial symptoms and causes and look for hidden root causes that might be avoidable in the future if acknowledged and identified on time. These root causes might be something as simple as unintended mismatches in personalities or harmfully overlapping role descriptions between strong individuals. Both could slowly grow into bigger conflicts during the critical stages of the journey. In some cases, however, the project has failed for reasons that are not so clear or easy to explain. Sometimes the team has been on the right track, and has been doing a good job in general, but hasn't reached the level of performance that was expected. If a project is terminated due to this type of underperformance, it would be pointless to try to identify a single reason for the failure. It would make more sense to prepare a list of things that will need improvement and see if something could be done about them. In these cases, it might be possible to assign the same team to a new project, for which they would just need to pick up their game.

Occasionally a project may be terminated due to external reasons, in which case the causes for the failure cannot be traced back to the team. There could be many reasons for such decisions. For example, a change in corporate strategy can lead to interrupting certain development projects, or some major changes in the market could result in re-prioritizing of R&D activities, which could bring an abrupt ending to several promising projects at once. For the team, this is obviously dissapointing, but on the other hand it leaves a solid ground for them to continue as a team if a suitable project can be found for them. The preparation for such a project would start in the follow-through, right after the failed project has been wrapped up and concluded.

Breaking the Container

There are many projects that are terminated before their scheduled completion. A lot can be learned from failures. What is more difficult is to get the people back on their feet and motivated for a new project. But the recovery[3] must start somewhere, and a formal, non-judgmental debrief is a good way to get this revival process started.

Whenever possible, it is a good practice to hold on to the positive team spirit during debriefs for successfully concluded projects. Then again, for projects that were prematurely terminated, the container might be contaminated. In such cases, the container needs to be broken to help release the negative emotions associated with the team. By breaking the container, we mean that the people are relieved from their team duties, allowing them to put the team experience behind them and move on as individuals. Only this way is it possible to take an objective look at what happened during the journey and figure out what could be learned from that project. The desire to help individuals move past negative expeirences is why debriefs for failed projects should be done in the opposite order from successful ones. There is a container-breaking event to bring a closure to the failed team, followed by individual and then team debriefs.

Individual debriefs provide a channel for team members to express their innermost feelings about the failed journey, but at the same time these feelings and emotions should not be allowed to take control or dominate the event. The individual debriefs serve two purposes. The primary purpose is to extract information about the events that lead the team to a failure, and the secondary goal is to prepare the individuals for having an efficient team debrief, regardless of how they might feel about their team. Expressing and analyzing emotions might help to achieve both objectives, especially if the root causes for the failure can be traced back to unresolved interpersonal conflicts. At this point, there is no reason for trying to solve these problems anymore. It will be sufficient to verbalize these issues, bring them to the surface, and honor their validity. Acknowledging and deeply listening to people's feelings is instrumental in helping them manage their emotions and grow from their experience.

Team debriefs for failed projects also have two objectives. Primarily they are needed to *validate the conclusions* made, based on observations and the individual debriefs. Secondarily, in contrast to the cool-down function that is needed for successful teams, there is a need for to *reboot* teams involved in failed projects. These are not failed teams, per se. They were part of failed projects. Although these are two very different things, people take failure personally no matter what the cause. The debrief can help teams get back on their feet after their efforts have been condemned unsuccessful.

Depending on the circumstances, these objectives might be difficult or even impossible to reach, but there are ways to facilitate positive progress. One key to rebooting the team lies in the order that the negative and positive issues are discussed within the team. As long as this order is constructive—starting from the negative issues and moving toward the positive ones—it will help the team to leave the session in a more positive mood than when it started. This does not interfere with the validation process, so there is no need for compromises in order to promote the team-reboot objective. If more emphasis needs to be given to rebooting the team, this could be achieved at the cost of reducing the validation requirements. If this is the case, the validation could be focused on the successful incidents identified at the individual debriefings, while the failures could be underrepresented or ignored completely.

Identifying Special Cases

In the previous chapter, we mentioned some special cases where the co-creative team had succeeded in most parts of the process, yet failed to deliver what was expected of them. The first such special case, which can be labeled as *bad team spirit*, is a skilled and diverse team that has produced a significant body of new knowledge but has been incapable of resolving internal conflicts, resulting in unbearable hostility, broken trust, and negative team spirit. The journey in these cases usually ends in a deadlock, where the team is unable to get passed the third stage of the journey because they are incapable of performing together as a team. At this point the project must be terminated, even though the team possesses some highly valuable knowledge.

A debrief in this case would have the ambitious goal of harvesting the knowledge from the team in such a way that it could be later utilized in other projects. This could be achieved through a process of conceptual design or project planning after the debriefing is over. Using conceptual design as a tool for knowledge harvesting means that the team is assigned for a special round of concept generation. Unlike regular concept generation, this time the team is expected to produce a whole line of high-quality concepts that are based on their collective knowledge. Through this effort, they will be able to capture and share at least some of their insights, which can later be assessed and evaluated by their colleagues—possibly even with some of their teammates. As the goal of the assignment is not to develop one but many concepts, there should be sufficient time reserved for finalizing the concept descriptions after an idea generation process has produced enough concept drafts for the team to work with. And even though a concept screening or prioritization is not required, a preliminary analysis of the concepts can aid future use of their insights.

This form of harvesting can be taken one step further by having the team use their collective insight to plan and prepare a follow-up project for their interrupted journey. This planning can be based on a complete or partial conceptual design process like the one described before, followed by a more in-depth analysis of what should be done with the selected concepts. After the harvesting is completed, the team can debrief and then be released through a wrap-up as described below.

To summarize, a proper order for the follow-up activities of this special case would be to begin by breaking the container, after which the team can be reassigned. The knowledge harvesting process would follow, and even though the harvesting might take a while, there would eventually be a wrap-up for the whole team.

The second special case concerns teams that have been doing all the right things and have found their way through all three Acts, but for some reason they just have not reached the level of performance that was expected of them. This special case of *underperforming teams* requires further examination, as the team might still have the potential to reach their target if given another shot at it. A debrief should identify their weaknesses and needs as a team, so that an appropriate boost could be provided to help them finish their mission. A boost could come in the form of giving additional resources to the team, making changes in the team structure or roles, or even something as simple as a moving the team to a new location. The debriefs are best conducted in the same order as they were done for the successful teams, starting with a team debrief and followed by the individual ones. Based on the debrief, the team could be either terminated or sent for a recharge as described below under follow-through.

Wrap-Up

Once the debrief rounds have been completed, it is time to bring a conclusion to the journey. Teams that succeed, fail, or carry on all need a sense of closure. Wrapping-up is largely a symbolic act. Its value lies in the rituals that will help us move on instead of clinging to the past. These are the final times for constructive feedback as members of *this* team in *this* context.

Rather than producing any direct value to the host organization, the wrap-up is first and foremost meant for the team. Its procedures and objectives follow this intention.

Bringing our theatrical metaphor to a close as well, the wrap-up is when the theater troupe sits down for one last dinner after a season of performing. The table is filled with delicious food and beverages, and the ambiance is celebratory. The emotional tone is mixed, reflecting the highs and lows of the journey just completed. Moreover, this may be the last time this team is together, and that tends to bring fresh sentiment to the surface. This night there will be celebrations, lamentation, tears, and laughter. Tomorrow the troupe will pack up their things and go separate ways, and so they appreciate what time they have left together.

The theatrical metaphor presents an ideal wrap-up scenario. It is one in which things went well overall. Celebration is easy in good times. The challenge for less successful cases is facilitating a wrap-up with positive personal and team outcomes. A large part of this art lies in contextualizing and reframing failures as opportunities for growth. Even in failure there are bright moments to celebrate, and these positives are drawn to attention in the wrap-up. Hopefully the team is preconditioned to this mindset. After all, from the very beginning we have emphasized celebrating failure. In the closing moments, we need to maintain this action learning attitude, sharing with each other what was good, what was difficult, and what we might do differently next time.

As with every other stage of the journey, there are a variety of tools that can be used at this point. Dialogue circles, peer feedback, intuition walks, and journaling are all means for reflection and growth. What these techniques share is a combination of looking back on the past and looking forward toward the future. "What has been learned?" and "What will you do?" are powerful questions that recontextualize the experience into growth trajectories. Here we explain one of the techniques we find valuable.

I like, I wish[4]

The procedure was quite simple. After a brief introduction, everyone was handed a bunch of feedback forms, and given about 45 minutes to fill them out. During this time, they wrote down all the things they liked, and the things that they wish to change, about each one of their teammates. They also wrote similar evaluations for the team itself. After the forms were completed, they then shared the content with their teammates.

I like, I wish is a facilitated team feedback method in which team members provide and receive positive and constructive feedback on both individual and team levels. The main purpose is increasing the feeling of togetherness by asking the team to reflect on everyone's role in the project and how they are bonding together as a team. The method consists of three consecutive feedback sessions that offer support for the internal communication of interdisciplinary teams working with challenging and innovative projects. The three parts are (1) writing down feedback individually, (2) sharing the feedback, and (3) reflecting on the feedback. According to the basic principles behind this method, feedback will be only be written and provided to the team members that are present in the session.

I like, I wish uses a facilitator who is not a member of the team. She or he is able to create a neutral setting. The main role of the facilitator is to provide a framework where it is safe and easy for the team to openly give feedback to one another. Especially in failure cases, a safe and trustful atmosphere is critical. The procedure follows a detailed format, where team members will share (and receive) both positive and constructive feedback on individual and team levels. Positive feedback ("I like …") refers to the strengths seen in a team member (or team), whereas constructive feedback ("I wish …") is about the potential seen in a team member (or team) that has not yet been fully utilized during the project. Note that all feedback is expressed in positive tones.

Sharing the feedback starts from individual-level positive feedback, as everyone is encouraged to share their likes with the one person at a time. It is important that the "I like" round is not interrupted at any time. The person receiving the feedback can share his or her feelings and thoughts after the round. After every participant has shared their likes with everyone else, the team moves on to sharing individual-level wishes in a similar manner, followed by a round of team-level wishes, and finally team-level likes. It is important to reserve sufficient time at the end of the session to give participants an opportunity to share their feelings regarding the session as well as to give time to reflect on the feedback shared.[5]

I like, I wish works on two different levels. For individuals, it acknowledges the role they played and the value it brought to the process while also giving them feedback on areas for growth. This small act can reframe their entire perception of the process, shift their emotional state, and empower them for their next role.

On the team level, it increases trust and mends wounds. Even if there are big, unresolved conflicts, this workshop can help in reducing their impact—if the container is still strong enough for authentic and respectful dialogue. Many of the self-doubts team members have about themselves and the assumptions they make about what the others in the team are thinking frequently prove to exist only in the team member's mind. Typically, all that is required to get rid of these disturbing issues is to take the time and speak them out loud in a safe setting. *I like, I wish* is one format for such expression, clearing the air before moving on.

Returning to Earth

What happens after the closing curtain of our performance? Part of the team might continue, with reinforcements, while others are assigned elsewhere. For everyone, this is a new start. There should be sufficient time reserved for recovery, even after successful projects, as the intensity of the co-creative process can result in temporary loss of energy. If a new co-creation project is starting right away, the participating individuals could be allowed and encouraged to start with a reduced tempo. We close the wrap-up by stepping out of the container and enjoying a period of calm in which everyone can renew their energies.

While our reserves are being renewed, through rest or plenty of Starbucks coffee, an equally important process of reintegration is occurring. In and Out of the Box, a creative technique we introduced earlier in the text, describes this phenomenon as "stepping back into the Box." This is an often-overlooked aspect of creativity that we want to draw attention to. Life would be impossible if we were thinking "outside the box" all the time. Our boxes are our models of the world. They give life coherence and meaning, without which we would be in a perpetual existential crisis. We need our boxes, not only for ourselves, but also to communicate with others and get things done. When we get outside our box, we have a chance to see it and change it, but we will always return to a box of our own fashioning. What that box is like is entirely up to each individual, and a lot of creativity and leadership training focuses on becoming the shaper of your own reality. But whatever that reality is, you must live in it most of the time.

The containers we build in co-creation are situated realities, special collective boxes that suspend normal reality for certain times in certain places, but they were never meant to last indefinitely. Just as individuals must return to their (hopefully redesigned) boxes, so too must the team return to their organizational boxes. A key difference is that it is unlikely that the time in the co-creative container has any effect on the organizational boxes you return to, so there will always be a period of adjustment as reality settles back in. How we make adjustments, to ourselves and our organizations, is the subject of follow-through.

Follow-Through

The follow-through of any co-creative process ideally connects its outcomes, tangible and intangible, to the organization and/or future projects. Tangible outcomes, the fruits of labor, manifest first in new products and services or a new organizational initiative. The debrief gives us another set of tangible outcomes, the good practices identified and documented. These raw materials will need to be further developed if the organization wants to learn from the past. This further development starts with an analysis of the documented materials and continues then by applying the results of this analysis to the planning and eventually preparation stages of forthcoming projects.

Intangible outcomes, the implicit insights and capacities developed by the team, are by contrast a form of tacit knowledge. They derive from the collective experience and cannot be easily shared through any form of documentation or explanation. Connecting tacit knowledge to the organization and/or future projects can be established by placing key individuals in suitable roles within new project teams and/or organizational structures. Through this their experience can influence activities from within the team. This in turn strengthens the culture of innovation by seeding it with highly skilled co-creators.

Looking at the effect of these follow-through actions overall, what becomes evident is that co-creation is a circular rather than linear process. We can visualize this iterative cycle as follows (Fig. 11.1, next page):

Our focus in the follow-through lies in the post-journey steps—the analysis, learning, and implementation that proceed a co-creative cycle.

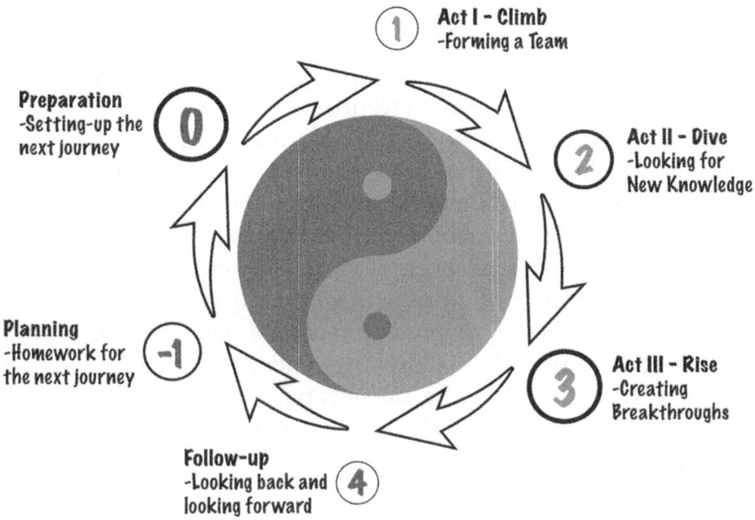

Fig. 11.1 The iterative cycle

Analysis of Debriefs

Analysis includes identifying key individuals and best practices. Key individuals hold skills and knowledge that can play a critical role in the success of any co-creation project. Best practices can include any combination of routines or processes that have enabled the team to reach a high level of knowledge and collective performance. These could be as simple as having an informal team lunch every Friday, dinner with executives once a month, having a designated routine for informing teammates about new insights or discoveries, and so on.

As we have stated throughout this text, while there may be an underlying grammar, or process architecture, for co-creation, the expression of that structure will vary by team and context. For this reason, it is helpful to analyze what worked for the team in the recently completed process, as a well as transferable skills and processes that can be applied in new contexts.

Of equal value is identifying what does not work and what was challenging. The debrief and feedback during the wrap provided opportunities to air out these concerns, and in the analysis it is time to figure out what can and needs to be done about them. In some cases, the analysis will have an immediate impact on implementation, while in other cases it might be archived as learnings to be applied to the next co-creative project.

Feedback forms that are kept as part of an organizational record are helpful in this regard. The written feedback created in *I Like, I Wish* is not appropriate to use for this purpose. Those materials, as well as personal journals, are for individuals and the team only. They are private to their experience, and to archive them for organizational development purposes would render them less valuable. For one, it breaks the bonds of trust by allowing outside eyes to see aspects of the inner team experience. Secondly, taking this feedback out of its context will surely result in misinterpretation. Instead, it is better to present more formal feedback forms that explicitly state their use. This allows team members to frame their replies in the context of the "It" (the organization) rather than the "We" or "Me." You will find that even when asking about personal experience, the answer will vary greatly if a person is writing their answer to the head of HR than if it were a personal journal with the same question.

One form of feedback we value is to ask the team to help us analyze the debrief. By making the analysis a co-creative act, we get a more holistic perspective as well as maintain the trust with the team. We operate as a collective from start to finish. The *Xd* can then work with the appropriate person to compile the diverse perspectives into a final report.

The report can become part of an organizational review. Singled-out issues can be read and handled at the executive level, in addition to a formal review of the completed (or terminated) co-creation process. In such cases the report should include actionable proposals for the organization to consider, to help them improve their processes based on the observations.

Individual, Team, and Organizational Learning

The title of the book refers to co-creation as an art because, like art, it requires practice to become skillful. Successful co-creation requires the cultivation of individual, team, and organizational skills and capacities. A shortfall in any one of these areas leads to marginal success and at times failure. Unfortunately, this is why co-creation is in many cases little more than lip service to an ideal that people struggle to live up to.

How do we get better at it? Well, as the old television show *GI Joe* says, knowing is half the battle (*hence this book*). The other half is practice. Improvement is about continually refining the shared experience and creating continuity so that the collective intelligence produced during the journey is transferable. Ensuring this requires proactive planning and preparation for the next steps.

Fortunately, we have been doing this all along. The learning model we have been advocating is that of action learning, the continuous process of doing and then reflecting on our actions with the intention of learning from the outcomes. Action learning is inherent within a design thinking mindset that always strives for better and better solutions. The trick is applying that same logic to yourself as well as the products or services you might be designing. In the follow-through, we enact this mindset by creating stable structures for continuous learning and growth. By structures, we mean cohesive groups such as transformation teams, peer coaching circles, and communities of practice that meet regularly to support organizational initiatives and each other's growth.

Structure may also include built environments such as the ones we described in Chap. 4: Staging the Environment. Having dedicated spaces that encourage and support creativity goes a long way toward establishing a culture of innovation. This is why organizations seek out design studios or build their own innovation labs. They are conducive to the types of creative processes needed. Designed environments are also conducive to learning and growth. They help people step out of everyday life and into the creative experience they were part of or may be about to join.

There are a lot of learning models to choose from, but among these there are some common denominators that serve as loose guidelines. First is the recognition that nothing ever goes exactly as planned. If it did it was not creative. This rule is just as true for the follow-up as it was for the creative process. Strategies and action plans have intentions and targets, but in the process of implementing these, there will always be some drift from the projected pathway. This is completely natural and should be expected.

Rather than worrying about this drift, an action learning approach accepts it and tries to identify what can be learned from it. Perhaps it needs correction and perhaps not. Or perhaps an error or failed delivery is a blessing in disguise. The post-it notes we all use are one such product, the result of a failed R&D project at 3M. Had the organization thrown out the results as garbage, they would have lost millions. Instead, they kept an open mind and identified an opportunity in failure.

A second guideline is to reframe successes and failures in more constructive terms. I OWN What's Next is a facilitation framework for action learning that posits, and we agree, that labeling unexpected outcomes as failure or luck limits what we can learn from them.[6] Instead, they illustrate outcomes as a range from less than expected to better than expected. These are less emotionally charged words, allowing us to look at results as part of an ongoing process rather than final outcomes.

I OWN What's Next facilitates new awareness and growth. First, it looks at our intentions and explores how we frame failures and successes. The primary objective of this inquiry is to clarify the positive intention and determine how success was measured. Revisiting goals and expectations sets the stage to draw out contrasts between expected and actual outcomes, which are then recast in new terms.

Although not part of the method, using a focused conversation here could collectively tease out distinctions between observable facts of a situation and the feelings surrounding it. The exercise can reveal just how much our worldview and corresponding emotional reactions shade our interpretations. Raising awareness in turn fosters personal growth, cultivating emotional intelligence and analytical skill.

The last step of I OWN What's Next focuses on taking ownership of the actions and attitudes that inhibit or support the intended results. Honestly identifying both is the foundation for growth. Recalling the discussion on authenticity in the Chap. 3 Creative Leadership section, authentic leadership is more than just being honest. You can be honest and still be a terrible leader. Authentic leadership, the capacity we encourage here, is being honest with oneself and then making the leadership decision that best serves the whole. If that means taking yourself out of a process, then take responsibility and do so.

Removal from the process is an extreme example, but for all of us there are areas of improvement. Action learning techniques help us identify what those areas are so that we can plan what to do and take the first steps. We can close the learning loop with a few guiding questions that help us in this regard. I OWN What's Next uses the following:

- What is our new intended result?
- How can we leverage what is working?
- How can we change what is not working?
- What new actions, attitudes, or behaviors can we try to improve our ability to get our intended results?

These are good team questions. A coaching angle might also add in some personal questions, such as[7]:

- What is my purpose?
- Are my heart, head, and hand (feelings, thoughts, and actions) aligned to my purpose?
- Do my external actions reflect my inner alignment?
- What has been the seed of the future that this experience has created for me?
- What are my next steps?
- How am I helping others realize their full potential?
- How do my needs integrate with the larger whole (team, organization)?
- How am I supporting its (the whole) needs and process?

These questions can be asked of the organization as well as individuals within it by substituting "we" or "our" in place of "my" and "I." In an action learning cycle, individuals, teams, and the organization then enact whatever actions they identify from the learning process, evaluate the change(s) they make, and begin the cycle again. Learning, like co-creation, is iterative. If people strive to continuously improve, their capacity for and skill at co-creation will grow. Perhaps more importantly, these changes are transferable, positively impacting every aspect of life.

Special Cases

The two special cases merit a bit more work in the learning cycle. Teams with bad team spirit need to be dispersed, but they can learn from their experience, perhaps more than the successful teams. For the organization, this is a time to reflect on how it supported or inhibited the team's success or failure. There will be times when the causes lie solely within the team, but at other times the negative spirit is due to external causes. Perhaps the team simply wasn't given the time resources needed. Being underfunded is a sure way to drop morale. And if each person has to spend 80% their energy on daily job tasks, how much can they be expected to give to the creative team? Or perhaps the compelling needs story wasn't all that compelling. Lack of engagement, or worse, boredom, is not a critical problem with a team. They are problems with the creative brief. In cases where some external factor affects the team spirit, care must be taken not to blame the team itself. Take the time to find out what happened, and openly address that with the team. This will help them move on and regain a measure of their confidence.

Depending on whether team members are expected to work together again, and the tensions that led to the bad team spirit, there may be a need for rehabilitation. Executives may, for example, be assigned to a transformation team that ultimately fails in their initiative. As executives, they still must work with one another. In the School of Design, we frequently managed team conflicts that reflect all too common issues in the larger field. Teams might form initially around a common interest or an engaging pitch, only to find out that they can't work well together. They may end up finishing the design project thinking that they won't have to see the others again, only to find themselves assigned to a team with the same tensions in the future. What can we do?

In best-case scenarios, people do take personal responsibility and steps to correct destructive attitudes and behaviors. If all parties attempt this, there is a good chance they will get past the initial tensions. Peer councils may assist this, in which the parties sit down and openly discuss what they are working on and how they feel … without critiquing others. Coaching and mentoring may also be called for. If none of these methods work, then the organization needs to operate with a level of awareness around whom they assign to teams and projects. That is why it is beneficial to engage senior leadership with the learning and feedback for special cases. At the very least they need to be aware of any lingering issues that could haunt future teams.

Underperforming teams need a different treatment. Teams that have had a good team spirit, but have not been able to get results, might need a proper pep-talk session and some tough love. In these cases, the team is unlikely to need peer counseling or mentoring. They work well together, but they lack motivation. What they need is someone or something to lift their spirits and re-engage their interest. Or, if they are just being lazy, they might need a swift, firm boot.

Regardless of the approach used to get the team going again, it is critical to identify what other factors (aside from motivation) have impacted performance. Just as we ask our team members to be authentic in their feedback and learning, so too must the *Xd* and the sponsoring stakeholders. If we can identify the underlying causes and remedy them, then an underperforming team can be put back on task better prepared to succeed.

Implementation

Analysis and learning are useful only if their results are spread and applied. These are best planned and initiated while the results are fresh. They are part of the larger implementation process, which is beyond the scope of this text. Implementation will vary greatly depending on the type of organization or project, leadership styles, sociopolitical and historical context, and other factors that we simply cannot anticipate here. What we can do is offer a few final guidelines that we have found make a difference between better and worse than expected implementations.

Keep Leadership Involved

Efficient application is based on acknowledgment by the directors who plan and prepare new projects and recruitments. Hence implementation should be a joint operation that is preferably initiated and executed by the executives. When further direct engagement from executives is not possible, there need to be clear channels of communication between the implementation team and leadership.

We have already discussed the value of leadership engagement in the co-creative process, and those same reasons hold true for implementation. This is especially true for change initiatives, which suffer without engagement from senior leadership.

> Our most common difficulty in launching a change process is that the organization is determined to keep the initiative in the human resources sphere. As long as the change process is in human resources it is like service in companies with a service department. Public story is that the change is everyone's business but who gets measured for it? Who gets rewarded for it? Human resources gets measured by program hours not change impact. It is the CEO who gets measured by the effectiveness of change and therefore they must be the ones behind the change process. It is a paradox of participatory change that to really sustain it requires leadership willing to lead it and willing to let it go.[8]

Leaders "in the dirt" with their teams have an opportunity to be much more responsive and leverage their skills to the benefit of the local (the project) and the whole (organization). They also tend to get more respect from the team and other employees who witness their willingness to lead from within rather than more top-down approaches. There are of course times when this is impractical, but even brief or symbolic presence can be instrumental.

Another benefit of engaged leadership is that they have full access to the collective knowledge and can become part of the collective intelligence. The wisdom of the co-creative process can then transfer to leadership, enabling wider organizational changes. We find this essential in scaling a culture of innovation from isolated projects, which may be anomalies at first, to more enduring qualities of the organizational culture.

Track and Lead

The ICA participatory action planning manual has very good guidelines on tracking implementation and leading change. These guidelines are appropriate in design and many other contexts[9]:

Build and Sustain Momentum

- Establish a rhythm of planning, accomplishments, and celebration.
- Plan an early success.
- Keep the purpose before the team.

Keep Everyone Informed

- Report regularly on progress.
- Keep calendar visible and updated.
- Keep all informed of meetings and events.

Meet Regularly to Update the Plan

- Which actions were initiated since we last met?
- What were the accomplishments?
- What have you learned?
- Were there any breakthroughs? If so what?
- Where are you blocked or challenged?
- Where do we need to focus now?

Motivate the Team

- Acknowledge all the little accomplishments and effort.

- See that everyone has an assignment or task.
- Use failures as learning opportunities.

Complementing these are tips that the nowhere group offers to help "implement with elegance." They describe enablers and disablers that affect change implementation.[10]

Enablers

- Deciding to act
- Cutting through inertia
- Aligning hearts, minds, and hands
- Maintaining flow and momentum
- Celebrating success

Disablers

- Analysis paralysis
- Working too hard and expecting everyone else to do the same
- Focusing on the task without resourcing people to do the new changes
- Moving too quickly to implementation (bypassing learning)

Together we find these lists fairly comprehensive and recommend them as useful team and organizational checks. Some of them, like using failure as learning opportunities, reiterate points of the debrief and wrap-up. Redundancy is precisely the point. Action learning requires continuously looping back and reevaluating where you have been, where you are, and where things are headed. Like the captain of a ship, the task is to take in all the information and make course adjustments as necessary. Leadership does not end with the closure of one creative cycle. It transforms into implementation actions that bring new value to project sponsors and other stakeholders.

Have a Framework

Lastly, implementation needs a framework. Depending on what you are trying to do, there are choices. The ACME team, for example, used a design process not unlike the PDP roadmap we offered in Chap. 7.[11]

ACME Epilogue

The co-creative journey was over and things were wrapped up for the team. For the next seven months, the entire team continued preparing the B-Beam platform for production, but DD and EE worked only part time. They had been assigned to planning the next product development projects, per the B-Beam road map. Two additional experts joined the team for this period.

B-Beam Beta prototype was finished in November, and it was immediately taken over by the market testing team, who were tasked with ensuring market fit and safety for the product. With the help of DD and EE, the next Alpha prototypes for the B-Beam Lite and B-Beam Display were finished in January and February, followed by a small-scale introduction day in end of February at ACME.

Production for B-Beam Standard started in February, after the Beta's had passed all safety tests. Marketing efforts lead into a big product launch event on March 2nd. At this point, the corporate executives had already taken over the show, and were enjoying their time in the spotlights. But for Dorothy and her team, this was just another day at the office, as they had already moved on to new challenges.

ACME's design process was nonlinear, reciprocal with extensive discourse; and used continuous experimentation and analysis before design decisions were reached. Production ensued and the original team moved on to the next design challenge.

Organizational change initiatives need a different framework. The consultancies we have referred to throughout this text each have their own, usually trademarked, models for change. For the ICA it is its LENS, a "double loop learning process."[12] In the ICA's Technology of Participation facilitation training, they recommend Kotter's Eight Stages of Change as a contextual piece to show people how change occurs.[13] The eight steps, combined with a set of tools and accelerators for each, give people a coherent step-by-step roadmap to follow. Given the enormity of most change initiatives, maps are welcome tools. These are often used in leadership coaching alongside capacity development. For us, that would be the creative leadership training that can occur as part of or complementary to a co-creative process.

An organization that strives for a culture of innovation needs an additional framework if it is to be sustainable. By sustainable we mean the ability to continuously innovate, not just a one-off project. The ICA and Kotter's models may be sufficient for implementation, but sustainability is another matter altogether. The nowhere group uses the "Innovation Spiral—a map and a guide for innovation."[14]

> It weaves together both the rational and intuitive to break through into higher orders of thinking, learning, and creating. The Spiral describes nine stages for creating a framework for deep and sustainable innovation... It can be used to fast-track key strategic projects, or to establish game-changing infrastructure for turning ideas into breakthrough solution.

This sounds amazing! "What does it look like?" you might wonder. We are not going to give away all of the nowhere group's secrets, but we can tell you that what they refer to is co-creation. The co-creative process architecture and techniques described in this book *are* the secret for sustainable innovation.

Breakthroughs are the highest expression of a culture of innovation. At times, they are accidental, but we strive to build the capacity for them into organizational culture. It requires a near-perfect performance ability that we call resonance. This resonant co-creation, the subject of our final chapter, is the Holy Grail for co-creative teams. As we will argue, resonance takes things to a completely different level, transforming the people and organizations involved.

Notes

1. By "implicit" we mean capable of being understood from something else though unexpressed.
2. Baum, Lyman Frank (1900). *The Wonderful Wizard of Oz.* George M. Hill Company.
3. Relevance of the recovery process is explained in Chap. 7—Supercompensation in physical training and in co-creation.
4. Rekonen, "Unlocking the potential of interdisciplinary teams," 91–102.
5. Details of the method procedure can be found at https://ilikeiwish.org/.
6. Source unknown. This method was given to us as a gift from a colleague in the Brains on the Beach network in Hong Kong.
7. For more possibilities, see co-active coaching at the Coaches Training Institute. http://www.coactive.com.
8. DEALING WITH THE WAY IT IS, from ICA experience. http://www.ica-usa.org.
9. Action Planning Manual. ICA Taiwan.
10. Leading Systemic Change Wheel, nowhere academy 2011.

11. See also Aspelund, *The Design Process*.
12. See http://www.ica-international.org/.
13. Based on Kotter, *Leading Change*.
14. See the nowhere group ltd. www.now-here.com.

References

Aspelund, Karl. *The Design Process*. Fairchild, 2010.

Kotter, John P. *Leading Change*. Boston: Harvard Business School Press, 1996.

Rekonen, Satu. "Unlocking the Potential of Interdisciplinary Teams." In *Passion-Based Co-Creation*, edited by T.A. Björklund, Laakso M., Kirjavainen S. and K. Ekman, 91–102. Helsinki: Aalto University, 2017.

PART III

The Perfect Play

Margaret Mead's famous quote, "Never doubt that a small group of thoughtful, committed people can change the world; indeed, it's the only thing that ever has" suggests the potential of collective intelligence, but what is it about the way these groups work that enables such powerful change?

In Part III we examine what qualities make for a great co-creative program. Here we introduce resonance, a perfect harmony among parts that lies behind the most memorable creative performances. These are what we all strive for, the unforgettable creative breakthroughs that inspire us and keep us up late at night pondering "How did that happen?" Resonance is our secret, and in Chap. 12, we discuss its origins and transformative power.

Rather than making closing statements, our Epilogue raises questions and possibilities for the future. We seek to end the book by opening new spaces for dialogue and creative exploration, to be enacted through educational programs and our continued online presence as the Co-Creation Initiative.

CHAPTER 12

Striving for Resonance

When an actor gets ready for the stage, they shed their everyday personhood and enter into a new role. They become, for a time, part of a story that is meant to provoke and entertain an audience. They step forth into the light in an effort to create an experience for others, and in their performance they must exhibit mastery of not only the script but also the moment. At the same time the director is behind the scenes holding it all together. They must orchestrate the multiple moving pieces into a seamless flow of events. If the story is well written and director and actors are successful, their work might make it to Broadway where its impact can reach the world. At the very least it will impact everyone involved in the experience co-created between the theater troupe, the space, and the audience. This is what most people call a memorable event.

As far-fetched as it might sound at first, design teams and business meetings can have the same impact. They can be transformative, both for the people involved and in the ideas that come forth. On the far end of what is possible, co-creation can generate breakthroughs. On the closer end, the more pragmatic "let's just get things done as a team," the desired outcome can be anything from incremental innovation to changes in organizational culture. Indeed, more often than not organizations seek out co-creation as a new way to address their everyday challenges than to discover the future. Yet in the same efforts there is space for emergence of something entirely new, and it is these moments of "ah ha" and "wow" that are most rewarding.

B. R. Rill, M. M. Hämäläinen, *The Art of Co-Creation*,
https://doi.org/10.1007/978-981-10-8500-0_12

These moments that we strive for are the outcome of resonant co-creation, when synchronicity and flow are perceptible to the team and insights seem to emerge from thin air. What is occurring are moments of creativity that spontaneously emerge when a group is resonant (frequencies in harmony) with itself. In other terms, resonance is an amplification of creative output resulting from a harmony among elements (Fig. 12.1).

Resonance is a product of harmony between an experience design, its facilitation, and talent development of the "actors." When combined just right (metaphorically creating a harmony), these three elements can transform worldview—the combination of beliefs, attitudes, and values that structure experience—to generate new conceptual and interrelational space among participants conducive to strategic innovation (i.e. breakthroughs).

When and if co-creative resonance occurs, creative ideas spontaneously emerge from the space between, the interintentional "field" in which all interactions occur. Given the different engagement, it follows that ideas that emerge from the collective will be different from the typical creative session where one or two people tend to dominate and others compromise. As Ruth Benedict once said about patterns of culture, "The whole is greater than the sum of its parts." In resonant co-creation, innovation is an emergent property, which in turn relies upon carefully constructed environments and practices that facilitate and hold the space between.

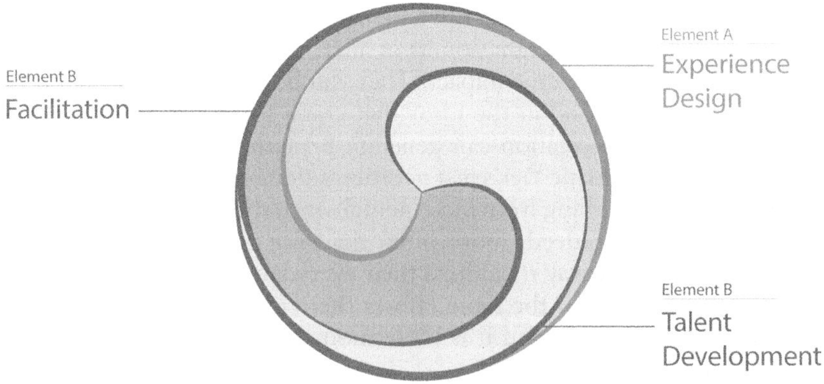

Fig. 12.1 Resonant co-creation

This chapter is an overview of the cultural and theoretical foundations to this approach, followed by a consideration of how to practice the art. The writing tone is more academic than previous chapters, in part because the authors are scholars who enjoy such musings. What we offer here is a result of many years of deeply thinking about the human nature, creativity, and the forces that help us seek out and reach our highest potential. Our writing voice reflects that philosophical journey.

Background

We developed the concept of resonant co-creation to meet a specific need, that being the transformation of interactional space and worldview required to maximize the potential of co-creation. According to Gouillart, who coined the term co-creation with Ramaswamy, "The idea of co-creation is to unleash the creative energy of many people, such that it transforms both their individual experience and the economics of the organization that enabled it."[1] Ramaswamy and Gouillart identify a wide range of organizational conditions to foster co-creation, and at the heart lies a "capacity to learn, nurture, share, and deploy knowledge across traditional boundaries" (both personal and institutional).[2] It is up to leaders to identify opportunities for new modes of engagement and then cultivate an ecosystem where co-creation can develop from initial seeds.

In their book *The Co-Creative Meeting*, Mandl and Mandl offer ideas on what co-creation looks like within organizational workspaces. They identify several core characteristics of a co-creative meeting:

> Participants are expressing their opinions openly; they are sharing their thinking to interpret information; they are acknowledging the wealth of divergent perceptions in the group; they are working through disagreements; they are challenging assumptions; and there is a deepening sense of connection, commitment, and participation within the team.[3]

As these authors indicate, co-creation incorporates several widely known aspects of collective ideation such as group sharing, empathy, working through disagreements, and building trust. This model of co-creation is widely sought and can bring instrumental change and innovation. The reality, however, is that co-creative meetings often do not go as imagined. Many attempts at co-creation bring suboptimal results because the people or organizations utilizing them do not understand what is required for it to work, or they fail to create the necessary ethos. As a result co-creation is at times no more than lip service to a nice idea with brand appeal, while in operational terms it is business as usual.

Although it is possible for anyone to implement co-creation as a set of practices to facilitate collective ideation, what is left unsaid in the co-creation branding trend are the necessary conditions for truly fruitful interactions to occur. How people *engage* co-creation has significant impact on the outcomes. Throughout this text we have argued that co-creative engagement is framed by how the *Xd* creates and holds the social space, the psychological states and capacities of the participants, and the dynamics of interactions between them that create (or dispel) creative energy. Within this argument lies a key difference between the received notion of co-creation and a more nuanced version that integrates world-view transformation. The latter is resonant co-creation, not only focusing upon the tapping into collective intelligence but also attending to developing the personal qualities necessary to co-create. In other terms, resonant co-creation focuses on transforming the space *within* people to tap into greater collective potential.

Resonant Co-creation

You can't solve a problem on the same level that it was created. You have to rise above it to the next level.—Einstein

Einstein's quote reminds us that breakthroughs require a shift in world-view. Resonant co-creation is a process that accomplishes this by shifting the level of consciousness of individuals and in interactions.

Seekers of resonant co-creation are often the key stakeholders in an organization and/or service chain, and the outcomes sought are aligned with the needs of these same stakeholders. Examples of organizational changes include restructuring vision and culture, adapting to disruptive market changes, developing or improving on communication channels, and leadership training. In design, the focus lies in coming up with breakthrough innovations that create new markets or revolutionize existing ones. Innovations of this scale are strategic in that they require fundamental shifts in thinking and often result in radical restructuring or novel approaches.

The roots of resonant co-creation lie in the push by several scholars and change catalysts to transform leadership and innovation capacities.[4] Recent texts such as *Leading with Spirit, Presence, and Authenticity* suggest that cultivating spirit, presence, and authenticity are essential to address global systems challenges.[5] Change begins with leaders, who "must learn to cultivate and transform themselves. This self-development results in enhanced internal capacities such as deeper intellectual understanding, perceptual capacity as well as a greater ability to innovate, self-manage, and self-direct."[6]

There is a body of evidence supporting the idea that developing these key skills does lead to greater insight and innovation.[7] In one of these studies, Brown interviewed several leaders and concluded that tremendous potential for strategic innovation lies in a worldview that he calls a "post-constructivist action logic." This type of action logic (i.e. worldview) is characterized by willingness to let go of old paradigms, intuitive insight, and adaptive design management. While Brown uses different terms, his argument echoes that of Peter Senge, Otto Scharmer, Laloux, Turner, and Udall,[8] scholars and organizational consultants who situate themselves as the forefront of what they see as a large-scale transformation of consciousness in management and leadership. Senge and others argue that profound worldview transformation cultivates the prosocial beliefs and behaviors that underlie creativity and innovation. Presence, authenticity, and empathy lie at the center of this transformation.

The choice of the term "resonant" stems from Marilyn Schlitz's model of the five developmental levels of social consciousness. Resonant consciousness is an expanded awareness that leads to prosocial experiences and behaviors, "in which people report a sense of essential interrelatedness with others—a field of shared experience and emergence that is felt and expressed in social groups."[9] Resonant consciousness requires shared attention, good feelings (such as trust and empathy), and synchrony, all of which are essential skills in co-creation.[10]

Resonant co-creation rests on a particular perspective on human consciousness. It accepts first that human consciousness is not an accurate perception of reality, but rather is a filter conditioned by biology and human experience. "Most of us think that what we perceive is the whole story, 'reality' unmitigated. It (our mind) screens, deciding which perceptions are significant and which are useful to the task at hand. It's only when we realize this and intentionally open ourselves to the wider picture that we begin to actively focus our attention."[11] That wider picture is an intersubjective, *interintentional* space. David Bohm, from whom many schools of dialogue derive, said[12]:

> Genuine judgments should come out of an act of perception rather than out of a reflex. But this will not be possible unless the reflexes of thought and feeling are suspended. Because the reflexes are so habitual, however, it is very hard to be aware that they are acting. Such awareness requires serious attention.

Bohm summarizes a core principle of resonant co-creation—the suspension of reflexive, conditioned thought and being present, or mindful, to the dynamics of the entire space. This requires setting aside the personal ego and its motivations temporarily and developing an awareness that can be described as an expansion of consciousness. Thus, although it builds upon the received notion of co-creation, and in fact it can occur in the very same activities, resonant co-creation requires the people involved have keen observation skills, empathy, and mindfulness. The Presencing Institute captures this sentiment well, stating, "The quality of results produced by any system depends on the quality of awareness from which people in the system operate. The formula for a successful change process is not "form follows function," but "form follows consciousness."[13]

Technique Foundations

> *Every profound innovation is based on an inward-bound journey, on going to a deeper place where knowing comes to the surface.—Brian Arthur, Santa Fe Institute*

The techniques to facilitate resonant co-creation derive from millennia-old cultural traditions ranging from Native American mythos to the Vedas of India. Experience designers often have decades of training in different wisdom traditions. There are several existing organizations and programs that draw explicit links between training in wisdom traditions and their development programs.

Among these are Naropa University's Authentic Leadership Center, the Co-active Leader Program offered by the Coaches Training Institute, the Theory U model for social change developed by MIT and the Presenting Institute, the nowhere group's Riding the Creative Rollercoaster leadership program, the Maharishi University of Management, and human potential programs offered by Insight Quests and the Social Artistry Foundation. These are but a few examples indicative of the growing "conscious business" and "conscious living" trends. It is hard to say what the outcome of these efforts will be in 20 years, but one thing we know for sure is that techniques to cultivate certain states and qualities of consciousness are becoming integral to leadership and creativity.

There are two qualities of awareness essential to resonant co-creation. The first—suspension—underpins Bohm's approach to dialogue. "Suspension of thoughts, impulses, judgments, etc., lies at the very heart of Dialogue. Suspension involves attention, listening and looking and is essential to exploration."[14] Suspension can be interpreted as a slight pause between thoughts. In that space between thoughts lies a vast emptiness, one without judgment or language. With practice, we can learn to extend that pause and apply the inherent equanimity that comes with it to observing what is happening within and around us. Some traditions call this cultivating the "witness," a neutral observer that sits in the eye of the hurricane of feelings and ideas rushing around.

As explained in Chap. 9, Bohm defined an approach to dialogue wherein open group reflection upon the aspects of human perception and ego is brought to the fore, rendering it possible for people to see and understand their internal biases and filters.[15]

Classic Bohmian dialogue circles consisted of a small group of people who met monthly to continually explore the inner and interpersonal filters that affected their speech and behavior. Everyone in the group acted as a mirror for the others, helping to draw out, identify, and address each other's reactions and the sources of them. Over time members of a dialogue circle would come to a deep understanding of the normally hidden operations of the mind that create reality.

In more recent organizational change literature, Bohm's approach is called "reflective dialogue." Jacobs and Heracleous argue for reflective dialogue as an instrumental means to achieve strategic innovation.[16]

Even when faced with entrenched positions, dialogue brings internal mental models to light in conversation and makes it possible to create new mental models. The result is worldview transformation.[17]

Throughout this text we have argued that, when used as part of a co-creative approach, dialogue is an integral tool for collective ideation. The intersubjective inquiry will "gradually build enough common understanding to allow the collective thought process to surmount the individual thought process."[18] This makes possible the type of creativity where new ideas emerge from the space between rather than individuals. In that dialogue encourages authenticity and shared vulnerability, it also tends to foster more positive interpersonal relationships.

The second essential quality of awareness is presencing, described first in the Creative Leadership section of Chap. 3. In presencing, action arises from a place of internal quietude wherein the stream of consciousness is silent and awareness connects with intuition. In this model of intuition, creativity emerges from deeply connecting with broader wholes. According to Senge et al., it is seeing past our mental models to a future whole that can emerge through us.[19] The Presencing Institute's Theory U of leadership "suggests a different stance of 'cocreation' between the individual or collective and the larger world. The self doesn't react to a reality outside, nor does it create something new in isolation—rather, like the seed of a tree, it becomes the gateway for the coming into being of a new world."[20]

Senge's perspective on the source of intuition has deep roots. Tracing these ideas to their origins requires looking far back into history. The *Tao Te Ching*, a sacred text in Chinese Taoism dated to some 2500 years ago, is arguably the first book to eloquently state the relationship between still awareness and creativity. According to Taoism, we all are creative. "The task is to tap into that creative ground of Originality at the root of our Being."[21] The text *Creativity and Taoism* argues that being creative is a process of connecting with, understanding, and emulating the Tao—the metaphysical origin of the universe.[22] We might understand this as manifesting the creative principle, or potentiality inherent within the universe, through our actions.

Cognitive psychologist Eleanor Rosch has attempted to translate the Taoist perspective into the language of contemporary science. The predominant problem solving model of creativity rests upon what she calls "analytic knowing."

> In the world consists of separate objects and states of affairs, the human mind is a determinate machine which, in order to know, isolates and identifies those objects and events, finds the simplest possible predictive contingencies between them, stores the results through time in memory.[23]

Contrasting this is primary knowing, which arises by means of "interconnected wholes, rather than isolated contingent parts and by means of timeless, direct, presentation" rather than through stored "re-presentation."[24] Primary knowing is possible because mind and world are aspects of an underlying unified field. This field, which Bohm described as the Implicate Order, is the Tao.

While they use different scientific and philosophical frames to understand this field of potentiality, the means of accessing it remains largely the same between the works of Senge, Scharmer, Rosch, and Lao Tzu 2500 year ago. How one does that is by cultivating *wu wei*, or non-action.

> …in this non action nothing is left undone. We are encouraged to create an attitude of responsiveness in lieu of over-assertiveness, which leads to effortless action. *Wu wei* requires a posture of non-contention and behavior that minimizes conflict by reducing the friction that accompanies an aggressive approach to a single preferred outcome. These conditions require a psychological state of creative quietude.[25]

Wu wei implies that a person's mind is so quiet and silent that it will not be disturbed by outside world. In everyday life people are influenced by many elements, including social pressures, attractions, and the ever-busy work schedule. A Japanese friend, CEO of an import-export company and lay monk, called this "noise." *Wu wei* is the stillness away from that noise. The emptiness of mind enables recognition that is rational and without bias. That is the mind Bohm found so essential to good dialogue. It is also the place of stillness that presencing takes one to and from which creativity and vision emerge. Senge and Scharmer call this emergence "letting come."[26]

Wu wei should not be mistaken for placitude or neutral observation. Huston Smith explains that *wu wei* is the "pure effectiveness that comes by combining within seemingly incompatible conditions: *supreme activity* and *supreme relaxation*."[27] The activity is the readiness and ability to act as needed. The relaxation is the mind empty of noise and capable of seeing things clearly as they are. *Wu wei* is thus the perfect concept to capture a state of being that facilitates resonance.

The challenge faced lies in the difficulty of cultivating qualities such as presence and *wu wei*. Studies demonstrate the resilience of normative patterns of thinking.[28] Human beings assimilate new experiences into preexisting models. Too much change upon the system meets with resistance. Given this, transformation of worldview requires techniques that focus on transcending—literally "crossing over"—our culturally and biologically conditioned worldviews.[29]

The task for experience designers is to first create the right context and facilitate the emergence of creative ideas from a deep inner source. "Only when people begin to see from within the forces that shape their reality and to see their part in how those forces might evolve does vision becomes powerful. Everything else is just a vague hope."[30] This is not just any container, but rather one designed to be strong enough to handle a deep and long dive in the Unknown.

Give a strong container, the *Xd* must use techniques to challenge and catalyze shifts in worldviews that underlie the ideas in the space between. By shifting the ground upon which ideas rest, the ideas themselves will be transformed. Common to most approaches are contemplative practices from traditions such as Transcendental Meditation, Zen, and Vipassana. These practices, focused on training awareness, are often combined with organizational leadership and change management practices that stem from the humanistic tradition, positive psychology, emotional intelligence, and integral theory.[31] Thus in some change approaches you might find presence training to be the principle methodology.[32] Another approach might use a redesign of the Native American medicine wheel to help people chart out their creative capacities and limitations.[33] Others might help people "tune" their consciousness to different fields of information, such as the somatic (physical sensory), psychological, mythic, and systemic "realms."[34]

Coaching and reflective dialogues complement practices derived from wisdom traditions. Coaching helps people turn the lens of perception inward to reflect upon and reframe one's worldview. In group contexts, reflective dialogue serves this same end. In reflective dialogues, the team examines closely what *within* them creates their perspective. Such dialogues are not only examining ideas, but the sources of them. Once we penetrate deeply into the cognitive models that structure our knowledge, we are more able to break free of them and explore.

Common to these approaches is a philosophical foundation that posits transformations in worldview foster an expansion of social consciousness—the awareness and sensitivity to the interconnectedness of people and their environments. This in turn leads to more effective leadership, creativity, and ultimately innovation.[35]

The challenge does not end with breaking down worldviews and reframing knowledge. Beyond reflective and explorative processes, the *Xd* must also help teams align, or tune, their intuition to the broader whole. The Presencing Institute refers to this as crystallizing intent.

> Crystallizing intent requires being open to the larger intention and imaginatively translating the intuitions that arise into concrete images and visions that guide action. … that's what entrepreneurship is all about—creating that compelling vision and force.[36]

The resulting shift of worldview to a resonant social consciousness opens up a new space for innovation to occur. The space between is no longer an exchange of ideas solely between participants. It becomes much larger field where ideas are exchanged between the particular (individuals and the team) and the whole (the organization, society, cosmos, etc.). When the needs of the whole (the larger intention) are present in the field, it aligns and focuses the creative process. The resulting innovations are far more likely to be strategic than those of a team without resonance.

Given that strategic innovation requires a break from the Known, it is only from the Unknown that new potentials can manifest. Highly engaged, present participants are more able to leave behind existing models and sit in the space of the Unknown, a space that many find uncomfortable because they are outside the expertise of their established worldviews. For this reason, resonant co-creation is more than a workshop. It is an art, requiring both practice and performance.

Practicing the Art

You don't have to be a monk to create resonance. It is true that many of the people we refer to in this book, from nowhere to the Presencing Institute, do in fact have long histories with one or more wisdom traditions. According to the *Harvard Business Review*, many successful business leaders engage in regular contemplative practices and credit these as part of their success.[37] There is clear correlation between cultivating oneself and effective leadership. And yet resonance does not require such practices. Anyone who is a keen observer of people and process can master the art.

Years ago, we were introduced to the In and Out of the Box facilitation framework developed by our colleague Jimbo Clark.[38] One day Jimbo asked if we would evaluate the framework and share our thoughts with him so that he could further improve it. We ran a short program with our design students that turned out to be transformational for many of them.

As an observer of the process, I was absolutely amazed at how fun and effective In and Out of the Box was in helping participants understand and identify the filters and biases that affect their ability to work in creative teams. Jimbo had, without ever reading Bohm or most of the other scholars we reference, developed a framework that accomplished the goals of Bohmian dialogue far more efficiently than any form of reflective dialogue we had seen. In and Out of the Box literally uses a box with preprinted illustrations that participants draw on and then wear on their heads while doing things with other team members. By externalizing the factors that influence human behavior, it completely changed the way everyone interacted. That, in itself, was an epiphany for many. By the end of a four-hour workshop, many of the design students were asking how they could become more aware of their internal filters and how they could practice empathy more effectively. If Jimbo were working with a client, he might offer coaching or other programs that met these needs. In and Out of the Box was the perfect entry point, opening people's eyes to what is often invisible to us as we interact with others.

Jimbo also taught us all that the Box—our filters, tensions, and other forces that affect how we experience and engage the world around us—is not a bad thing. The Box makes sense of the world, protects us, and helps us be successful. While it is good to think outside the Box, equally important is how we repack and use our Box in everyday life. We cannot, after all, be outside of our Box on a continuous basis. So key questions arise, such as "What kind of box do I have and what do I want to create?" or "How do I develop the capacity to see and step outside my Box as needed?"

There is a tremendous wisdom to In and Out of the Box, and it didn't come from years of arduous practice under the tutelage of a wisdom tradition master. It came from Jimbo's observations of life, which is the real teacher. Wisdom traditions simply capture what life has to offer in a set of teachings to be passed on. They are valuable in that they make wisdom accessible, but the lessons contained within them are freely available to anyone who pays attention. Likewise, resonant co-creation requires careful attention but not superpowers.

Creating Resonance

There is a place for linear thinking in business, but it is not for new creative breakthroughs and insights. This is the realm of delving into the chaotic unknown and allowing new things and ideas to emerge.—Benjamin Butler

In the introduction to this chapter, we stated that resonance is the product of harmony between an experience design, its facilitation, and talent development. Resonance then generates new conceptual and interrelational space among participants conducive to breakthroughs. Parts I and II of this text are dedicated to explaining each of these three elements that, together, can create resonance. The art lies in the weave.

The weave begins with having all the right components in place. If an *Xd* has taken all the guidelines offered herein into consideration, then they will have a process design that began by setting a core question and/or challenge to frame the coming activities in dialogue with key stakeholders. This framing question/challenge is compelling enough to engage all the stakeholders and participants in the co-creative process. High levels of initial engagement are necessary for participants to take on the challenge of worldview change that underlie this approach to innovation.

Given that resonant co-creation explores the Unknown and challenges existing structures, the process can be perceived as a threat to established systems and power relations. Resonant co-creation thus requires strong container. Team building cannot be understated. It is worth taking the extra time to create a group identity through shared experience, empowerment, and co-creation of a central symbol (e.g. a team logo or shield). A shared identity greatly helps people shift from the ego-centered "I" into the co-creative "We" mindset needed. Without a combination of trust, authenticity, respect, empathy, and freedom in that space, resonant co-creation can spin off track and will likely fail. It is not enough to set up a collaborative space and facilitate gameplay that reframes the challenge. The container must be set correctly, for it is within this space that participants go through a developmental journey to cultivate a deep inner knowing and a meta-awareness of the contextual factors that shape collective innovation processes. When this is achieved, collectively, the results can be profound.

In resonant co-creation, a key objective for the *Xd* is to create a space between wherein a high-level awareness (presence) fosters deeper engagements between participants. Resonant co-creation adds emphasis on cultivating meta-awareness of internal and external factors that influence collective ideation. Cultivation of such awareness enables perception and action from a place still alertness, increases empathy, and taps into intuitive modes of thinking from which new ideas emerge. When combined with other facilitation techniques to challenge or reframe knowledge, presence has the potential to open up new spaces for creativity and communication. It taps into and engenders the shifts in collective intelligence that underlie breakthrough innovations.

The ability to create and hold a strong container and a resonant space between we call "perfecting appropriateness." The phrase suggests that it is not so much the tools that you have that make the difference, but rather how you use them. Throughout this text we have used the metaphor of a theatrical performance as the glue that binds all the different pieces of co-creation together into a coherent process framework. We use this metaphor to suggest that facilitating co-creation is best approached as an art rather than a science. Resonance requires the skills and insight of an artist who knows how to take whatever elements he or she is working with and create something amazing. Translating this principle into practice, perfecting appropriateness is that near-mystical quality that some facilitators, coaches, and leaders have to use exactly the right tool at exactly the right time. It can be a question, a subtle shift in program, or even silence.... Whatever the tool is, perfect appropriateness is the use of that tool in just the right way to help the group go where it needs to.

Talent development in the form of coaching, contemplative practices, or other training enhances the capacity for and likelihood of resonance. Perfecting appropriateness, for example, requires the qualities described in the section on creative leadership in Chap. 3. An *Xd* cannot make such subtle shifts without a high level of awareness, empathy, and vision. They must embody PACE and be the tuning fork for the groups they work with. People will respond to the quality of presence that a creative leader has, subconsciously entraining to what they bring into the process.

Creative leadership is especially important for those that sponsor co-creation in an organizational change initiative. In that "the people involved in redesigning work imagine new, positive experiences for themselves and develop interactions that did not exist before," co-creation can lead to enduring changes in organizational culture and business processes.[39] Such change requires more than the occasional workshop or consulting. It mandates a leadership that creates and holds the co-creative space. Leaders, as much as the *Xd*, must have the capacities and skills to do this if resonance is to be maintained.

When a team also has opportunities for talent development, it can change how they interact exponentially. Team talent development often comes in the form of short workshops aimed at training specific skills, and these can be included in the co-creative process. From experiences such as appreciative inquiry workshops to sensing journeys, a goal is to help people learn to "step into" the felt experience of others. Reflective dialogue is one of our favorite tools because it creates empathy while simultaneously leveling up the whole group's awareness. Being reflective while engaged in ideation is time consuming and requires a great deal of attention, but it dramatically improves the quality of dialogue.

In our designs, we take every opportunity to integrate capacity building and training of transferrable skills. In most cases, we don't have the time for extended training sessions, so instead we make it part of the larger program. On day one we might teach people about design thinking with the Backpack Challenge, a two- to three-hour workshop in which people run through a rapid design cycle to make a cardboard and tape prototype of backpacks. In that one session they gain an understanding of the larger process they are about to engage in. We might also have everyone do a self-assessment of their personalities and work styles, then share this with others to build teams. In the process they learn some of the tools of leadership and negotiation. We can also integrate presence training at various points throughout a program, beginning with basic techniques on day one and adding nuances to their abilities daily. These are just a few possibilities among many. The point is that we are consciously integrating talent development throughout the process, not only to help in delivering the desired results but also to facilitate personal and professional growth. We want to finish a co-creative process with great outcomes and empowered teams. Creating growth opportunities serves both ends.

Conclusions

An experience design aimed specifically at profoundly shifting consciousness, facilitation with perfect appropriateness, and talent development of both leaders and team members are the ideal ingredients for a resonant co-creation cocktail. If only our work was as straightforward as a mixed drink, we could reliably create resonance. We could engineer breakthroughs.

Unfortunately, creativity is not so predictable. It is times like these, after carefully laying out every possible factor we argue can unleash the creative power of teams, that we must remind ourselves of the basic truth that physicist Neil deGrasse Tyson pointed out, "In science when human behavior enters the equation, things go non-linear." This quote reminds us that human behavior is so incredibly complex that we cannot ever engineer precise outcomes from any human-centered process. If we could, we might as well be robots, and creativity would be ... well ... not very creative. The beauty of our species is that, as predictable as we can be at times, human always have the capacity to surprise. Resonant co-creation is often experienced as a surprise because it happens so rarely. And yet most of us have at least one team experience where we can clearly remember that feeling—the "eureka" moment of a true collective breakthrough. In this chapter, we have uncovered much of what underlies the art of creating resonance, but we still acknowledge and respect the mystery.

This work is but one step in the continued journey by scholars and practitioners to unlock the secret of creative breakthroughs. The theory of resonant co-creation is our contribution to that effort. We hope that anyone and everyone can master the art of co-creation, building resonance in teams and organizations. The human species needs resonance and other tools if we are to meet the challenges of our times. How much or little co-creation can be of value in this effort and what applications it might have are the subject of our closing chapter. There we shift our tone from explanation to exploration, inviting you the reader into a larger dialogue about the future.

Notes

1. Ramaswamy and Gouillart, "Building the Co-Creative Enterprise," 100–109.
2. Ibid., 252.
3. Mandl and Mandl, *The Co-Creative Meeting*, 11.
4. Cook-Greuter, "Making the Case for a Developmental Perspective." Laloux, *Reinventing Organizations*. Brown, "Conscious Leadership for Sustainability."
5. Schuyler et al., *Leading with Spirit, Presence, and Authenticity*.
6. Hunter and Chaskalson, "Making the Mindful Leader," 195–220.
7. Brown, "Conscious Leadership for Sustainability." Hunter and Chaskalson, "Making the Mindful Leader." Senge et al., *Presence*. Schlitz et al., "Worldview Transformation and the Development of Social Consciousness."

8. Senge et al., *Presence.* Scharmer, *Leading from the Emerging Future and Theory U.* Laloux *Reinventing Organizations.* Turner and Udall, *The Way of nowhere.*
9. Schlitz et al., "Worldview Transformation and the Development of Social Consciousness," 23.
10. Tickle-Degnan and Rosenthal, "The Nature of Rapport and Its Nonverbal Correlates."
11. Mandl and Mandl, *The Co-Creative Meeting*, 10.
12. Bohm 1991 *in* Mandl & Mandl, *The Co-Creative Meeting*, 10.
13. www.presencing.com. Accessed August 2014.
14. Dialogue Proposal Copyright © 1991 by David Bohm, Donald Factor and Peter Garrett. http://www.david-bohm.net/dialogue/dialogue_proposal.html, 5.
15. Dialogue Proposal, 3.
16. Jacobs and Heracleous, "Answers for Questions to Come," 342.
17. Ibid., 343.
18. Schein, *Process Consultation Revisited*, 203.
19. Senge et al., *Presence.* Kindle Location 1271.
20. Ibid., 1296.
21. Dance, "Creativity and the Tao Te Ching," 3.
22. Chang, *Creativity and Taoism.*
23. Eleanor Rosch 2001 *in* Senge et al., *Presence.* Kindle Location 1378.
24. Ibid., 1378.
25. Dance, "Creativity and the Tao Te Ching," 4.
26. Senge et al., *Presence.* Scharmer, *Leading from the Emerging Future.*
27. Dance, "Creativity and the Tao Te Ching," 4.
28. Dunbar et al., "Do Naïve Theories Ever Go Away?" Freeman, *Societies of Brains.* Turner and Whitehead, "How Collective Representations Can Change the Structure of the Brain."
29. Recognizing this challenge, a small but growing sector of consciousness-based consultancies have developed techniques that explicitly claim to transform worldview. Examples include the Eliad Group, the Presencing Institute, People Brands, Nowhere, and Sally Anderson. Signature toolsets have been developed from research at interdisciplinary research centers such as the Institute of Noetic Science Future Centers, the Conscious Business Institute, the Maharishi University of Management, the Co-Creation Initiative, and the Esalen Center for Theory and Research. Communities of practice such as Conscious Capitalism and the Society for Organizational Learning support the growth of this paradigm.
30. Senge et al., *Presence*, 1852.
31. Bohm, *On Dialogue.* Maslow, *Toward a Psychology of Being.* Rogers, "A Theory of Therapy, Personality and Interpersonal Relationships as

Developed in the Client-Centered Framework." Goleman, *Leadership: The Power of Emotional Intelligence.* Wilber, "An Integral Theory of Consciousness."

32. The Theory U framework developed by MIT and the Presenting Institute is one example.
33. The nowhere group ltd. uses a variety of models derived from Native American medicine wheels. They combine these with contemplative practices from Zen.
34. This example stems from Social Artistry, developed by Jean Houston, and the Five Realms, developed by Nic and Susie Turner.
35. Berman, *Children's Social Consciousness and the Development of Social Responsibility.* Schlitz et al., "Worldview Transformation and the Development of Social Consciousness." Laloux, *Reinventing Organizations,* Zimbardo, *The Lucifer Effect.*
36. Senge et al., *Presence,* 1864–1875.
37. Harvard Business Review. Issue Unknown.
38. www.innogreat.com.
39. Ramaswamy and Gouillart, "Building the Co-Creative Enterprise," 11.

References

Berman, Sheldon. *Children's Social Consciousness and the Development of Social Responsibility.* Albany, NY: State University of New York Press, 1997.

Bohm, David. *On Dialogue.* London: Routledge Classics, 2004.

Brown, Barrett Chapman, and Development Fielding Graduate University. The School of Human and Organization. "Conscious Leadership for Sustainability: How Leaders with a Late-Stage Action Logic Design and Engage in Sustainability Initiatives." 2012.

Chang, Chung-yüan. *Creativity and Taoism: A Study of Chinese Philosophy, Art & Poetry.* New York: Harper & Row, 1970.

Cook-Greuter, S. R. "Making the Case for a Developmental Perspective." *Industrial and Commercial Training* 36, no. 6/7 (2004): 275.

Dance, Robert. "Creativity and the Tao Te Ching." In *Mindful Essays,* 2011.

Dunbar, K., J. Fugelsang, and C. Stein. "Do Naïve Theories Ever Go Away? Using Brain and Behavior to Understand Changes in Concepts." In *Thinking with Data,* edited by M. Lovett and P. Shah, 193–205. Mahwah, NJ: Lawrence Erlbaum Associates, 2007.

Goleman, Daniel. *Leadership: The Power of Emotional Intelligence: Selected Writings.* 1st ed. Northampton, MA: More Than Sound, 2011.

Freeman, W.J. *Societies of Brains: A Study in the Neuroscience of Love and Hate.* Hillsdale, NY: Lawrence Erlbaum Associates, 1995.

Jacobs, Claus, and D. Heracleous. "Answers for Questions to Come: Reflective Dialogue as an Enabler of Strategic Innovation." *Journal of Organizational Change Management* 18, no. 4 (2005): 338–352.

Hunter, J., and M. Chaskalson. "Making the Mindful Leader." In *The Wiley-Blackwell Handbook of the Psychology of Leadership, Change, and Organizational Development*, edited by H. S. Leonard, R. Lewis, A. M. Freedman and J. Passmore, 195–220. Oxford: John Wiley & Sons, 2013.

Mandl, Christoph E., Markus Hauser, and Hanna Mandl. "The Co-Creative Meeting: Practicing Consensual Effectivity in Organizations." Berlin; New York: Springer, 2013.

Maslow, Abraham H. *Toward a Psychology of Being*. 2nd ed. Princeton, NJ: Van Nostrand, 1968.

Laloux, Frederic. *Reinventing Organizations: A Guide to Creating Organizations Inspired by the Next Stage of Human Consciousness*. First edition. ed. Brussels, Belgium: Nelson Parker, 2014.

Ramaswamy, Venkat, and Francis Gouillart. "Building the Co-Creative Enterprise." *Harvard Business Review* 88, no. 10 (2010): 100–109.

Rogers, C. "A Theory of Therapy, Personality and Interpersonal Relationships as Developed in the Client-Centered Framework." In *Psychology: A Study of a Science. Vol. 3: Formulations of the Person and the Social Context*, edited by S. Koch. New York: McGraw Hill, 1959.

Schein, E.H. *Process Consultation Revisited: Building the Helping Relationship*. Reading, MA: Addison-Wesley, 1999.

Scharmer, Claus Otto. *Theory U: Leading from the Future as It Emerges: The Social Technology of Presencing*. Cambridge, MA: Society for Organizational Learning, 2009.

Scharmer, Otto, and Katrin Kaufer. *Leading from the Emerging Future: From Ego-System to Eco-System Economies*. San Francisco, CA: Berrett-Koehler Publishers, Inc., 2013.

Schuyler, Kathryn Goldman, John E. Baugher, Karin Jironet, and Lena Lid Falkman. *Leading with Spirit, Presence, and Authenticity*. San Francisco, CA: Jossey-Bass, 2014.

Schlitz M, Veiten C., and E. Miller. "Worldview Transformation and the Development of Social Consciousness." *Journal of Consciousness Studies* 17, no. 7–8 (2010): 18–36.

Senge, Peter M., Claus Otto Scharmer, Joseph Jaworski, and Betty Sue Flowers. *Presence: Exploring Profound Change in People, Organizations, and Society*. Kindle Edition ed.: The Crown Publishing Group, 2005.

Tickle-Degnen, Linda, and Robert Rosenthal. "The Nature of Rapport and Its Nonverbal Correlates." *An International Journal for the Advancement of Psychological Theory* 1, no. 4 (1990): 285–293.

Turner, R., and C. Whitehead. "How Collective Representations Can Change the Structure of the Brain." *Journal of Consciousness Studies* 15, no. 10–11 (2008): 43–57.

Wilber, Ken. "An Integral Theory of Consciousness." *Journal of Consciousness Studies* 4, no. 1 (1997): 71–92.

Zimbardo, P.G. *The Lucifer Effect: Understanding How Good People Turn Evil.* New York: Random House, 2007.

Epilogue

We would like to end this book with a quote from Bob Marley, "Some people have hopes and dreams. Some people ways and means." Co-creation is our ways and means, a difference that can make *the* difference. This is a bold statement, and in these last pages, we will consider some of the possibilities for this to be true in the present day and into the future.

Some say that success is built on the shoulders of others. The art of co-creation is most definitely so, and the giants that inspired us come from the fields of design, organizational change, anthropology, psychology, knowledge management, and consciousness studies. As our work is first and foremost grounded in design thinking, we look to the role of it in the world today to identify aspects of design thinking that can make *the* difference.

Texts such as *Change by Design* and *Designing for Growth* illustrate the value of design thinking beyond the boundaries of the field of design. In contrast to the skills required to be a designer, which require years of learning and practice, design thinking "can be practiced by anybody. There is no reason why everyone, up to and including the 'C-level'—CEOs, CFOs, CTOs, and COOs—cannot master these thought processes as well."[1] As design thinking has transcended its disciplinary boundaries, it has found new life as a way of thinking and process that can not only improve life in the present but also help us envision and enact the future. Its reach is now far beyond the design of products and services. Design thinking is being increasingly used in business contexts it was once seen as

B. R. Rill, M. M. Hämäläinen, *The Art of Co-Creation*,
https://doi.org/10.1007/978-981-10-8500-0

antithetical to. The reasons for this are many, but one of them is a global business climate that demands innovation. It is now easy to replicate strategies, so innovation capacity has become one of the sole differentiators left. In an age of "innovate or die," design thinking has entered the picture as somewhat of a savior. "Getting new results requires new tools—and design has real tools to help us move from talk to action."[2]

Tools and processes are one aspect of adopting a design thinking approach, but more importantly is the mindset that comes with it. Designers live in a world of possibility and exploration that artists enjoy matched by the real-world constraints, analysis, and need for generating value of business. Their discipline requires cross-disciplinary, integrative thinking. *Designing for Growth* explains the contrast between design and business mindsets as follows:

> Most managers are taught a straightforward linear problem-solving methodology: define a problem, identify various solutions, analyze each, and choose one—the right one. Designers aren't nearly so impatient—or optimistic. They understand that successful invention takes experimentation and that empathy is hard won. So the task is one of learning.[3]

Designers learn to embrace uncertainty and welcome in a degree of chaos, for these are necessary ingredients for creativity. The need for deliverables, spelled out in concrete terms before the finance department will approve a "creative" project, is a surefire way to kill an innovation process from the start. Managers who adopt design thinking either eliminate that criteria or do as one of my academic mentors once told me to do with research proposals that expect the same—write them to get the funding and then promptly throw them out. Ethnography, like design, is a process of discovery. You will only find new things if your eyes are open to possibilities beyond anything that you could have foreseen. This is part of being comfortable with the Unknown. It is the realm of possibility from which new things emerge, given the right conditions.

We feel it is worth restating the proposition in *Designing for Growth* that *both* mindsets are integral to the managerial toolkit of innovative organizations. Co-creative processes and tools are uniquely suited to identifying and acting on opportunities, and analytic ones help run the organization effectively.[4] In many businesses this balance already exists, a validation of the value design thinking can bring to any organizational sector.

Building Success Stories

There is a lurking danger to wholeheartedly adopting design thinking and parading it around as a "savior" within any organization. The danger lies in what Tim Brown calls "the politics of new ideas."[5] We quote here at length to preserve the integrity of his argument.

> More good ideas die because they fail to navigate the treacherous waters of the organization where they originate than because the market rejects them. Any complex organization must balance numerous competing interests, and new ideas, as Harvard's Clayton Christensen argues, are disruptive. If it is truly innovative, it challenges the status quo. Such innovations often threaten to cannibalize previous successes and recast yesterday's innovators as today's conservatives. They take resources away from other important programs. They make life harder for managers by presenting them with new choices, each with unknown risks—including the risk of making no choice at all. Considering all of these potential obstacles, it is a wonder that new ideas make it through large organizations at all. At the heart of any good story is a central narrative about the way an idea satisfies a need in some powerful way: coordinating a dinner date with friends on opposite sides of town; making a discreet insulin injection during a business meeting; converting from a gasoline-powered to an electric-powered car. As it unfolds, the story will give every character represented in it a sense of purpose and will unfold in a way that involves every participant in the action. It will be convincing but not overwhelm us with unnecessary detail. It will include plenty of detail to ground it to some plausible reality. It will leave the audience with no doubt that the organization "narrating" it has what it takes to make it real.

We have argued, as Brown does, that good storytelling is instrumental in overcoming organizational resistance (i.e. structural resistance). A compelling needs story or breakthrough question is what creates engagement for co-creative teams. Similarly, a story that involves and connects to stakeholders throughout an organization, or users in a market, is needed for them to engage something new with enough interest to cut through the inertia of habitual patterns. A good story highlights the integration of needs we have argued for. It connects the "Me, We, and It" in a language that everyone can relate to. A designed narrative can be inspirational, a burning bridge scenario, or anything else, but a good one touches the human heart. It is the heart that leads all real change. The mind will follow.

Another approach is to co-create the story. Value co-creation brings producers, stakeholders, and users into a larger collective engagement where value is created through the use of (or involvement in) the product, service, or initiative. The value in such cases lies not only in articulating how needs are met or processes improved but also in the social relationships created. One of the benefits of value co-creation is the ability for an idea to diffuse on its own, going viral through stakeholder communities because they feel partial ownership of the idea. They want to spread it. Win win.

Success stories also require a culture of optimism, a belief that co-creation will actually work. The organization or project team needs to be curious enough to try it with an open mind. Cynicism is its opposite. While we need critical analysis and feedback during a co-creative process, a cynical attitude demotivates those with the courage to take risks and openly explore the Unknown. If people are only engaged in projects or processes that they are sure to advance their agenda, or avoid uncertainty and potential shame, they will be of little value until they get past that attitude. It is thus imperative to build a culture of optimism in the creative team early on. Equally vital is that this optimism is supported by leadership. With these conditions met, it is possible to build successes even in organizations with structural resistance.

We refer to small successes in resistant environments as "anomalies," drawing from Thomas Kuhn's study of scientific progress.[6] Kuhn found that contrary to the popular notion that science progresses gradually with ever-increasing knowledge, the prevailing situation is far more like tribal warfare. Paradigms defend themselves with great passion and fervor in the face of epistemological and/or ontological challenges, which begin as anomalies that resist explanation in the existing paradigm. Anomalies are at first ridiculed and rejected, but they tend to persist and grow larger. At some point, anomalies reach a critical mass and overthrow the old paradigm. They then become the new paradigm, and the cycle repeats itself through time. Gradual progress is an illusion based on the fictional assertion that people accept change. We don't, at least not without resistance. That is why a good story and optimism are so beneficial. People will adopt what they perceive to be good for them, even with the difficulties inherent in any change. But they need a positive perception, and that starts with leadership and culture. "People have to believe that it is within their power (or at least the power of their team) to create new ideas, that will serve unmet needs, and that will have a positive impact."[7] Design thinking is instrumental in organizations where the culture and strategy support it.

Harnessing Human Potential

Our work also owes a debt to disciplines that help us understand the most important ingredient for co-creation—people. A deep understanding of human needs and motivations, of relationships to each other and organizations, of how they create and share knowledge, and of what inspires and drives excellence are all essential if we are to grasp how to tap into and harness creative potential.

Looking beyond the borders of individual disciplines, we identified the cutting edge of innovation leadership—transforming consciousness. Consider the challenge raised by Otto Scharmer[8]:

> We live in an age of profound disruption where something is ending and dying, and something else is wanting to be born. What is ending and dying is a civilization that is built on the mindset of maximum me, or bigger is better, and of special interest group driven decision making that has led us into a state of organized irresponsibility. What is being born is less clear. It is a future that requires us to connect with a deeper level of our humanity… How can we build the capacity to sense and actualize the future?

Answering Scharmer's question lies at the heart of the U.Lab course offered by MIT and the Presencing Institute.[9] This online course, and the growing movement of which it is part of, address a critical issue of our time. We live in a global reality that is increasingly VUCA (volatile, uncertain, complex, and ambiguous). "Many of the complex challenges leaders face exceeds their ability to perceive, understand, and adapt to them with their current schemas."[10] In our introduction we mentioned that strategic, rather than incremental, innovations are needed to meet the challenges we face. Yet "fundamental strategic innovation, and the substantial organizational changes it entails, requires that organizational actors' mental maps of their industry, strategy and organization undergo a shift so that they can see things in new ways unconstrained by history."[11] If that is the case, then worldview transformation is integral to contemporary innovation platforms. It can be, particularly with resonant co-creation. The capacity to sense and actualize the future that Scharmer calls for is what we have described as creative leadership. When shared by a co-creative team and enacted collectively, the resulting resonance transforms the creative process, its outcomes, and the people and organizations it is part of. We can expect transformation of individuals to include increased empathy, improved communication skills, honed intuition, and greater awareness. Organizational transformations include improvements in:

- Leadership—Cultivation of mindful and authentic leadership
- Innovation—Tapping into and harnessing potential at will and with skill
- Vision (Purpose)—Clarification of the "Why" behind the "What" and "How" that aligns the energy and efforts of the organization
- Environment—Sustainable organizational practices (e.g. continuous innovation, conscious business)

Resonant co-creation is transformative, *by design*. When we intentionally design experiences that skillfully transform consciousness, we imbue our process with a greater potential for breakthroughs. This, for us, is what lies at the heart of innovation leadership. It is not just about coming up with the next great product, service, or strategy. It is about building cultures of innovation. Resonant co-creation is a ways and means to meet these hopes and dreams.

The Art Lies in the Weave

The value our work brings to the table lies in the integration of insights from across disciplines. In *Change by Design*, Brown argues that "we need to invent a new and radical form of collaboration that blurs the boundaries between creators and consumers. It's not about 'us versus them' or even 'us on behalf of them.' For the design thinker, it has to be 'us with them.'"[12] Co-creation is that, but we replace "consumer" with the more inclusive term "stakeholder." "Us with them" is the ***We*** that the entire experience design is oriented around and serves.

The focus on experience rather than process design is what differentiates our work from most current design thinking. We say "most" because design thinkers at IDEO and other places do in fact take the human experience quite seriously. That is what human-centered design is all about. And yet, as we explained in detail in Chap. 2, there are subtle differences that we feel have a major impact. Human-centered and other participatory design approaches tend to focus on the designer-user interaction. Our emphasis is on the experience of the creative team itself.

Having a great creative team need not rely on the leadership skills and charisma of a design lead whom all others follow. That is not co-creative. Nor are participatory design practices that invite other stakeholders into a process to give inputs to the design team, then be sent off on their way while the "professionals" do the designing. Co-creative design, or co-design, begins with a careful consideration of how to tap into and harness the full creative potential of the team. The answer is not process. It is experience, because all insights emerge from experiences. Process can generate such experiences, but they are not the experience itself. Recognizing this fact begs the question, "What else can we do to enhance the creative experience?"

Our research and practice have resulted in three contributions to this effort. The first is the Co-Creative Journey model, a process architecture that underlies the collective journey of a creative team. That journey has three aspects: knowledge, emotional, and interpersonal (team dynamics). Most design thinking focuses on the knowledge aspect, because at the end of a process it is knowledge that is harvested in the form of new products, services, or initiatives. The unfortunate consequence of this emphasis is that the emotions and interpersonal dynamics among people are often relegated as less important. Whatever serves the knowledge journey is what needs to be done, and so it is.

Such approaches can result in very cold, insensitive design processes wherein people are told to "suck it up" or "level up your game" if they are perceived to be underperforming. While authoritarian approaches do work at times, they usually leaves a bad taste in everyone's mouth. No one wants to work with jerks. And from an organizational perspective, people need to get along and be able to work with others.

We prefer an inclusive approach that humanizes the creative process by giving equal emphasis to all three aspects of the journey. This may seem like rather minor difference, but the implications for program design are quite significant. Disciplines such as organizational change facilitation and psychology have robust methods for working with emotional and interpersonal dynamics, and we weave those in as part of a co-creative process.

While the methods we cite are not unique to our work, what is new is the cross-disciplinary integrative framework posed. Using a performance theater metaphor, we brought a wide range of ideas together into a comprehensive model that will help professionals design and lead programs that maximize creative outputs. The Co-Creative Journey model serves as a universal grammar that experience designers, leaders, and facilitators can base their program design on. The accompanying guidelines help to understand why, how, and where to use the variety of possible techniques, as well as offering support on how to manage creative teams.

Our second contribution is the Space Between model, an illustration of the interactive components required to establish the space between—the field of potential from which insights arise. Part I of the text explained how to work with People, Environment, and Process (PEP) when designing for co-creation. A powerful space between maximizes the potential that attention to each component can bring. What we strive for is an experiential field full of ideas, emotions, intuitions, and other dynamics that lead to the "ah ha" moment of an insight. The more potential inherent within the field, the more creative ideas and insights will manifest.

Harnessing the full potential of the space between begins with designing a total experience. A total experience is more than just process, or even the techniques that we have laid out. It is a mix of hard work, play, entropy, and serendipity. It is an emotional rollercoaster with highs and lows, breakdowns and breakthroughs. Designing this type of experience is large part of the art of co-creation. The best designs weave program pieces seamlessly together to facilitate the dance between the Known and Unknown from which insights arise.

An *Xd* is the playwright, director, and sometimes actor, a master of process and presence. Like a director, they must be able to lead the journey that they design. This calls for creative leadership and facilitation skills. We are not referring here to design or other skills that one can learn through a masterclass or corporate training. Capacities are the qualities of "being" that lie behind all "doing." Essential are the personal qualities of awareness, empathy, sensing and moving with flow, and the ability to let go of a process design. With time and practice, an *Xd* may develop what we have dubbed "perfecting appropriateness"—the ability to use the right tools at precisely the right time.

Our thoughts on creative leadership and capacity development are the third contribution to improving the co-creative experience. If and when you get all three just right—the experience design, the facilitation, and the talent development—you may be fortunate enough to experience resonance. That harmony among elements is a special feeling, one that no one ever forgets. It was the quest to understand these experiences that inspired our journey into collective creativity. Now that we have reached the end, we hope to inspire you with a few thoughts on what co-creation can do.

Let's Build an Anomaly

It is befitting to bring this text to a close by mimicking the cyclical nature of co-creation and looping back to where we began. We have come full circle. "Why co-creation?" was the subject of our first chapter, and there we looked at what it has done that makes it so special. Here we look to the future and wonder out loud what comes next.

In Design

If we look at design as a process, then we can see co-creation as a specific, highly beneficial way of executing this process. Co-creation builds on the collective intelligence of a group of people rather than relying on the individual performance of assigned experts. This approach enables the group to rush through fields of uncertainty by committing to an iterative process of internal knowledge sharing, collective decision-making, and constructive experimentation. As co-creation relies on the collective capabilities of a group in decision-making, the explorative journey of design will be guided by the shared insight rather than the strongest individual. When exploring uncharted territories, this type of a lean steering mechanism is superior to any hierarchical, rigid decision-making structures that large organizations are generally bound to follow. Hence co-creation fits the managerial needs of a design process quite well.

The simultaneous involvement of a diverse range of stakeholders also makes it possible to advance the design process in several parallel fields at the same time. The extensive body of shared knowledge can be utilized throughout the design process, rather than forcing the designers to wait for experts to point out possible flaws in their design only after they have been submitted for review. When experts participate in the design process themselves, most design flaws can be dodged before they have time to accumulate into serious problems. This saves time and reduces the number of iteration cycles required to achieve a favorable outcome.

The field of design has already embraced co-creation, and we see its presence worldwide in initiatives such as *Horizon 2020: Europe in a changing world—inclusive, innovative, and reflective societies.* The first part of this effort, which took place at CERN in 2016–2017, was "co-creation for growth and inclusion." Co-creation *is* the strategy to engage European cities and communities in a social design. And with the help of works like this book, co-creation will continue to thrive and grow. It is part of the larger movement that acknowledges and leverages the power of collective creativity.

In Organizations

Organizations of all types have recognized the power of the collective creativity. We are seeing more and more adopt design thinking, as well as allocating resources for creative teams and environments. The Harvard Business Review has labeled this trend in large corporations "The fourth stage of innovation."[13] Co-creation is uniquely suited to this endeavor. Collective engagements lead not only to better outcomes but also to better leadership, communication, and culture.

Co-creation can be instrumental in creating and sustaining a culture of innovation. Yet structural resistance is a challenge that most organizations face in the attempt to change. In the face of resistance, changing the system can begin through concentrated units with a critical mass of experiential learning. Greenleap, an instance of the iLead+Design program led by the Eliad Group, was one such anomaly that led to a complete overhaul of an educational system. In our experience, creating an anomaly is more successful than attempting system-wide change. Beginning with something small allows people to engage it with less fear of consequences, which tends to open hearts and minds to possibility. If it makes a difference, then it becomes scalable. If it doesn't, no harm no foul.

If we consider what role co-creation best plays within the larger field of organizational change, it fits well within the conscious business movement.[14] The trend of conscious business is largely attributed to Fred Kofman's text *Conscious Business: How to Build Value Through Values.*[15] The term conscious business implies that a business will seek to be conscious of its impact on the world in various spheres. It requires an awareness of the needs of others and the dynamic interrelationship between people, organizations, and the world. A conscious business considers both short-term and long-term effects of its actions or inactions and chooses to be of benefit to the world and to function with awareness.

Conscious business begins with a transformation of leadership. "Leaders must learn to cultivate and transform themselves. This self-development results in enhanced internal capacities such as deeper intellectual understanding, perceptual capacity as well as a greater ability to innovate, self-manage, and self-direct."[16] In the past decade there has been a growth in innovation strategies that cultivate these and other characteristics. Such approaches to innovation focus on personal and organizational transformation through a restructuring of worldview, or action logic.[17] Approaches that facilitate this type of transformation are referred to as "consciousness-based."

Conscious business also calls for the development of nourishing organizational environments. "Innovation *per se* cannot be designed, but can be designed for, where the conditions fostering innovation can be put in place."[18] In co-creation we design and build such environments and then support them by setting the container and holding the space for insight to emerge. In that resonant co-creation develops the innovation leadership capacities called for by the conscious business movement, we would suggest the co-creation be more widely used in organizations that seek to live up to such ideals.

In the World

We consider ourselves fortunate to be living in a time when co-creation is desperately needed. In an age of global volatility, uncertainty, complexity, and ambiguity (VUCA), leaders are looking for new approaches to address challenges large and small. For businesses, the concern may be the need for continuous innovation in a climate where creative capacity is the only real differentiator left. For educational institutions, it may be the need to remain relevant and competitive when digital technologies and culture are rapidly moving away from traditional models. For governments, the concerns are even more complex. They must figure out how to support their populations in the face of resource scarcity, global warfare, changing social dynamics and technologies. One might put their head in the sand like an ostrich, but we prefer to see such challenges as opportunities. Now, more than ever, we need to work collectively to solve problems and identify opportunities that help us all.

> Today we have an opportunity to take their example and unleash the power of design thinking as a means of exploring new possibilities, creating new choices, and bringing new solutions to the world. In the process we may find that we have made our societies healthier, our businesses more profitable, and our own lives richer, more impactful, and more meaningful.[19]

Co-creation, like design thinking, transcends the field of design. It is a "meta" level process applicable to any endeavor that seeks to tap into the collective potential of a group of people. But just how ambitious should we be? Can it bring together corporate and world leaders to co-design solutions to the BIG problems of our time? Can professionals be Big Kids, using play instead of pressure to innovate? Can co-creation be an organizational structure, or is it a special "other" space that we engage from time to time to excite new possibilities? These questions ponder the role and potential of co-creation, and we invite our audience to engage us further.

Community of Practice

This book is the first step in the development of programs that can help designers, change facilitators, and leaders to improve upon themselves and the practices they employ to tap into the potential of their teams. The 12 chapters give practicing professionals everything they need to design for and lead co-creative programs. The "Art" is complete, for now. "What happens next?" is an open question that we hope our readers and the broader community of practice will help us with.

The Co-Creation Initiative (CCI) online platform (www.cocreation.world) is the digital space where we present what we know and what we are continually learning, bringing clarity to what co-creation means, highlighting exemplary works, and continuing the discourse. CCI is meant to be living, breathing space for continuous co-creation. We maintain the open source mindset that we have held throughout our research and the writing of this book. All our materials are free for anyone to use under a Creative Commons License. The only caveats are we ask that no one claim our ideas or models as "theirs" and that credit is given when referring to any of the source materials (ours or others). In the spirit of hope, we invite you to take what you have learned here out into the world and be a difference that makes *the* difference.

Notes

1. Brown, *Change by Design*, 150.
2. Ogilvie and Liedtka, Designing for Growth, Kindle Locations 169–171.
3. Ibid., Kindle Locations 230–234.
4. Ibid., Kindle Locations 368–453.
5. Brown, *Change by Design*, 136–137.
6. Kuhn, *The Structure of Scientific Revolutions.*
7. Brown, *Change by Design*, 76.
8. Scharmer, EdX, 2015. U.Lab: Transforming Business, Society, and Self.
9. Ibid.
10. Kegan and Lahey, *Immunity to Change*, 5.
11. Jacobs and Heracleous, "Answers for Questions to Come," 338.

12. Brown, *Change by Design*, 57–58.
13. Anthony, "The New Corporate Garage."
14. Kofman, *Conscious Business.* Laloux, *Reinventing Organizations.* Schlitz, "Conscious Business as Transformative Practice."
15. Kofman, *Conscious Business.*
16. Hunter and Chaskalson, "Making the Mindful Leader," 6.
17. Brown, "Conscious Leadership for Sustainability."
18. Jacobs and Heracleous, "Answers for Questions to Come," 341.
19. Brown, *Change by Design*, 242.

References

Anthony, Scott D. "The New Corporate Garage: Where Today's Most Innovative - and World-Changing - Thinking Is Taking Place (the Big Idea)." *Harvard Business Review* 90, no. 9 (2012): 44.

Brown, Tim, and Barry Katz. *Change by Design: How Design Thinking Transforms Organizations and Inspires Innovation*. Adobe Digital Edition ed. New York: Harper Collins e-books, 2009.

Brown, Barrett Chapman, and Development Fielding Graduate University. The School of Human and Organization. "Conscious Leadership for Sustainability: How Leaders with a Late-Stage Action Logic Design and Engage in Sustainability Initiatives." 2012.

Cook-Greuter, S. R. "Making the Case for a Developmental Perspective." *Industrial and Commercial Training* 36, no. 6/7 (2004): 275.

Hunter, J., and M. Chaskalson. "Making the Mindful Leader." In *The Wiley-Blackwell Handbook of the Psychology of Leadership, Change, and Organizational Development*, edited by H. S. Leonard, R. Lewis, A. M. Freedman and J. Passmore, 195–220. Oxford: John Wiley & Sons, 2013.

Jacobs, Claus, and D. Heracleous. "Answers for Questions to Come: Reflective Dialogue as an Enabler of Strategic Innovation." *Journal of Organizational Change Management* 18, no. 4 (2005): 338–352.

Kegan, Robert, and Lisa Laskow Lahey. *Immunity to Change: How to Overcome It and Unlock Potential in Yourself and Your Organization*. Boston, MA: Harvard Business Press, 2009.

Kofman, Fred. *Conscious Business: How to Build Value through Values*. Boulder, CO: Sounds True, 2006.

Kuhn, Thomas S. *The Structure of Scientific Revolutions*. Chicago: University of Chicago Press, 1996.

B. R. Rill, M. M. Hämäläinen, *The Art of Co-Creation*,
https://doi.org/10.1007/978-981-10-8500-0

Laloux, Frederic. *Reinventing Organizations: A Guide to Creating Organizations Inspired by the Next Stage of Human Consciousness.* First edition. ed. Brussels, Belgium: Nelson Parker, 2014.

Ogilvie, Tim, and Jeann Liedtka. *Designing for Growth: A Design Thinking Toolkit for Managers.* Columbia Business School Publishing. Kindle Edition: Columbia University Press, 2011.

Schlitz, Marilyn. "Conscious Business as Transformative Practice." 2013. Accessed December 10, 2014.

Index

B. R. Rill, M. M. Hämäläinen, *The Art of Co-Creation*,
https://doi.org/10.1007/978-981-10-8500-0

The manufacturer's authorised representative in the EU is Springer
Nature Customer Service Centre GmbH, Europaplatz 3, 69115 Heidelberg,
Germany. If you have any concerns regarding our products, please
contact ProductSafety@springernature.com

Printed and bound by CPI Group (UK) Ltd, Croydon, CR0 4YY
30/09/2026
02225442-0017